August Henry Keane, Wilhelm Junker

Travels in Africa During the Years 1875-1886

August Henry Keane, Wilhelm Junker

Travels in Africa During the Years 1875-1886

ISBN/EAN: 9783744753609

Printed in Europe, USA, Canada, Australia, Japan

Cover: Foto ©Andreas Hilbeck / pixelio.de

More available books at **www.hansebooks.com**

TRAVELS IN AFRICA

DURING THE YEARS
1879-1883

BY

DR. WILHELM JUNKER

TRANSLATED FROM THE GERMAN BY

A. H. KEANE, F.R.G.S.

ILLUSTRATED

LONDON: CHAPMAN AND HALL,
LIMITED
1891

RICHARD CLAY & SONS, LIMITED,
LONDON & BUNGAY.

CONTENTS.

CHAPTER I.
FROM EUROPE TO KHARTUM 1

CHAPTER II.
JOURNEY FROM KHARTUM TO MESHRA ER-RÊQ . 32

CHAPTER III.
JOURNEY FROM MESHRA ER-RÊQ TO DEM SOLIMAN 62

CHAPTER IV.
FROM DEM SOLIMAN TO PRINCE NDORUMA'S . 91

CHAPTER V.
RESIDENCE AT PRINCE NDORUMA'S, AND BUILDING OF THE LACRIMA STATION 133

CHAPTER VI.
FROM NDORUMA'S TO THE WELLE-MAKUA . 178

CHAPTER VII.
RESIDENCE AT PRINCE MAMBANGA'S, AND JOURNEY EASTWARDS TO TANGASI 224

CHAPTER VIII.
FROM THE WELLE BACK TO NDORUMA'S AND LAST STAY IN LACRIMA 265

CHAPTER IX.

FROM NDORUMA'S THROUGH A-MADI LAND TO THE A-BARMBOS AND BACK TO THE A-MADI 308

CHAPTER X.

RESIDENCE WITH THE A-MADIS AND JOURNEY TO HAWASH STATION   356

CHAPTER XI.

NEGOTIATIONS FOR PEACE WITH MAMBANGA AND STAY AT HAWASH STATION 395

CHAPTER XII.

JOURNEY TO THE CHIEF BAKANGAI FROM HAWASH STATION .   440

Dr W. JUNKER'S EXPLORATIONS
CENTRAL AFRICA

HOME MEMORIES.

CHAPTER I.

FROM EUROPE TO KHARTUM.

Departure from the Civilized World—Corfu—Alexandria—Cairo—No News from Gordon—A special Farmān needed for the Journey—Rude Reception at the Ministry—Start for Suez and Sawākin—Fellow-travellers—Despatches from Gordon—Departure for Berber—Berber—Trip to Khartum—News from the South—Abu Khamsa Miyeh's Residence—Europeans in Khartum—Arrival of the *Ismailia* from the Bahr el-Ghazal.

ON my return to St. Petersburg in September 1878, after my first journey to Egyptian Sudan, nothing was further from my thoughts than a second visit to that region. Yet within a twelvemonth my preparations for another expedition to Central Africa were well advanced, and on October 10th, 1879, I found myself on board the steamer *Progresso*, bound for Alexandria.

On the 16th I again landed on African soil, my immediate goal being Khartum, which I hoped to reach without delay by the Sawâkin-Berber route. The heavier boxes packed in Berlin for the caravan transport were sent from Alexandria straight to Suez, and the rest despatched to Cairo. With these and other articles, which could best be procured on the spot, I intended making up some additional camel-loads in the Egyptian capital. Mr. Pirona again in the most obliging manner adjusted my instruments for taking meteorological observations.

RODA ISLAND, CAIRO.

I also obtained from M. Marquet some more accurate information regarding my collections, which had been damaged on the way to Europe in 1878. M. Marquet, younger brother of the French trader at Khartum, to whom the things had been entrusted,[1] and who had since died there, now told me that

---

[1] See vol. i. p. 515.

many of the boxes had been swamped during the floods at Berber, that they had afterwards been abandoned by the cameldrivers on the road between Berber and Sawâkin, and, lastly, that on reaching Sawâkin, they had been detained by the authorities as presumably belonging to the elder Marquet, who was reported to have committed suicide. Hence it was found impossible to forward them to Europe till the Russian Consul interfered, and caused inquiries to be instituted by the Egyptian Ministry. Thus it was that the specimens had at last turned up in St. Petersburg in the deplorable condition already described.

In Alexandria I also met Herr Maximo, who had lately settled as a trader in Sawâkin. He was now returning to that place, where, on my subsequent arrival, he was of the greatest service in forwarding my interests.

At Cairo I had the pleasure of renewing acquaintance with George Schweinfurth, who had returned to Egypt by the last steamer from Europe. I profited much by the advice and suggestions of this distinguished naturalist, in whom I found a true friend and instructor.

Although much still remained to be seen in Cairo, all my thoughts and energies were absorbed in maturing the plans for my approaching expedition to the interior. Despite my anxiety to be on the road without loss of time, delays still intervened, and before anything could be done I had to procure the necessary papers from the Khedival Government. On November 2nd the Russian Consul-General von Lex procured me an audience with the new Viceroy, Mohammed Tewfik Pasha, who had lately succeeded Ismail Pasha, and who now promised that the necessary orders would be issued to the Sudanese officials. It may be incidentally mentioned that just then Gordon Pasha was absent on a mission to Abyssinia, from which he was not expected to return for a few weeks. Hence the Khedive suggested that it might be well to put off my journey till the end of the month, when he would probably be back. This suggestion fell in with my own desire for another personal interview with Gordon before my return to the Sudan, and my departure was accordingly postponed.

Meantime I went leisurely about the final preparations for the expedition. But when everything was ready, and there was absolutely nothing more to be done, we were still without news from Gordon. On the other hand, it was urgently necessary for me to reach the Negro lands before the rainy season set in. A steamer belonging to the Rubattino Company was advertised to sail from Suez to Sawâkin towards the end of November, and unless I availed myself of this opportunity, my departure might be indefinitely delayed.

I accordingly telegraphed to Khartum for tidings of Gordon, but at the same time learnt from another source that he had again returned from Galabat to Abyssinia. Hence there was no prospect of his return to Cairo for the present, and nothing remained except a faint hope of possibly meeting him in Sawâkin. I therefore informed his Highness, at a second audience on November 22nd, that I had decided to start forthwith, and renewed my application for the viceregal farmân.[1] The Khedive informed me that, while on his way back to Galabat, Gordon had been obliged to return to Abyssinia by order of King John, and approved of my resolution.

I had now to get the papers in all haste from the ministry, for the feast of Bairam was approaching, when all official work would be suspended for a few days, while the steamer was announced to sail at the end of the ensuing week. Being already sufficiently well acquainted with the relations in Sudan, I knew that a formal document, drawn up in the usual way and full of detailed instructions for travellers, would be of little service to me. Hence I had applied to the ministry for a paper embodying certain special provisions, such as—

1. Free rations for myself and servants at the Egyptian stations in Sudan, wherever there were no markets or opportunities for purchasing provisions.
2. Free supply of the necessary carriers in Negro land.
3. Right of settling and erecting huts wherever I pleased.
4. Privilege of accompanying, for the object of my explor-

---

[1] Farmân, فرمان, order, decree, edict—Persian.

GARDEN OF THE HÔTEL DU NIL, CAIRO. (*From a photograph by L. H. Fischer.*)

ations, any expeditions organized at the stations for procuring ivory, or for any other purpose.

3. Official responsibility for my safety in Egyptian territory, but not on or beyond the frontiers, with full permission to cross those frontiers at my own discretion without let or hindrance on the part of the authorities.

An order containing these clauses seemed all the more desirable now that I was not to have an interview with Gordon, whose return to Khartum as Governor-General, after his Abyssinian journey, seemed to me more than doubtful. What I asked for was in reality less than what Gordon had himself freely granted me on my first expedition, and had promised to renew on future occasions.

Those unfamiliar with the state of affairs in Sudan might perhaps think my demands somewhat exacting and unreasonable. In fact, so they appeared at first sight to the Cairo officials, who are themselves little acquainted with the true relations in those remote provinces. But under the circumstances prevailing in the Egyptian Sudan, it was highly important for the explorer to be quite independent of the local authorities, and in no way subject to the caprice of the governors and superintendents at the stations. The service required of carriers is compulsory, a kind of *corvée* without claim for compensation; the corn represents the tribute of the negroes, while the flesh is the result of the yearly raids amongst the unreduced tribes. Hence my demand involved no sacrifice on the part of the administration, nor was it in any way a charge on the Treasury.

Fearing, however, that there might be a difficulty in granting my request, I had solicited the friendly offices of the late D. Bey, an influential European in the Egyptian service, who was himself present during my audience with the Prime Minister. Nevertheless my reception was far from courteous, the minister constantly interrupting the proceedings, and insisting that such demands were never made or granted, that there were many travellers to whom it would be impossible to make all those concessions. Thereupon my friend remarked: "But, your Excellency, the doctor is not going to Zagazik" (a town in the Nile delta, meaning thereby that I was not an ordinary tourist making a trip in Lower Egypt); "nor does he ask more than Gordon had already formerly granted him," and so on.

At this I handed up Gordon's farmān, which the minister at

A STREET IN CAIRO.

first refused to recognize, and then declared that it did not matter; Gordon might do what he liked in his province, such demands could not be granted here. Then, after another interruption, turning directly to me, he asked would I be satisfied with an order or recommendation drawn up in the usual way, and addressed to the Sudanese officials.

Feeling hurt at the way I had been treated, I answered somewhat warmly: "Excellency, I must needs be thankful for any recommendations you may be pleased to favour me with. Even without any such official aid to my undertaking, I would, nevertheless, adhere to my plan in the interest of science, and even of your country, by the cartographic work I propose to carry out in Egyptian territory. Although in the absence of distinct instructions to the authorities the difficulties of my journey will be doubly increased, I am still determined to reach my goal, even if I have to travel as a mendicant, seeing that a vaguely-worded order merely recommends me to the favour of the officials in Sudan."

No immediate answer was made to these remarks; but, ultimately, to my surprise, the minister stated in a few words that he would have the papers prepared according to my wishes, adding, however, that I would have to pay duty on my effects in Sawákin. But another official readily granted me exemption from the Custom-house charges, and my last days in Cairo were brightened by an unexpected meeting with Gerhard Rohlfs, who had just returned from his arduous journey to the Kufra oasis in the Libyan desert.

Shortly before starting, I decided, on the advice of my friends, to engage the services of Bohndorff to help in preparing the zoological specimens, and in obtaining biological collections. Besides my servant, Farag 'Alláh, he was the only assistant who accompanied me from Cairo, and later my only European companion in the wilds of Africa.

As the vessel was to sail on December 3rd, I at once despatched twenty boxes of all sizes to Suez, whither thirteen large cases had already been sent direct from Alexandria. Our party followed by train on December 1st, accompanied by the good wishes of my Cairo friends, who had assembled at the station to see us off.

In Suez there was the usual delay, and we did not get away till December 5th. I whiled away the time with repeated visits to the bazaar, picking up amongst other odds and ends an Indian basket-chair, which afterwards proved of the greatest service during my long wanderings in the interior.

Recently the Rubattino Company had established a regular steam service in the Red Sea, a ship sailing every twenty-five or thirty days from Suez for the ports of Jidda, Sawâkin, Massawa, and Hodeida, and returning the same way. Our boat, the *Palestina*, did not touch at Jidda, in order to escape the quarantine which had been proclaimed at Sawâkin for ships from that port during the pilgrimage season to Mecca. Nearly all the few first-class cabins were occupied, the passengers including two Englishmen and a Pole going on a hunting

DEPARTURE FROM CAIRO.

expedition to the interior, and the Italian trader, Conte Sapelli, who was bound for Khartum, and who joined our party at Sawâkin. The deck was crowded chiefly with two troops of Nubians, who were returning home after having entertained the Parisian and Berlin public with their performances during the summer. At the last moment a Greek and a Nubian came on board, and were afterwards the cause of an unpleasant delay of twenty-four hours' quarantine at Sawâkin.

The weather, at first cool and refreshing, became oppressively hot during the day. But the moonlit nights were delightful, and

MOUNT SINAI. (*From a drawing by L. H. Fischer.*)

on the third evening the lunar crescent, rising above the horizon on the distant waters, gave occasion to a perplexing optical delusion. The two limbs of the crescent, bathed in a flood of glowing light, became larger and larger, and at last seemed, as it were, to burst into flames. At first sight the appearance was curiously like that of a burning vessel seen in the distance.

Any marked indentations in the contour-lines of the coast or of remote islands, or even ships or other prominent objects, often produce a weird effect on the observer. The visions are not exactly aërial phantoms in the ordinary sense, conjuring up the forms of some "baseless fabric" that has no existence, but are rather

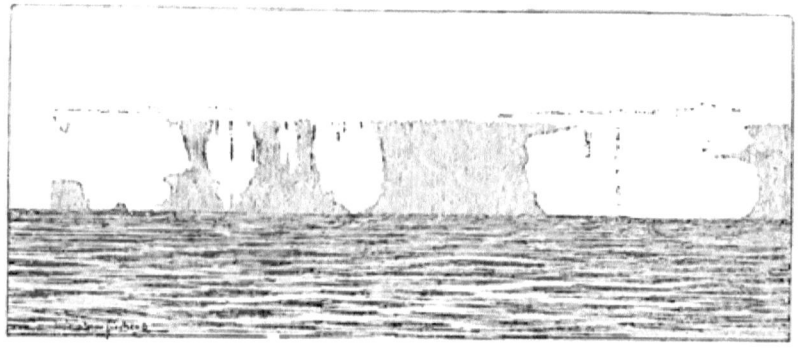

OPTICAL DELUSION ON THE SEA.

distorted views of real objects seen under peculiar atmospheric conditions. Such "insubstantial pageants" are doubtless the result of terrestrial radiation acting in combination with the refraction of luminous rays. Under these conditions the objects often stand out distinctly above the watery surface, or else their continuity is broken, their outlines raised, extended, distorted, and decomposed in diverse fantastic ways.

On the fourth day we again sighted the western coast-line. The dark mountain masses of the mainland were enveloped in gray clouds, and for long stretches could scarcely be distinguished from each other. Later the banked-up clouds assumed a deeper gray-blue colour as they gathered round the neighbouring rocky headlands, while the sun shot down radiant streaks of light in the foreground. To all appearances it was raining on the coast-lands, while above us stood the canopy of a cloudless azure sky.

At last the white-washed houses of Sawākin became visible in the distance, standing out in the glaring light of the setting sun. The approaches to the harbour are here endangered by shoals and coral reefs; but the channel is carefully indicated by several piles of dazzling white coraline blocks.

On December 8th the *Palestina* cast anchor, and received the customary visit from the sanitary commissioner, who, much to our surprise, imposed a quarantine of twenty-four hours, apparently because the names of the two last passengers were not entered in the captain's papers. The incident gave rise to some unpleasant inquiries, and a document complaining of the official's unwarranted action was signed by all on board.

In Sawākin I met both Messrs. Marquet and Maximo, and was also agreeably surprised with a visit from Herr Kohn, the dealer in wild animals, whose acquaintance I had already made in Upper Nubia, and who was just now staying with his little daughter in Sawākin. I had no difficulty in getting my things through the Custom-house, and was soon installed in the vacant house of a Greek trader.

As a convoy of gum-arabic and other wares had just arrived from Berber, I had my pick and choice of camels returning to that place, and might have started at once for the interior. But I was detained by the report that Gordon had reached Massawa, or at least was soon expected there. I telegraphed at once to that place, and in a few days came the answer: "Start, as my coming uncertain. Gordon."

Simultaneously came an order from Gordon to the Sawākin officials to push forward the arrangements for my journey. I at the same time telegraphed my approaching arrival in Khartum to Herr Giegler, who had lately been appointed Gordon's representative in that province, with the title of Pasha.

My few remaining days in Sawākin were fully occupied in getting everything ready, and securing the boxes, all of which were carefully sewn up in stout matting.

Under all circumstances the traveller will do well as far as possible to conform to the local usages, especially in the matter of diet. Those who can thoroughly adapt themselves to the native food have already won half the battle, and when their own supply of provisions runs out or gets scarce, they escape many troubles and trials, such as have often proved disastrous even to otherwise well-planned expeditions. In the course of the present narrative, I shall consider it my duty to introduce the experiences acquired on this point during my long ramblings in the interior, for it too frequently happens that travellers, wedded to old habits and prejudices, neglect to make the most of the products of the land. I will even go so far as to assert that by conforming to the simple fare of the natives, the European may preserve his health in those regions better than by indulging in the best cuisine of civilized countries.

The first choice *entrée* in my bill of fare was borrowed from the camp life of the Sudanese Bedouins. The soft skin of a young goat, such as is used for the *girba*, or leather water-bottles, of the Arabs, is three-quarters filled with the very hard little whey-cheeses retailed at a cheap rate in the Arab markets, and then filled up with fresh milk, salt, red pepper, or other native seasoning being added according to taste. During the journey the skin is suspended to the saddle of a camel, by whose motion the contents are thoroughly and uniformly shaken together. In the course of days, or even weeks, the hard cheeses get ground down by friction, while the milk thickens, and the whey or watery part evaporates, this process of evaporation keeping at a low temperature the contents, which have gradually acquired the consistency of porridge.

After a hard day's march I have constantly experienced the benefit derived from this refreshing mess of half-liquid cheese and curds taken with bread. I have often even preferred such a frugal meal to meat and preserves. In the Sawâkin market I was able to procure a supply of these cheese-skins, besides bread, dates, and the large but mild onions, which may be freely consumed without risk in the form of a salad. To these dainties was added the long variety of Arab cucumber (*Cucumis melo* L. var. *K'hate*).

I again bought an ass for my own use, and hired nineteen camels at six and a half thalers each for the whole journey to Berber, four and a half payable in advance, and two on reaching that place. Since my visit to Sawákin four years previously, a decided improvement had taken place. At that time the island of Sawákin was connected with the mainland at Géf only by small boats; now a wide embankment had been constructed, so that goods could be shipped close to the harbour.

On December 14th my caravan set out, and was joined in the evening at our first camping-ground by the Italian trader, Sapelli, who was anxious to make the journey in our company, but whose few pack animals were not ready in time for all to leave Sawákin together. An unexpected despatch also arrived from Gordon, ordering the authorities to supply me with camels free of charge, both for the present journey to Berber, and for my return in case I came back by that route. But I was unable to avail myself of this last act of kindness on the part of Gordon; I had already paid more than half of the cost of hire to the camel-owners, and I discharged the rest in Berber.

A detailed account of the journey from Sawákin to Berber may be dispensed with after the exhaustive description of this route by Dr. Schweinfurth. For this and other reasons I even neglected to survey the road, which I afterwards regretted, as in the eastern section the route followed by me differed considerably from that traversed both by Schweinfurth and Von Heuglin. At several difficult points and passes over the eastern hills the camel-track had been much improved by Gordon, and Marquet had also begun the construction of his carriage-road across the district. Thanks to these works, the Sawákin-Berber route would certainly have been recognized as the best for the export and import traffic of Egyptian Sudan, but for the untimely revolt of the Mahdi, and the hasty abandonment by England of all civilizing efforts in that region. Had a permanent roadway been laid down between Berber and Sawákin, it would have been at once chosen as the most convenient line of communication, and immeasurably preferable to that across the Bayúda steppe from Kerreri below Khartum to Dabbeh in

Dongola, or across the waterless Nubian desert from Abu Hamed to Korosko.

These three long-established routes are the only commercial highways worth discussing as at all practicable between Egypt and the Sudanese provinces. On my return from my last journey I learnt something of the track across the Bayúda steppe; the Korosko road leads through an inhospitable wilderness, where water occurs at such long intervals that it is practicable only for small, rapidly-moving caravans. Hence it was never used by me on any of my journeys, and I also avoided

BERBER ON THE NILE.

the direct road from Sawâkin to Kassala, by which the Red Sea is connected with Upper Nubia and Eastern Sudan. My first journey to this region, as already fully described, was made by the roundabout way of the Báraka Valley to Kassala.

Since the close of the Abyssinian War commerce had resumed its normal course, and we now almost daily met long convoys of camels all the way to Berber. As previously explained, the carrying trade is monopolized by various tribes, which so jealously guard their respective districts that trespassing often leads to sanguinary reprisals. But the increasing traffic and a better administration were gradually getting rid of these troubles, and camel-owners from the most diverse tribes with their pack-animals were now peacefully assembled in Sawákin. Other improvements in the transit trade had also been made, especially through the efforts of M. Marquet, who was the first to introduce a machine for cleansing and sorting the gum-arabic intended for the European market. The same trader also first adopted the practice of sorting ostrich feathers according to quality, and the uses they were meant for, thereby of course securing better prices for the finer kinds.

In the eastern parts of the hilly district crossed by the route to Berber, the soil is sufficiently watered to yield a rich vegetation, and the scenery in some places may even be described as charming. Here the routes of travellers often diverge in various directions, afterwards converging in a single track on the plateau. Thenceforth the path to Berber leads across a barren district dotted over with a few straggling acacia-trees. Here long, trying marches have to be made between the watering-places, and the road is often strewn with loose, weathered rubble-stones, a foot or so long, which if removed, a good carriage-way might easily be constructed. But greater difficulties would be experienced farther west, where the route traverses a broad zone of dunes and drift-sands, which for several days before reaching Berber form irregular chains of hills.

The whole region between the coast and Berber, but especially the eastern part, is roamed by the Hadéndoas, whose settlements here also are met at many points along the route. We reached Berber on December 27th, the journey having occupied fourteen days, while each day's march averaged seven hours.

I was hospitably received by the Mudir Mani Bey, whose acquaintance I had already made in Khartum. The boxes and bales were at once transferred from the camels to the hold of a small steamer from Khartum, which had been placed at my service, and on board of which I also took up my quarters. Although suffering from an attack of ague, I was unable to escape an endless round of visits, some coming merely to pay their respects, others as patients for consultation and physic, or else to obtain introductions to the officials in Khartum.

An evening stroll about Berber revealed nothing remarkable, although it ranks as one of the chief Arab towns in Sudan. Many newly-erected little brick houses reminded me of last year's sudden freshet and inundations, which had even sapped the foundations of some of the larger structures, and had also wrought havoc with my collections.

On December 29th we weighed anchor for Khartum, and on January 4th, 1880, reached Kerreri, where, eighteen months previously, on my return journey to Cairo, I had quitted the Nile and entered the Bayúda steppe. By this time the fever had disappeared, and I reached the metropolis of Sudan in the full enjoyment of my wonted health. As we neared the port I found that I had narrowly escaped being bitten by a huge yellow scorpion, which had crept in amongst the bed-clothes in my berth.

My further movements were now dependent on the reports which I awaited in Khartum on the state of affairs in the Negro lands, and on the condition of the communications with the south. The *sudd*,

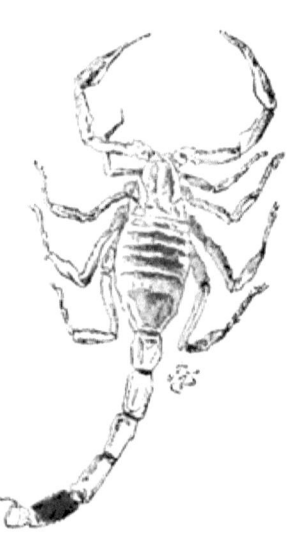

A SCORPION.

or grass-barrier, in the upper reaches of the Nile (Bahr el-Jebel) had not been cleared away, and for over a year the waterway had been closed between Ladó and Khartum. For several months Ernest Marno had been hard at work with steamers, boats, and numerous hands trying to get rid of the obstruction. Yet the re-opening of the regular highway to Ladó seemed as far off as ever, so that I had to give up the project of reaching Mangbáttu Land from Ladó, and thus connecting my explorations with my previous researches in the Makaraka country.

In the Bahr el-Ghazal also, which afforded a water route between Khartum and the western regions subject to the Egyptian sway, the navigation had for some months been obstructed by grass-barriers. These, however, could be easily forced, so that the communications in this direction had not yet been completely closed, and a steamer returning from that quarter was daily expected in Khartum.

During the course of the past year Romolo Gessi had succeeded in completely quelling Soliman Bey's revolt in the Bahr el-Ghazal region, where he was now residing as Governor of all the Equatorial Provinces, including the territory adminis-

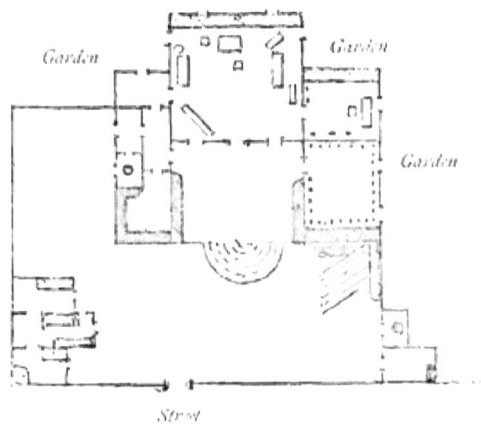

PLAN OF MY RESIDENCE IN KHARTUM.

tered by Dr. Emin, now promoted to the rank of Bey. I accordingly at once decided to make the Bahr el-Ghazal the starting-point of my next expedition, and to proceed thither by the next steamer leaving Khartum for the south.

Anticipating a protracted detention in the capital, I forthwith installed myself in the house which had already been engaged for me, and which was well known to all Khartumers as the residence of "Abu Khamsa Miyeh," that is, "Father of the Five-hundred." This was the nickname of a former mudir, owner of the house, who was in the habit of awarding a "round five-hundred" when sentencing culprits to the bastinado. The structure, which lay somewhat off the river-bank between the Government palace and the Mudiriyeh, contained some spacious apartments arranged in the Khartum style, which was very convenient for storing or packing my effects.

At the entrance into the court the kitchen lay to the left, apart from the main building. A few semi-circular steps led to a veranda, which ran round the living-rooms, and opened on the court. Every available space was soon filled with camp-tables and stools, angarebs (Sudanese bedsteads), hammocks, boxes and chests of all kinds; straw mats were spread over the clay benches, and I had soon fitted up a special workroom and a divan or reception-room, whose windows overlooked a neighbouring garden. Bohndorff installed himself on the right of the veranda, while the loads prepared for the journey were all arranged in rows in a well-secured space on the left.

During the ensuing weeks the veranda, which was covered in overhead, served as a convenient workshop during the day, and in the cool of the evening, when swept and garnished, I here entertained my friends. Of the former circle, Consul Rosset had died in Dar-Fôr, where he had lately been appointed governor, and Gessi was still detained in the Bahr el-Ghazal province. But there remained Giegler Pasha and Consul Hansal, besides Dr. Zurbuchen, a Swiss physician, who had lately removed hither from Wâdi-Halfa. There were also the Italians, Messadaglia Bey, Rosset's successor in Dar-Fôr, whence he had just been recalled, and Zughenetti, who had accompanied Gessi to the Bahr el-Ghazal, but had returned before the outbreak of hostilities.

Marquet still held his ground at the head of the commercial community, and the Catholic Mission had undergone several changes, fresh arrivals from Europe taking the place of others who had proved unsuitable for the work.

For the period of my stay in Khartum I engaged a servant and a female cook, the latter afterwards accompanying the expedition to Negro land. Ernest Marno's official report on his tedious operations undertaken to clear the main stream had already induced me to alter my plans, and take the first opportunity of proceeding to the station of Meshra er-Rèq on the Bahr el-Ghazal. Meantime Gordon had arrived in Cairo from Massawa, and the report now came in that he would not return to Khartum, where he was to be succeeded as Governor-General by Rauf Pasha.

THE SYLVESTER FEAST IN KHARTUM.

News also came from Gessi by the land route, *viâ* Shekka, that Richard Buchta had returned to the Bahr el-Ghazal from his expedition to the south, and that the missionaries, Dr. Felkin and Wilson, had also reached the same district from Uganda. The two missionaries had continued their journey by Shekka to Khartum, while Buchta intended to leave for the north by the next steamer from Meshra er-Rèq.

The Russo-Greek New Year's Day had now arrived, and I resolved to keep Sylvester-eve by inviting my friends to a feast, at which a great surprise was in store for them. The place was gaily decorated with a Russian flag and many-coloured Chinese lanterns suspended round the walls. But the reader will perhaps smile to hear that the real surprise which I had prepared for my guests consisted in potatoes served up in three different ways. With the view of introducing the cultivation of this tuber into the Negro lands, I had brought a basketful all the way from Europe. But some now began to sprout, and after such a lapse of time had become useless for my purpose; so rather than lose them altogether I hit upon the idea of treating my friends to a dainty fare, such as had never before been seen in Sudan. First came a smoking dish of mealies cooked in their "jackets"; then some sliced "roasters" with "anise seed and cumin," winding up with a potato salad, prepared by myself, with a dash of sardine sauce and some mixed pickles "chopped fine."

A HORSE'S ORNAMENTAL COLLAR FROM DAR-FÓR.

Giegler Pasha, to whom I was indebted for much assistance in promoting my plans, was the only member of the European society at that time settled in Khartum that I was destined again to see alive. The very next year Dr. Zerbuchen fell a victim to the treacherous climate; Marquet died later in Cairo; Consul Hansal and most of the rest perished during the horrors attendant on the revolt of the Mahdi.

On January 18th we were surprised by the arrival of the *Ismaïlia* from the Bahr el-Ghazal, bringing good tidings of Gessi Pasha and Emin Bey. But what pleased me most was the announcement that within a fortnight the steamer would leave again for the same region. Now all was bustle and activity in preparation for the expedition. For several days a carpenter had been at work in the veranda, putting together boxes of suitable size for the transport by carriers in Negro land. I had already procured in Berlin a number of long boxes adapted for conveyance by camels, and several of these had now to be broken up into two or three of smaller size for carriage by porters. The deal boards required for such purposes are dear in Khartum, having to be imported from Europe; ordinary lengths prepared for the trade cost three Egyptian thalers apiece, so that on the former occasion the boxes needed for my collections had formed a serious item in my expenditure.

TRAVELLING BASKET WITH TIN INSET.

These boxes and all other packages were numbered according to their size in white, blue, red or yellow figures, to make them more "legible" for my Negro servants. On some I even drew in distinct colours such devices as a snake, or some other animal or human form, which impressed themselves more vividly on the native mind than figures or ciphers, of which they had no clear conception.

During my previous journeys I had ample opportunity of

HELMET FROM DAR-FÔR.

noticing the numerous defects in the various types of boxes—iron, tin, or wooden—which were used by Gordon, Gessi, Lucas, Sir Samuel Baker, and other African travellers. In preparing my general outfit on this second occasion in Berlin, I accordingly took a new departure, introducing stout basket-work, such as is already common enough in Europe, covering it with the strongest canvas, well oiled a grayish colour, and adding movable tin linings. Such trunks I found most serviceable, light, yet durable, and in every way far preferable to the metal boxes, which, if of iron are too heavy, if of tin too fragile and apt to bulge and crack.

Travellers should provide themselves with trunks of various sizes and capacity, as the different objects themselves vary greatly in weight. For a certain number of these boxes I had myself adopted a definite system of packing in Berlin. The more indispensable articles were divided into ten equal parts, and stowed away in as many separate loads, so that each such load was made up of exactly the same quantity of the several articles. In other words, each box contained, for instance, an equal proportion of pens and stationery, of the more necessary medicines and supplies, such as compressed soups, tea, tobacco, body linen, timepieces, revolver with its ammunition, and so on. The advantage of this plan was obvious, for in my circular expeditions it enabled me to leave the great bulk of the baggage at head-quarters, and in case of fire or other accidents, though some packages might be destroyed, the risk of losing all the more urgently needed articles was reduced to a minimum. On such excursions I always took several boxes, each packed with these miscellaneous contents, so that if only one escaped destruction in a possible disaster, I should still possess at least a proportionate supply of indispensables.

My experiences were of course mainly confined to the regions north of the Equator, where the conditions are in many respects totally different from those prevailing in South Equatorial Africa. In the remote provinces of Egyptian Sudan, contact with civilization was not effected gradually, or through the medium of legitimate trade; but lawless and plundering traders from the contiguous Arab districts rapidly overran the Upper Nile regions, where they developed a system of compulsory labour, regardless of the advantages to be derived from better regulated commercial relations. Even the Egyptian administration itself, which from the first was tainted by the evils of the previous state of things, had lacked the strength and vigour required to eradicate long-standing abuses and introduce salutary reforms in the Negro lands.

These deplorable relations in the provinces about to be explored by me were doubtless in a pecuniary sense advantageous, relieving me from the heavy tribute exacted by independent chiefs, as well as from the regular pay and support of the carriers, as these were for the most part supplied by the authorities for a few marches, and were then replaced by others. Nor did I require, like travellers starting for the interior from Zanzibar, to encumber myself with bales of cloth, glass beads, copper or brass wire, needed for the regular barter trade, or for paying hired carriers. These marketable wares I was enabled to replace by articles suitable for presents, or in payment of occasional services required on my own account from the natives.

It may here be remarked that owing to the general scarcity of manufactured wares, articles of this sort had an exceptional value in the Equatorial Provinces, where trade in the ordinary sense had as yet merely got beyond the rudimentary state. When mention is made of goods imported from Khartum to Ladó or the Bahr el-Ghazal region, by this expression is to be understood the retail business carried on with the permission of the Government by private dealers occasionally visiting the country, and supplying the personal wants of the local Arab and Nubian officials; or else the goods forwarded by the administration in Khartum for the requirements of the functionaries and troops stationed in those remote provinces. Of all such imports, probably less than ten per cent. in beads, cloth, and copper went to the native chiefs in payment of the ivory supplied by them.

Thus regular trade and barter remained for the most part

confined to the inhabitants of the Government stations. Elsewhere the Negro populations continued during my residence in the country to be enslaved and oppressed by statutory labour and other exactions to meet the requirements of the public service. Commodities are never imported from Khartum in sufficient quantities to develop a normal traffic with the natives, and thus the best intentions of Emin Bey and others were entirely defeated. All the more was this the case that none of the Egyptian officials had any interest in welcoming innovations, by which they foresaw that their own selfish dealings would be interfered with.

Owing to these relations, the traveller in the Equatorial Provinces required a far smaller quantity of such wares as cloth, beads, and copper, all of which could be procured in Khartum. I was thus enabled to provide myself with considerable supplies of articles which, although not absolutely necessary, had never yet been introduced into North Central Africa, and which, however trifling in themselves, were calculated to give the natives quite a different idea of our European industrial arts. I also hoped that the Negro, who in many respects remains a child to the end of his days, would be amused by the sight of such curious novelties, and thus brought more readily to co-operate in the furtherance of my plans. With few exceptions, none but the cheapest and worst European wares are prepared for the African markets. Such, for instance, are the amazingly cheap razors, knives and scissors, but of such vile quality that they are far excelled by the native cutlery, and a false impression is thus produced of the European industries. Consequently, besides the necessary and useful, I also took care to be provided with other articles of better workmanship, which might serve both as presents for the local Arab officials and as a means of entertaining and instructing the natives.

Thus from Berlin I bought, besides my personal outfit, a far greater quantity of white and blue enamelled kitchen ware, plates and dishes, than was required for my own personal use, rifles of several different patterns, and a whole magazine of miscellaneous items, from needles and thread to smoothing irons and mincing machines. Amongst them were dried fruits, jams, tea, a large supply of seeds from Erfurt, cutlery, looking-glasses, hunting-knives, bronze chains, retailed by the yard and afterwards found to be in great demand, as were also the numerous tin whistles, pipes, jew's-harps, accordions, and other musical instruments, including a large full-toned barrel-organ, added in Cairo. There was also an extensive assortment of amusing or instructive toys, animals, ships, houses, soldiers, a railway train, pictorial illustrations of the whole animal kingdom in clear, bright colours,

OM-DERMAN.

crackers, in which were cunningly concealed whole costumes, or else frightful masks of human or animal heads in diversely-tinted tissue-paper. Then came scientific instruments from London; camp-beds, hammocks, a huge umbrella, a camp table, and two chairs put together in pieces, from Paris.

My "stock-in-trade" was completed in Cairo and Khartum by the addition of oil and vinegar in flasks, powder and shot, saddlery, chemicals, salt, sugar, rice, macaroni, soap, candles, a large supply of ship-biscuits, tubs, kettles, washing-gear, cotton goods, and many other things, by which my *impedimenta* at last assumed formidable proportions. Hence, I already began to be anxious about the question of carriage, all the more that the difficulty would probably be increased by the war with Soliman Bey, which had only just been concluded.

Towards the end of January everything had been packed, and two days before the departure of the *Ismaïlia* I sent on board about one hundred and thirty separate packages, all with few exceptions arranged to suit the requirements of transport by carriers in the Negro lands. A social gathering at Consul Hansal's was followed by a final *réunion* of my Khartum friends at my house the evening before we parted, in most cases for ever. None of us could at that time have foreseen the terrible calamities which were pending, and in which nearly all were overwhelmed. While a merciful Providence protected and guided me through countless perils back to my home, most of the others were swiftly overtaken by a premature death, leaving nothing to me but the memory of the pleasant days passed in their society.

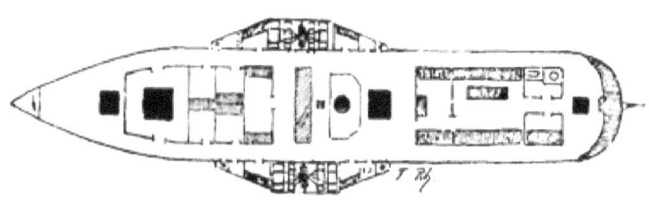

THE *Ismaïlia*.

CHAPTER II.

JOURNEY FROM KHARTUM TO MESHRA ER-RÊQ.

On Board the *Ismaïlia*—Bohndorff's Career—High Water on the White Nile—Shifting Scenery—Mosquitoes and Rats—Stay in Fashoda—The Steamers *Burdeïn* and *Ernest Marno*—A Steppe Fire—A Grass-barrier—Farewell to Marno—We enter the Bahr el-Ghazal—Dreary Wastes in the Nuer Territory—Countless Grass-barriers—*Varia africana*—Papyrus—In Collision with a Crocodile—Turtles *versus* Rats—Ambatch Forest—A Colony of Darters—The Bahr el-Arab—Mouth of the Jur—Flooded Savannahs—Arrival at Meshra er-Rêq—Cartographic Survey of the River—Gessi's Disastrous Journey down the Nile—Origin of the Grass barriers—Arrival of Gessi Pasha—The Carrier Question solved.

ON January 31st I sent on board all the remaining things, together with the three mounts and additional fodder for the asses. On this occasion the *Ismaïlia* was accompanied by the *Embâba*, another Nile steamer, with several boats in tow, which were intended to bring back to Khartum a considerable quantity of ivory, besides a number of Nubians and rascally Arabs, who had been ordered by Gessi Pasha to clear out of the Bahr el-Ghazal district.

During my previous excursions on the Nile I had acquired some experience of the *Ismaïlia*, where the only available space for stowing our effects was the deck of the stern, with the arrangements shown on the accompanying plan. Besides the cabin, two side-berths, and a table, there was a saloon also with a long table and couches, affording sleeping room for four persons. But most of the space was so encumbered with Government supplies destined for Fashoda, that we were obliged to cram nearly all our things into the cabin, leaving scarcely any room for stretching our legs till a clearance was made at Fashoda. A great part of the steamer was also occupied by an upper deck, which was protected by an awning from the glare of the sun.

Warned by my experience during the previous expedition, I had taken care to hire no Arab servants in Khartum, and besides Farag 'Allâh I was accompanied to the Upper Nile regions only by a negress, my cook Saida. I hoped to find in the country itself young natives suitable for my purpose, who could soon be trained to perform their simple duties. Our trip was much delayed by the time consumed at the various stations in taking in fuel for the *Ismaïlia* and the other craft following slowly behind. Such occasions were utilized for short hunting expeditions along the wooded banks of the river, or with fishing with rod or net. Thus were captured many specimens for my collection, besides guinea-fowl to keep the pot boiling.

The monotony of the journey was also somewhat relieved by conversation with Bohndorff, in whose account of his past career I naturally felt some interest. Born in 1849, at Plau in Mecklenburg, he had started in life as a goldsmith's apprentice, but soon took to wandering, passing from Hamburg through Cologne to Switzerland, and thence to Savoy. Here he was arrested during the Franco-German War as a "Prussian spy," and escorted in chains to the Italian frontier, and soon after obtained employment in Genoa. But, yielding to his roving propensities, he now found his way to Tunis and Egypt. In Cairo he again worked some time at his trade, and in 1874 entered Gordon's service, accompanying him to Gondokoro as a kind of steward or store-keeper.

At the end of 1875, as I was about to start on my first expedition to Sudan, Bohndorff offered to join me; but I was at that time obliged to dispense with his services, having already engaged Kopp as collector and dresser. Nevertheless, soon after my departure from Egypt, the restless adventurer set out— in May 1876—on his own account, proceeding from Cairo through Dongola straight for Dar-Fôr, and so on to the western parts of the Niam-Niam territory. Here he reached his westernmost point in the Nsakkara district, west of the Shinko river, at a temporary station founded by Rabeh, one of Zibêr's captains, who figured somewhat prominently in the revolt of Soliman. In consequence of this revolt Bohndorff had to return, but was plundered on the way, and barely escaped with his life to Shekka, where Gordon happened to be staying at the time. With his assistance Bohndorff made his way back to Cairo shortly before my arrival in 1879, when, as already stated, he entered my service.

It may here be mentioned, to complete the history of his venturesome career, that owing to constant illness requiring his return to Europe, I sent him back from the Niam-Niam country at his own request in October 1882. But owing to the revolt of the Dinkas in the Bahr el-Ghazal province, by which the route to Meshra er-Rêq was blocked, Bohndorff was unable to leave the Negro lands before December 1883.

After a short stay in Europe, he took service under the Congo State, and was for some time engaged as superintendent at the station of Manyanga. When the Austrian Expedition of 1885, under Dr. O. Lenz and Dr. O. Baumann, was preparing to reach Emin Pasha's province from the Congo, Bohndorff received permission to accompany it. Thus it happened that he found himself at Quillimane on the south-east coast in 1887, after crossing the Continent with Dr. Lenz. Finding it impossible to settle down in Europe, Bohndorff was back in Egypt in the autumn of the same year, and has since found active employment in the service of the German East African Company, under the Imperial Commissioner, Major Wissmann. His surveys in the Niam-Niam domain and the Bahr el-Ghazal province were published by Dr. B. Hassenstein in *Petermann's Mitteilungen* for 1885.

Owing to frequent interruptions we were ten days making the trip from Khartum to Fashoda, which place we reached on February 9th. Compared with previous years, this section of the Nile presented in many respects a somewhat novel aspect.

FASHODA ON THE WHITE NILE.

The river was still considerably swollen, so that its banks at Kaka, which formerly stood high above the surface, were still under water. This was due to the exceptional height of the White Nile during the present year.

Other striking changes were also noticed. The masses of grass vegetation drifting down stream warned us of the presence of these obstacles on the upper reaches, where the stagnating waters in tracts exposed to the inundations promote a fresh growth of floating masses, while other parts, naturally or artificially detached, drift far to the north on the swollen current of the Nile. Thus, a few days south of Khartum, we met large grassy islands, some, so to say, moored to the banks, others borne along by the stream. In this way the papyrus could now be seen floating away with other vegetable refuse far from its southern home.

South of Kaka began the plague of the large gadflies, whose sting is extremely painful. They obliged me during the day

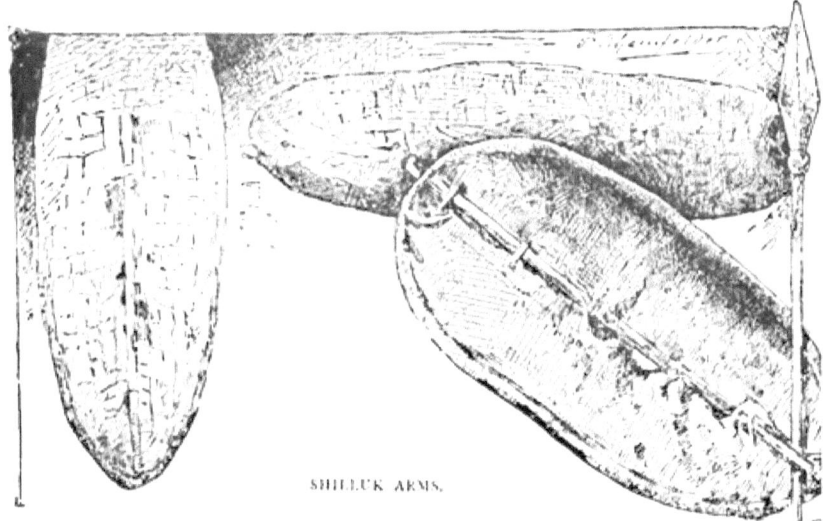

SHILLUK ARMS.

to work under my mosquito-net, and I had even to protect my riding animals both from these pests and from the swarms of midges who took their place at sunset.

But a worse plague, on board the *Ismaïlia*, were the rats, against whom everything had to be carefully secured during the night. Towards evening they generally began to run riot among the boxes piled up in the cabin, clambered up the ropes to reach objects suspended from the roof, and even went impudently scampering up and down the couches, and on the very table as I sat reading. However, I was occasionally able to restore a little order by a successful discharge of shot from my pocket-pistol.

The non-arrival of the *Embâba*, with its string of barges, detained us some time at Fashoda, during which I gave my saddle-asses a little exercise every day ashore. We frequently landed, though there were but few attractions in a place which seemed suited for nothing but a penal settlement, for which purpose it was in fact maintained by the Administration. During the rainy season it is little better than a dismal swamp; but just now we could at least get about without sinking ankle-deep in the mud.

Here also a pleasant surprise awaited me. The steamer *Burdehn*, so named from a place in Upper Egypt, where the former Prime Minister, Sherif Pasha, had a large estate, had arrived unexpectedly from the south with Ernest Marno on board. He had come for more ropes and fresh supplies of all sorts for the men employed higher up in clearing away the grass-barriers. Although Marno had repeatedly visited Egyptian Sudan, and had even been my precursor in Makaraka Land, I now for the first time made his personal acquaintance. He gave me much accurate information on the present state of affairs in the Upper Nile regions, and I was especially indebted to him for useful sketches of several river valleys. Since my last visit the territory of the Shilluks had been made almost entirely tributary to the Egyptian Government, and it was stated that with an escort of a few soldiers a traveller might now reach a part of that domain called Tungu in a three days' march in a south-westerly direction from Fashoda.

In Fashoda, almost on the verge of civilization, I made a few final purchases, such as coffee, sugar, salt, butter, soap, dates, and the like, which I was glad to procure from the Greek trader, Jussuf, settled in that place. To my stores were also added some fresh vegetables, a sheep, and twelve chickens, these last costing only one thaler.

At last, on February 15th, the long-expected flotilla arrived with a full supply of fuel, and next day all the steamers started southwards, passing the mouth of the Sobat on the 17th. A few hours later we reached a new station, where some soldiers were at work stacking fuel for the boats engaged in getting rid of the *sudd*, or grass-barriers, farther south. The men had built themselves some huts, and thus had sprung up a regular settlement, where the steamer *Manssura* lay at anchor. Thus as many as four steamers, with a large number of smaller craft, were now assembled in this inhospitable district.

At this season of the year the exciting spectacle of a steppe fire may here be witnessed almost every evening. One night one of these conflagrations, away to the north of Fashoda, assumed an aspect of terrific grandeur. Between us and the raging sea of flames stood the Jebel Akhmet Agha, its massive slopes partly concealing the all-devouring element. But as the night advanced the dark mountain mass stood out sharply against the horizon, its outlines vividly traced in gold, while the blazing fire flared up, and was reflected almost to the zenith on the overhanging blue sky. We stood spell-bound at the overwhelming spectacle.

After taking in a fresh supply of fuel, we found to our amazement that the whole breadth of the White Nile at the so-called Maiyeh bita Signora [1] was obstructed by a grass-barrier over three hundred yards wide. This fresh formation had accumulated during the last few days, for the vessels which had recently descended from the Bahr el-Jebel had found the river at this point quite free from obstruction. A few hours, however, sufficed to force our way through the *sudd*, which had not yet had time to form a dense mass, but still floated somewhat loosely about.

In the evening we cast anchor in the lake-like basin of the united Bahr el-Jebel and Bahr el-Ghazal, the lake No of the older maps, now known as the Maqren el-Bahūr, or "Meeting of the Waters." [2] The *Manssura* had already left us to resume operations at the great obstruction on the Bahr el-Jebel. She was soon followed by the *Burdehn*, with Ernest Marno on board. To him I wished all success in his arduous undertaking, and bid him a farewell, which proved to be final. A few years later

---

[1] A backwater so named from the intrepid traveller, Miss Alexine Tinné, who was the first to explore it.

[2] From قرن, to join or unite, and بحر, sea, river, water.

PAPYRUS THICKET AND HIPPOPOTAMUS.

(August 31st, 1883), he also fell a victim to the Sudanese climate, which he had so long resisted.

With our entrance into the Bahr el-Ghazal began the serious work of the expedition. The Bahr el-Jebel I had already ascended as far as Ladó; now I was to visit the second great head-stream whose junction with the other forms the White Nile. It was my intention to make a careful survey of the Bahr el-Ghazal, which had hitherto been neglected, whereas the course of the Bahr el-Jebel had been accurately traced by Chippendall and Watson in 1874, and again recently by Marno while engaged in removing the grass-barrier. For this purpose I had already several times taken the log of our steamer; but this did not help me much, owing to the tremendously difficult conditions of the navigation in the Bahr el-Ghazal. Hence I was at last obliged to depend upon averages based on rough estimates.

We started on February 21st, and I began at once to record the angle measurements of the fluvial channel, and to sketch any salient features in the course of the river and its immediate vicinity. During the rainy season the whole region of the Moqren el-Bahūr forms an extensive lake, whereas at low water it is divided into two sections, which communicate through a channel a little over half a mile long. Even after entering the river, properly so called, the observer seeks in vain for any conspicuous object, or even a mere bush from which to take his bearings. On both sides extensive tracts are permanently flooded; but the river gradually narrows apparently to half or even a third of the lacustrine depression; nevertheless it still for some hours of steam navigation maintains a clear waterway at least fifty yards wide. Throughout this stretch nothing was visible except a dry patch on the right side occupied by a wretched fishing hamlet, whose Nuer inhabitants led a sort of amphibious existence.

A little higher up there came into view, also on the right side, the Maiyeh bita Komundári (the Keilak of the older maps), branching off like a river far into the interior. A second back-water followed still on the right side, and soon after the Maiyeh bita er-Rêq on the left. Smaller channels of like formation, and communicating with the main stream, also occur for a long way on both banks; but they are so little conspicuous that it is often difficult to say whether they are the mouths of tributaries or merely backwaters.

PARRA AFRICANA.

An apparently endless uniformity is the prevailing feature of the landscape, the low grassy mere scarcely broken by a few tall papyrus stalks. Amid the water-lilies (*Nymphœa lotus*) and other characteristic growths of those swampy regions, the graceful little *Parra africana* may be seen daintily tripping about on the broad foliage of the floating plants. An open expanse which I noticed penetrating far into the grassy steppe, our *reïs* (pilot) told me was the Khor Deleb. Half an hour beyond it we sighted another wretched Nuer fishing village. With the field-glass I could descry some ten huts, on which about thirty of the natives had swarmed the better to observe our steamer. In the immediate vicinity the main stream is joined by an important affluent, which would appear to be a northern branch of the Khor el-Arab.

Shortly before noon we passed two Deleb palms (*Borassus flabelliformis*), forming on the left side a distinct landmark near the mouth of the already mentioned Khor Deleb. Some scrub and a few old termite hills, rising above the grass on the distant horizon, indicate the locality where this dreary watery region begins to merge in more solid higher ground. The termites' nests are often built against such scrub; when they stand isolated near the water they frequently look as if whitewashed by the droppings of the birds. Now and then a darter (*Plotus melanogaster*) may be seen perched on one of them, preening itself in the sun.

In the course of an hour we passed the third Nuer hamlet in this region—a group of some twenty mud-huts with straw roofs peeping up above the grass. The stream, which had hitherto presented a free surface at least fifty yards wide, now assumed a sudden and surprising change. The navigable open track seemed to trend sharply round to the right; hence my astonishment when we made straight for a narrow opening in the grass, which would have escaped any but a sharp eye familiar with the locality. We thus suddenly passed from a broad waterway to a narrow channel, where the steamer's paddle-boxes grazed the herbage on both banks. This was the continuation of the Bahr el-Ghazal, whereas the apparent main stream turned out to be only the Bahr bita el-Arab branch.

The open current was only fifteen, or in the broadest places at most fifty yards wide, and pond-like expanses were but rarely met. Nor was it often possible to detect the true river-banks, or distinguish the parting-line between land and water. The higher grounds, rising like islands above the grassy plains, were indicated more by their scanty brushwood and ant-hills than by their actual elevation; while the region exposed to inundation stretched in many places far into the dreary waste.

In the midst of this oppressive monotony it was a relief for the eye to rest on a few clumps of trees away to the south-west. The trip itself had hitherto been made, if slowly, at all events without any interruption. Now, however, began our troubles, floating grass getting entangled between the paddles, which had every now and then to be cleared, or else the whole waterway becoming obstructed by floating masses which required more or less effort either to break through or remove. Hence the rate of progress varied greatly, thus considerably increasing the difficulties of my survey.

About three o'clock we met the first real grass-barrier, which, however, was surmounted in the course of twenty minutes, during which the ropes of the boats in tow snapped several times. Later followed other loose accumulations, which, though easily removed, still caused much delay; one more compact mass especially took fully an hour to be mastered. At sunset we cast anchor, to give the *Embába* time to overhaul us.

Early next day, February 22nd, I resumed my observations, while the puffing and snorting engine continued its struggles with the grassy obstructions. Now for the first time we noticed a stretch of woodlands near the left bank, followed later by another on the same side, while on the opposite bank two solitary trees served as clear landmarks for my calculations. Beyond the Ghaba Jer Dekka, a little grove close to the river, the stream meanders incessantly through the monotonous plains, nowhere relieved by a single conspicuous object. Here the floating obstructions thickened; but towards noon we unexpectedly reached a good broad waterway, and after another sharp bend a large Maiyeh (backwater) was passed on the right, soon followed on the left by a large tree, grouped round which were a few Negro huts.

Our experienced pilot now drew my attention to the new barriers, which had been formed since his last trip, and which required considerable efforts to set aside. Those on the other hand which have once been pierced are always more easily overcome, though they may have partly closed up again. But although the way was thus to some extent cleared by our vessel, the *Ismaïlia*, the *Embába*, with the boats in tow, found great difficulty in getting through the sedgy masses in our wake.

Towards sunset I noticed in the distance one of those curious long-legged and "whale-headed" waders (*Balæniceps Rex*), whose range seems confined to these swampy regions of the Bahr el-Jebel and Bahr el-Ghazal. I was very anxious to secure this specimen, and the captain, yielding to my wish, cast anchor for the night. Unfortunately the helmsman, Ibrahim, who went in pursuit, lost his way in the swamp and tall grass, and had to return at dark empty-handed.

Next day, after getting through some smaller masses, we were arrested for several hours by a huge barrier of a felt-like consistency, and nearly the third of a mile in extent. In the course of another hour's steaming through open water, we reached the confluence of the Maiyeh bita el-Deleb, as I was assured by the pilot; he also informed me that this watercourse is joined by a stream from the south, presumably the Jau, which rises far to the south in Abakáland.

The Maiyeh is fringed by strips of woodland, and the prospect is also relieved by euphorbias, which occur here somewhat frequently. The papyrus also grew more profusely, and in the shallower parts of the stream along the river-banks this reed was associated with a young growth of ambatch (*Herminiera elaphroxylon*). The wooded banks of the Maiyeh are occupied by the Nuers, whose huts were visible from the steamer. Here we had a long wait for the *Embába*, whose white funnel at last came within the focus of my field-glass. But a flag of distress was also flying half-mast high, and it presently appeared that the *Embába*, with all the boats in tow, had stopped short at the last great barrier. They remained in this position all night, but next day all were got through with our united efforts.

After forcing another extensive mass, we all ran an imminent risk of destruction through the heedlessness of one of our men, who, in spite of my warnings, had rashly set fire to some of the grass, which at this season of the year is quite dry on the surface. In a moment we were encircled by a sea of flames, which had to be extinguished by letting the water play freely on the floating vegetation lying nearest to our steamer. But this did not afford much help to the boats we had in tow, and even less to the *Embába* and its barges, which were still some distance behind. The fire had now reached the withered herbage on the left bank, and the flames, fanned by the breeze, were already licking the sides of the boats. Fortunately, however, the danger disappeared as quickly as it had sprung up, and in a few minutes the conflagration had burnt itself out.

The last great barrier, some 2000 yards long, was soon followed by another fully as large. We anchored before it for the night, and here we noticed a crocodile floundering about near the surface, apparently injured by collision with the steamer. But though the men gave chase in a boat, it managed to get clean off, and soon disappeared in the grass.

The *sudd* at which we were now arrested was of a peculiarly tough consistency, and being about a mile and a quarter long, it took nearly a whole day of combined efforts to force it. The barrier occupied a bend in the river, leaving only a narrow channel in the centre free of herbage. Some distance off stood a stately *Balæniceps Rex*, apparently sunk in deep contemplation, but doubtless on the watch for any passing prey. Having lately engaged the services of a large tortoise, I felt so relieved from the plague of rats that I was now able to continue my work till midnight. As soon as dark set in the tortoise would begin to potter about in the cabin, and this seemed to have the effect of restoring order amongst the unruly rodents; at least I was henceforth far less disturbed by their boisterous riotings.

On February 26th, after passing another *sudd* nearly 500 yards long, I took soundings, and found the Bahr el-Ghazal at this point ranging in depth from twenty to thirty feet. A little higher up the fluvial scenery assumed a different aspect. The river gradually grew wider, while the banks stood out more distinctly, being both higher and better wooded than lower down.

Some native dwellings also came into view, and at one point the north side was fringed with a regular forest of ambatch, a plant which had already been passed some days previously. Here for the first time the observer is able to form some idea of the actual size and volume of the river, which in some places was nearly 350 yards wide between its wooded banks.

An interesting spectacle was here presented by a large colony of darters all living peacefully together. Hundreds and hundreds of the black, snake-headed birds, disturbed at the approach of the flotilla, suddenly rose on the wing and kept whirling in dense clouds round about a cluster of high, leafless trees; the unfledged broods peeped eagerly from countless nests, while the fledgelings in a first attempt at flight came flopping down on the banks of the river or in the water. But for our hungry crews they proved a "windfall," in the strictest sense of the word; many dozens, at all stages of development, were knocked on the head and brought on board, some of which found their way into my stock-pot, while others went to increasing my collections. The flesh had a smack of train-oil.

BALÆNICEPS REX.

At the Ghaba bita 'l Arab, on the north side, the main stream is joined by the Bahr el-Arab; owing to the slight incline the confluent waters here expand into a spacious basin, which appears, from a communication made to me by Schweinfurth, to have had no existence at the time of his explorations (1869-71). Farther on follows another expanse of stagnant waters, beyond which the open channel contracts at first to fifty or sixty and then to a little over twenty yards. Here also the woods become thinner, and at last again give place to boundless flooded grassy plains with patches here and there of tall ambatch.

In the narrow channel we were again delayed two hours by a mass of *sudd* about 160 yards deep, above which the stream broadens to fifty-five yards; but nothing is visible except an endless expanse of grass and ambatch. At this season the stouter ambatch stalks grow to the thickness of an arm, or even a leg, and rise from twelve to eighteen inches above the water. From the top sprouts the tufty foliage, the stem proper, from ten to fifteen feet long, lying below the surface.

In the vicinity of the arboreal vegetation shallow water may generally be expected, whereas the ambatch reed often shoots up from considerable depths. Just now it was beginning to blossom, and the tufts were already in many places covered with a pretty yellow flower. With the extremely light stalks the Shilluk negroes make their primitive river craft. The plant is not an annual, but lasts several years, and when full grown attains a height of sixteen feet. In its lower part the stem bulges out to a thickness of ten or twelve inches; it greatly resembles the Indian *Aeschynomene*, which is used for making summer head-gear, dainty toys, house-models, and the like. Hence ambatch is certainly one of the future resources of Africa, as a material that may come into use for technical purposes. The tangle of felt-like root fibre growing about the foot of the stem is built of little bulbs or tubers, whose purpose is not quite evident, as they neither produce sprouts nor appear to increase the buoyancy of the fibrous radicles.

Towards sunset of February 27th, we passed the confluence of the river Jur coming from the south-west, and next day brought us to the end of our journey. During the last few hours the Bahr el-Ghazal had in many respects again assumed a different aspect. Beyond the mouth of the Jur there was little to suggest a river in the ordinary sense of the term. The "Kit," as this section is called, presents the appearance of a boundless sea of grass and sedge with an open expanse winding away to the head of the steam navigation at Meshra er-Rêq. The real navigable channel can be detected only by those familiar with the locality, so sluggish is the current, though the Kit is joined farther south by the Molmul. This relatively flat expanse, spreading out like an inland sea, is to be regarded as a result of the pent-up waters of the Jur, increased by the

PLAN OF MESHRA ER-RÊQ.

contributions of the Molmul also from the south-west, and probably by a branch of the Torij, which permanently flows to the south-eastern part of this labyrinth of water, grass, and sedge.

Early on the 28th I was shown the spot, indicated by no particular landmark, to which, and even beyond which, the waters had retired after the heavy rainfall of 1878. The steamer from Khartum had on that occasion to cast anchor at this place, where, the water still continuing to subside, it was soon left high and dry above the stream. At that time people could go all the way by land to Meshra from this station, which stands at the head of the low water navigation, and which has received the name of Matrak el-Vapor, or "Place of the Steamer."

The almost stagnant expanse of the Kit is in many places carpeted with the superb lotus, nymphæa, and other aquatic plants. Of an evening the peculiar crackling sound is frequently heard, with which the magnificent milk-white calyx of these huge water-lilies bursts into bloom. Here and there the surface is broken by dry spots, which are partly nothing more than flooded termites' nests, a proof that in previous years the Kit had long remained free from the inundations. But some of these dry places are also real islands, on which the tall *Balæniceps Rex* may occasionally be seen mounting guard in his peculiarly motionless attitude.

At some distance from the left bank I noticed a Negro village, beyond whose conic mud-huts the southern horizon was bounded by a semi-circular fringe of woodlands, a sure indication that we were at last approaching more elevated dry land. Presently our weary eyes were gladdened by the sight of the straw-thatched huts and the masts of some Nile boats grouped about the landing-stage. Before reaching the goal our attention was attracted to the right side by a herd of ten or twelve elephants on a scrubby island, which seemed to be connected by a stretch of shallow water with the mainland. On coming within half a mile of the spot I sent several bullets amongst the huge pachyderms, one of which seemed to be hit; but pursuit was rendered impossible by the swampy character of the flooded ground.

Four hours after leaving our last anchorage below the Kit, we reached the new station of Meshra er-Réq, a little to the south-east of the now-abandoned Meshra el-Tujár ("Landing-place of the Traders"), which was formerly the starting-point for all expeditions to the interior. The *Ismaïlia* cast anchor for the last time off a little island, on which nothing was to be seen except a few Government huts. Beyond it the flooded land still stretched away southwards to the already-mentioned amphitheatre of low-wooded rising-grounds.

MESHRA ER-REQ; AMBATCH THICKET IN THE RIGHT FOREGROUND. (*From a drawing by L. H. Fischer.*)

We had entered the Bahr el-Ghazal on February 21st, consequently we had taken nearly eight days to ascend the river, owing to delays caused by the numerous floating obstructions. In order to render possible the cartographic survey of the river, I estimated for the *Ismaïlia* six different rates of speed, and in my calculations applied this scheme according to the nature of the obstacles. The course of the stream, as determined by 1781 angular measurements, I found to be 214 kilometres, or say, 130 miles long. It may be incidentally remarked that these results were found to agree in a surprising manner with a chart afterwards prepared by Marno, as well as with the section surveyed by Lupton Bey.

Before leaving this watery domain, a few words may be acceptable regarding the formation of the *sudd* in the Upper Nile regions. How disastrous such obstructions may at times prove, was shown by the fatal issue of the voyage undertaken the same year by Gessi Pasha from Meshra er-Req to Khartum. The steamer *Sasia* had left Meshra on September 25th, 1880, taking in tow some boats with over four hundred Arabs and officials, leaving the Bahr el-Ghazal province after the war with Soliman, and the whole flotilla got completely hemmed in by a grass-barrier near the Ghaba Jer Dekka, some distance below the Bahr el-Arab confluence. All efforts to get disentangled were in vain; provisions soon fell short; famine and typhus combined swept away over half of the men; the others lived on the flesh of the dead, and not one of them would have ever seen Khartum again, had not Marno appeared with the steamer *Burdehn* as an angel of deliverance on January 4th, 1881, bringing succour to the survivors after months of unspeakable horrors and misery.

As regards the firmness of their texture, the grass-barriers show considerable diversity. Some are loose enough to be forced by a powerful steamer at the cost of much patience, toil, and help, while others resist all such efforts. The latter type is more easily developed in the Bahr el-Jebel, which abounds far more than the Bahr el-Ghazal in isolated or stagnant back-waters and lateral lagoons. Such tenacious masses are, in fact, more frequently formed in the Bahr el-Jebel, while the looser kinds are more characteristic of the Bahr el-Ghazal.

It is abundantly evident that the vegetation itself does not spring up spontaneously on the spot where it becomes solid enough to dam up such a mighty river as the Upper Nile, whose breadth, depth, and current would necessarily prevent such a growth. Few rivers in the world have so slight a fall as the Upper Nile, and its western affluent, the Bahr el-Ghazal. In its course across many degrees of latitude, the former traverses a uniform level region, and in many places the current is maintained merely by the pressure of the streams descending from the more elevated parts of the Bahr el-Jebel basin.

Through the periodical rise of the Nile, which differs considerably in volume from year to year, being determined by the amount of the rainfall in the tropics, the low-lying riverain tracts are flooded, and these consist in many places of flat depressions where the Nile waters lodge after the general subsidence. Such depressions often continue even at low water to communicate with the main stream, of which they form, as it were, so many inlets; or else they become transformed in the dry season to small lakes and ponds, which resume their connection with the Nile at each returning rise. These are the "old" or backwaters, the Maiyehs of the Arab boatmen, which are constantly changing their level and assuming a different aspect with the rise and fall of the flood-waters. They form hundreds of *culs-de-sac* of all sizes, by which the difficulties of the navigation is greatly increased. Such conditions do not occur in the Sobat with its high and regular banks, but are partly found in the section between the Sobat and the Moqren el-Bahūr, and especially on the Bahr el-Jebel, as far as and beyond the station of Bor. Other conditions prevail in the Bahr el-Ghazal, where the Maiyehs are doubtless rarer, but where broad flooded expanses are more frequent.

The periodically replenished lateral lagoons and depressions naturally promote a rank growth of aquatic plants, and the Maiyehs are in fact the hot-beds and nurseries of all the grass islands which drift away to the main stream when the communications are re-opened. But at other times the same stagnant waters serve to retain the masses which, being rooted very lightly to the ground, gradually form floating islands. Such islands, continually growing in thickness and solidity, would in fact become stable, and in course of time fill up nearly the whole of the Maiyeh, but for the fact that at each periodical flooding they get detached from the bed of the depression and raised to the surface. Then they drift away before the high

AZOLLA.

winds, and reach the Nile in various states of development. During our detention at Fashoda, strong north winds had constantly prevailed, and under their action all the floating masses along the northern bends of the river would be inevitably driven into the main stream.

In a word, the favourable conditions for the development of the *sudd* in the Upper Nile basin are :—

1. A rise of the flood-waters above the normal level in order to bring the backwaters into free communication with the river, and at the same time detach and raise the floating masses to the surface.

2. Favourable winds to further detach and drive these masses into the river, where they either drift harmlessly with the currents, or else coalesce together into formidable barriers. At the same time, the winds, as is obvious, may have a contrary

ISMAIL EYUB PASHA, EX-GOVERNOR OF KHARTUM.

effect, arresting as well as propelling the masses, breaking up as well as building up the barriers; hence the constant changes that these formations are subject to through the shifting of the winds, as well as from the varying character of the periodical floods.

3. The growth of those innumerable little plants, which spring up in still and sheltered waters, and then drift away to enlarge

or render more compact the tangle of the floating masses. Such are, for instance, the Azolla, Pistia, Aldrovanduà, Lemna, Ottelia, Ultricularia, Ceratophyllum, Potamogeton, Naias, Lagarosiphon, and others.

But even under the most favourable conditions a protracted damming up of the Nile is of relatively rare occurrence, as, however deep the barrier may be, the current always flows underneath. In the opinion of long-experienced Arab boatmen, the prevailing relations in the forties and fifties were much the same as at present, though in those years the obstructions were never so compact as some of those occurring in recent times. The best known were those of 1863, at the time of Miss Tinné's visit; of 1870 and 1871, by which Sir Samuel Baker's expedition was delayed, and which was ultimately cleared away by the vigorous action of Ismail Eyub Pasha in 1874; of 1878, at my first excursion, when the Nile rose to an unusual height, and caused extensive floodings in the delta.

It may be mentioned that in the lower reaches of the White Nile the current is too strong to allow of any accumulations. Here the smaller masses, breaking away from the southern barriers, are carried swiftly along to and beyond Khartum. But very little reaches Egypt itself, most of the floating growths being either arrested in the recesses along the banks, or else becoming waterlogged and sinking to the bottom, where they are slowly decomposed.

In the composition of the *sudd*, the prevailing element, at least in the Bahr el-Ghazal region, is the so-called Om-Suf, or "Mother of Wool" (*Vossia procera*), an aquatic grass, which, to the unscientific eye, looks more like a reed. It is a favourite food of animals, and in its midst grow patches of papyrus, but very little ambatch, which generally shoots up from deep water and enters only casually into the composition of the *sudd*.

The varying texture of these obstructions depends largely on the different conditions under which they have been brought together, on their age and general constituents. Their tenacity is at times so great that huge amphibia, such as the hippopotamus and crocodile that occasionally get entangled in their meshes, are unable to free themselves, and thus perish of hunger or want of air. As a rule they are more compact, and consequently present greater obstacles to navigation, in the Bahr el-Jebel and White Nile than in the Bahr el-Ghazal. In this river we were generally able to force our way through such impediments, even though steaming against the current. But in the Bahr el-Jebel the steamer alone is often helpless, and requires the aid of special apparatus to break through.

In most cases the object aimed at is simply to get through, leaving the obstruction to close up again or not behind the steamer. But when systematic and continuous operations are undertaken to clear the waterway, the course adopted is to break up the

CLEARING AWAY THE GRASS-BARRIERS.

masses piecemeal, and send the fragments into the current to prevent them from again coalescing, at least in the same place. Solid masses can be attacked successfully from the north side only, that is, operating against the current. In this case most of the work is in fact done by the stream itself, by carrying off the fragments as they get detached by the men at work on board the steamer. But were the steamer to force its way with the current into the tangle, the detached pieces could not drift away, and the ship would run the risk of being caught, as in the pack-ice of the Arctic regions, by the fragments closing in from behind. In November 1878, Emin

Bey was thus arrested with his steamer on the journey down to Khartum, and being unable to overcome the obstacle, had to return to Ladó. To the same circumstance was due the already described disaster that befell Gessi and his people in the Bahr el-Ghazal two years later.

The usual plan is for the steamer to select a suitable point of attack, and go full speed into the elastic *sudd*, if possible through some opening between the shore and the barrier, where the elastic parts are generally more easily detached. Some of the crew help with long-forked poles, guiding all released masses sternwards, while others co-operate on the barrier itself just in front of the prow, pressing it down below the surface and thus facilitating the progress of the steamer. They work breast-deep, steadily moving forward or clambering up to get the higher parts under-water. During these operations the progress of the vessel is scarcely perceptible, although the paddles are continually kept going.

But should all efforts fail, recourse is had to another process which, though tedious, aims at clearing the waterway to the utmost. As before, the steamer drives at full speed into the yielding tangle, in which, however, it soon gets hemmed in. Then all dead inflammable matter, such as dry papyrus stalks, is fired; and when consumed two diverging cables are made fast to the floating mass at a distance of thirty to fifty yards from the prow. The ropes are secured by being wound round long stakes, which are driven right through the thick mass at an oblique angle to prevent them from yielding when the steamer begins to back off. After one or two efforts this manœuvre generally detaches a large floating island, which either at once drifts away down-stream, or else is taken in tow by another steamer, and sent adrift at any point where the current is strong enough to carry it down.

Should even this method fail, then the whole mass is broken up and torn away bit by bit by the steamer. Such operations are excessively tedious, and Marno was occupied from September 1879 to April 1880, with four steamers and several hundred men, in clearing the Bahr el-Jebel.

To these aquatic growths the White Nile, as well as many other sluggish streams of tropical Africa, owe their characteristic aspect. The White, which is the "Clear," is so named in contradistinction to the Blue, that is, the "Dark" or "Turbid" river, which contains a large proportion of inorganic matter kept constantly churned up by its rapid current and eddies. In the White Nile, on the contrary, as well as in its numerous affluents, the floating vegetation acts like a filter, purifying the troubled flood-waters of the rainy season, and sending them down in almost a limpid stream as far as and even beyond the Blue Nile confluence.

Our arrival in Meshra er-Réq brought fresh trials to my patience. The advent of the steamers was at once reported to the remote southern stations; but we had still to wait for Gessi Pasha with the carriers required for our heavy baggage. But in the whole district there were absolutely no settlements, beyond a small station which had been founded on the mainland some seven or eight miles off in connection with the steam navigation of the river. At the present dry season there was a decided lack of water at that place, and I consequently resolved to remain on board the *Ismailia* during my enforced stay at Meshra.

In my report to Gessi I endorsed the opinion of the captain and pilots, that the grass-barriers on the Bahr el-Ghazal should be seriously taken in hand, and more men engaged for the return trip. Richard Buchta had returned from Ladó after his expedition to the south, and was now at the little inland station awaiting the next steamer for Khartum. He came on board, and we passed several pleasant days together, looking over the beautiful photographs and other pictures which he had brought back from the Magango and Makaraka regions, and numerous specimens of which adorn these volumes.

But the heat was oppressive, and after sunset we suffered dreadfully from the mosquitoes. The rats and black-beetles were also extremely troublesome. Lock up as I would, they still found their way into cases and coffers, and fouled the sacks and baskets of *buxmat*, or biscuits, which I had procured in Khartum. It was also annoying to find that my mercury barometer, brought so far with such care and trouble, now proved useless. The quicksilver had become decomposed into minute, almost invisible, little pellets, for which there was no remedy.

To my joy Gessi arrived on March 10th. Our long conversations were unexpectedly disturbed by a fierce thunderstorm, accompanied by a tropical downpour, a rare occurrence at this season of the year. My table-top was swept overboard, and the steamer itself dragged its anchor. But Gessi relieved me of all anxiety regarding the carriers, by placing at my disposal the men who had brought to Meshra the ivory destined for Khartum. I now regretted not having brought more supplies, but with my remaining cash bought a fresh supply of salt and cloth from the ship's crew.

On March 13th I was able to send off a first convoy of one hundred and five loads to the station of Jur Ghatta, our provisional destination.

DEPARTURE FROM MESHRA ER-RÊQ.

CHAPTER III.

JOURNEY FROM MESHRA ER-RÊQ TO DEM SOLIMAN.

Fatal Consequences of the lack of a Stronghold at Meshra er-Rek—Gessi's Vigorous Administration—*Balœniceps Rex* and Chimpanzee—Departure from Meshra in a Dug-out—Gordon's Warning—Order rules the Universe—Dried-up Morasses—Nuers and Dinkas—The Flooded Lands of the Tonj River—Island Oases—Residence in Jur Ghattas—Westward Ho!—Jurs and Bongos—Kuchuk Ali Station—Wau Station—The Bati People and the Bahr el-Ghazal Tribes—Biselli Station—March to Ganda—Excursion with Gessi to the Dem Soliman Province.

OUR two steamers had brought some Government supplies for the Bahr el-Ghazal province, and these had to be conveyed to Jur Ghattas in order to be thence distributed amongst the stations. Since the first appearance of the Arab traders, this was the nearest strong post that had been erected throughout the wide domain of the Dinka tribes. The trading stations at Meshra, near the place made memorable by Schweinfurth's historical journey, were merely temporary refuges for the traders while awaiting the arrival of their convoys, and for the use of the few men left behind with the boats. A similar purpose was at present served by the little zeriba which had been erected a few hours inland from the Meshra landing-place.

But for a great distance round about no fortified post had anywhere been established, although such a stronghold was urgently needed for the control and administration of the surrounding Negro lands. The disastrous consequence of this oversight was seen a few years later in the fate of the ill-starred Lupton Bey, who, even before falling into the hands of the Mahdists, had to carry on a desperate struggle with this very section of the Dinka people. Such was the prevailing disorder that at that time the road from Meshra er-Rèq to Jur Ghattas could not be traversed without an escort of 800 men, and the traveller Shuver, venturing forward without sufficient protection, was here murdered by the Dinkas.

However, at the time of my arrival a military guard was scarcely needed for the journey to Jur Ghattas; but to secure their good-will the natives throughout the whole district had hitherto been exempt from the burdensome *corvée* as applied to the transport service. Trained carriers could only be formed in the course of years round about the fortified stations, where the chiefs were under the control of the administrators.

After the transfer of the stations in the Bahr el-Ghazal region to the Egyptian Government, the establishment of a fortified settlement in the vicinity of Meshra er-Rèq had become more urgent than ever. Gessi's successful campaign against Soliman, son of Zibér, entailed for some time at least as regular a steam-boat service with Khartum as possible. Unfortunately the erection of such a post was neglected both during the ensuing short administration of Gessi, and at the commencement of Lupton's vigorous rule, which was so soon followed by the rebellion of the Dinkas.

Lupton had the misfortune of succeeding to the government of the Bahr el-Ghazal after the Arab "reign of terror," and the sharp reaction under Gessi, who fell into the opposite error of making too many and too sudden concessions to the Negroes, while pitilessly crushing the Arab system. Gessi placed an almost blind confidence in the Negro hordes, whom, during the war with Soliman, he had stirred up against everything Arab, that is to say, Mohammedans, Sudanese, Nubians, and the like.

At first these Negroes naturally showed themselves extremely loyal and submissive to their champion and liberator. But after his sudden departure, Lupton's task was undoubtedly rendered more difficult by the ensuing change of system, and especially by the introduction of the *corvée*, however necessary this institution may otherwise be in those regions.

After the Dinka revolt, and towards the close of Lupton's administration, a strong garrison was at last placed at Meshra er-Réq. But it was already too late. The Mahdists knew well how to take advantage of the situation, and, making common cause with the Dinkas, soon made themselves masters of the Bahr el-Ghazal province. After their irruption early in 1884, it was at once seen that all the heroic efforts of Gessi and Lupton had been in vain. These brave men could leave no lasting fruits behind them; but they left a name that cannot soon be forgotten, for both fought might and main in the best interests of humanity.

As already stated, I was now able to send forward to Jur Ghattas most of my effects by the carriers who had arrived in Meshra from the south, mostly laden with ivory for Khartum. This and other cargo was at once put on board the steamers, which in a few days steamed down the Bahr el-Ghazal for the Sudanese capital.

My repeated efforts to secure a specimen of *Balæniceps Rex* were at last crowned with success. A boatman brought me two young birds, both of which had been shot in the neighbourhood of Meshra. One having been badly injured received the *coup de grâce*, and went to increase my collection; the other, which had only been winged, soon recovered, and both on board the steamer and later at Jur Ghattas proved a source of much amusement. I had some fish placed daily in my large bath, and it was curious to observe the great "whale-head" for some time stand perfectly still, then dart forward with his huge bill, and in a flash snap up a fish a foot long, which, without any apparent effort, vanished down his capacious throat. He developed a surprisingly sedate and phlegmatic disposition, was from the first far from timid, and soon allowed people to come near, though easily startled at any sudden change or noise. He would mostly take his stand in some particular place, as if buried in thought, and could with difficulty be driven from the spot. Extremely comical was his attitude towards two young chimpanzees, which had been captured for Gessi, and which evinced an unconquerable dread of the bird. This proved

SPUR-WINGED GOOSE. (*Plectopterus gambensis*).

to be rather convenient for us, as the anthropoids often behaved like unruly children, especially at meals, with their shouting, grinning, and biting, actually driving us from the table and then falling on the victuals themselves. But a check was soon put upon their unseemly importunities by the stern demeanour of our phlegmatic "policeman," as Gessi now insisted on calling him. Later, whenever the chimpanzees ventured to renew their pranks at meal-times in Jur Ghattas, we had only to shout "police," when order would be immediately restored by the appearance of our preserver of the peace, who would stalk in and assume a position of imperturbable gravity without condescending to take the least notice of the boisterous romps. On my departure for the interior I left the bird with Gessi, who gradually accustomed it to eat flesh as well as fish. He afterwards informed me that it was one of the victims of the terrible disaster in the Bahr el-Ghazal, serving at least to furnish one meal for a few of his famished people.

Another aquatic bird more frequently met on the White Nile and its numerous affluents is the spur-winged goose (*Plectopterus gambensis*), so named from the powerful spurs with which its wings are armed. But the flesh is tough and rank, tasting of train-oil.

On March 18th, 1880, I took a temporary leave of Gessi, whom I was again to meet in Jur Ghattas. But it was no easy matter to reach this station from the little island at which the steamers rode at anchor. From the Meshra landing-stage, a shallow, swampy expanse, in parts reaching to the waist, and here and there concealed by reeds or aquatic plants, stretched some three or four miles southwards to the fringe of woodlands visible in the distance. To a dug-out scarcely twenty inches wide I could trust myself, but not my mathematical instruments, compass, chronometer, and the like. These were carefully packed and consigned to the carriers, who went off in Indian file, Bohndorff, servants, and all plunging with a light heart into the flooded morass. Then I stretched myself full length in my frail bark, bare-footed and bare-legged, to be ready for a possible capsize or other accident. The dug-out was taken in tow by a long-legged Dinka stripling, my servant, Farag 'Alláh, and a few others shoving along on either side. Thus I reached firm ground with no further mishap beyond a pair of blistered legs, half roasted in the broiling sun.

A few hours' march through a stretch of open woodlands

brought us to the southern station, situated in an arid, waterless district, as if to support the reputation of Africa as the "Continent of Contrasts." For months together we had had water more than enough, and now we already began to feel the pangs of thirst. I say now, in the dry season, for a few months later the torrential rains will again convert these hard-baked plains into an almost impassable quagmire.

Towards sunset, however, we came upon a few water-holes in the open forest, where we encamped for the night. The helplessness of my followers, still but roughly trained for the work before them, here reminded me of the warning words uttered by Gordon at our very first interview: "Trust in no strangers for help; in these lands learn early to help yourself, if you would avoid continued loss or damage to indispensable things either difficult or impossible to be replaced." The constant complaints of African travellers regarding such mishaps are undoubtedly, in many cases, due to careless packing, combined with the temptation to leave too much in the hands of ignorant or indolent assistants. During my first expedition I once discovered a fellow hard at work trying to shorten a metal peg with a chisel, the result being that both peg and chisel were spoilt.

Our southern march was resumed next morning through a level grassy plain, where the tamarind, Kigelia, Cordia, and a few other representatives of the African tropical forests, already began to appear. Various marshy depressions, though now nearly dry, were crossed with difficulty, especially where the deep footsteps of elephants had become hard as stone. In some places a little water still remained from the recent heavy rainfall, which for the time of year was somewhat exceptional.

After leaving Meshra er-Réq, we at once found ourselves in the wide domain of the powerful Dinka or Janghah nation. Behind us we had left the Nuer people, whose numerous but detached groups occupy the low-lying marshy tracts along the lower courses of the streams flowing to the White Nile and Bahr el-Ghazal, nearly the whole way from the affluent eastwards to the Sobat. Our route had afforded us only a few glimpses of these tribes, which even reach farther south to the districts between the Jau and the lower courses of the Rol and Bahr el-Jebel; here their territory is conterminous with that of the Dinkas, at or about 7° 30′ north latitude.

The broad tract between these rivers is still almost entirely unexplored, and but rarely traversed even by the Arab cattle-lifters. During my first expedition I had already come in contact with several of the south-western Dinka groups, where they border on the Moru, Mittu, and Bongo peoples. I had now an opportunity of observing a part of their western territory between the Tonj and Molmul rivers, which is inhabited chiefly by the Réq group, who give their name to the Meshra er-Réq landing-place.

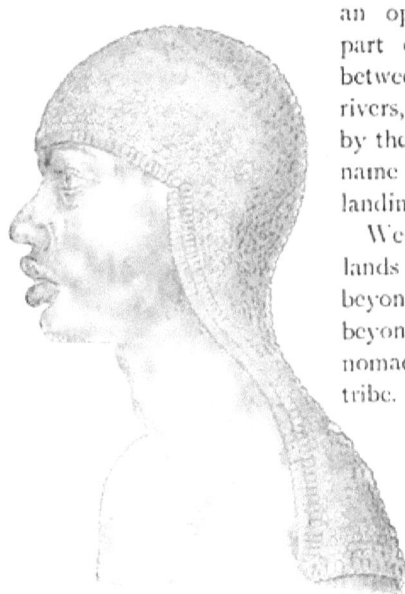

A DINKA (RÉQ TRIBE).
(From a drawing by Dr. Schweinfurth.)

West of the Molmul the Dinka lands stretch still far to the north beyond the Bahr el-Jur, bordering beyond 9° N. latitude on the nomad Arab Bagara el-Homr tribe. This district also still awaits detailed exploration, although, owing to their wealth in cattle, these Dinkas were especially exposed to the raids of the ivory and slave-hunters from the first days of the Khartum trading expeditions. Most of the slaves captured at that time belonged to the various Dinka groups, and the yearly forays in these harassed districts had the result of greatly diminishing their herds.

Our present route through Dinka Land lay in the narrow tract between the Molmul and Tonj rivers, a tract long traversed by most of the expeditions going to and coming from Khartum. Between Meshra er-Réq and the more westerly stations formerly founded by Khartum traders, there are no doubt other caravan routes trending south-westwards, such as that followed in 1863 by Miss Tinné's expedition; but the direct, and consequently most frequented, road to Jur Ghatta, lay through the district of the Rêq tribe. But here, also, other parallel ways ran southwards, some more to the west in the direction of the Molmul, others more to the east towards the Tonj. My present route lay to the east of that followed in 1869 by Schweinfurth.

Good progress was made on March 19th, through an open level country diversified with thickets of scrub and stretches of park-like scenery, but nowhere presenting any conspicuous

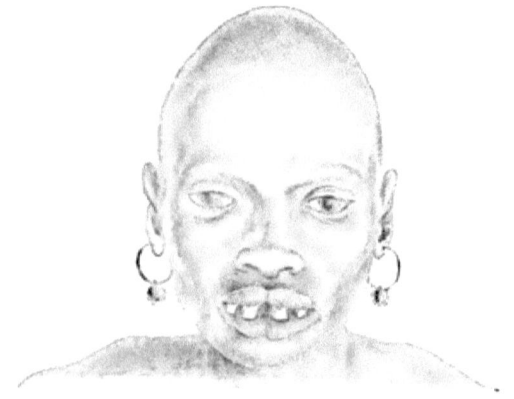

A SOUTHERN DINKA. (*From a drawing by Dr. Schweinfurth.*)

rising grounds. A short spurt next morning brought us to the village of Kûj, a noted Dinka chief; and the following day, after passing several settlements belonging to a chief, Melau, we reached the station of a third Dinka princeling, Matiang. The park-lands and tracts under tall yellow grass, harbouring numerous flocks of guinea-fowl, besides antelopes, giraffes, and ostriches, had suddenly given place to a boundless low-lying region, the first sight of which showed that it was subject to periodical inundations. At present this depression, which lies within the Tonj basin, was for the most part dry. In some places, however, I noticed large ponds which, after the subsidence of the flood-waters, must contain an abundance of fish.

But this region, which stretches for miles east and south to the Tonj, and which at high-water assumes the aspect of an inland sea, is especially remarkable for the large number of eminences rising from its bed, and often clothed with a rich forest vegetation. These heights, forming islands of refuge during the floods, had now the appearance of oases, whose tall umbrageous trees were in some places mirrored in the waters

DINKA COW. (*From a drawing by Dr. Schweinfurth.*)

of still flooded cavities. On one of them we passed the fourth night with Chief Matiang, and next day reached the Tonj, advancing in a south-westerly direction.

At the crossing this river is joined by a small affluent, which drains a part of the island-studded depression, and which sent down a little water. Crossing to the north-west side, we at last reached Jur Ghattas on March 23rd; here my cartographic surveys were connected with those of my first expedition, as I had already visited this place in the year 1877.

Pending the arrival of Gessi, who was to come on after the Khartum steamer had started from Meshra, I settled down in Jur Ghattas, where, despite the war with Soliman, I still recognized several familiar faces. I was glad yet pained again to meet my old friend Atrush Bey, ex-administrator of Makaraka, now broken down in health and spirits, and under arrest for breach of discipline during the war. An affection of the lungs was making rapid progress, and I had at least the sad consolation of brightening his last days with a few attentions in return for the many little acts of genuine kindness formerly received from him. Gessi arriving on March 28th, I put in a word on his behalf, and thus was granted the dearest wish of his heart—leave to set out for Khartum; but, as I afterwards learnt, he was released by death from his sufferings and sorrows before starting from Jur Ghattas.

Now, for the first time, I was able to mature the plans for my future operations in Negro land. My original intention was to visit the Mangbattu country south of the Welle; but the block of the Bahr el-Jebel by the *sudd* had obliged me to make Meshra er-Réq the starting-point. Otherwise I should have gone up the river to Ladó,

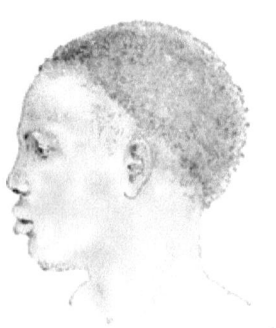

A SOUTHERN BONGO. (*From a drawing by Dr. Schweinfurth.*)

as on the former occasion, and proceeded thence through Makaraka Land to my destination. From Jur Ghattas the most frequented and safer route to that region runs by Rumbak and up the Rol valley through the Abaka country.

But I had already explored the whole of this region, and was all the more reluctant again to follow this route, that I was anxious to visit the Niam-Niam (A-Zandeh)[1] lands on the way south. This project had even been facilitated by the war with

---

[1] A-Zandeh is the plural form of Zandeh, *a* being the plural prefix in many Negro languages north of the Equator; it thus answers to the *wa*, *ba*, *va*, &c. of the southern Bantu idioms, as in Wa-Ganda, Ba-Lunda, &c.

Soliman, friendly relations having since then been established with some chiefs in the Niam-Niam domain. Ndoruma, a powerful prince in this region, had received in a friendly spirit the overtures of Gessi Pasha; hence his court became the first goal of my expedition.

My shortest and most direct route thither would have been southwards through the Bongo and Bellanda Negro territories, but I preferred first to accompany Gessi to Dem Soliman, capital of the Bahr el-Ghazal province, and then start from Dem Bekir for the A-Zandeh lands. The bulk of the baggage was to be sent with Bohndorff, and the servants by a shorter road from Ganda to Dem Bekir. In carrying out these arrangements I met with every assistance from Gessi, who also, at my request, sent forward a messenger to inform Ndoruma of my visit, and request him to have some of his people to meet me at Dem Bekir.

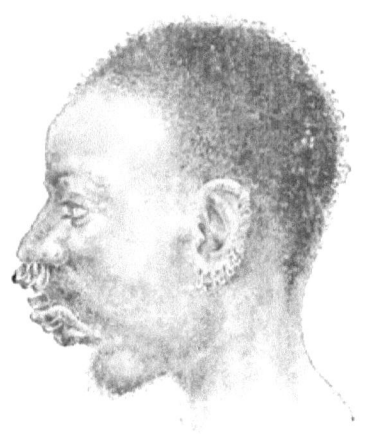

A BELLANDA CHIEF.
(*From a drawing by Dr. Schweinfurth.*)

Owing to various circumstances connected with the late war, the death or disappearance of numerous Arab traders, the emancipation of a multitude of young slaves who scarcely knew what to do with their freedom, I had no difficulty in procuring any number of men willing to enlist in my service as carriers. At least a dozen of such young men had followed Gessi all the way to Meshra, merely for their food. Many were natives of Mangbattu Land, and on hearing of my intention to proceed thither, they offered of their own accord to accompany me. I was thus enabled to make my selection at the landing-place itself, and later required only to engage a few young men as assistants. Bohndorff also made choice of two Mangbattu boys, who were to attend exclusively to the collections, and help in the preparation

CHIMPANZEES SCARED BY KALANICE'S REX. (From a drawing by Fr. Rheinfelder.)

of bird-skins. I took charge of two other Mangbattus, and a young Niam-Niam, and throughout the whole journey we kept a few Negro girls constantly employed in grinding corn and preparing the thick porridge for our followers.

The few days of our stay in Jur Ghattas were occupied partly in working up the results of the journey already obtained, partly in completing the preparations for our further advance. Many things had to be unpacked and repacked in more convenient form, and there were many other things which I left behind for Gessi. I gave him half of the seeds I had brought with me for growing European vegetables at the different stations in the Bahr el-Ghazal province, and I also parted with the rest of the potatoes, which had already begun to sprout.

Many pleasant hours were also passed in the society of our host, Gessi Pasha. My *Balæniceps Rex*, who had accompanied us from Meshra, kept strutting with his measured pace up and down the court, still a constant terror to the little chimpanzees. During the last few days the latter had joined the family circle, all the members of which continued to afford us much amusement. Many anxious moments, however, were caused by a half-grown but strong and surly chimpanzee, who, like all the others, had been brought in a stout cage from the western Niam-Niam Lands. In the station a little wooden hut, with door and fastenings, was fitted up for his accommodation. But one day, as we sat at table with Gessi, he managed to get out, putting to sudden flight the servants and others in the court. Expecting to have a tussle with our anthropoid friend, we armed ourselves with some stout sticks lying at hand; but he took very little notice of us, and went with surly mien moving slowly about from hut to hut.

Meantime some soldiers posted outside hastening up, I directed them to empty the contents of our plates into the chimpanzee's house. The ruse took effect, and he at once withdrew to enjoy the meal we had surrendered to him. In future, however, we took care to keep him more securely under lock and key.

The young chimpanzees which pass a brief and sickly existence in our Zoological Gardens are not to be compared with this specimen, for, despite their formidable teeth, they are really as harmless as little children. Although only half-grown, our ape already displayed amazing muscular power. Later I killed many fully-developed specimens during our wanderings in the denser parts of the forests.

At last the time came to leave Jur Ghattas. Several days previously I had sent forward to Ganda station 130 loads under the charge of some dragomans, and I now proceeded to the same

AN EASTERN BONGO. (*From a drawing by Dr. Schweinfurth.*)

place with Bohndorff, my newly-engaged servants, and the rest of the loads. But Gessi was again prevented by official business from accompanying us; he promised, however, to overtake us later on, and then take up his head-quarters with us in Dem Soliman.

We set out on April 5th, my Dinka carriers of the Madiok

tribe leading the van, milch goats with their kids, goats and sheep for the shambles, and baskets of flour following in the rear. The first day brought us, by a route with which I was already familiar, to the little zeriba Drar (Abu Gurun). At the ford we found the Molmul dry; but under both banks were several large pools teeming with fish, which were being captured by the soldiers of the neighbouring station as we crossed over. The Negroes of this district belong to the Jur tribe, and are subject to a chief named Fin, whose settlements we passed next day. In the little station a number of invalided Egyptian soldiers had been assembled, awaiting the departure of the next steamer for Khartum. They presented a pitiful sight, scarcely with rags enough to cover their nakedness.

The first light rainy season for this latitude had already begun, and it may here be remarked that in the region we were now traversing, the seasons are separated by two rainy periods, a light and a heavy. The former, somewhat more irregular, lasts from March till April, while the latter usually begins about the middle of May and often continues far into October. For weeks the weather had been threatening, but we had mostly experienced little beyond light showers. To-day, also, the horizon was overcast, and we journeyed under clouded skies, though no rain fell.

During my first expedition I had taken the road from Drar to Awet. But this station having been destroyed during the late war, I now made a bend to the south, passing by the villages of the Jur chief, Fin, to the residence of the Bongo prince, Jabai. The frontiers of the various Negro territories can scarcely be indicated even approximately, the relations having been fundamentally altered by the founding of new stations and of Arab settlements. Thus, in this district, Dinka communities are found in the midst of Jur populations, while the Bongo Sheikh Jabai, with his followers, has become a subject of Fin.

To show how chiefs in the vicinity of the stations may be satisfied with the merest trifles—for they receive next to nothing from the Administration—I may mention that Jabai was evidently delighted with my almost valueless gifts of an empty cigar-box, two biscuits, a lump of sugar, a few matches, and a shred of cloth, given more in joke than seriously. The Bahr el-Ghazal Negroes eagerly accept pieces of cloth, which they by no means despise, as do so many tribes on the Upper Nile, such as the Bari, who prefer a handful of tobacco to a strip of cloth, with which they might cover their nakedness. Unfortunately, the quantity of cloth sent by the Government to Negro land scarcely suffices for the most urgent wants of the officials. Hence only a few of the more favoured natives were now and then honoured with such presents.

My people revelled to-day in the somewhat rare luxury of a

PEACOCK-CRANES (*Grus pavonina*).

meat meal. Being by no means fastidious as to choice in this matter, they seemed highly to relish a peacock-crane, which we had knocked over. The flesh, however, of this bird, feeding mainly on grain, is not to be altogether despised, despite its blackish colour; even in many parts of South Europe the common gray crane is esteemed a dainty dish.

On the other hand, the fare to which Bohndorff and myself were now reduced might be described as somewhat meagre, compared with the well-filled flesh-pots of our hospitable friend

Gessi in Jur Ghattas. I allowed none of the sheep or goats to be killed, as they were reserved for Ndoruma, and I was quite aware that in the Niam-Niam country we might pass years without tasting "butcher's meat."

We again came upon the old track in the neighbourhood of the ruined zeriba Awet. The place recalled to my mind a little adventure of my Negro boy, Morjan, who had here been kidnapped by some slave-dealers, but had escaped during the night and found his way back to me. On the river Jur I came upon the first entrenchments that Gessi had thrown up in this district during the war against Soliman, while the rebels still held the station of Kuchuk Ali. From this point they were driven by Gessi steadily westwards from one stronghold to another, until at last the decisive engagement was fought at Dem Soliman. Here the rebels, after a resolute stand, were utterly routed with great slaughter, and Gessi entered Dem Soliman in triumph, while Soliman Bey Zibēr sought safety in flight, without, however, escaping the fate that soon overtook him. How this rebel captain, son of the Zibēr still interned in Cairo, was run to earth by Gessi, captured and shot with others of his kindred, are events which belong to the special history of these lands.[1]

Wading across the Jur, which was at that season only two feet deep, we soon reached the newly-erected station of Kuchuk Ali, the old zeriba formerly visited by me having also been destroyed during the war.

The Jur people are still distinguished by their industry in smelting the iron ores and their skill in working up the metal, qualities already observed by the first European visitors to their territory. Along the route we frequently noticed the little primitive furnaces constructed for this purpose. In other respects the road to the station of Wau, which I had previously traversed, presented no new features calling for special remark. Between the rivers of Jur and Wau (the latter had also fallen to about two feet) great masses of bog-iron ore crop out. This formation, however, should rather be described as laterite; at least no

---

[1] R. Buchta, *Der Sudan unter ägyptischer Herrschaft*, 1888.

difference appears to exist between the specimens of reddish stone from the Upper Nile and Congo basins, which are found in European museums. Apart, however, from their ferruginous property and prevailing red colour, these ores are very diversely constituted.

In this district a barren soil is by no means the necessary consequence of the presence of laterite. In deeper places, with rocky bottom, some moisture, and even pools of water, had already been collected since the rainy weather had set in. Over such depressions hovered swarms of bright, many-coloured butterflies, a spectacle which in Africa occurs only periodically in certain damp localities. Here, also, the landscape was varied with fine woodlands and a rich growth of tall timber.

I may take this opportunity of referring to the state of the water in both rivers during my first journey. At that time, the

WOODEN SIGNAL HORN OF THE BONGOS.

BONGO WOODEN MASK.

rainy season being well advanced, we required boats to get across the streams, whereas now we were able easily to wade through their shallow beds. The contributions received throughout the year from thousands of trickling springs and brooks are insignificant compared with the tropical downpours, to which the floods are entirely due.

Hitherto I had enjoyed tolerably good health, but now began to suffer from sleeplessness. In my sleep I was disturbed by strange and vivid dreams, which generally brought me back to my native land; on the other hand, if I sat awake over the nightly camp fire, I became a prey to hallucinations till again overcome by weariness; then, as I dozed, dreamy visions were again conjured up and again dispelled as I started up to gaze distraughtedly on the dying embers and brood over the sober realities.

As the reader may remember, Gessi Pashi had the intention of making Wau the chief station of the Bahr el-Ghazal province. For this position it was well situated at a point of the river, whence large flat-bottomed craft could convey goods throughout the year down to Meshra er-Rèq, and bring back the stores and supplies sent up from Khartum. During the floods even steamers might ascend as far as Wau. By such a fluvial service the natives would also be gradually relieved from the oppressive obligation of carrying heavy loads, involving a great waste of time, which might be more profitably bestowed on their fields and homes. An outlet would, moreover, be obtained for many products of the Upper Nile regions, such as the excellent timber, which could not bear the cost of transport by carriers.

In this connection it may be remarked that in abundance of natural resources the Bahr el-Ghazal province and conterminous backlands far excel all the regions bordering on the Bahr el-Jebel. The populations themselves stand on a higher level of culture, and are both more capable and more eager to rise in the social scale than those of the White Nile. The Bari people of Ladó, for instance, are still characterized by the inherent defects of the Negro race, a perfect type of indolence and apathy, whereas the Makarakas are far more progressive, forming the transition between the eastern and more advanced western Negroes.

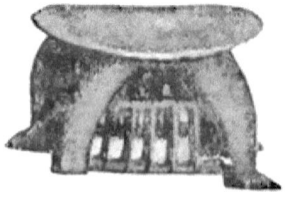

WOODEN STOOL OF THE BONGOS.

At Wau we were overtaken by Gessi, who, however, was again detained by his official duties. Hence we again left him behind and started by an entirely new route towards Biselli. During my former visit to this province I had advanced a short distance to the west and then retraced my steps to Wau; now, however, we pushed forward in a north-westerly direction to Biselli, through a thinly-wooded district strewn with fragments of laterite, and more broken than hitherto. After a moderate march we camped the first night at the huts of the native chief, Mediok, entering the zeriba next morning.

The Jur people, as well as the Wau tribe, which is settled in this district, and which gives its name to the river and the station, store away there winnowed grain in large earthen vessels several yards high, and similar in form to the *burmas*, or ordinary water-vessels. These granaries are set up in the huts chiefly as a protection against mice and other animals, which are unable to gnaw through the clay sides of the receptacles, even though not hardened by the action of fire. Such receptacles, which serve also to keep the corn dry, are in general use amongst the Mohammedan tribes of the Sudan, where they are usually called *gugas*. In his excavations on the site of Troy, Dr. Schliemann found some earthenware vessels which served a similar purpose. In the huts set apart for provisions, wooden stands, in the form of high tables with a wooden grating, are set up for drying the flesh of wild animals, which is first cut into shreds and then placed on the stand over a smouldering fire. The grass thatch and rafters of these huts acquire a dark chestnut or almost black colour from the smoke and heat, and the whole inner side of the roof shines like lacquer-work.

The new zeriba Biselli is pleasantly situated somewhat farther north than the old station visited in 1871 by Schweinfurth, whose tracks I frequently followed on the journey to Dem Bekir. Before his time the whole district had already been explored in 1863-4 by Miss Alexine Tinné and her companions, Theodore von Heuglin and Dr. Steudner. Many of her party perished on this occasion, amongst others, Dr. Steudner himself, whose grave

FIELD MOUSE, MERIONES BURTONII A. WAGN.
(*From a drawing by Dr. Schweinfurth.*)

lies towards the east near the Gitti ("Little Wau") river. South of the station the view is broken by some low hills; but northwards the eye sweeps over the Gitti valley and the fine leafy woodlands which reach right up to the zeriba. The district is occupied by a mixed Jur and Bongo population, while west and north dwell the northernmost tribes of the widespread Bongo nation, which intervenes between the Jur, Dinka, and Mittu-Madi peoples on the one hand, and the Niam-Niams on the other. Some of the Bongo women in these parts wear enormous wooden pegs from an inch to an inch and a half in diameter in their under-lip. Apparently to give support to this heavily-weighted member they often let it rest on the knee when assuming a squatting position.

In Biselli Gessi again overtook us, though again prevented by official business from accompanying us at our departure. Before we started, Biselli was also visited from the northern station of Dembo by Gnaui Bey, who had inherited from his father a number of zeribas in the north. In the remote western territory of the Banjia people, his kindred also maintained a series of posts, which had not yet been officially transferred to the Egyptian Administration. Gnaui was now the only Khartum trader who still retained possession of his stations and people as his private property. Gessi had hitherto hesitated to take over all this property, because the powerful and wealthy owner had accepted the new order of things, and had joined with all his people in the war against Soliman. Negotiations, however, had at last been begun with the view of having all these private stations and their effects made over to the Government.

From Biselli, so named from its former owner, the route towards Dem Soliman lay for some days almost constantly in a westerly direction. Soon after setting out we twice crossed the Gitti river, whose bed at this season contained only a few isolated hollows, filled with water. But indications were not lacking of the great size of the stream in the wet season, when it overflows into lateral morasses, where the water afterwards becomes stagnant. As we might now be overtaken at any time by the rains, at our next camping-place our people, for the first time on this journey, erected grass huts. But the weather still continued clear and fine. In Biselli I had unexpectedly met my old Makaraka friend, the Turkish officer, Mohammed Effendi (Hamdi) from Kabayendi, who was now serving under Gessi in Dem Soliman, and who accompanied us from Biselli to that station.

Next day the road continued to traverse a wooded district, which prevented me from getting a view of the Kosanga mountains, figuring on early maps to the south of our route.

In these regions the traveller frequently meets the *Erythrophlæum guineense* a middle-sized tree with acacia foliage and white berries, the bark of which possesses remarkable properties. This is the bark which is used by various Negro tribes in the western parts of the Continent in the preparation of their poisonous fetish potions. The extract (*erythrophlæin*) is said to be a most efficacious anæsthetic in relieving local pain. There may, consequently, be a great future for the plant as an article of the African export trade.

After crossing the Pongo, an unimportant stream except when swollen by the rains, we again encamped in an inhospitable wilderness. But our sportsmen, who had previously missed a young wild boar and a buffalo, were now more fortunate. Adatam brought down a small antelope, and Hamdi's people bagged a young giraffe, so that our flesh-pots were well filled, and much excitement prevailed round about the camp-fires. We greatly relished the tongue and a cutlet of the giraffe at our evening meal. One of the hams I converted into jerked-meat for future consumption, by having it cut into strips and dried over the fire. The Arabs call flesh cured in this way *sharmut*, or "shreds"; if properly prepared, it will keep for months together on journeys.

Next day the route still continued for some time to traverse a thinly-wooded district, beyond which we entered a magnificently wooded country, which here and there resembled an English park. The land, hitherto level or slightly rolling, became more and more broken towards the west; here also the laterite surface is more frequently interrupted by granite or gneiss masses cropping out above the surface.

On the third day after leaving Biselli a short morning march brought us to Dem Idris or Ganda. Here also the old station had been destroyed in the war with Soliman, and the new zeriba had been recently built a mile or so farther east. We had already passed from the Bongo into the Golo territory, and the district now traversed showed signs of good tillage, without, however, effacing all traces of the havoc caused by the rebellion. The numerous huts and rich banana plantations of the Golo chief, Kasa, inspired a certain respect for the power of this Negro potentate. In this rolling land we enjoyed a somewhat wider prospect over the level depressions and wooded knolls away to the low hills in the distant north. The road leading to the station is skirted on the right by a line of bare gneiss eminences.

In Ganda I found my loads that had been sent forward from Jur Ghattas. Here the route trended southwards by the Ziber Adlan station to Dem Bekir, whence we were to proceed direct for Ndoruma's. I accordingly now despatched Bohndorff with everything that could be spared and the greater part of my people straight to this station, while I continued my westerly journey to the Mudiriyeh Dem Soliman (formerly Dem Ziber). Later I overtook Bohndorff's convoy by the road leading from Dem Soliman through Dem Guju southwards to Dem Bekir.

In Ganda I was rejoined by Gessi, with Gnaui Bey, and Saati Effendi, ex-Mudir of the Bahr el-Ghazal province, all of whom accompanied me to Dem Soliman. On the eve of our departure I entertained a jubilant audience with the varied programme of my barrel-organ. Many other objects of my equipment excited much wonder, while a few useful little European articles were distributed amongst a grateful public. In the neighbourhood Gessi showed me over the ground where his little batteries had compelled Soliman to abandon his fortified lines and beat a rapid retreat on Dem Soliman.

A good day's march brought us from Ganda to the river Kuru, which was crossed next morning, and the journey continued to the Mudiriyeh. On the way the caravan was, for a moment, thrown into some disorder by the sudden cry of "Bees, bees!" raised by the people in the rear. Everybody now rushed wildly forward, and even we put spurs to our mounts until it was discovered to be a false alarm. Gessi later informed me that people had frequently been attacked and badly stung by swarms of bees in this district.

At present the bed of the Kuru, partly sandy, partly rocky, had only one foot of water. One of its tributaries has received from the Arabs the name of Silek, from a species of tall tree which grows on its banks, and which has also given its name to several streams in the district between Ladó and Makaraka.

Beyond the Kuru we crossed the Khor el-Ghanam ("Goat River"), at a point where it develops a horse-shoe bend between steep rugged banks. It was here that Gessi inflicted his last crushing defeat on Soliman, afterwards triumphantly entering the station, at that time called Zibér Rahama, but now re-named Dem Soliman. To-day, also, the place was entered in solemn procession by Gessi Pasha, with ex-Governor Saati, Gnaui Bey, and numerous other officials and natives, all arrayed in their best attire. I had reached this provincial capital on April 17th, having left Jur Ghattas twelve days before.

Dem Soliman is the most important of all the Arab settlements of this class visited by me in these Negro lands. Soliman Bey Zibér had undoubtedly greatly strengthened the place, especially in recent times. Around the whole zeriba runs a double and treble palisade, 26 feet high; within this enclosure the several courts are separated by matting almost hard as boards, and behind them are grouped the high and spacious dwellings surmounted by conic roofs. Soliman's residence, now occupied by Gessi, was built in the style of a two-storeyed house in Khartum; there were also several other strong brick structures, besides magazines well suited for their purpose.

The day after our arrival being my birthday, Gessi honoured the event with a sumptuous repast, including an excellent plumpudding. Next day followed another *asuma*, or banquet, at Saati's, winding up with an evening entertainment given on the eve of our departure by Hafifi Effendi, an officer whose acquaintance I had made in Makaraka. But I had a twofold object in visiting Dem Soliman, first to survey the district, and then to avail myself of Gessi's offer to place at my disposal any of the stores in that important station which might be of service

MUDINIVEH DEM SOLIMAN. (Drawn by L. H. Fischer, from a photograph by R. Buchta.)

in my further wanderings. Having already spent all my hard cash in Fashoda and on leaving the steamer, Gessi made me an advance, afterwards repaid in Cairo, with which I now purchased from the Government stores soap, candles, rice, cigars, tobacco, percussion-caps, powder, shot, and Arab clothes. From private sources I also procured an excellent express rifle, with 1500 cartridges, a smaller rifle, some other firearms, and an ass more inured to this climate than the animal brought from Khartum.

On behalf of Gessi I took charge of several presents for Ndoruma, including a big Turkish drum, an Arab burnoose, an embroidered shawl, and a gun with some cartouches. Before starting I also forwarded despatches for Khartum and Europe by the Shekka route. This road, which runs northwards to Kordofan and through Hofrat en-Nhas to Dar-Fôr, was followed by the Arab traders from the earliest times, and by it no doubt most of the slaves were exported northwards. The traffic along the western highway had considerably increased, especially of late years, since the outlet down the Nile was more strictly watched.

A parting line between the Golo territory and that of the Krej nation stretching westwards from Dem Soliman, might be somewhat arbitrarily drawn north and south at about a day's journey to the east of this station. I say arbitrarily, because so great a mixture of tribes has resulted from the Arab rule, that it is no longer possible to lay down accurate frontiers between the several populations. The Kuru river, however, somewhat approximately marks the eastern limits of the Krej people, who are divided into numerous small groups, among which are interspersed various other communities, some long settled in the country, and already subject to the dominant race, others immigrants or fugitives since the Arab ascendancy in the western districts.

My stay in Dem Soliman was prolonged from the 17th to the 23rd of April, during which my health was thoroughly restored under the hospitable roof and in the genial society of Gessi Pasha. At our leave-taking I received from him the thoughtful gift of a milch cow with her calf, together with a Dinka boy named Farag, to look after these animals and the goats. The Dinkas, being great cattle-breeders, understand these things, whereas the Mangbattus, Niam-Niams, and others not engaged in the rearing of live stock, make but indifferent herdsmen. But wherever cattle are bred in Negro land they are always tended and even milked by the men, never by the women.

IPOMŒA ASARIFOLIA.

PARTING FROM GESSI.

CHAPTER IV.

FROM DEM SOLIMAN TO PRINCE NDORUMA'S.

Final Parting from Gessi—Krej Huts—Relation of the Negroes to the Arabs and to Gessi Pasha—Forced Labour indispensable in dealing with Negroes—Unexpected Arrival of Ndoruma—Solemn Reception, Festivities—Departure of Ndoruma to prepare his People for my Arrival—Dem Bekir—Unfriendly Reception by Abd es-Sit—Ascent of Mount Du—The great Nile-Congo Divide—" Gallery" Woodlands—Chief Jissa—Ascent of Mount Ghasa—Ndoruma's Frontiers—Korumanda District—Head-streams of the Mbomu—The last Affluent of the Bahr el-Ghazal—Chief Gassande—Arrival at Ndoruma's.

WE made rather an imposing exit from Dem Soliman, escorted by Gessi mounted on his mule, and accompanied by many of his officials. Many of those who remained behind, aware of my intention to spend some years in wandering over the southern Negro lands alone and unattended by the customary bodyguard, doubtless gave me up for lost. All Arabs entertain the greatest mistrust of Negroes, and consequently had little hope of my return. At our final parting beneath the shade of a mighty forest-tree, this sentiment found expression in the silent leave-taking, a mere grasp of the hand and the usual Arab farewell greeting for the native officials, a warmer embrace for Gessi as a dear friend, and the last European it might be my fate to meet for many a long year. Gessi himself I never saw again. The days of this brave, noble-minded Italian were numbered. His already enfeebled health never recovered from the effects of the disastrous return journey to Khartum, and on May 1st, 1882, little more than a year after our parting, he ended in Suez his active and useful career.

As far as Dem Soliman we had mainly followed a westerly course to Jur Ghattas; but we now turned southwards to Dem Guju, the route lying the whole way through a rolling country covered with bush, and watered by numerous streams flowing north-west to the Biri. This route was different from that followed by Schweinfurth, who had penetrated west, crossing the Biri, and then curving round to Dem Pekir, whereas I never crossed the river, Dem Guju lying considerably more to the east. On the march we met a number of carriers and the Zandeh chief, Zemio, whose territory lies south-west from here, and who was now travelling to Dem Soliman with ivory, caoutchouc, poultry, honey, and other produce. Many of his people showed the unmistakable Zandeh type, their appearance reminding me of the Makaraka and Bombeh tribes. With Zemio, whom I here met for the first time, I entered later into active relations, and of all native rulers he proved to be my best and warmest friend.

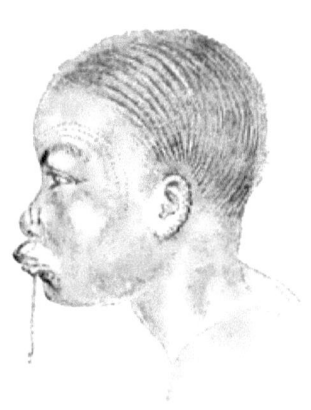

SERE WOMAN.
(From a drawing by Dr. Schweinfurth.)

In the halcyon days of the independent traders, when Zibēr and other ivory merchants of Khartum had grown powerful enough to impose tribute on many of the western and southern lands,

Dem Guju was a much larger and more important place than at present. It was the starting-point of numerous excursions, which were more in the nature of plundering and slave-hunting raids than trading expeditions. Hence, at that time, Dem Guju was practically a slave-market where the Jelabas, or settled retail dealers, brought up the living wares for further distribution on their own account.

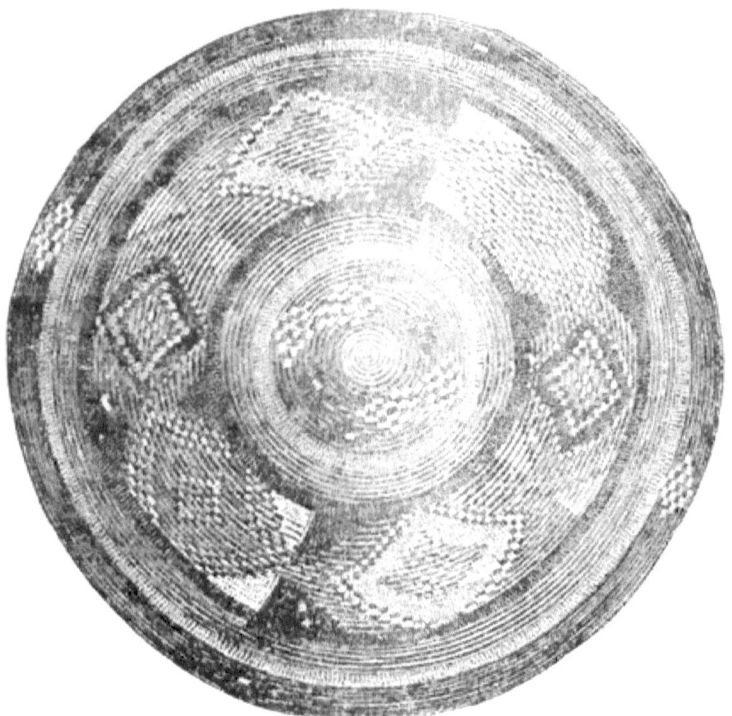

WICKERWARE FOR KISRA AND DINNER PLATES; DAR-FOR WORK.

Thanks, however, to the increased watchfulness of the authorities, these relations have in later times been greatly modified. But before Gordon had taken energetic measures to prevent the export of slaves, both by the Nile and the main caravan route through Shekka and Hofrat en-Nhas, the traders sent their slaves by the tracks leading directly northwards from the remote western lands beyond the Bahr el-Ghazal province. All those western lands and the regions to the south of them were collectively known to the traders by the name of Dar-Fertit, a common Nubian expression, which indicated no particular country with any definite limits. On the clandestine traffic in those days carried on by the Dar-Fôr traders in the western districts entirely unknown to the officials, I shall have more to say when I come to describe my wanderings in the Far West.

At the time of my visit Dem Guju was inhabited, besides the few Government officers, by some of the still surviving Nubian and Dar-Fôr traders, with their female slaves. Here a little wickerwork industry had been developed, and a chief speciality were very pretty, bright-coloured baskets, ornamented with glass beads, and also a kind of substitute for a dinner service, worked in diverse patterns. Some of these I procured for my own use and for my ethnographic collection.

SMALL BASKET : DAR-FÔR WORK.

A short march brought us (April 26th) from Dem Guju to the Krej prince, Gaggo's, the route trending from south to south-south-east over the water-parting between the Biri and Kuru basins, and retaining this direction to Dem Bekir, and in fact all the way to Ndoruma's. My rapid march through these districts, whose inhabitants have for the most part kept at a distance from the beaten tracks of the traders, prevented me from giving more than a hasty glance at the social life of the Negro tribes in the Bahr el-Ghazal region. But their dwellings, weapons, implements, and industrial products are reproduced in a masterly manner by Schweinfurth in his *Artes Africanæ*.

I noticed that all the huts in these northern regions are round and covered with a more or less pointed conic straw roof. The doorways of the Krej huts are so low that they can be entered only on all fours. Near them are seen miniature straw roofs on stands scarcely a few spans high, and under these are little utensils similar in form to the large water-vessels. Such objects, which look like children's toys, and which are also found in diverse forms but of the same fundamental type amongst other neighbouring populations, are indications of a dim perception of mysterious powers. They suggest the easily formulated but difficult question whether the Negroes of this part of Africa really believe in a higher, invisible being? The Arabs settle the matter right off by telling us that such things are the Negroes' "Allah" or Kujur, that is, his fetish, who can cause good or evil. Whether we are justified in concluding that these objects are associated in the savage mind with any deeper conceptions of the supernatural, I shall endeavour to ascertain after a more extensive comparative study of all the facts.

The next march brought us from Gaggo's to the village of Ganago, another Krej chief near the upper course of the Kuru. The source of this river lay a day's journey farther south, and is followed westwards by that of the Bitti or Biri. This district is geographically important as forming a part of the water-parting between the Nile and Congo, the two largest African rivers. The streams flow north and north-west to the Bahr el-Ghazal, south and south-west through the Mbomu to the Welle-Makua.

At this season heavy dews fell every night, so that the tall grass, already over three feet high, drenched us nearly to the hips on the morning's march; but both grass and clothes were soon dried by the warm sunshine. Here I found a portable iron bedstead very serviceable in the Krej huts with their small entrances, which rendered useless the larger Sudanese angareb. Nevertheless I passed many sleepless nights, and envied my little black Saida snoring away on the straw mat at my side.

On April 29th we reached Dem Bekir, where we rejoined Bohndorff and found the loads all in good condition. On the route we crossed the Kuru, here ten paces wide, and beyond it two smaller water-courses. It was a rolling, little diversified country, with much bush preventing extensive prospects. As far as I could judge, the whole region is but thinly peopled, the recent wars having perhaps driven the inhabitants to quit their settlements and withdraw beyond reach of their foreign oppressors.

The Dem Bekir zeriba lies on the little river Duro, which here flows eastwards through a broad grassy depression, dotted over with the habitations of the Golo tribe. The superintendent, El-Maas, had received orders from Gessi to assist us in every way, and he was well aware that in doing so he was consulting his own best interests. I had scarcely expressed my satisfaction at the arrangements made for our accommodation when he related all his wants, including diverse petitions to the Pasha, which he expected me to back up. In Dem Bekir I took up my quarters for a few days, awaiting the messengers from Prince Ndoruma, to whom my approaching visit had already been announced from Jur Ghattas.

Owing to the innovations introduced by Gessi the position of the Egyptian Negro States and their rulers had just then entered on a period of transition. The Bahr el-Ghazal populations, and especially the Zandeh kingdom, already shaken to its foundations by sanguinary intestine strife, as well as all eastern and western lands where the Khartum traders had founded settlements, or organized plundering expeditions, had in the course of years been enslaved, and laid waste by these foreign usurpers; the peoples themselves had also been largely deprived of their personal freedom and compelled to render compulsory service to their new masters. The enforced contributions of corn and other local produce, the incessant raids on the cattle of the Dinkas, Nuers, and other pastoral tribes, the kidnapping of their women and children, and similar outrages, must have created amongst all the Negro populations a feeling of profound discontent, which under other relations would certainly have led to open revolt and the expulsion of the hated intruders.

But the Negroes are incapable of either defending or recovering their freedom, as the case may be, for their immense preponderance of numbers is neutralized by lack of cohesion and disunion. Were they fused in a single nationality, or capable of understanding the necessity of common action for the common good, they could easily withstand the few armed forces sent against them, and all the powder and shot hitherto expended in assailing and enslaving them would never suffice to save their oppressors from extermination.

As it was, they now naturally hailed Gessi, vanquisher of the great slave-trader Zibér's son Soliman, as a benefactor. At the beginning of the war they had held aloof, and often even betrayed hostile feelings towards these new invaders, who for them seemed to forebode nothing but fresh misery, and who as yet held out no promise of better times. But after the first successes, and when they saw that Gessi was smiting their former oppressors hip and thigh, emancipating the kidnapped slaves and even calling in the natives to hunt down the enemy that had taken refuge in the bush, then they welcomed the conqueror with shouts of jubilant exultation.

At that time mistaken notions of the new order may have dimly dawned on the excited brain of many natives. Some assuredly expected relief from the obligation of statute-labour, and improvement of their material condition, hopes which were not realized, and which under prevailing conditions cannot be realized, even by the mildest possible system of government. The efficient administration itself of a Negro province requires increased labour on the part of the native, and this labour he will not submit to freely, for after all he is mainly indolent and indisposed to work. The prosperity of the land and of the individual, the so-called "Negro culture," is impossible without the compulsory labour of the Negro himself. According to European notions this may seem an infringement on personal freedom, and cried down by sham philanthropy as only a lighter but still inadmissible form of slavery; nevertheless for generations to come enforced labour must remain a primary condition of all successful attempts to improve the condition of the African.

After Gessi's successful campaign against Soliman, the remote chiefs and princes in the Niam-Niam country everywhere displayed a friendly spirit, spontaneously sending envoys and ivory to the new governor, and even presenting themselves personally at the stations to declare their goodwill. But this natural action of rulers whom he had liberated from their oppressors, inspired Gessi with too much confidence in certain transactions, and especially in the dismissal of numerous Negro soldiers who had served under Soliman and the Arabs. At that time he frequently spoke to me of his conviction that, after having as far as possible eliminated the Arab element, he would no longer need any great armaments in the province; the Negroes, he felt assured, would continue to show themselves submissive, and in case of need readily accept military service.

On the other hand he would be able considerably to lighten their burdens when the standing army was reduced to a minimum. It was accordingly his policy to maintain as few men as possible at the expense of the native populations. Hence he dismissed not only the slaves who had taken refuge with him and the former retainers of the Nubians, but also many young Negroes who had served in the war, and now desired to return to their homes. He went even further, and allowed many of these men to keep their arms. However, he still retained an adequate force of native troops, some consisting of young men recently enrolled in remote districts, others who had years before been torn from their homes, and who had voluntarily joined the standards.

But many of these disbanded soldiers took advantage of their freedom, not only to recover their homes, but also, with the truculence characteristic of Negroes, to play the part of swashbucklers, ready to take service with petty chiefs for lawless purposes, or else undertake freebooting expeditions on their own account. In the interior of the country I had later many opportunities of noticing the insolence and overbearing conduct of these disbanded natives.

For the moment, however, Gessi's policy secured the friendship of the Negroes and their rulers, who placed themselves freely at his service. Some of the fire-arms taken from Soliman he handed over to several of the more powerful Zandeh chiefs, such as Zemio, Sasa, Ndoruma, and others; he thereby strengthened their hands against rival potentates, and also enabled them to reduce refractory tribes, and procure ivory for the Government by filibustering expeditions. They were also expected to bring tribute of caoutchouc, cereals (durra, maize and telebun), palm-oil, ground-nuts, honey, pulse, to the Bahr el-Ghazal stations.

In a word, he aimed at limiting to the utmost the expeditions formerly organized at these stations, and despatched under Nubian leaders to plunder the southern lands, relying on the chiefs themselves whom he had furnished with fire-arms to bring in the ivory, but of course abstain from slave-raiding! Many of the old commanders of zeribas, Arabs from the time of Soliman or of his father Zibér, who anticipating Soliman's overthrow had remained neutral, or even helped Gessi, were now allowed to

ROMOLO GESSI PASHA. (*From a photograph by R. Buchta.*)

remain as administrators at their posts in the remote western districts. Such were Rafai, Abd Allah, Ali Kobbo, and others; and this was but another proof that neither Gessi nor any other Governor could dispense with the Arab and Mohammedan elements in the administration of Negro land.

In carrying out his innovating reforms Gessi trusted to his lucky star, and he was anyhow actuated by the highest motives.

In the case of chiefs such as Zemio and Sasa, he may not have had cause to regret his confidence in the loyalty of native vassals. But the disbanding of the black troops and dismissal of former dragomans, and especially the granting of arms to the smaller chiefs of the Dinka tribes, was to say the least premature, and not justified by the circumstances. I do not go so far as to assert that the disastrous Dinka revolt which afterwards broke out under Lupton Bey was precipitated by this mistaken policy; but the success of the Dinkas was certainly facilitated by the concession. I would here express my dissent from Gessi's fundamental principle, that the traffic in slaves is entirely promoted and mainly carried on by the Arabs. And as he aimed at the suppression of this traffic in his province, it was at least risky to grant the more highly-favoured native rulers the right of organizing distant expeditions, which, without the proper restrictions, were practically plundering raids. I myself later accompanied such native expeditions, and I can therefore certify that all Negroes make a more reckless use of the power entrusted to them than do the half-caste Sudanese Arabs. On such occasions they commit many outrages associated with their superstitious practices, such as human sacrifices, which they consider themselves bound to make in honour of the dead. They are also more ruthless than the Arabs, and recognize no law except that of the strongest.

The action of the natives in connection with Gessi's successful campaign acquires special interest in the light of recent events in East Africa, where the Germans are engaged in a similar conflict. It is to be hoped that they will take warning from the consequences of Gessi's misplaced confidence, and not allow themselves to be deceived by apparent successes, or by the passing emotions of impulsive Negroes.

But while touching on these relations I am far from desirous to detract from Gessi's great merits. I am myself too well aware how hard it was at that time to eradicate inveterate abuses, and direct existing institutions to better purposes. Gessi's efforts at improvements, like those of Gordon, Emin, Lupton, and other well-meaning reformers, were thwarted by the lack of sympathy and co-operation on the part of his underlings, and by the absence of that vigilance which was necessary to control both officials and subjects in the exercise of their rights and the performance of their duties. However, the friendly disposition of the Negro rulers towards the new Governor, Gessi Pasha, promised the best results for myself and my journeys to the interior.

As I had anticipated, messengers from Ndoruma arrived in Dem Bekir, though I was amazed to learn from them that the prince himself was following close behind. I hastily made every preparation to give him a worthy reception, and when he soon after entered the station, the reason of his personal visit at once became evident. He wanted to be certain of the object of my expedition, and ascertain if I had any hostile intentions, or was accompanied by a large force that might be dangerous or burdensome to his people. He could not at first understand my intention of visiting his country with quite an insignificant escort. This was even later a perpetual wonder to him, for strangers had hitherto traversed his territory with hundreds of armed men ever ready for war or attack.

For the solemn reception my little suite had quickly donned their best—Russian peasant costumes, bright cotton shirts and trousers, of which I had brought several dozen as presents. With the Turkish fez, on the possession of which every Negro prides himself, my few followers made a brave show, as they drew up and presented arms, while I advanced with Bohndorff, the superintendent El-Maas, and others to give Ndoruma a hearty welcome, and lead him by the hand to a seat in the hut set apart for the reception. Such was my first meeting with this powerful Niam-Niam ruler, who had several times struck terror into well-equipped Arab expeditions, two of which he had nearly annihilated in 1871.

On his first appearance Ndoruma presented a somewhat comical sight, arrayed in an eccentric costume, which he had apparently put on expressly for this occasion. He had squeezed his long muscular legs into a pair of crimson trousers which were far too short and narrow for his brawny limbs, and which seemed to have at one time formed part of a huzzar's uniform. Over this he wore an Arab gelabiyeh, which was also far too tight a fit, compressing shoulders and arms into the smallest compass, and leaving chest and paunch fully exposed. Yet so calm and dignified was his bearing, so imposing his colossal figure, that I soon forgot his laughable appearance and at once became deeply interested in this striking personality.

He involuntarily reminded me of the Mangbattu king, Munsa, as described by Schweinfurth in his *Heart of Africa*. On the countenance was stamped the unmistakable Niam-Niam type— sharp, vigorous traits, animated eyes bespeaking a resolute spirit, combined with prominent cheek-bones and broad nostrils, which imparted a strange wildness to his Negro features. The lips, however, were but moderately everted, and were moreover relieved by thin mustachios, and a shaggy beard merging upwards in a sparse growth of whiskers. The hair, arranged Zandeh-fashion, though somewhat carelessly, in tresses, projected under a tarbush round the occiput. Like all the Niam-Niam chiefs of the early period, Ndoruma scorned all personal ornament, his ordinary dress being the customary "rokko" which is prepared from the bark of a species of fig (*Urostigma*), and which is generally worn by many peoples of Central Africa. The Zandehs wear a comparatively small garment of this type, which is brought forward between the legs and fastened behind by a girdle, so as to spread out on both sides, and fold round the hips like a loose loin-cloth. In this national rocco Ndoruma's tall handsome figure showed to the best advantage. When seated he affected a somewhat careless attitude, though by no means awkward, but on the contrary displaying a certain natural dignity in every movement.

In recent years Ndoruma had been brought into frequent contact with the Arabs and Khartum traders, and had already acquired some familiarity with their language. Some eighteen months before our interview his independence had been broken in war by Rafai Agha, the Mohammedan governor of Zibēr's former zeribas in the West Zandeh lands, a person who had played a leading part in the history of Egyptian Sudan. But though compelled to recognize the suzerainty of the Nubians,[1] Ndoruma, like the vanquished chiefs, had gladly welcomed the new relations growing up under Gessi's administration. Hitherto, however, he had apparently met no Europeans, but Egyptians alone. Hence I was evidently an interesting object in his eyes, and I was aware that he had shown great curiosity to see me. At first, however, despite his self-conscious attitude, he had been unable altogether to conceal that suspicious shyness which is inborn in every Negro. But the feeling soon wore off, and when my frank declarations enabled him to grasp the true situation, he showed undisguised pleasure at being able to put aside all needless fears. Every word and gesture also betrayed his astonishment at my appearance, and at the many objects entirely new to him, as well as at my expressed intention to visit his country and other strange lands alone and without escort of any kind.

The prince had already on a former occasion visited Dem Bekir with a convoy of ivory, and had even been as far as Dem Soliman, but at a time when Gessi was absent. At present he was accompanied only by a small following, having, as he explained, started in all haste on the arrival of my messengers. During our interview I expressed great hope that, under the new relations in the Bahr el-Ghazal region, better times were also in store for the Negro lands. I gave him, as far as seemed necessary, all information regarding Gessi's good and friendly intentions towards the native princes and chiefs, at the same time communicating Gessi's personal greetings, and informing him that I was bearer of the Pasha's presents to himself.

At a second interview I produced all these gifts and solemnly presented them to him. Each of my attendants, arranged in a semi-circle, advanced with one of the articles, while I enlarged on my proposed visit to his country, my object and friendly intentions, also pointing out that I would be attended by a small

---

[1] It may be mentioned once for all that by the expressions Nubians, Sudanese, Sudanese Arabs, Mohammedans, Khartumers, Egyptians, are to be understood all the Muslim intruders, who had penetrated from Khartum through Shekka or Hofrât en-Nhâs into Negro land.

Government escort only as far as the frontier of his territory, and merely as a protection for my numerous carriers. After that I should expect, as a harmless private traveller, to be aided and safeguarded by the native rulers, of whom he, Ndoruma, was the first; in him I placed every confidence; to his loyalty, after entering his territory with the few followers whom he here saw,

PRESENTATION OF THE GIFTS TO NDORUMA.

I wished unreservedly to confide my safety, as well as that of my people and property. All this I dwelt upon in one of those lengthy palavers which are so dear to the heart of the Negro, employing all kinds of figurative language, such as during the course of years I had picked up from the natives themselves. In conclusion, I assured him of my satisfaction at personally greeting him here, instead of through his envoys, hoping thus to learn from his own lips that he was willing to receive me as his guest, for on no other condition should I venture to enter his country.

Thereupon followed the presentation of the gifts, and as I had anticipated, Ndoruma gave me all the assurances and promises that I could possibly desire. At the same time they were the promises of a native, which my long experiences in the Negro lands had taught me to estimate at their proper value. But even so, I was well pleased at this meeting with Ndoruma in Dem Bekir, the more so that we had come to a clear understanding on many urgent and weighty matters.

He was now anxious to get back without delay, in order, as he assured me, and as I readily believed, to prepare his people for my arrival, and to set their minds at rest regarding my intentions. Then I might follow in a few days with my men and effects, for my approaching visit was already widely known.

I was naturally desirous to part with him on the best of terms, to make the most favourable impression on him from the first, and let him clearly see how greatly we Europeans differed from the Arabs in all our views and actions. My purpose was fully accomplished during the ensuing daily interviews, at which long personal conversations were carried on by the aid of my interpreter, Farag 'Allâh.

A little feast also, which I improvised for him on the eve of his departure, and at which he saw for the first time many wonderful things, was partly intended to give him a slight insight into our European ways, to impress him with a sense of our superiority, and supply him and his people with topics for discussion on their return to their homes. For this purpose I had unpacked several curious things, which at the evening entertainment did not fail to excite the wonder and amazement of these children of nature. Here were all kinds of musical instruments, illustrated books and other objects, which now and for years to come I found useful in amusing my black audience and securing the goodwill and co-operation of the natives in furthering my views. At dusk we arranged a little procession with gay Chinese lanterns, introducing with great effect comical and animal masks, which even caused momentary alarm, until a little reflection enabled the spectators to enter into the fun of the thing. Then their outbursts of jubilant delight were suddenly arrested by the deep notes of my barrel-organ; all was hushed, while every ear listened to the unwonted strains of the *Wacht am Rhein* rolling harmoniously over the wilds of Africa.

I had done my best to honour my newly-acquired African friend, the ruler of the cannibal Niam-Niams. He took his departure next morning, May 3rd, not merely relieved of all further anxiety regarding our visit, but apparently now troubled only with the fear that we might not come after all. At our parting he promised on his return to have everything ready for erecting the huts and preparing the station for our accommodation; the building, however, of these structures was at my special request put off till our arrival. After this first meeting with Ndoruma I felt relieved from many cares which had hitherto preyed on my mind. But

DUKKA (*Sorghum vulgare*).

in Africa when one trouble is over another is sure to take its place; nor had I long to wait for fresh causes of anxiety.

After Ndoruma's departure the time passed quickly in preparations for the journey. My property was now increased by forty-five additional loads of durra (*Sorghum vulgare*) and flour, for it appeared that not much corn was grown in Ndoruma's country, and although telebun (*Eleusine coracana*) could be procured, durra especially was scarce. I may mention that telebun, widely cultivated in tropical Africa, in India, and South Arabia, is a cereal with short stalk and ears disposed like stars.

I also took enough corn for the period of our first stay with Ndoruma, in order, especially at first, not to be a burden to his people, and if necessary live on our own supplies.

Dem Bekir, which we left on May 7th, after a week's stay in the place, was the southernmost settlement of the Arab traders in the Bahr el-Ghazal region properly so called. After leaving Meshra I had hitherto mostly followed Schweinfurth's route of 1871, on his return journey from Dem Bekir, north-eastwards to Wau. Before my expedition the vast regions stretching south from Dem Bekir was known only from the inquiries made by Schweinfurth and Th. von Heuglin, and from the reports of the Arab traders; hence its broad features alone had been roughly, and of course quite inaccurately, figured on our maps. No European had yet set foot in those lands, which comprise the largest section of the Zandeh domain. Schweinfurth's memorable expedition to Mangbattu Land beyond the Welle river merely touched a spur of those uplands considerably more to the east. Here, also, the Italian collector, Piaggia, had made a lengthy stay; but although he was the first to bring back accurate information regarding the Zandeh nation, his cartographic data are worthless.

The western districts of the Zandeh and Bangia territories explored by me had a few years previously been traversed by the Greek physician, Dr. Potagos, already notorious for his romantic travels in Asia. His fantastic descriptions and cartographic errors are all embodied in the first volume of his *Dix*

Années de Voyages dans l'Asie Centrale et l'Afrique équatoriale, Paris, 1885. About the same time my present companion, Bohndorff, had made his already-mentioned journey beyond the Shinko river; but no particulars are extant of that expedition.

During my travels Lupton Bey, successor of Gessi Pasha as Governor of the province, had also traversed the western parts of the Bahr el-Ghazal region—a region, however, with which we are here scarcely concerned.[1] But most of his notes unfortunately perished with him, for he also was one of the victims of the Mahdi's revolt. To these names, for the lands lying south of the Welle-Makua, may be added those of the Italian traveller Miani, of the Italian Captain Cassati, whom I met later in Mangbattu, and lastly Emin Bey. These exhaust the short list of those European travellers who have visited parts of the region explored by me. Thus the new routes followed by me during the next few years traversed many unexplored districts and lands hitherto known scarcely by name.

On May 7th, 1880, we soon crossed the bed of the Jih, headstream of the Pango, which we had already passed on our way to Ganda. Here it was about six yards wide, with very little water in its channel. The gradually ascending track leads through a wooded hilly district, over a saddleback of laterite, between Mounts Daingirri and Chito, and so on through fine, park-like woodlands and several small plateaux down to the valley of the river Katta. This stream, which despite its small size contained several feet of water, was frequently crossed by our route.

Here the western horizon was bounded by chains of wooded hills, while the land sloping eastwards presented a broad open prospect. At the village of the Golo chief, Jenge, may be approximately drawn the southern limit of the Golo territory, which is here conterminous with that of the Sere or Bashir people, as the Zandehs call them. Here the scene suddenly changes with an abrupt fall in the road. The gaze now sweeps uninterruptedly for miles and miles over the clumps of trees dotted over the low-lying region rolling away to the south.

---

[1] *Proceedings of the Royal Geographical Society*, 1884, p. 245.

Our first halt after leaving Dem Bekir was made south of Mount Luh, at a bend of the Endese rivulet, which still contained some water. We found that the wooded, hilly, and mountainous country south of the Jih lies on the water-parting between the Pongo and Wau basins. The Endese itself was the first head-stream of the Wau; and all the brooks crossed during the following days, and flowing north-eastwards, combine to form the upper course of the same river.

At the camping grounds I generally set up my quarters on some shady spot beneath a branching tree, or on the bank of a wooded stream. Here were brought table, chair, books, maps, and writing materials, and here were posted up my daily notes, while the camp-fires were kindled for the evening meal. This supper, preceded by the always welcome cup of tea, was the most substantial meal of the day, for on the march we were usually satisfied with a little *abré* (thin, dry durra bread) steeped in water, cheese, milk and kisra (bread), Khartum *buxmat* (biscuits), and tea. But while writing up my diary I had to keep a watchful eye on the surroundings. The young hands I had engaged were still novices, careless and happy-go-lucky, like all Negroes, and needing instruction in the simplest duties. Hence the work would be constantly interrupted with questions and orders—have the animals been watered, fodder cut, firewood collected, the cow attended to, the goats tethered, and so forth. Such matters require to be constantly seen to by all travellers who wish to save themselves from continual losses.

Next day, May 8th, brought us to the station of the dragoman, Abd Allah, one of El-Maas' sub-inspectors, who had founded settlements of Bongos, Diggas (Zandehs), and Seres round about, and whose duty it was to look after the interests of the Government in this district. Here was the largest stream we had yet crossed, the Buseri, a head-water of the Wau, which collects several other brooks, and which at this place is already fifteen yards wide. But at that season its banks, fourteen or fifteen feet high, contained a current not more than six yards broad and half a foot deep.

The route, here as everywhere in Negro land scarcely a foot

wide, now left the hills and entered a rolling country with alternating stretches of bush and forest growths. By the latter expression ("Hochwald") I mean close woodlands with tall timber in contradistinction to the patches of bush or scrub, often separated by considerable stretches of herbage, and either growing round some solitary forest giant, or else forming continuous thickets by themselves. Forests, in our sense of the word—that is, consisting of a single species—are rare in this region,[1] where the woodlands are of a mixed character, the prevailing forms being combretaceæ, cæsalpinieæ, and rubiaceæ.

Occasional openings through the woods afforded distant glimpses of the Nbia Daragúmba[2] away to the south; a rising ground farther on also afforded a wide prospect of low-lying land stretching eastwards. To avoid repetition in describing the general aspect of the land, I may remark here once for all that a rolling formation is characteristic of all these regions. But the contour lines of such rolling grounds may be short or long, high or low, and are distinguished accordingly. Where the conformation is different, or the rolling character is scarcely perceptible—as, for instance, the extensive grassy savannas in the South and Far West, or the hilly and mountainous tracts—the special features of the land will be described in each case. Broad open plains, in the strict sense of the term, are here of the rarest occurrence; but characteristic of the lowlands is the alluvial formation traversed by the lower course of the larger streams flowing to the Bahr el-Ghazal.

Here, also, the respective southern and northern frontiers of the conterminous Sere and Digga territories can only be approximately drawn through the district in charge of Abd Allah. In these border lands, under the administration of dragomans, the populations of the Bahr el-Ghazal province have become so

---

[1] This reference is less applicable to England than to the European Continent, where extensive pine, fir, birch, oak, chestnut, and other forests are common. Elsewhere the author, like other travellers, compares the African scenery to that of England, with its park-like aspect and woodlands of diverse growths.

[2] In the Zandeh language *nbia* means rock or mountain. Hence many watercourses bear the name of *nanbia*, that is, *na-nbia* = "on, or over, rock," in reference to their rocky or stony beds.

intermingled during the last ten years, that it is no longer possible to draw hard and fast lines between the several ethnical groups. The northern Diggas have long been brought into relations of dependency on the Government of the Bahr el-Ghazal province; they now live peacefully side by side with the Sere, Bongo, Golo, Pambia, and other tribes, all of whom had formerly been vassals of the warlike Zandehs.

At this station Abd Allah provided us with five loads of durra, and some lugma (thick porridge) with seasoning was served out to my people, as was customary when the Arab convoys passed through all these stations. A tiring march brought us before noon next day to the settlement of Abd es-Sit, another dragoman subordinate to the superintendent El-Maas. He had charge of the southernmost posts on the road to Ndoruma's territory, and had been several times at this chief's residence to take over the consignments of ivory. I had already met him in Dem Bekir, whence he had been sent forward to get everything ready for our reception, and to make arrangements for the continuance of our journey; for El-Maas had given orders that the carriers from Dem Bekir were to be changed here, and that Abd es-Sit was to personally accompany us on the next stage.

But it soon became evident that the rascal, formerly one of Kuchuk Ali's slaves, had made no preparations of any kind. On my arrival he presented himself before me drunk and smoking a pipe, and began a rambling statement nothing to the purpose. So I cut matters short by first of all chucking his pipe into the next bush, which seemed to stagger him a little, and then taking the work in hand myself. A few huts were cleared out for our accommodation, while a *dahr et-tor*[1] or shed was run up to shelter the baggage. Later Abd es-Sit came up somewhat dejected, protesting that he had not expected us so soon, that he was not himself ready to travel just yet, and had been unable to procure any carriers, but would arrange for those who had come so far to remain in my service. Though apparently in a penitent mood, he still asked for a day's delay, and as I was

---

[1] Literally an "ox-back," in reference to its sloping roof.

anxious to scale a neighbouring mountain I granted his request. He did not again present himself before me, but probably sought consolation in the beloved merissa (native beer) for his slighted feelings.

The inhabitants of this district are less heterogeneous than in the north, the indigenous element being the Diggas, a northern branch of the Zandehs. Their territory, bordering north on the Sere and Krej lands, stretches far to the west, and they still occupy in that direction a part of the country figuring on Schweinfurth's map as Mofio's, where is the Ombanga zeriba. But wherever the Nubians have been long established we find the same hopeless mixture of tribes, and here also the Diggas have ceased to be the dominant race. Some of their chiefs settled in the neighbourhood came with their people to welcome us. I could detect no distinctive Zandeh features in their appearance, and I believe that the Diggas, at least in many districts, are already a mixed race.

Next day I ascended Mount Du, which lies an hour's march to the south-east of Abd es-Sit. On the road we crossed the Kommo, which rises close to the Busseri, flowing, after its junction with that river, to the left bank of the Upper Wau. Although only a few hundred feet high, Mount Du commands a wide prospect, and gave me an opportunity of taking several angular measurements. It terminates in a rounded granite or gneiss summit, whence the eye ranges over an open bushy region bounded in some directions by rising grounds.

Short as was the trip, I returned tired and languid with an uncomfortable feeling, which proved in a few days the forerunner of an attack of fever. Abd es-Sit was still sulking, while a chorus of complaints rose against him on all sides. The carriers who at his command were to continue in my service, whether they wished or no, were clamouring for their corn rations. So I sent for him, and with an accuracy of judgment rare in such cases, the knave informed me that he was *sakrān* ("drunk"), again imploring me to put off our departure for a day. My growing indisposition obliged me to make a virtue of necessity, so I consented, but insisted on the men getting their corn, though doubtless he had little intention of keeping his word.

Next morning still no corn, so that I began to fear they would all run off, while it was rumoured that Abd es-Sit intended to delay our departure still longer. Enraged at the insolence of this lying and deceitful upstart, I had six loads of corn from my own stock forthwith served out to our two hundred carriers, with the promise that come what may a start should be made next morning. Thereupon the men expressed their willingness to accompany me farther, only they hoped I would let them get back as soon as possible to look after their fields.

I sent word to Abd es-Sit that, unless he wished to make the acquaintance of my kurbash, he was not to venture again into my presence, but to refund in full measure the corn which I had distributed to the carriers; if this was not done at once, I should there and then inform the Pasha by letter of his criminal conduct. This brought him to his senses, and in a twinkle five small loads of Dukhn (*Penicillaria*) were produced. But the intense irritation had aggravated my general indisposition to fever point; nevertheless I personally superintended the necessary arrangements for our departure next day.

I had passed a somewhat sleepless night, and still lay weary and feverish on my camp-bed, when Bohndorff started early on May 12th, at the head of the convoy. Pulling myself together with an effort, I followed in half an hour with the servants and the loads containing the daily requisites. Reaching camp about noon I laid up for the rest of the day, and after a dose of quinine felt strengthened for next day's march.

Meanwhile our vigorous action had also brought Abd es-Sit to reason; he followed somewhat later, and towards evening unexpectedly entered the camp with a number of carriers bearing loads of corn. This man was for me another instance of the fact that the Negro raised to a responsible position and left to himself often abuses his authority more than the Arab. The complaints of those subject to his jurisdiction plainly showed that his sole aim was to administer the district for his own exclusive benefit.

Next day's route traversed rolling ground overgrown with open brushwood. Along the banks of the numerous rivulets crossing our track, and sometimes flowing in deep beds, the vegetation assumes a more exuberant character; the thinly-wooded savanna was here changed to a narrow selvage of tall forest growths, lining the river banks. These conditions again became modified farther south, and the contrast was very marked a few days' march beyond Abd es-Sit's. On the day after leaving Mount Du the edge of a new fluvial basin was reached some distance south of 6° north latitude. The development of animal and vegetable forms frequently undergoes a striking change about the main water-partings of great hydrographic systems; for the occurrence of distinct species is often associated with the area of drainage of a given river, while in this connection climate, character of the soil, and other determining causes are naturally important factors.

Apart from the little river Jih, which had been crossed south of Dem Bekir, the numerous streams or brooks met along the next six days' line of march all belonged to the same fluvial basin, flowing north-eastwards, and combining to form the Wau. But the Wau itself is only a tributary of the Bahr el-Ghazal, and that again of the Nile, so that during the last few days my route lay about the head-waters of one of the largest Nile affluents. But a single day's march west of the route hitherto followed south of Dem Bekir leads to the great divide between the Nile and Congo basins. All the streams beyond this divide flow in the opposite direction to that already indicated—that is, to the south-west—and lower down constitute a section of those rivers that go to form the Welle-Makua-Mobangi—that is, one of the largest Congo affluents.

Above the part of the divide here under consideration there rise, in order from north to south, the three Mounts Makámba, Daragúmba, and Baindiri. Under 6° 45′ N. the route crosses the water-parting, and then traverses lands belonging to the Congo basin. Hence this hydrographic parting-line had for me the greatest possible interest. During my travels in Makaraka Land I had for the first time crossed streams flowing to the Congo in the territory of the Mundu Negroes, and again also in Kalaka. To be sure at that time I had still no suspicion that the Welle-Makua ultimately finds its way to the Congo. But here in this western region I was already able approximately to determine the divide between the two great fluvial systems. During the following years my movements in the southern lands lay in close proximity to this important divide, so that I was enabled to insert in the map of Africa the Nile-Congo water-parting in its main direction and nearly in its entire length. A glance at the

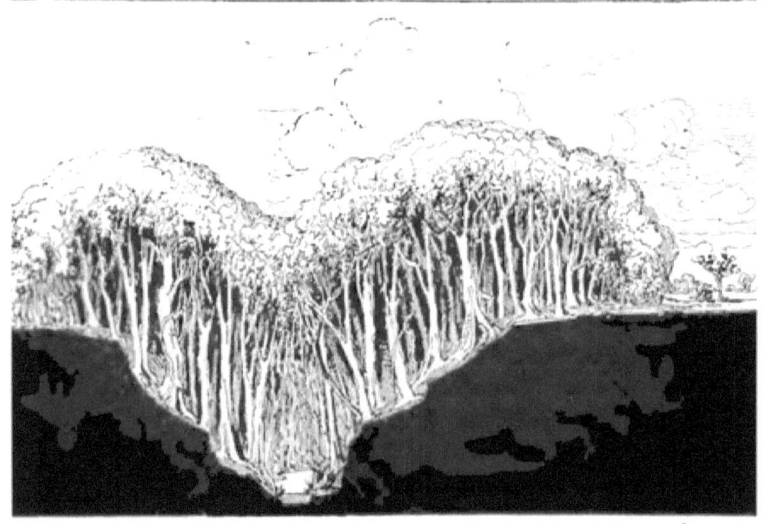

SCHEMATIC SECTION OF A FLUVIAL AVENUE.

map shows that it runs from about 2° N. latitude west of Lake Albert Nyanza north-westwards to 8° N. latitude, having a total length of some 745 miles.[1]

Where we traversed it, the region south of Dem Bekir is at present for the most part an uninhabited wilderness, except in the settled districts under Abd Allah and Abd es-Sit. As the

---

[1] A more detailed account of this hydrographic feature will be found in Petermann's *Mittheilungen*, Supplement No. 92.

Khartum slave-hunters advanced, the primitive populations were driven to emigrate in large numbers, and place themselves under the protection of the native rulers farther south. During our many days' journey to and beyond the water-parting we nowhere met any Negro settlements, but noticed at various points clear traces of former habitations. Thus a day's journey south of Abd es-Sit's we entered the former territory of the chief Ingo, who, like others, had escaped from the Arab *razzias* and from the detested *corvée* by taking refuge with the Zandeh prince, Mbio.

On the slight rising grounds between the rivers and rivulets the almost universally ferruginous soil of the wooded savannas is of a reddish colour. But it has not yet acquired that intense brown-red or brick-red hue, which is characteristic of the more southern lands, and from which probably the greater part of the surface of the Continent might be described as of laterite formation.[1] In some places underlying the laterite are granite or gneiss fragments, though here and there the hard rock also crops out in small bare eminences. Frequently the current flowing in deep channels causes an underwash and polishes the rocky surfaces in the river bed. Between these are formed in the dry season little pools, which to me seemed like so many natural aquariums full of vigorous life.

We always gladly rested under the shady trees of these wooded streams, or else pitched our tents in the vicinity. The bottom was often covered, as with a green carpet, by dainty water-plants, such as *Lagarosiphon*, *Naias*, *Ceratophyllum*, *Utricularia*, *Chara*, and others. Little fishes an inch long could be seen darting about amid these plants, water-beetles diving to the lower depths after taking in a fresh supply of air at the surface, small crab-like creatures peeping out from their hiding-places, and there was even a real hermit-like crustacean, a longish blue fresh-water shell-fish, which would every now and then open ever so little the aperture of his abode.

---

[1] Laterite, from *later* = brick, tile, is a reddish earth derived from the disintegration of various rocks, hence is of various constitution, but is usually strongly impregnated with sesquioxide of iron, and sometimes contains hæmatite and bauxite.

Where we crossed it, the Nile-Congo divide presented the aspect of a broad-crested rising ground, which sloped gradually eastwards, and which here sent its farthest little affluent down to the Wau. Beyond the rising ground a broad prospect was unfolded towards the west, and here the Badua, the first tributary of the Congo, was soon crossed. Here also the above-mentioned change in the physiognomy of the water-courses and in the character of the riverain vegetation was very striking. Probably it was due to the southern aspect of the land, which, being exposed to the trade winds, receives a more copious rainfall than the opposite (Nile) water-shed. But it may perhaps be also due to the steeper incline of the divide on its south-west side. This would produce a tendency in the streams flowing to the Congo to excavate deeper channels along their upper course, whereas the gentler slope on the Nile side would diminish the erosive action of those trending northwards.

But whatever be the cause, we here again enter that marvellously exuberant vegetable world, where tropical forms, now intermingled with new species, display a scarcely-expected development along the moist slopes of trough-like dales, cutting deep into the ground, and where half visible streamlets flow in everlasting gloom along the bottom lands lined on both sides by perennial swampy depressions promoting a rich vegetable growth. Such increasingly lavish vegetation is stimulated especially by the formation of the deep, dank fluvial beds. Tropical exuberance finds its full expression along the course of these channels in the magnificent "gallery forests," such as are seldom rivalled farther north. The term "gallery," first applied by Piaggia to these tunnel-like woodlands lining the river banks, was afterwards adopted by Schweinfurth, and has since come into general use.[1]

The Badua, the first stream met on the southern water-shed, already shows this remarkable change in the general character of the vegetation. We encamped (May 12th) for the night in its vicinity, and found that here the rains had set in earlier and more copiously than in the north. The grass was already as tall

---

[1] This statement is true; nevertheless "gallery forest," being both un-English and unintelligible, is here replaced by the expression "fluvial avenue."—ED.

as a man and yielded material for roofing our temporary huts. Here also after a long interval game was again obtained, so that my Khartum cook Saida had to try her hand at the higher branches of the culinary art; for our simple frugal fare was now

CAVE AT YISSA'S.

varied with antelope cutlets and joints of other large game.

On May 16th, after our long journeying in the wilderness, we were at last gladdened by the sight of human habitations in the district of the Zandeh chief, Yissa. Then we crossed the Rongo, the first considerable Congo affluent, which has here a westerly trend; its bed, which like all the others winds through a deep trough, was about fifteen yards wide, but contained a current scarcely six yards wide. The Rongo, after collecting the other waters of the district, joins the Boku, which is itself tributary to the Mbomu, the largest northern affluent of the Welle-Makua.

In the development of the fluvial avenues along the banks of the Rongo, nature has put forth all her grandeur and magnificence. For the first time since my journey to Kalika Land I was here again struck with amazement at that characteristic parasitic growth which clings to the huge stems of the forest giants. It is the *Platycerium*, a tropical African fern, one species of which, the elephant-ear (*Elephantotis*), was first discovered by Schweinfurth.

Some twenty minutes before reaching Yissa's settlement I visited a spacious cavern, the approach to which lay near our track. In a small circumscribed depression the vaulted entrance, about five yards wide, gives easy access to a large front chamber, from which a broad lofty passage on the left leads first down some steps sideways, and then along even ground forward. I had penetrated scarcely ten yards through this passage when I was arrested by innumerable large bats, which, scared by the smoke of our torches, whirled incessantly round our heads, and in their fright even clung to my clothes. I had great difficulty in keeping them off, while beating a hasty retreat. In the rocky walls of the cave I noticed many quartz veins. The natives are said to have frequently taken refuge in this place from the raids of the Nubians, which seems probable enough, for the part visited by me would alone afford a safe retreat to several hundreds. I had no difficulty in capturing some of the bats, and popping them into the flasks of spirits of wine which were always kept ready for such opportunities.

Yissa had been to Dem Bekir with Ndoruma. His promise made in that place to have everything ready for my arrival he had also kept more honourably than had Abd es-Sit. At the foot of the northern slope of Mount Ghasa we found a large space cleared of grass, on which huts had been built for us, a *dahr et-tor* for the loads, and a *rekuba* or awning. Here the chief and his people gave us a friendly welcome with their national song.

I had every reason to be satisfied with this reception given me by the southern Zandehs, who are already in this district more independent than their northern kinsfolk. Still I was detained in the place longer than I could have wished, owing to the ever-recurring carrier question. Those belonging to Dem Bekir now returned in all haste to attend to their plantations, for the ground had already been loosened by the late rains. Our little camp at the foot of Mount Ghasa was this evening for a time bathed in the light of the moon, whose beams struggled through the banked-up moisture-bearing clouds. Later it cleared up, and the pale moonshine was diffused over a peaceful scene, with the phantom-like crags of the neighbouring mountain towering abruptly above the plains.

Next morning I ascended this eminence in company with Yissa and some of his Zandeh subjects acquainted with the locality. The ascent was made from the east side, but even there it was so steep that in some places I had to clamber on all fours. In the grassy clefts of the rocky slopes we got on better, while elsewhere our progress was much impeded by the numerous weathered blocks piled up one on the other. Nevertheless, in half an hour we found ourselves on the rocky summit, which formed a table about 150 feet broad, and which presented an uninterrupted prospect in every direction. I was specially attracted by a mountain range in the east running in a south-easterly direction. The land in that quarter I was told belonged to the Digga nation, and more particularly to the Pambia tribe. I recorded a number of peaks with their names, and by taking the altitude of other heights, I obtained some valuable measurements for my cartographic work.

Ghasa, like Du, has a relative height of scarcely more than 500 feet. On the rugged terminating plateau the bursting of the hard rock (gneiss?), the peculiar grouping of the boulders, weathering and erosions, had given rise to some natural basins, which were again in their turn disposed in secondary divisions by small dams and ridges of stone. As the rain-water cannot here filter through, while the loss by evaporation is constantly replaced by periodical rains, the summit of Mount Ghasa is studded with lovely little tarns, all teeming with life. After completing my observations, I spent some enjoyable hours about

PANORAMIC VIEW FROM MOUNT CHASA. (*Drawn by L. H. Fischer.*)

the margins of these natural aquariums perched on the summit of a rocky eminence. As in the already described basins of the small water-courses, the bottom was here also strewn with a carpet of green aquatic plants; while the water, clear as crystal, was alive with insects, beetles, and other small organisms, specimens of which were soon transferred to my flasks. On Mount Du I had seen some baboons at a distance, but none on Ghasa, although they were said to frequent this hill also.

ENCAMPMENT AT MOUNT GHASA.

Next day, no carriers being ready, we had again an opportunity to practise the virtue of patience. Although we were in the territory of the former powerful prince Solongo, Yissa himself seemed to exercise authority over a mere handful of subjects. The remnant of the nation lives in small communities scattered over the bush towards east and west. According to national custom, Solongo had been succeeded by his eldest son, Yissa, some of whose brothers had remained as superintendents of districts; but two of them, unwilling to accept the rule of the Arab raiders, had migrated, like so many others, southwards to Prince Mbio. Solongo's youngest son was in the service of El Maas at Dem Bekir, and Yissa himself was no longer anything more than a humble vassal of the Nubians. In the evening my barrel-organ was produced, to the wonder and bewilderment of his people.

It will be remembered that Abd es-Sit had received orders to accompany us as far as Ndoruma's. But fresh complaints were here urged against him, while Yissa assured me of Ndoruma's deadly hatred of the fellow, whose high-handed dealings had in fact raised up enemies on all sides against him. I was even told that Ndoruma had designs upon his life. All things considered, I was anxious to dispense with his further attendance, which had become very irksome; a lucky circumstance now came to my aid, but for which I should have had some difficulty in getting rid of an underling who was naturally afraid of acting against the orders of his superior in authority. A Negro soldier unexpectedly arrived at this opportune moment from Dem Bekir with an Arab letter, which I was unable to decipher. But the messenger supplemented it with a rambling account of troubles which had broken out in the north. The frequently-recurring words Arab, Shekka, Rabay, helped to throw a little light on his confused report, though I doubted its truth, the experience of years having long taught me to receive with suspicion all such statements, whether made by Arabs or Negroes. I may here incidentally remark that Rabay had at one time been the first and most distinguished captain of the rebel Soliman Zibér, after whose overthrow he had turned westwards, no one knew exactly whither, still a powerful and dreaded warrior at the head of many thousand Negro troops. At least so it was reported, and since then rumours, inspired by the dread of his possible return with hostile aims, were constantly in the air, to the effect that Rabay was again on the war-path. During my later wanderings in the north-western lands I was never able to ascertain anything definite regarding his movements. Possibly he may have sought a new home with his followers in the remote regions south of Baghirmi.

FLUVIAL AVENUE.

From the messenger's verbal communications I gathered so much that anyhow Abd es-Sit was to return; only he seemed to think that a similar command affected me also. Naturally I took all the less heed of this assumption that there were no distinct communications from Gessi Pasha. But, to my great joy, I was henceforth relieved from the further attendance of Abd es-Sit, about whose recall there was no doubt.

Although the carriers were not yet all at hand, I sent off Bohndorff, on May 20th, with about 200 men. The move, however, did not spare me much troublesome contention with those Negro soldiers who had been told off to escort me as far as the frontier of Ndoruma's territory. So I now gave them the option of continuing with me or going back, whereupon some decided to return with Abd es-Sit, while others remained a few days longer to guard my effects. I started next day with the remainder of these, and overtook Bohndorff in the afternoon.

On May 22nd, the united company pushed forward, and the same day we reached Ndoruma's frontier district, which was ruled by Kommunda, one of his foremost vassal chiefs. On the route we had passed a few wretched hovels belonging to the widely-scattered A-Barmbo nation, whose chief tribe we shall meet in the region south of the Welle river.

The streamlets crossed by the route between Mount Ghasa and Kommunda's converge farther west in a single channel, which joins the already-mentioned Boku. Here, also, are seen numerous magnificent fluvial avenues, often overshadowing quite insignificant brooklets flowing in deep ravines.

We had scarcely reached the first huts in Kommunda's district when the carriers furnished by Yissa at once laid down their loads, and went off in hot haste. Though the chief's residence was still some distance off, he soon made his appearance, and promised forthwith to send us some carriers to convey our things to his own station, in the neighbourhood of which he had erected our huts. He further informed us that it was Ndoruma's intention to come in person and bring us thence to his capital.

South of Abd es-Sit's district—that is, in the domain of the Zandehs proper—my relations with the natives and carriers underwent a complete change. In the Egyptian provinces both carriers and the inhabitants generally had shown themselves favourably disposed through motives of fear. But the influence of the Administration was extremely limited in the southern lands, and in the Zandeh country scarcely nominal. I was consequently aware that henceforth I should be exclusively dependent on the various local rulers. Hence all my efforts were now directed to securing a good understanding with them. In my calculations I took into account the personal weight of a European acting justly and according to law.

Nevertheless, both now and later I had naturally to contend with many prejudices, and needed all my tact and skill to open and keep open the way into the country, and at the same time to represent the interests of the Egyptian Government, which I felt it my duty to promote.

My relations to the carriers were so far changed, that henceforth the men, otherwise little accustomed to such service, could be engaged only with the sanction of their several chiefs. But the suspicions created by the truculent conduct of the Arabs were at first extended also to me. Hence the severe treatment hitherto occasionally required had now to give place to patience, forbearance, and kindness.

Kommunda had brought with him many of his sub-chiefs and other persons, all eager to see me, and doubtless also anxious to satisfy themselves that I had not come with any hostile intentions. I accordingly endeavoured to convince them of my friendly feeling towards land and people. An excellent effect was produced by my solemn assurance that the military escort from Dem Bekir was to proceed no farther. In fact, some complaints having been made of their unruly conduct, I dismissed them one and all, sending them back with Yissa's people. As explained in long conversations with Kommunda, I wished the Zandehs to see for themselves that I did not want to be a burden to them with so many followers; that the Egyptian soldiers were not to eat up the bread of the people; that, on the contrary, I desired to enter their land confidently and without any escort, relying on the protection of the Zandehs themselves, which I regarded as more efficient than a number of troops. Had I not Ndoruma's word and promise? How, then, could I doubt that the hospitable Zandehs would meet my just wishes, and also that the carriers would cheerfully and without fear lend me their services?

For the most part my long speeches made a visible impression on the people, though too often my oratory remained without biding results.

At Kommunda's disquieting rumours reached my ears, which sounded ominously for my future plans. The hostile relations between Mbio and Ndoruma were threatening to break into open war. Our visit to Ndoruma, an event already known far and wide, had presumably aroused deep distrust in Mbio; nor could I doubt that Ndoruma's people fanned the flame of this distrust amongst Mbio's subjects on the border lands by lying statements and exaggerations of all kinds, so that false reports of my intentions could not fail to reach him.

But the hostile feelings of the two most powerful Zandeh rulers at that time had broken into open feud, especially since Ndoruma, vanquished and hard pressed by Rafai's forces, had been fain to show himself more obsequient to the Egyptian Administration. In their sore distress during this war with Rafai, Ndoruma and his people had received neither aid nor protection from Mbio's subjects. Hence Ndoruma's deadly hatred of Mbio, a feeling which had since been fostered by sanguinary conflicts along the frontiers, so that it now threatened again to burst into open hostilities.

Characteristic of the present situation was a bundle of twenty sticks which were brought to me, and which were intended to indicate the number of Ndoruma's people who had in recent times been killed by Mbio's subjects in the border lands. This method of representing units and higher numbers by so many material objects is practised by many native tribes, abstract reckoning being always a difficult process for the Negro.

The fluvial avenues of this district are inhabited by several species of apes, amongst others the beautiful black-and-white long-tailed *Colubus Guereza*, whose skin is worn as a striking and original national adornment by the Zandehs. We succeeded in taking many fine specimens.

Beyond the Bamunga rivulet, crossed on the way to Kommunda's, we came upon a few native huts embowered in the riverain gallery, which a few evenings before had been the scene of a tragic event. A man-eating leopard had broken into one of the huts and carried off to a neighbouring thicket a woman near her confinement. Farther on an extensive rising ground of laterite was followed by some broken land with detached hills, while sparsely-wooded savannas continued to be the prevailing feature between the rich vegetation lining the river banks.

Near Kommunda's dwellings we noticed an open space cleared of its grass, on which stood several new huts apparently erected for our accommodation. In fact Bohndorff had already deposited some of the loads, and I had myself begun to settle down comfortably with the rest of the things, when my patience was again put to a severe trial. Not only was Ndoruma's arrival delayed for several days, but when he at last made his appearance he brought no carriers with him. Several more days were thus wasted, during which I had to console myself with the wearisome promise of "To-morrow." But this "to-morrow" grew into a week and more, while the wet season was advancing, and the increasing rains penetrating into the huts. The inquisitive natives, by whom we were constantly beset, found much to amuse them in my person and the curious foreign things lying about, while I sat moodily awaiting the "morrow."

Here I for the first time made the discovery, afterwards confirmed by repeated experience, that with all their assumed despotism the Zandeh chiefs had really a very limited authority over their subjects. Ndoruma himself seemed enraged at the long delay, and I at last induced him to look up the carriers himself. Some of the things I had been able to send forward in charge of Farag 'Alláh, and Ndoruma's departure was followed by the arrival of more carriers, with whom I started at once without waiting his return. Bohndorff remained behind with the rest of the baggage, and thus it happened that we ultimately arrived in three separate parties at Ndoruma's residence, to which he had himself meantime returned.

Beyond Kommunda's the route still lay through broken ground, rising imperceptibly south of the Bada rivulet, where a broad prospect opened over a low-lying region stretching westwards. Here the head-stream of the Mbomu trends first to the north-west, then to the west, and after collecting many tributary waters becomes a potent affluent of the Welle-Makua.

Although only a few head-waters of the Mbomu were afterwards crossed, the district stretching south-eastwards to Ndoruma's station possesses considerable hydrographic interest. All the streamlets hitherto met on the Congo slope of the water-parting flow westwards to the Mbomu, while those to the south of Ndoruma's go to join the Welle-Makua, but north of that station we again come upon a little tract which is comprised within the Nile catchment basin. It is drained by the Bikki (Beki), which flows to the Such (Jur) affluent of the Bahr el-Ghazal, whose furthest sources were thus passed by our route north of Ndoruma's station. The first of these sources struck by us was the Yubbo, flowing east through the Bikki to the Jur; but the station itself stands on the upper course of the Werre, which again belongs to the Welle-Mobangi-Congo system.

An extensive rising ground here affords a boundless prospect towards the east, where a few isolated crests rose on the horizon. Amongst them were Mounts Keddede and Nango, while close to our track stood a small cone, near which is the site of Ndoruma's former settlement.

We reached Chief Gassande's late at night, just in time to get under cover from a fierce thunderstorm. But the only available shelter was a little barn, where the next night also had to be passed, while storm followed storm, one more violent than the other. When at last I tried to get a little sleep, we were assailed by millions of ants, either out on a roving expedition or, like ourselves, escaping from the rain.

Our progress was now arrested by the sudden flight of several carriers, who, however, to my agreeable surprise, were replaced next day. Thus, after a toilsome march through the tall grass, which in swampy depressions becomes stiff and almost woody, we at last reached Ndoruma's on June 9th. Where the Bikki was crossed it was six yards wide with a sandy bed eighteen inches deep. Judging from the districts already traversed and the few scattered huts visible along the route, I concluded that Ndoruma's country must be very sparsely peopled.

At the same time the absence of settlements along main highways gives no clue to the actual density of the population in Negro lands. Taught by experience, the natives generally keep aloof from these highways to escape requisitions and plunder from passing hordes. Habitations and tilled land became more frequent farther south, and beyond the Bikki we passed a number of huts belonging to Chief Sindia. Then followed a hilly district merging southwards in a rising ground, which separates the last little head-streams of the Bikki from a few wooded brooks flowing from the southern slope of the rising ground down to the Werre. Ndoruma's huts lay on the other side of this river, scattered over the thinly-wooded savanna. The new huts which were destined to serve as our first quarters stood somewhat nearer to the river, and here Farag 'Alláh, in charge of the first convoy, had already stowed away some of the loads. The people were still at work on a large shed, so that Bohndorff, who arrived next day with the rest of the things, was also able to get under shelter. Ndoruma, informed of our approach, received us at our quarters accompanied by a number of his chiefs and retainers.

A STOOL.

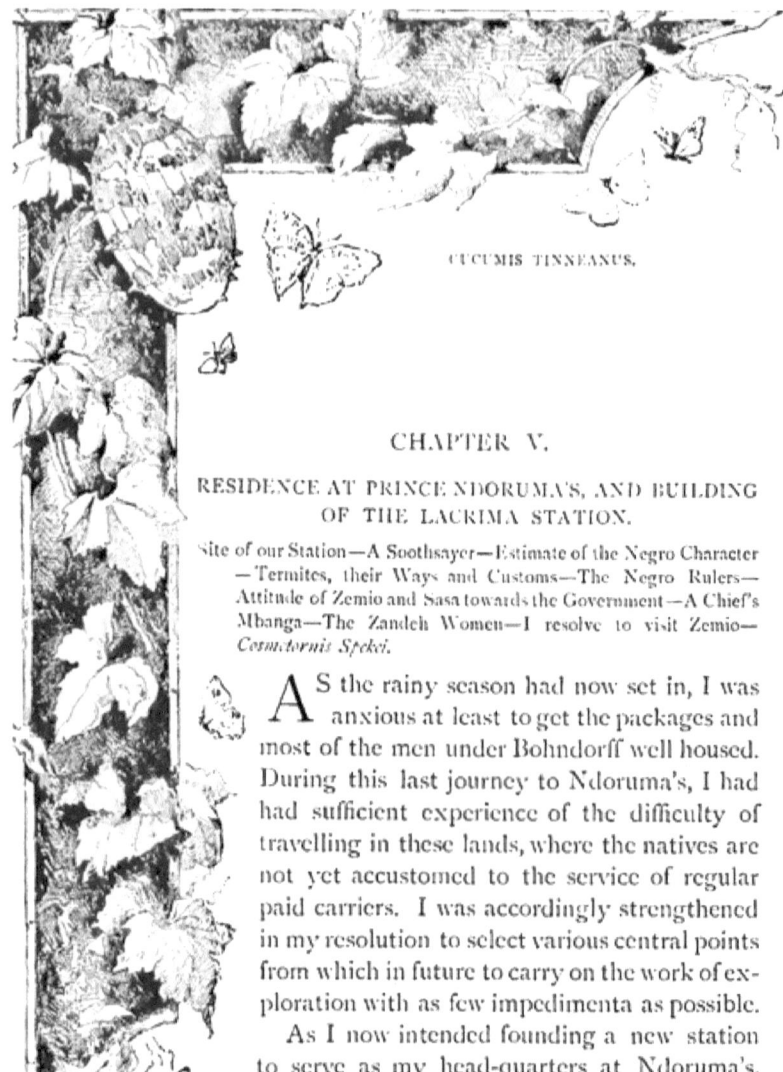

CUCUMIS TINNEANUS.

CHAPTER V.

RESIDENCE AT PRINCE NDORUMA'S, AND BUILDING OF THE LACRIMA STATION.

Site of our Station—A Soothsayer—Estimate of the Negro Character—Termites, their Ways and Customs—The Negro Rulers—Attitude of Zemio and Sasa towards the Government—A Chief's Mbanga—The Zandeh Women—I resolve to visit Zemio—*Cosmetornis Spekei*.

AS the rainy season had now set in, I was anxious at least to get the packages and most of the men under Bohndorff well housed. During this last journey to Ndoruma's, I had had sufficient experience of the difficulty of travelling in these lands, where the natives are not yet accustomed to the service of regular paid carriers. I was accordingly strengthened in my resolution to select various central points from which in future to carry on the work of exploration with as few impedimenta as possible.

As I now intended founding a new station to serve as my head-quarters at Ndoruma's, similar stations could be erected from time to time in other places for the reception of my people and the heavy loads. I could thus make flying expeditions round about the different provinces, while

Bohndorff remained at head-quarters in charge of everything. The erection of the central station at Ndoruma's would take several weeks' hard work; but until it was completed no fresh excursions could be undertaken.

The site had already been cleared and temporary huts run up. The position was well chosen on a piece of ground gently sloping northwards towards the Werre, so that the rain-water could be easily carried off by cutting a few drains down to the river. But although the few trees and bushes had already been cut down round about, timber for the erection of better huts was still wanting, Ndoruma having failed in his promise to have it ready.

BUILDING OF THE STATION.

At our first interview I spoke freely of my annoyance at the worries I had already been subjected to, and especially the great delays caused by the constant want of carriers. As the promises, on the strength of which I had dismissed my escort on the frontier, had not been fulfilled, I expressed a hope that his people would at all events show a more friendly spirit in the erection of the new station.

The first and most essential point was to make the place secure by constructing a stout palisade, for the district abounded in leopards, whose nightly depredations had to be guarded against. I therefore marked off a space eighty paces long from east to west, and sixty broad from north to south, entrusting the

four sides to the retainers of four different chiefs. Stakes, thick as the arm or leg, and ten to twelve feet long, were set close together and planted two feet in the ground and further strengthened with beaten earth raised to a height of eighteen inches on both sides.

A few days after my arrival I consented, at the request of Ndoruma, to allow a Zandeh *binsa* (soothsayer or wizard) to deliver his oracles to the people gathered round my huts. His vaticinations had reference chiefly to myself, our arrival and residence in the country, their general tendency being to impress upon his audience the advantage of our appearance in Ndoruma's land. In this he doubtless shrewdly calculated on my gratitude, and was of course not disappointed.

But I was also personally interested in the fantastically-arrayed old prophet, who had decked himself with all manner of odds and ends, charms and amulets, crowning all with a Niam-Niam straw hat. The spacious *dahr et-tor* near my huts was crowded with a choice company of Zandeh chiefs, anxious to witness the theatrical performance of the wizard. Ndoruma with his attendants was of course also present, while the common folk found standing room in the open.

The performer, taking his stand in the centre of the audience, began with a dance to the accompaniment of the never-failing tamtam (kettle-drum), first in slow, measured time, and off and on inclining his head in a listening attitude towards the ground. Gradually the step was quickened, becoming wilder and wilder, the gesticulations also increasing, until at last he exhausted himself in furious bounds and contortions. And he still kept listening for the messages from the potent underground spirits.

But he now suddenly interrupted his frantic caperings, wiped the perspiration from his face, approached our circle, and began his speech. This was repeated after every dance, the oration being each time addressed to some particular person, or else some topic selected at random. At first he dwelt at length on my good qualities, announcing that all my intentions were of a peaceful, benevolent nature; that, thanks to our arrival, all fear of further Arab forays would be dispelled; that the people could henceforth cultivate their fields in peace and enjoy the fruits of their own labour; and, lastly, that the Zandehs might now confidently begin to build new huts, as no Rafai, no outlandish foes would again come to plunder them, since our coming had brought them luck and should inspire them with confidence.

In another discourse the seer gave forth that he had heard from the invisible spirits that in the houses of a certain chief there was somebody harbouring evil intentions and entertaining malicious designs against certain persons. Then in another bombastic harangue he foretold that several persons, amongst others my servant Farag 'Alláh, would be overtaken by sickness. But in all these utterances his prophetic eye seemed involuntarily to avoid my searching and perhaps contemptuous gaze.

Meantime my station was progressing very slowly. Ndoruma had told off a number of his chiefs with their people to take in hand the various parts of the work. The natives are accustomed to such combined labour in erecting their own huts, but although by this plan very little work falls to the share of each individual, that little takes a long time to do, owing to the universal indolence and laziness of the people. Notwithstanding my constant vigilance, much of it was also indifferently performed, so that it had later to be altered and repaired.

Pending the completion of my hut I had to take up my quarters in the open *dahr et-tor*, where exposure to the damp at night brought on many light but still troublesome attacks of ague. Ndoruma visited me every day, often several times, while I constantly complained of the people's neglect of their work, and at the same time communicated from letters to hand Gessi's expressions of goodwill towards him and his land. In reply he would deplore the remissness of his subjects, who were unaccustomed to finer and more difficult operations, as, for instance, the construction of palisades. Such zeribas were scarcely known in the country, for the Zandeh never surrounds his dwelling by any enclosure.

Before my arrival in Meshra an ivory expedition, under Osman Bedawi, had started southwards from the Bahr el-Ghazal region, and had passed through Bellanda Land to Ngettua's. This was Ndoruma's uncle, a weak but independent chief, whose territory lay to the east, where it was conterminous with Mbio's. From Ngettua's Osman Bedawi had advanced still southwards to Prince Binsa's, son of the aged Prince Malingde, whose country borders to the south on Ndoruma's. The objective point of the expedition was the Zandeh Prince Bakangaï's, south of the Welle; but the ivory so far procured had been left under guard in Ngettua's and Binsa's territories, to be picked up on the return journey northwards. Belahl, the Arab in charge of the store at Ngettua's, now sent me greetings, and I, on my part, forwarded him letters for Osman Bedawi, which had reached me from Dem Bekir.

But more important for me was a satisfactory understanding

ZANDEH WAR DRUM.

with Ndoruma. Since my arrival I had already given him the first presents usual on entering a chief's territory. He seemed specially delighted with a revolver in a case and a quantity of ammunition, and to this were afterwards added several other European objects. Nevertheless the days still went by while operations at the station were almost at a standstill. At last my energetic expostulations and even threats caused a general resumption of the work, while I went about encouraging here, blaming there, now and then distributing a little tobacco or a few cigar-stumps—in a word, doing everything to keep the men in good humour.

In all this I could again notice how like children the Negroes are in many respects. Once at work they seemed animated by a sort of childlike sense of honour. They delighted in praise, though even a frown or a word of reproach could also excite their hilarity. Thus a loud burst of laughter would, for instance, follow the contrast between a piece of good and bad workmanship. Like children they would point the finger of scorn at each other, and in some other characteristic features they almost showed themselves in a more favourable light than the civilized European. They are certainly less prone to those feelings of rancour and sullen anger which with us so often result in deeds of violence, crime, and murder. In this connection the prevalent custom of tribal vendetta is not to be confused with the petty feelings of personal vindictiveness caused by some real or fancied injury. The former has its *raison d'être* in deeply-rooted traditional customs, and also assumes more the character of a standing feud regulated by established use.

During the operations we had to clear away a number of small termites'-nests affecting the form of huts or mushrooms, and about the size of a man's head. Such structures, which are widely scattered over the interior, are so compactly built that they can be detached from the surface by a violent blow and removed in a solid block. On the march they serve the purpose of hearth-stones, three placed in triangular form together making an excellent fireplace.

In a day or two the men again began to grow remiss, whereupon one morning Ndoruma had the great Zandeh war-drum beaten. Its rattle is distinctly heard far and wide, and according to the number and character of the strokes, the prince's orders are conveyed to the surrounding chiefs to gather with their people for the hunt, war, or some festive purpose. Formerly, when the land was more densely peopled, the men, always ready for war, could by this means be rapidly mobilized to the remotest frontiers of the state. On the present occasion, the signal being taken up and repeated from village to village, the people soon presented themselves from all quarters, ready with shield and spear for battle. But on learning the nature of the summons they burst into loud laughter, and putting aside their weapons, the doughty warriors went quietly to work.

LACRIMA STATION. (*Drawn by Fr. Rheinfelder.*)

The palisade was now soon finished, and further strengthened against prowling leopards by some thorny scrub along the outer sides. I now carried out a long-cherished purpose, laying out a certain space in the interior as a kitchen-garden, taking this occasion to instruct the natives in the use of European spades and rakes. In this I was aided by Farag 'Alláh, who had already seen such work in Europe, and in a few weeks both divisions of the garden were thoroughly tilled and sown with various European seeds.

On the west side of the station, behind Bohndorff's quarters, were several small huts for the saddle-animals, and to avoid the risk of utter ruin by fire I had the loads distributed in several huts, instead of being stowed away in the large house originally intended for them. My private quarters, last to be finished as being the least urgent, stood at the southern entrance to the station, and I was very glad to remove to them from the exposed *dahr et-tor*, where I had hitherto passed many an uncomfortable night.

The end of June was now approaching, and many things still remained to be done; so I plainly told Ndoruma that I should quit his land for ever unless everything was completed to my satisfaction within ten days. This had the desired effect, and next morning a number of fresh hands were again hard at work.

My dwelling was constructed in the style prevalent in this part of Africa—round, with pointed conic roof, but much larger and stronger than is usual. A passage ran round the outside, with sloping roof, which merged upwards in the roof of the main building. In the accompanying illustration may be seen the various stages of its erection under my guidance. The first drawing shows the ground plan, from the centre of which two circles were described with a kind of compass made of a string attached to a pointed stake. On these circles holes a foot deep were sunk at regular intervals for the posts of the main wall and outer passage, while a deeper hole was made for the stout central pole, which was about the thickness of a man's thigh. In these holes the forked posts were so placed that all the prongs radiated towards the central pole, which was higher than

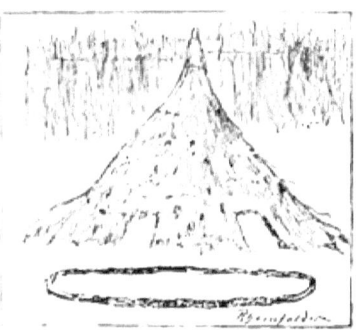

BUILDING OF A HUT.

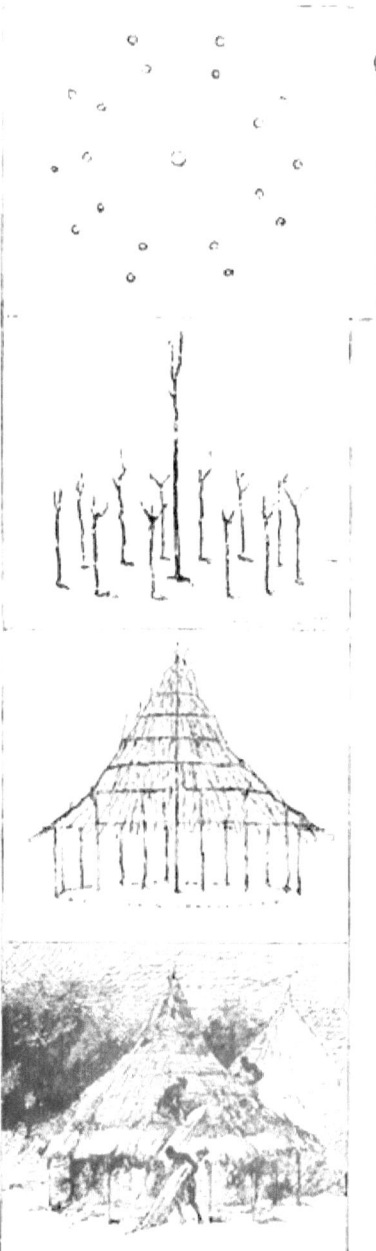

the others, but, like them, terminated in a fork. Then a crown or hoop, made of long pliant rods bound together, was made to rest firmly on the forked posts, and at the joints were inserted long rafters converging, pyramid-fashion, on the fork of the central pole. The roof itself was strengthened by several similar crowns, continually decreasing in circuit and made fast to the rafters on their inner edge. Three such crowns, with an outer and smaller hoop over a yard in diameter, and serving as a support to the rafters at their upper ends, sufficed to impart great firmness to the whole framework of the roof. In the interstices of the converging rafters were introduced thinner laths, long pliant little saplings and bamboos, all similarly wedged into the lower crown, and on the outside secured on the other crowns to the apex of the roof. Some, however, were not carried right to the top, but terminated at the several crowns, this being done to avoid encumbering the apex with useless materials and thus giving it an irregular, unfinished look. In the mud walls were introduced twelve small round window-openings, like the port-holes of steamers, and closed with firmly-inserted wire grating. The wall facing towards the middle of the station had two doorways, while the outer passage was left open except overhead, where it was inclosed by the roof, which rose nearly five feet above the sustaining walls.

Owing to the heavy tropical rains, special care has to be bestowed on the grass thatching, which prevails in most Negro lands throughout North-east Africa. The best time for collecting the material is the rainy season, when it has already acquired a considerable growth. Amongst the Zandehs, as in many other regions, before being used it is bound together in convenient form, the bundles being then unrolled and secured to the framework of the roof. During this process the stalks are always disposed point downwards, and the upper layers are made to overlap the lower by about a third of their length, the thatch being thus rendered quite waterproof. For the binding work many materials are used, amongst others a red-brown bast which grows under the bark of certain trees, such as the *bauhinia* and various species of the *grevia*, which closely resembles the European linden. But the best material is the outer involucrum of the ratan (*Calamus*), collected in the green state, while it is very pliant and tough; when dried it retains its strength and never yields, so that the binding never becomes slack.

In the draining operations care was taken to prevent any flooding of the low-lying kitchen-garden, and also to avoid stagnant pools. Small gutters were dug round each hut for the reception of the water from the roofs, and with these and other precautions the ground was kept quite dry.

These round huts with conic roofs are the prevailing style everywhere as far as the A-Madi country in the south-west and the regions south of the Welle, where they are replaced by the square gable-roofed dwellings. The latter style I preferred both here and elsewhere, being more airy and allowing a better escape for the smoke of the fire which is kept constantly burning on the hearth. But they have to be made larger and stronger than those of the natives to meet the various requirements of the European, and to afford him better shelter from wind and rain.

Those of the Zandehs, though of light structure, are often very elegant and clean, mostly with their round walls quite smooth, but without framework, and surmounted by a light roof resting on a few posts.

The first few weeks spent at Ndoruma's gave me considerable insight into the character of the Negro in general, and his capacity for free labour, for Ndoruma himself was powerless to exercise any real compulsion over his people. The experience now acquired already sufficed to modify my preconceived views regarding Negro emancipation, the golden freedom of the natives, mild treatment, kindness, and forbearance, principles of conduct which can have no result except in the case of human beings endowed with a sense of honour.

During those days I learnt a hard lesson, but one which later proved of great service to me. It enabled me gradually to master that impatience to which doubtless all travellers in Negro lands at times give way and which defeats its own object, whereas the native may really be guided by steadfast patience, and compelled in us Europeans to recognize his masters.

It may seem strange that I should have gained this experience now for the first time; but it should be remembered that the expeditions described in the first volume of this work were undertaken under totally different conditions. They were confined to regions which had for years been occupied by the Sudanese Mohammedans, regions where the Negro had been compelled through fear to accept the yoke of statute labour. At that time all my wants and wishes were attended to by the superintendents of the Government stations and their underlings. Those expeditions were carried out in the suite of Egyptian officials, or under the escort of plundering troops.

On such journeys, as for instance from Ladó to Makaraka Land, later in the Bahr el-Ghazal province, and again to Kalaka Land, no full and just estimate could be formed of the Negro, of his inclination or capacity for free labour, or of his good and bad qualities in general. Now, however, ample opportunity was afforded of studying his true character in its strong and weak points, though doubtless at the cost of much patience, forbearance, worry, and annoyance. The philanthropic sentiments inspired by love and sympathy for our fellow-men, and strengthened by the heartless treatment of the natives by their Mohammedan oppressors, must undergo some change, when tested by the actual relations and in the light of the Negro's true character. I am far from excusing the brutal conduct of his taskmasters, which springs from pure selfishness and displays itself in acts of plunder and treachery, nor can I utter a word on behalf of those truculent Nubians who inflict so much wrong on the natives. But the Negro also has doubtless a sufficient sense of right and wrong so far as regards the *meum et tuum*, though not where there is a question, for instance, of domestic slavery. To this relation he naturally adapts himself, having grown up under similar conditions of dependence on his own rulers. I therefore repeat that for the next generations the natives can be raised to a higher state of culture by statute labour alone, by a well-regulated system of *corvée* kept under due control.

After the station was completed special precautions had to be taken against the constant attacks of the termites. One of the most important duties of the servants who had daily to sweep the house, was to remove the galleries which during the night these pests constructed along the posts. Thanks to assiduous care and attention, I had the satisfaction of knowing that after years of residence my effects had escaped the ravages from this cause, which are the constant subject of lamentation on the part of most travellers. But the result can be achieved only by incessant vigilance in small matters and great. Thus I never omitted when retiring for the night to hang up my shoes or place them on a stool.

The voracious termites must have a special instinct, or an

extremely delicate sense of smell to emerge from the ground exactly under any object lying about and begin their depredations in the darkness. They avoid the light of day, and on coming to the surface they immediately begin to construct a tunnelled passage on any object, such as a tree or a post, which they wish to ascend. As the tunnel and the ascent go on simultaneously, they are thus always at work in the dark, and when the top is reached a hard crust of hollow earth is found to extend all along the post or stem. But what a sensitive feeling must they possess to go from their underground dwellings straight to a pair of boots, for instance, lying under the bed. Or, besides the fighting and working classes, can they also possibly have an organized "intelligence department"? Perhaps there may not be a single white ant visible in the whole house, yet when we go to pick up a shoe, we find it cemented to the ground by fresh earthen passages, and the sole already partly devoured during the night.

ZANDEH STOOL.

It is difficult to form even an approximate idea of the life and habits of these tiny underground organisms, their prodigious numbers, industry, and incessant work, work which in the course of ages cannot fail to have had its effect on the slow but continuous modifications of the crust of the earth. A characteristic aspect is imparted to many regions of the Continent by the innumerable ant-hills strewn over the surface, and often forming the only break on the boundless plains.

During those weeks I never failed, after the day's work, to entertain Ndoruma's people with the products of European industry, or else distribute trifles amongst them. The sight of pictures, musical-boxes, organs, and the like, was a constant source of attraction. In this way, and by hinting at other wonders not to be produced till the station was finished, I endeavoured to keep them in good humour.

Some time was also devoted to more serious matters, and I often sat up late drawing up reports to Gessi Pasha on administrative affairs, and on the relations in these districts. Such labour was not without its practical results, as, for instance, on the transport of ivory, which had hitherto been forwarded to Jur Ghattas by the roundabout way of Dem Bekir instead of by the direct route through Wau. This certainly brought upon me the wrath of El Maas, superintendent of Dem Bekir, who derived certain perquisites from the transit trade; but it saved the Government the cost of porterage from Dem Bekir to Wau.

And now my little settlement in the African wilderness, evanescent though it might be, as lacking all the elements of stability, had to be named. At that time my memory was constantly haunted by a song of the olden days, whose touching words would rise to my lips even while at work, but especially in the still evening hours, when my eyes gazed dreamily over the smouldering night-fire. This was Stighelli's charming song of the "Tears" (*Lacrima*), whose plaintive melody seemed at the time to echo all my deeper sentiments. Thus it happened that this lay, as it were of itself, became the name of my new station, the erection of which had cost me plenty of care and worry, and drops of perspiration also, if not actual "tears." So at the first hoisting of the flag I christened my station in Zandeh Land "Lacrima."

Meanwhile the report of my arrival at Ndoruma's without a military escort had spread to the remotest confines of the Niam-Niam domain. Favourable accounts of my peaceful attitude, and of my regard for the person and property of the natives, had also produced the desired effect. Numerous messages reached me from distant princes, inviting me to visit their states also, their motive being the hope of my protection from the incessant raids of the Nubians.

Envoys arrived from Binsa, son of the aged Prince Ngerria, in the south; from Prince Wando, also advanced in years, whose territory lay farther east; and from others in the west. Wando especially implored my protection against the despotism and exactions of Abdullai, nephew and successor of Abd ez-Zammah, the latter of whom had accompanied Schweinfurth on his expedition to Mangbattu, while I had journeyed with the former to Jur Ghattas in 1877.

Thus all roads were open to me, except towards the east, where the powerful Prince Mbio still held aloof. Rumours and whisperings constantly reached me of this ruler's hostile designs and intention of falling on Ndoruma's territory and seizing my station. But experience had taught me to receive with many grains of salt the reports of the natives, mostly exaggerations or lies, often inspired by motives of fear.

And here a circumstance may be mentioned which, during my subsequent circular journeys in these lands, was to me a

HEAD OF A ZANDEH DOG. (*From a drawing by Schweinfurth.*)

source of much embarrassment and endless worries. The dismemberment of the great Zandeh kingdom into a number of petty states had resulted in constant feuds and warfare. No prince any longer ventured to leave his territory through mistrust of the neighbouring rulers. This mistrust Ndoruma now endeavoured to foster in me, obstructing my intercourse with his rivals by false reports, and later, when I declared my intention of visiting them, by exaggerated anxiety for my safety. On the other hand similar make-believe sentiments were expressed by the other potentates in regard to Ndoruma, so that none of them entered his territory, although at that time there were no open hostilities between them. Mbio alone, Ndoruma's old rival, was still in recent times showing feelings of animosity, while Ndoruma himself, better informed on the state of affairs in the Bahr el-Ghazal province, had, after a useless struggle with the Nubians, displayed a more friendly spirit towards Gessi. Hence he had also given me permission to enter his state, whereas Mbio, badly informed as to my intentions, continued to regard me with suspicion. In later years, after Mbio's defeat and capture by the Egyptians, I was able to visit his territory also, and then, when it was too late, his sons admitted their blind stupidity, caused by their crediting all those false and exaggerated reports. Had they shown more wisdom I also should have doubtless been better prepared for coming events.

Of the neighbouring princes Ngettua, Ndoruma's uncle, was alone on "visiting terms" with him. He went about accompanied by an old red-brown Niam-Niam hound, whose inseparable associate was a red-haired ape. Whenever they set out it was amusing to see the simian mount the back of the dog, having thus instinctively and without any training secured the services of a riding animal.

North-west of Ndoruma's and north of the Mbomu river stretched the domain of the Zandeh prince Zemio, whom I had met on the journey hither from Dem Soliman. He had long been a vassal of the Arab traders, and was now a loyal adherent to Gessi's government. Trained to the *corvée* system under Zibér and his son Soliman, Zemio, as well as his southern neighbour Sasa, had obtained extensive powers from Gessi; each of them possessed about one hundred rifles, and they were now permitted, or rather ordered, to make expeditions for ivory in the southern regions.

On such occasions they plotted the overthrow of independent chiefs, and after procuring the ivory required by Government, they also looked after their own interests. I am not here making any formal charge against them, and it should be borne in mind that many things in the dealings of such men as Zemio and Sasa may not seem justified according to our notions of right and wrong. But here we have Negro rulers seeking to subvert their compeers in defiance of native custom itself, and without treating the vanquished a whit better than the haughty Arab.

Compared to many others Zemio at heart was a well-meaning person, and later proved himself a loyal friend to me. At this juncture he happened to be in the districts of the chiefs Palembata and Badinde, south-west of Ndoruma's, whom he had already reduced to a state of vassalage, and on whom he was again levying contributions. He was unaccompanied by any Arabs, but in his long intercourse with them he had learnt their language, and had under their instruction trained his subjects to the use of fire-arms. From him I now received an envoy with the present of a girl, and the request to visit him at Palembata's. His further demand for percussion-caps I was able to comply with, and also promised to visit him later, but sent back the girl.

I had impressed upon Ngettua, whose district bordered on Mbio's, to be vigilant, and to keep us informed of any threatening danger. We were later kept frequently in suspense by false alarms, to which at last I almost ceased to pay any heed. But Ndoruma himself was largely to blame for this, all his thoughts and schemes being exclusively directed towards the destruction of his deadly enemy Mbio. His constant hope was that at my instigation Gessi would send troops to take part in a joint expedition against him. I, on the other hand, still fancied that the reduction of the one remaining powerful Zandeh chief might be brought about by peaceful ways, nor did I give up the hope of later putting myself in relation with Mbio, and obtaining leave to visit his country from the south, that is, either from Wando's or Ngerria's.

There were certainly substantial reasons for Ndoruma's hatred of Mbio. During the struggle with Rafai, Ndoruma had escaped to Mbio's territory, whence, however, he had been expelled, and thus obliged to come to terms with Rafai. But many of his subjects had at that time remained in Mbio's, and here they were afterwards joined by others, especially women, eager to escape from Rafai's exactions, and for other motives. Mbio's thus became in course of time a land of refuge for various broken tribes and family groups, refugees not only from Zandeh Land, but also from other native oppressors and from the Nubians.

Meantime the days of freedom and independence were numbered for Mbio himself. My departure from Ndoruma's in January 1881 was followed by a sanguinary war, in which he was vanquished by the Egyptians, and two years later I traversed his wasted territory. After his overthrow Mbio turned eastwards to Emin Pasha for help, but it was too late. His territory was comprised in the Bahr el-Ghazal province, which had withdrawn from Emin's jurisdiction. Since then the fate of all those lands has been shrouded in mystery.

After getting through his other work Bohndorff was usually occupied with skinning birds. Every object in this region was still new to us, and the shady shrubwood of the Werre was especially alive with a rich avifauna, specimens of which could easily be secured. For this purpose the young men were instructed in the use of fire-arms, but every suitable capture represented a large expenditure of powder and shot. My collection was here enriched by the helmet-bird (*Corythaix leucotis*), and the horn-raven (*Tmetoceros abyssinicus*), a member of the hornbill family. The former has probably the most gorgeous plumage of all the larger species in this region.

The black-and-white colubus (*C. guereza*), which inhabits the leafy avenues of the Werre, was also obtained, and I was always glad to secure the beautiful skin of this variety. Owing to a lingering fever, causing weariness and apathy, I had much difficulty in assisting at any manual labour at this time. Bohndorff also was now subject to less frequent but more violent accesses of ague, which rendered him at times unfit for work the whole day.

At Ndoruma's *mbanga* (trysting-place) there daily gathered a number of his subjects to discuss burning questions of Niam-Niam jurisprudence or high politics, or else to lay before him their personal grievances about such matters as an elopement or an abduction, the theft of a few maize cobs, and similar weighty private or public affairs. The assembly usually accompanied Ndoruma on his visits to me, but on such occasions the women never came. The wives of the Zandehs, especially in the upper circles, enjoy a less elevated social standing than, for instance, those of the Mangbattu people. Those who visited me individually or in groups were always reserved, timid, and well-behaved.

I had already given Ndoruma's wives all sorts of glass beads and trinkets, such as captivate the heart of all Negro women. Now I produced various toys, not of course for Ndoruma's numerous olive branches, but for the entertainment of the parents themselves. The adult black, with a generation of years behind him, is still, so to say, in his teens so far as regards his mental capacity. His experiences are in fact all one-sided, and he has no understanding for many things with which our children are already familiar. How much more must this be the case with inexperienced youth itself?

HELMET-BIRD.
(*Corythaix leucotis.*)

In point of fact I never noticed any indications of pleasure in the native children at the sight of European playthings. Hence my large assortment of toys served rather as plastic

COLUBUS GUEREZA. (*Drawn by Fr. Rheinfelder.*)

illustrations of Western culture for their elders, and whatever I produced and distributed had also to be explained as in a kinder-garten school. These objective lessons would often elicit shouts of delight, and then would echo the long-drawn-out *akoōh*, an exclamation with which the Zandehs would express wonder and amazement if not intelligent appreciation of the strange things placed before them.

At the same time the blacks, like others, are diversely endowed, showing various degrees of quickness in grasping the purpose of such novelties. They, of course, lack the training and education which give rise to so much difference in the mental capacity of our own social classes; nevertheless here also the higher circles, princes and nobles, are the most highly endowed with intellectual qualities. This is doubtless due to the fact that, despite his limited sphere of action, the Negro ruler is still compelled to think and act in his capacity as judge, lawgiver, and captain, whereby his cerebral activity has more play than that of the common folk.

To this must be added the fluency acquired by the long parliamentary speeches at the *mbanga*, a sort of witenagemote, where the winged word, often embellished with simile and metaphor, stimulates thought and promotes readiness of expression. The lower classes are doubtless also present at these assemblies, but in their slavish dependence assist only as dumb spectators, except when called upon to speak as plaintiff or defendant. Special gatherings and meetings of the commonalty to deliberate on any topic of general interest are unknown to these peoples. Every question is discussed at the place of assembly in the immediate vicinity of the royal residence, or at the *mbanga* of the vassal chiefs.

But the *mbanga* serves also for social gatherings, which either precede or follow every serious deliberation, and which last the whole day for the convenience of those coming from a distance. Even the women are influenced by such festive reunions, at least amongst those peoples who allow them to associate with the men. Their superiority over the Negro women is seen in the case of the Mangbattus, whose women struck me as more capable of thought and judgment, more quick-witted, and altogether more cultured than their Negro sisters elsewhere. For instance, the Zandeh women, who hold a more abject and servile position, are prevented by fear from raising themselves above their narrow mental range, their dullness and indifference.

Speaking generally, the black race cannot be denied those intellectual qualities which, under guidance and example, might render them capable of higher moral development. The question Is the Negro susceptible of a higher degree of culture? needs no answer; but the views regarding the means of raising him to a better social position need consideration. Competent and incompetent writers have theorized upon this subject; but those alone who are thoroughly acquainted with the actual relations prevailing in Negro lands can satisfactorily deal with such questions.

Amongst the novelties displayed before Ndoruma and his people was an okarina, which took the form of a fish, and from which, despite my elementary knowledge of instrumental music, I managed to extract notes, which were received with rapturous applause and the ever-recurring "akoōh," expressive of breathless surprise. Astonishment was also produced by children's penny whistles, while a large accordion caused universal amazement. This was in later years my *pièce de résistance*, in which I had fortunately the assistance of another amateur, my servant Farag 'Alláh, who really played with some skill and possessed an accordion of his own.

The performance, especially of the musical-boxes, usually struck the listeners dumb with amazement, so that a solemn stillness would pervade the audience. Occasionally, when the soft and weird-like notes were suddenly emitted, and when I myself feigned surprise, looking round about the hut to discover the agency at work, my visitors would be overcome by an unmistakable sense of fear and alarm at the uncanny sounds, and would stealthily disappear one after the other. Most Africans of course firmly believe in witchcraft, and in the magic power of certain individuals. But a magician who never brought harm on any one was doubtless a new phenomenon among these peoples, and they soon came to be convinced that these series of surprises were all fair and above-board. My action thus helped somewhat to diminish the witchcraft craze, and I was doubtless the means of shaking the belief of many natives in that delusion. The fame of all these things went before me on my wanderings, so that we were often asked to rehearse our concerts along the route.

HORN RAVEN. (*Tmetoceros abyssinicus.*)

One night about this time we had a characteristic African experience in a regular attack of robber-ants, whose marauding expeditions we had later frequent opportunities of witnessing. These forays may even lead to little tragic episodes, such as came under my own notice. I was also at this time subject to some typical accesses of fever; in the lighter attacks I abstained from the use of quinine, in order not to accustom my constitution to this remedy, and reserve it for more serious cases. All travellers should be warned against its too frequent use, which tends to diminish its efficacy, while on the other hand giving rise to other troubles, such as ringing in the ears and hardness of hearing.

Now the aged Zandeh prince Wando again sent envoys, amongst others one of his brothers, to complain of shameful outrages and attacks on the part of the Nubians. Wando's son, Hokwa, had played the traitor, and for his own purposes made common cause with the intruders. During his expedition this year to Mangbattu Land, Abdu'lallahi, nephew of Abd es-Sammat, had joined Hokwa and his followers in a raid on the territory of Hokwa's brother, Mbittima, for Wando had already distributed his possessions amongst his sons, to be held by them in feudal tenure. The consequence was that Mbittima had been carried off in chains to Mangbattu Land, while Wando, in his old age, had escaped to the wilderness, and was now with his brother Ngerria.

Abdu'lallahi was also reported to have brought away many slaves, girls and women, though what chiefly grieved Wando was the captivity of his best-loved son Mbittima. He now implored me to report these matters to the Pasha, and to pay himself a personal visit, in order to exert my influence in his land, where Abdu'lallahi had stationed several Arabs and soldiers to support the traitor Hokwa. I could just then do nothing for Wando beyond holding out a hope of being able soon to come and help him.

I mention these occurrences to show how deeply rooted were the old abuses, seeing that such things could take place after Gessi's reforms in the Bahr el-Ghazal, where in fact his authority was little more than nominal. Here again his good intentions were thwarted by his own officials, for after the war with Soliman, Abdu'lallahi had been made administrator of the eastern districts as far as the Rol, and was well aware of the Pasha's orders and wishes, but acted in direct opposition to them. It was his policy, by constant petty exactions, to force the native rulers into revolt, in order then, by misrepresenting the true relations, to justify himself, if needs be, with the central authorities. Amid such complications I had myself to play the diplomatist in order not to imperil my own position; for in my further wanderings in those lands I had often to reckon with both parties. In emergencies I endeavoured to act as mediator in reconciling all interests.

The station being now completed, I fitted up a meteorological observatory, where I took records thrice daily. These after my departure were continued by Bohndorff, so that they cover the six months of our stay at Ndoruma's to the end of 1881.[1]

The envoys were now dismissed with a few presents for Wando. From Ndoruma, during my long residence, I received only an occasional piece of venison. This scarcity of game, both here and elsewhere, shows that the surrounding regions are inhabited not by hunting, but by agricultural and pastoral peoples. Compared with other tribes, the Zandehs themselves are no doubt keen sportsmen, but they by no means depend mainly on the products of the chase. They would be reduced to sore distress if corn did not form their staple food at least during certain seasons of the year.

The durra and Kaffir corn of the northern regions is here replaced mainly by eleusine (*E. coracana*), a small grain like flax or canary-seed. The thick, blackish porridge prepared from this cereal serves as the chief article of diet both for prince and people. About half the crop is used in brewing the beloved native beer, which is so nourishing that for days together a liberal allowance will enable them to dispense with other food. After poor harvests, for which the thriftless Negro is badly prepared, and also during favourable hunting seasons, flesh is certainly the chief support of the people; it is mostly preserved in the dried state, and is unquestionably preferred by the Niam-Niam to all other kinds of food. Besides eleusine, maize is also everywhere grown in small quantities, and at Ndoruma's it was also occasionally supplied to us.

In our own garden were sown, besides pulse, maize, theosinte (*Euchlæna luxurians*), carrots, beetroot, celery, parsley, &c.

---

[1] See Dr. Schmidt, *Petermann's Mittheilungen*, Supplement Nos. 92 and 93, part II.

SYLVAN LANDSCAPE ON THE WERRE.

However, I was not too sanguine of the results, especially as the experiment was confined to a single spot. I could have wished to lay out another plot in a more suitable locality near the river, but feared that the clearing and tilling of the ground would prove too great a tax on the energies of Ndoruma's people. In any case my chief aim was to instruct my men, and accustom them to regular work, while giving Ndoruma and his subjects an insight into our system of husbandry, and affording ourselves an opportunity of useful bodily exercise against the monotony of zeriba life. If after that we also obtained any material result, our efforts would be doubly rewarded, and fresh experiences acquired regarding the acclimatation of northern cultivated plants in tropical Africa. On July 15th we first enjoyed the pleasure of knowing that the seeds had germinated; on that day the young plants were at last seen struggling into light in several parts of the pea and bean plots.

More envoys, this time from Zemio. He was still at Palembata's, and also wanted me to visit him. I put him off, like the others, and asked him to send again in a fortnight, when I might be able to arrange for a journey to him. Binsa, son of the aged Prince Malingde, and our nearest southern neighbour, also sent people to greet me. Such messages were often inspired merely by the curiosity of the chiefs anxious to get some direct information regarding me, and to satisfy themselves regarding my harmlessness.

During these months (July and August) the temperature was very agreeable at Ndoruma's. Great heat was rare, and far less than in more northern lands, such as Egyptian Sudan, Khartum, or the Red Sea coast lands. During the day the glass seldom rose in the shade above 77° or 78° F., falling at night to 59° or 60°. The early morning and the evening hours especially were very pleasant. Thunderstorms occurred mostly in the afternoon, but also in the evening and at night, but rarely during the forenoon. These favourable conditions are partly due to the fact that Central Zandeh Land stands at the greatest relative altitude (2440 feet), being in fact the divide where many considerable streams have their source, and flow in various directions.

Ndoruma's dwellings, which lay scarcely five minutes from my station of Lacrima, were in no way distinguished from the ordinary native huts. Ndoruma himself, in accordance with the good old Zandeh custom, displayed the greatest simplicity in all things. His favourite dress was the "rokko," which had certainly seen better days, and which was fastened by a stout twisted bast cord. On his visits he was followed about by two or three boys carrying an old musket, the revolver I had given him, and a large Mangbattu *trumbush*.

The humble style of his dwellings was no doubt partly due to the fact that the Zandehs often abandon their settlements after a few years, and remove to another place. Ndoruma himself had not long been here and his huts were of a temporary character. During Rafai's successful expedition against him, the land had been frequently wasted, and the former habitations destroyed or abandoned, while the fear of renewed attacks from the Nubians had prevented the erection of more substantial dwellings.

It was owing to this fear that Ndoruma had come forward to meet me at Dem Bekir, whence he had hastily returned to reassure his subjects, who soon perceived that my residence amongst them would even afford some protection against the Nubians. I frequently heard them remark that they now looked forward to better times, and could attend to their fields and habitations with a greater sense of security. On my return at the end of the year from my first circular journey, I found Ndoruma's new huts even enclosed by a palisade, such as had never before been erected by any Zandeh tribe. Stout enclosures prevail mostly amongst pastoral peoples, as a protection against beasts of prey, and to prevent the cattle from roaming over the land. But the Zandehs keep neither cattle nor goats, and are too indolent to erect efficient barriers against the nightly attacks of leopards.

During my last eastward journey through Ndoruma's district, three years later, I scarcely found a trace of the structures at my station of Lacrima; Ndoruma also had again abandoned his settlement, and founded another a little farther east on the Werre plateau. Of his former huts nothing was visible. Thus everything in tropical Africa warns us of decay and oblivion; but within us bides the depressing feeling that perhaps after all the continued efforts of Europeans may produce no fruit, and that these children of Nature may themselves pass away before any lasting improvement can be effected in their condition.

Our household was now disturbed by the illness of my cook Saida, whom I had brought all the way from Khartum. She was a member of the Berta tribe on the Blue Nile, and had become somewhat proficient in Arab cookery, too much so, in fact, for our present simple mode of living. Hence during the long attack of rheumatism which now incapacitated her for work, her place was taken by Farag 'Alláh, who knew enough to prepare our frugal fare under my daily instructions.

ZANDEH WOMAN AND CHILD.
(*Drawn by Fr. Rheinfelder; from a photograph by R. Buchta.*)

Thanks to the friendly invitations of the surrounding princes, the way was now open to renew my ramblings in various directions. I was aware that Ndoruma, through motives of fear and petty jealousy, would be unwilling to let me set out just yet; the difficulties, in fact, which he threw in my way caused me no little vexation and annoyance. So I was determined, on the arrival of another envoy from Zemio, to visit him. His intention was to go southwards in quest of ivory, and I hoped to join the expedition.

Here I may be permitted to give a brief sketch of our quiet life at the station. In these latitudes daylight lasts about twelve hours, without perceptible difference throughout the year. The sun rises shortly before six, reaches the zenith about noon, and sets again towards six, dawn and dusk being of short duration compared with our higher latitudes. As day follows quickly on night, daylight in its turn is quickly succeeded by darkness, unless a more gradual transition is effected by the friendly light of the moon. Of the full power of this luminary in tropical lands our northern peoples scarcely form an adequate conception. In our artificially lighted towns, the great majority scarcely trouble themselves at all about lunar phases or starry skies. But in the southern regions millions of Nature worshippers, under a dim foreboding of an all-ruling Power, choose the period of the full moon for mystic rites, fantastic dances, and festivities. They recognize the advantage of not having to pass half their lives in impenetrable darkness.

Our daily work began for the most part when the last feeble light of the moon was extinguished in the glowing rays of the rising sun. All had their daily appointed tasks, which constantly returned, and which had to be got through before anything else could be done. The maid-servants had their huts, the kitchen and its approaches to look after; the boys had to keep the grass cut and cleared away, while the little Dinka lad, Farag, took special charge of the sheep and goats. My hut and the open space where we gathered in the evening were constantly watered and swept clean, and every morning the tunnels constructed during the night by the termites were carefully removed.

In the early morning water had to be brought by the girls in large pitchers from the Werre, and this duty had to be again performed several times during the course of the day, according to circumstances. These porous vessels, of various size and mostly of round plump shape, keep the water at an agreeably cool temperature; such a *burma*, as the Arabs call them, always stood on the stem of a tree in my hut.

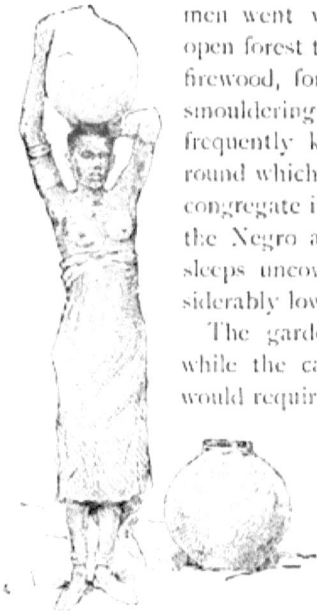

EARTHENWARE WATER VESSELS.

After the morning work some of the young men went with their axes to the surrounding open forest to collect bundles of dry and decayed firewood, for I always kept a fire burning or smouldering night and day. Another was also frequently kindled in the open before my hut, round which the young people were allowed to congregate in the evening. A blazing log is for the Negro almost indispensable at night, as he sleeps uncovered, and the temperature is considerably lower than during the day.

The garden also needed constant attention, while the carefully-cut trenches and channels would require to be cleared of the mud and slush washed down every other day by the fierce thunderstorms. The natives themselves required to be constantly looked after, especially at first; they did nothing spontaneously, but had to be told over and over again to perform the same daily routine work. Their duties were neglected, not so much through malice or obstinacy, as through sheer indolence, want of training, and, in the case of the young people, an unlimited faculty for forgetting. The Negro will put off everything, and dream away the day basking lazily in the sun, although he knows quite well that water, fuel, and other necessaries have to be provided.

My effects of all kinds were always kept under lock and key, and the daily rations were distributed by myself from the provision chests. Even the salt had to be thriftily doled out, for this important condiment cannot be procured in the Zandeh country. Here the natives season their food with the alkali of wood-ashes. Hence our kitchen salt is a great luxury, is everywhere highly valued and eagerly devoured, like sugar by our children. I had consequently brought twenty "head" of salt, about four loads, from Khartum, and increased my stock at Meshra.

Most manual labour is left in Africa to the women, except when they are fortunate enough to become the favourites of princes or chiefs, in which case they are often exempt from all work. The female slaves, especially in the service of Arabs, whose domestic needs are greater than amongst the Negroes lead a far more toilsome existence than the men. These have, in many cases, no special work to perform, and in the houses of wealthy Arabs are often more ornamental than useful.

Apart from field operations, the hardest and most time-consuming duty of the women is the grinding of corn in their primitive fashion. Meal is of course the chief article of food, whether taken in the form of thick porridge (*lugma* or *assida* of the Arabs), or of *medida* (thin gruel), or of thin cakes (*kisra*, or when dry, *abré*) prepared only in Arab households; or, lastly, in the form of solid, round little loaves, as in the northern Arab lands.

SALT BLOCK FROM KHARTUM; NINE INCHES HIGH.

But the primitive mill, universal in Egypt and amongst the Arab Bedouins, is found only in the larger towns of East Sudan, while it is absolutely unknown in the Negro lands. Here it is replaced by the *funduk* (a kind of stamping mill or trough) for the larger and harder cereals, which have to be first husked and prepared for the grinding-stone. This funduk is a hollowed block of wood of varying size up to three feet or so high, or else a thick wooden trough prepared somewhat like a dug-out. But in either case heavy wooden pestles are used for pounding the corn.

In the houses of the Zandeh chiefs are seen elegant ivory pestles a foot long with ornamental thick ends, and these are amongst the choice objects of primitive Negro art. They serve also especially for pounding vegetables and condiments, and for preparing the termite messes. Thus the time-consuming work of braying corn and other food for a large household requires a great many female hands; and as the Arab expeditions in Negro lands are accompanied only by a limited number of the female slaves, it follows that on the march an extra share of work falls to the lot of the free women themselves. I have often

TROUGHS FOR BRAYING CORN.   ZANDEH IVORY MORTAR.

seen and heard the girls laboriously pounding away at their grinding troughs late into the night. They have often even to get up in the small hours to have the kisra or assida ready for the early breakfast before the start on the next wearisome march. The ordinary proportion is one corn-grinder for every three mouths; but it frequently happens that one slave-girl has to provide for as many as ten hungry stomachs.

In Egyptian Sudan corn-grinding is left exclusively to the women; but on the route to Zanzibar, south of the Equator, this work is done by the carriers themselves. The Sudanese Negro willingly undertakes kitchen work, but his self-respect requires him to draw the line at the mortar and pestle. He would prefer eating his durra uncrushed, either roasted over the fire or parboiled, to the indignity of having to bray it himself. Taught by my former experience, and in many respects guided by the example of the Arabo-Nubians, with whose customs I usually conformed, I always engaged female hands on these expeditions.

I soon got used to the simplest kinds of Arab fare, and especially to kisra and the other kinds of bread. This was always prepared by the women under my inspection, and remained for years the chief article of my diet, greatly to the benefit of my health. By the exercise of a little study and invention, the European may here easily increase his bill of fare, and from the dark, bitter telebun (*Eleusine coracana*) I myself succeeded in preparing a fine, sweet, and snow-white meal, which tasted quite as good as wheat-meal. Maize also I found, by husking and reducing in size, made an excellent substitute for rice.

The season when the ants take wing was now at its height, and the already-mentioned mess of termites was a good test of my power to adapt myself to native fare. At this time Ndoruma's contributions were limited to maize and large quantities of dried termites, little else being in season. These female termites, about a third of an inch long and of cylindrical shape, but varying according to the species, are very fat, and are boiled down in water to the consistency of a thick porridge. To prevent putrefaction after being gathered, they are immediately dried over a fire, when the long wings all fall off, and they are often eaten in this state. Those received from Ndoruma, about fifty loads in the month of June, were very acceptable to my people as an accompaniment to their porridge, for this food is not liked by the natives taken by itself. Soon I had it served daily at our own table; it tasted something like meat-stuffing, and we took it mixed either with kisra or with rice. I had it also cooked with beaten eggs as a termite omelette, or as a substitute for flesh in meat-pies, the *fatir* of the Arabs. In this dish, however, the Arabs themselves never use termites, which the Mohammedan detests, although he cannot regard them in a religious sense as unclean, being sprung from eggs.

Our daily menu was varied with European provisions, such as lentil, pea, and bean soups, which I had brought both in the form of condensed tablets and dried in little bags. Julienne in either form may be strongly recommended to all travellers. When nothing else was available, it served as a welcome accompaniment to the kisra, taken with a little dried game. There were also macaroni and rice, and tinned vegetables of all kinds, as well as tunny-fish, salmon, lobsters, tongue, sardines, though such delicacies were only produced on special occasions, and in small portions. Dried and compressed fruits, such as apples, apricots, and plums, were also a great treat in illness, and cooked with rice made a capital Sunday dish. On the other hand, fresh meat was rare, as I avoided as far as possible encroaching on our little stock of goats and poultry.

At Ndoruma's we had coffee with milk and sugar every morning, and two regular meals during the day, but no wine, the little I possessed being reserved for emergencies. The sugar ran out in a few months; after putting aside a little for cases of illness, I used up the rest freely, for it is a useless and heavy burden on the march, and may be replaced by honey on the spot. On the other hand the Khartum biscuit (*buxmat*) keeps well, and we usually took it soaked in water with our morning coffee and afternoon tea. Tea itself was our most refreshing beverage during all our wanderings, and the kettle was always kept simmering on the fire in the stations, the camping-places, the native huts, or wherever we happened to be staying. I do not say that it acted as a preventative against bowel complaints, from which I never suffered, but I do maintain that weak tea taken frequently (the English drink it too strong) is to be highly recommended to travellers; it enables them almost entirely to dispense with cold water, which is often bad and charged with the germs of typhus or dysentery.

Three days towards the end of July (22nd, 23rd, and 24th) were occupied with long palavers chiefly about Binsa, son of Prince Malingde, who refused to give up a store of ivory which had been left in his charge by Osman Bedawi, and which was to have been consigned to Ndoruma. Binsa was also accused of other high-handed dealings; but after much deliberation, and despite the explanations of Binsa's envoys, it still remained doubtful where the truth lay.

About the same time Prince Wando sent me another message and the gift of four fowls, with a renewed and urgent request to visit him at his brother Ngerria's, where he was still a refugee. All this helped to give me a better insight into the relations of the Zandeh rulers, as well as the hostile designs harboured by Mbio against Ndoruma and even myself. I was able, however, to form a more correct estimate of his reported intention to fall on and destroy my station, when viewed in the light of Ndoruma's avowed desire to break Mbio's power by the aid of the Government troops. At the same time I clearly saw that amidst all these intrigues it would be impossible to treat on a friendly footing with Mbio from my present residence, for it was reported by Ngettua's envoys that he would not receive my messengers.

At this time Ndoruma's *mbanga* was attended by several distant feudatories, amongst others his brother, Mbima or Mbansuro, ruler of a south-western district on the border of Palembata's territory, where Zemio was just then residing. They came chiefly to greet me and offer me little presents, which I usually distributed amongst the people for themselves and their women.

On those occasions the station was all astir with excitement, for my visitors would resolutely refuse to withdraw till they had seen some of the white man's marvels, the fame of which had spread far and wide over the land. They were specially interested in those magic boxes and instruments (accordions), from which such mysterious yet attractive sounds were emitted without the touch of human hand. Then they would admire those wonderful books and pictures, in which they recognized their own dwellings and weapons, their wild animals, the worm, the fly, the bee and beetle, the birds on the wing, the fishes in the water, the dreaded snakes, and their very elephants, these last a never-failing source of irrepressible jubilation. A painted cardboard marionette, about three feet high, which I had hung up in my hut, often gave rise to the liveliest scenes. During the ladies' visits, whenever I suddenly and stealthily pulled the string, they would rush screaming and yelling from the hut, and could with difficulty be won from their terror. I mention these things, trivial enough in themselves, to illustrate the low mental state of these aborigines, and to show that we must look on the Negro as a child, and regulate our treatment of him from this point of view. For instance, when I set the barrel-organ going, many supposed that I alone had the power of extracting the notes. Hence all the greater was the exultation when I invited one of themselves to turn the handle and produce the same sounds, to his own bewilderment.

When the plants began to spring up in the numerous garden plots with their trim borderings and tidy walks, I took Ndoruma and his guests round the enclosure to show them our methods of gardening, and make them acquainted with some of our culinary plants. To the few who displayed any special interest in such matters, I even distributed several varieties of maize for their own plantations.

Ndoruma, who intended to start with a convoy of ivory for Gessi Pasha, kept putting off his departure from day to day, solely through fear of my going to Binsa's and Wando's in his absence, and perhaps then open communications with Mbio himself. He feared for my safety, as was the burden of his song; but had I followed his advice I should have still remained long inactive at the station. Hence, for the moment, I no longer spoke of my own plans, but rather urged him to depart on his journey to the Governor.

Soon after he actually did make a start, giving out that he would first of all collect the ivory from the chiefs in the northern part of his territory. At the same time he expressed his fear that after my departure Rafai might possibly return and again levy contributions on his people. It thus became evident to me that all his efforts were aimed at keeping me permanently in his territory. The same troubles I afterwards again experienced amongst other rulers, so that it was often not only difficult to reach their districts, but still more difficult to get away again. They were always glad to retain me with them, as a protection against hostile neighbours and against the exactions of the Nubians.

A brood of chicks which had recently been hatched now began to attract the attention of predatory birds, amongst others

COSMETORNIS SPEKEI.

the *Cosmetornis Spekei*, of which I was very anxious to secure a specimen. It belongs to the family of goat-suckers, and about this time I saw it for the first time swooping over the station on several evenings towards dusk. On one occasion the winged termites buzzing about a neighbouring ant-hill soon attracted several of these long-tailed nightjars. It was highly interesting to observe their peculiar flight, their long flag-feathers giving the impression of two small birds always flying at their side. They circled swiftly and noiselessly round and round the ant-hill, darted upwards, and then dropped as suddenly down, so that it was scarcely possible to get a good shot. At last I managed to bring one down, but it fell in the tall grass, and when it was recovered some days afterwards it was found to be useless as a specimen, having been half devoured by the ants. Meanwhile its companions disappeared, and were not again seen near the station.

On August 2nd envoys presented themselves for the third time from Zemio to say that he was on the point of leaving for the south, but would still expect me before starting. Now I made up my mind, and sent the envoy back with the assurance that I would set out in a few days. I even retained one of his people at the station to act as my guide. My preparations were soon completed, my light equipment enabling me to dispense with a numerous following. It was important that I had chosen the road to Zemio's, where Ndoruma could not pretend to entertain any alarm respecting my safety. He knew that Zemio held a prominent position, enjoyed the confidence of Gessi Pasha, and was acting on behalf of the Government.

I now gave Bohndorff all necessary instructions regarding the work to be continued at the station during my absence, and handed him the inventory of all the effects, with duplicate keys of the boxes. I also instructed him in the reading of the meteorological instruments, which enabled him to continue the systematic observations during the following months.

On August 5th all preparations were completed, and a package of letters addressed to the postmaster of Khartum had been sent off to Ndoruma, who was still sojourning in the northern parts of his territory. I at the same time informed him of my approaching journey to Zemio's, recommending to his care my assistant Bohndorff, and all the people left behind at the station.

I now engaged fifteen carriers to be ready by the 7th, but that day and the following passed in useless waiting. Farag 'Allâh, whom I had despatched to the neighbouring chiefs, brought back the news that Ndoruma had plainly forbidden them to let me have any carriers. This I had not expected, and the attempted indignity was the last straw which well-nigh caused me to lose all patience.

Later, when Ndoruma's sons with a few chiefs called on me, I expressed myself in the harshest and most plain-spoken language on the subject. In this I played the part of an injured and outraged person, and declared that after such an experience I should no longer remain at the station, but the very next morning should start with my servants alone for Zemio's, and bring back carriers from him to bring away all my things and leave Ndoruma's for ever. And I clenched the matter by asking who would dare to prevent me, adding that the Pasha should be at once informed of Ndoruma's high-handed attempt to oblige me to remain, and that all the other Zandeh chiefs should hear of his conduct.

A messenger from Wando happened just then to be at Ndoruma's *mbanga*. I sent for him there and then, so that Wando also might be forthwith informed of the occurrence. But his followers were already so alarmed at my determination to carry out my expressed intentions, that they also now began to make revelations on their part. This result I had expected; nevertheless I kept them long in doubt as to my action, and at last required the carriers to be supplied by sunset, failing which I should carry out my project by daylight, perhaps even go straight to the Pasha and return with troops and carriers from the Bahr el-Ghazal province. In that case I should need none of their carriers, but travel like all other Zandeh, Pambia, and Barmbo people; and then the lazy Zandehs, who were no men, but women, might stay at home with their wives.

After these words, uttered in a towering passion, Ndoruma's sons and the others present hurried off, and brought the carriers before sunset. But the rain now set in, and after all my departure was delayed until August 10th.

DOUBLE WOODEN BASIN.

CROSSING A SWAMP WITH PLANKS.

CHAPTER VI.

FROM NDORUMA'S TO THE WELLE-MAKUA.

Off at Last—Chimpanzee Hunt—Zandeh Cannibalism—Journey to Mbima's—Ndoruma's Vassals—Swampy Woodlands—Mbima's Territory and surrounding District—Zandeh Habits and Customs—Ndoruma's Arrival—Journey to Zemio's—Palembata's Territory—Family Alliances of the Zandeh Princes—Negotiations with Badinde—The Mangballa Borderlands—Nazima and his Schemes—The Gurba River—Bangusa—Swamps—Mbruole River—First Sight of the Welle—Shifting of our Headquarters.

I HAD tarried full two months on the banks of the Werre, where my station of Lacrima had been founded. Our European garden was already clothed with verdure, and I was gratified by the pleasant sight of our tender seedlings springing into new life when the time approached to leave our comfortable quarters in an inhospitable land, and renew our wanderings through the wilderness. But I could scarcely hope to reap what I had sown with my own hands, although the finest deep red radishes were already promising to reward us for our loving care.

When the carriers were at last obtained, they behaved in a

pitiful manner over the comparatively light loads assigned to them. Many even began to cry off, and try to escape the service by lies and shamming sickness or lack of strength. Our first march was a short one, and, to the surprise of Bohndorff and the others who had remained behind, the same afternoon saw us back again at the station. This, however, was due to a lucky event, the capture in fact of a chimpanzee, which I was anxious to have properly preserved as a specimen by Bohndorff.

The chimpanzee is indigenous in the southern and western parts of Zandeh Land, or about between 25° and 28° E. longitude, and reaching north to 5° or even 6° N. latitude. Although not exactly rare, he is not easily met, owing to his habit of frequently moving from place to place; nor, despite all inquiries, had I yet succeeded in securing a specimen. Stalking him in the almost impenetrable thickets or along the swampy river banks is a very laborious pastime. He dwells exclusively among the lofty forest trees of such districts, which offer him a safe retreat, so that his capture is mostly a matter of chance. And so it was with me on this occasion, when my good luck threw in my way no less than three of these apes, one of which was undoubtedly amongst the largest representatives of the race.

CHIMPANZEE HUNT.

It happened in this wise. We had proceeded scarcely half an hour on our journey from the station, when we found ourselves surrounded by a broad swampy sheet of water. I had brought with me a plank, thirteen feet long, for the purpose of crossing such places, where a few dry spots occur at intervals round about the snags or roots of trees. Beyond the morass the natives reported the presence of chimpanzees in the neighbourhood. Eager to observe them in their natural environment, and possibly to secure a specimen, I called a halt, and followed the guidance of the people across bog and slush, forcing my way with difficulty through bush and briar and snake-like creepers, emerging at last on a spot overarched by the summits of gigantic forest trees.

The movements of the animals had meanwhile been noticed by some natives, who received me with the repeated exclamation: *Yá, hó! mansúruma* ("There, there's the chimpanzee"). But the indicated tree was so high that it was some time before I could detect him moving about in the foliage. My first shot was followed by an unearthly yell and a shower of good-sized branches, which the animals broke off and flung down at us. Then one of them showed itself, and I distinctly noticed a young one clinging to its breast. The mother again quickly sought cover, crouching in the fork of two huge branches in such a way as to shield her offspring with her body. The fifth shot brought her down, though I afterwards noticed that she had been hard hit several times. In her extremity she had at last even put aside the little one, which remained unharmed on the top of the tree, so that at first I hoped to take it alive.

Some of the people climbed up, but before they had got half way returned in hot haste, reporting that the adult male was lurking in the tangled foliage of the summit. After in vain endeavouring to spot him, I at last fired a charge of heavy shot at random into a dark mass of leaves. I had hit the right spot, for the animal at once left its cover with a yell, and was then brought down with a few more shots. It proved, however, not to be the old male, but a second and smaller female. The first surprised me by her solid build; although only four and a half feet high, she presented an enormous muscular development in the arms and legs. I failed to capture the young one, owing to the laziness of my people, who refused to climb the tree.

The strength even of young chimpanzees is amazing. On one occasion I had the greatest difficulty in wrenching a stick from one, which was but half grown, and a suckling will cling so tightly to your finger that the greatest effort will be needed to get free. I have seen many of these anthropoids, some of which I have kept at the stations or carried about with me on my wanderings. They afforded me many an hour's distraction, and I shall have more to say of them later. The older it grows the darker becomes the chimpanzee's skin on face, palms of the hands, and soles of the feet. The face of adults is of a dark brown inclining to blackish, and often speckled, while the hairless parts of the very young are, on the contrary, of a light colour.

Once their retreat is discovered, chimpanzee hunting is easy enough. They move slowly and cautiously amongst the branches, so that they can scarcely escape a sportsman armed with a good gun, as can other apes, such as the nimble Colobus, who often travels faster overhead from branch to branch and tree to tree than his pursuer can follow through the dense undergrowths. The chimpanzee, on the contrary, always seeks cover, and will even descend to the ground, where he can more easily disappear amid the thick brushwood. Here he will apparently even show fight. Such is his physical strength, and so formidable are his teeth, that in single combat the Negro finds him a dangerous foe. On the other hand, the natives, armed only with spear, bow and arrow, are scarcely able to bring down the chimpanzee when he keeps to his arboreal retreat; hence all the greater was their astonishment at the range and efficacy of my rifle.

On the march back to the station the large chimpanzee was brought back bound to a long plank, and received with acclamations. The specimen was at once skinned, while some of the carriers waited eagerly for their share of the game. Not all, however, for although the Zandehs are undoubtedly cannibals, some amongst them will touch neither man nor chimpanzee, probably because of its human appearance; at least they do not refuse any other kind of monkey, and also devour many other repulsive things. In the present instance all my carriers rejected the flesh of the chimpanzee, except the members of the A-Barmbo and A-Pambia tribes, who, as elsewhere stated, live scattered about in small communities amongst Ndoruma's people.

Our route now trended south-westwards in the direction of a station belonging to Mbansuro (Mbima), a brother and vassal of Ndoruma, on the south-west frontier of his territory. This settlement, which was reached in a few days, lay midway between Ndoruma's and Zemio's temporary encampment in Palembata's country.

After crossing another shallow swamp by means of the plank, we reached a deep broad morass where this expedient proved useless. I had therefore to wade across over rough ground strewn with much underwood, and could not but secretly envy the well-seasoned soles of my carriers, who went steadily forward, slow but sure, while I floundered about, helplessly sprawling and stumbling at every step amid the tangle of roots and slush. Chief Kunna awaited us at his huts on the opposite bank, where I got rid of the mud and dirt while our people were being fed. Another short march brought us to chief Gumba's, where I passed the night in a tiny little hut, with no room even for my work-table, the top of which had to be placed on a basket at my bedside.

Next morning the carriers were changed, which caused more delay, and as the rain came on in the afternoon we got no farther that day than the station of chief Gallia (Balia).

All the swampy tracts between Ndoruma's and this place, as well as the streamlets crossed the following days, drain northwestwards to the Werre. Notwithstanding its low elevation (2440 feet above sea-level), the district about Ndoruma's residence, lying between 4° and 5° north, 27° and 28° east, comprises one of the most important water-partings of the hydrographic system in this part of Africa, a sort of nucleus or central point for the sources of most of the streams flowing south to the Welle for the Congo, and north to the Sueh-Jur for the Nile.

On the route to Gallia's I met only one small swamp stream

ZANDEH WIZARD.
(*Drawn by Fr. Rheinfelder; from a photograph by R. Buchta.*)

flowing in a different direction from the others, that is, southwards to the Gurba, an independent affluent of the Welle-Makua. During this first circular journey I crossed its lower course later on. In the neighbourhood of Gallia's huts, on the scarcely perceptible water-parting between the Werre and Gurba, formerly stood the residence of the powerful Prince Yapati, who at one time held sway over a great part of the Zandeh nation, and from whom had sprung many of the still living Niam-Niam rulers. His son, the aged Malingde or Bunza (not to be confused with Binza's father, Malingde, whose territory lies between the Gurba and Mbruole rivers), gave me much valuable information on the history of the Zandeh peoples. He and Balia were now the only

LAYING THE GRASS.

surviving sons of Yapati. A little south of our route there also stood a residence of Prince Mbio, whose domain was said to have some decades ago reached this point.

The hut here placed at my disposal was so small that there was no space to rig up my mosquito-net, so that for the night I was at the mercy of these pests. These Negro hovels are mostly crowded round the residence of some prince or chief, and between the groups there stretch miles of uninhabited tracts. In many Zandeh districts, and especially round about the much-frequented settlements of the chiefs, the tall grass growing eight to ten feet high gets completely beaten down along both sides of the narrow track; but beyond this they rarely take the trouble to clear away the grass itself and widen the path. They even seldom resort to the practical method of laying the rank herbage by means of a stout branch or sapling held by a cord, both ends of which are attached to it at a third of the length from either extremity. The heavy stick is thus easily raised and let down and pushed along with the foot, a process which, aided by the weight of the body, effectually breaks and flattens the tall stalks, as clearly shown in the accompanying illustration. In such places locomotion is easy enough; unfortunately they are confined to few localities, and elsewhere the traveller has to force his way for miles through the thick, sharp grass, holding his right arm in the attitude of a combatant to protect his face and eyes.

The third day's march brought us to the territory of Gangura, another brother and vassal of Ndoruma. Here ended the immediate domain of the paramount lord, that is to say, the district round about his residence within which the petty chiefs and their subjects attend the mbanga (royal assembly), and consult it in all judicial matters. Over the more remote districts are placed, as rulers, especially brothers of the prince, who as vassals yield obedience to his orders. The Zandeh prince is addressed by the title of "Bia," which is also extended to his brothers, to chiefs, and, in fact, to all distinguished persons. It answers to our "Sir," and was even used by inferiors in addressing me. "Baiki," the Zandeh word for chief, is not employed in conversation.

In Gangura's district we at first followed the water-parting between the two already-mentioned affluents of the Welle-Makua. Instead of the troublesome swampy tracts and rivers, we here traversed many broad stretches of woodlands, which took the direction of the streamlets crossing our track farther on. In their exuberant growth and vegetable forms these woodlands partly display the characteristic features of the fluvial avenues; but they lack the deep troughs or gorges in many places disposed in terraces, whose bed is occupied by swampy ground or limpid brooks. Within their limits the all-pervading moisture still percolates underground, appearing lower down as surface streams.

We passed the night with Peru, a chief subject to Gangura.

Here also the huts were wretched, though the settlement presented a comfortable appearance from its enclosure of magnificent bananas, whose fruit, a foot long, forms the staple food of the Mangbattu people. We also noticed some well-tilled tobacco-fields, all the more pleasing to the eye that the ground under other crops is generally neglected after sowing-time.

Next day we reached Gangura's settlement, having again to cross running waters and swampy tracts, for here the water-parting lay to the south of our route. The rise was scarcely perceptible between the streams, all of which flowed to the Werre.

At Gangura's I was accommodated with a more spacious hut; but here, as elsewhere, the door had to be secured with blocks of wood and boards, against the attacks of prowling leopards. While the hut was being put to rights, I passed the time, as was my wont, under the shade of a tree, surrounded by a number of admiring and inquisitive natives. During our stay in this place my rifle supplied me with a few guinea-fowl to supplement the ordinary diet of gourds, sweet potatoes, and maize. The chiefs, who furnished these provisions, received in return sundry little presents, such as glass beads, cheap razors, small looking-glasses, brass rings and bracelets, bad penknives, and in special cases cloth, all of which things were gladly accepted.

Beyond Gangura's district follows south-westwards that of Mbima (Mbansuro), Ndoruma's most distinguished brother and vassal. I had already made his acquaintance, as well as that of Gangura and of several other chiefs whom I met on this journey, at my station of Lacrima. Mbima gave us a grand reception, coming with his people some distance to meet us. His territory is considerably larger and more populous than those of his other brothers, and forms on the west and south the border-land of Ndoruma's domain. Here I took a day's rest to repair the damage done to my clothes during our wanderings through the coarse, tall grass.

In the vicinity were some extensive fields, which at this season yielded mainly gourds, yams, sweet potatoes, and maize, abundant supplies of which were received from Mbima. He also sent us a leg of buffalo beef, which, however, was too high for my taste, though relished by my people. I noticed a marked difference between the natives of this district and those of Ndoruma's and the other territories hitherto traversed. Many of them were undoubtedly full-blood Zandehs, who are advantageously distinguished from other tribes by their strong muscular development, and are also much better nourished. On the other hand, I found many half-famished, miserable-looking A-Pambia and A-Barmbo settled in Ndoruma's country.

The unexpected report that Ndoruma was on the road hither, that he had already reached Kuru's, and wished to see me before I went further, induced me to prolong my stay at Mbima's. Nine chiefs, all tributary to him, are included in his territory. South of Ndoruma's, and separated from it by an extensive uninhabited wilderness, stretches south-west and north-east the land of the aged Prince Malingde, who, however, had at that time already handed over the administration to his sons. Of these, Bagbarro, Mange, and Mbilli were stationed south of Mbima's, between the middle courses of the rivers Gurba and Mbruole. The district of his fourth son, Sungiu, lay to the south of the Mbruole, while that of his fifth son, Binsa, was situated, as already stated, to the south of Ndoruma's residence. Mbima's district extends from his chief settlement about a day's journey to the west, where it is conterminous with that of Prince Badinde, who had been made tributary by Zemio. Towards the north Yabikumballo's land forms the boundary of the district which, in that direction, borders on the territory of Mbellebil, a third brother and vassal of Ndoruma. Eastwards follows the tributary state of Toto, a fourth brother of the paramount chief, while other brothers have their settlements farther to the north-east.

Ndoruma's arrival was delayed for several days; nor should I have waited any longer, but that I hoped through him to get news of the Bahr el-Ghazal, and possibly also receive some anxiously-expected despatches from Khartum and Europe. Meanwhile Mbima's mbanga was visited by many of his tributary chiefs. They feasted their eyes on the white man, and on all of the marvels he had brought all the way from Europe. They were never weary of listening in amazement to my musical instruments, and contemplated with ecstasy the coloured pictures of the mammals known to them. So great was the commotion both here and afterwards in other places, that my stay at a prince's residence often became a source of revenue to him; for whether ordered or not, his tributary chiefs seldom came to court empty-handed. Their offerings comprised corn, flour, fruit and vegetables according to the season, game, bananas, red, that is, fresh unclarified palm-oil, beer, palm-wine, honey, tobacco, and the like. With the abundance of such presents my own store of provisions waxed or waned.

ARMLETS OF THE ZANDEH WOMEN.

To the polygamous habits of so many Negro princes is due their numerous progeny. Amongst the Zandehs and many other tribes, the wives after the chief's death become attached to one of the legitimate sons, generally the most distinguished of the household. Thus one of Aeso's numerous wives, Ndoruma's mother, lived with him, and the same relation existed between Mbima and his mother. In these western districts the women wear nothing but a bunch of fresh foliage, often replaced by a narrow leathery leaf. Their ornaments are restricted to a few iron anklets and bracelets; only a few of more distinguished position rejoiced in spiral iron rings wound round arm and leg; copper rings also are reserved for the favoured few, even the cheap strings of glass beads of European manufacture are by no means common.

The taste for these beads, as well as their value, varies throughout Africa according to their style and abundance, the period, the tribes, and similar conditions. Amongst the Negroes beads are in fact a question of fashion, and it may be stated in a general way that their market value tends to be depreciated by the introduction of other more useful or more esteemed wares. Thus their price has fallen considerably in regions where the traders have imported fire-arms, ammunition, spirits, and cloth.

Hence in the north equatorial lands, here under consideration, where no trade in foreign wares has yet been developed, beads and, to some extent, shells, are still highly prized, their value varying, as stated, according to quality—that is, size, form, and colour.

As I had taken care to provide myself with a rich assortment of the coloured beads, I was able to offer the natives many novelties. The love of adorning, in many cases one should rather say disfiguring, the person, is common to all Negroes. But the local arts and industries are quite incapable of meeting the demand for finery, and as most of the body is exposed, the natives have sought and found in the natural pigments a means of supplementing art. Red, black, and white colours are available for painting the body, and with these slender resources some tribes achieve great effects. Red and black are yielded by the vegetable kingdom; for white many utilize hyæna droppings bleached in the sun, while from potter's clay is obtained a light gray, a favourite means of daubing the face, especially for masquerading purposes.

Amongst the Zandehs both sexes show a preference for black and red, the latter being procured from a dyewood ground to a powder, which is either lightly dusted over shoulders, neck, and back, or else kneaded with fat and rubbed into the whole body. In a few days the glaring red coating scales off, leaving a beautiful light copper brown, which scarcely any longer suggests an artificial coloration. For the red pigment the Zandehs manufacture various receptacles, of which the accompanying illustration reproduces a rare and artistically-carved specimen. The pulpy fruit of a *Gardenia* (*blippo* of the Zandehs) yields a black cosmetic much in favour with all ages and sexes. Those who still fancy that the Negro's skin is really black, may think it strange that he should need a black pigment. But I would here repeat that a decided black complexion nowhere occurs, and that it would be much more correct to speak of a brown, a copper, or chocolate-coloured, than of a black race in Africa. The black pigment in question is laid on in an endless variety of designs, but, compared with the Mangbattu patterns, those of the Zandehs are for the most part very irregular. They are punctured, spotted, striped, smeared over whole surfaces, or else the sap is simply squeezed on to the shoulders, back, and breast, and then allowed to stream irregularly down the body. Such bedaubed figures look like fiends, and in fact the men try to make themselves as frightful as possible with this blippo, especially in battles and combats.

The postponement of my departure from Mbima's gave Zemio an opportunity of sending me fresh envoys. In the meantime I had myself opened up relations with the sons of Malingde, who ruled in the southern districts, whither I had despatched messengers with small presents, to allay the fears entertained of possible

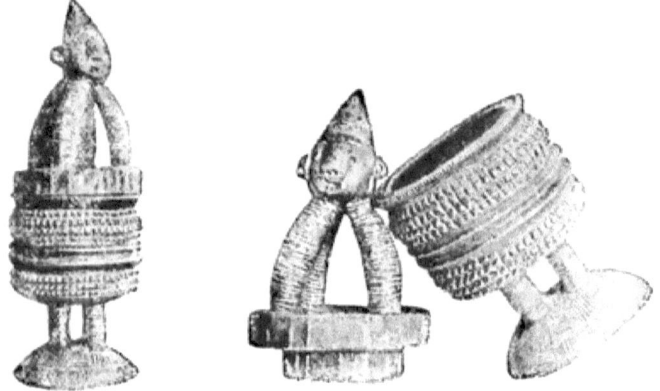

ZANDEH WOODEN BOXES FOR RED PIGMENT.

hostile intentions on my part. New friends were thus secured, and the roads to those parts kept open for future use.

Thence also came the news that Osman Bedawi had returned from Bakangai, and had marched farther eastwards through the territory of Mbilli. Messengers also at last reported the approach of Ndoruma, who sent me some far from pleasant tidings. Both of Bohndorff's assistants had decamped, while some unseemly bickerings had occurred in connection with my female cook from Khartum; but still no news either from Gessi or from Europe. Ndoruma would even now have still kept me back; but he soon saw that this was impossible, and had to listen to some bitter home-truths on the subject of his vindictive action towards me.

After a stay of four days at Mbima's, I set out on August 20th for Zemio's. The objective of our first day's journey was the settlement of the frontier chief Bani, who showed himself very obliging. He had prepared for our reception some large new huts, which we reached just as a heavy downpour came on. His entertainment was equally good, and included even a fowl, at that time a rare treat for me.

Bani accompanied us on our route next day, evidently at Ndoruma's request, his object being to sound me on my further intentions regarding Zemio. On the road to Bani's we had crossed the Buye, which, after collecting all running waters of the district, flows like all those streams north-westwards to the Werre. A common feature of the rivers in this district also was their broad, deep, trough-like channel fringed with a rich vegetation. The banks are mostly swampy, although the limpid rivulets often flow over sandy beds. Here again Africa appears as "the Continent of Contrasts."

These marches were rendered very wearisome by the constantly recurring difficulties with the carriers. Even when all were got together in the morning, one or another would try to shirk duty, so that we were often unable to start before ten or eleven o'clock.

South of Bani's residence the route traverses an extensive tableland, where I enjoyed a wide prospect, a rare feature in these regions. On the ferruginous soil the grass fails to reach its full development, a fact which greatly facilitated the march. The rising ground forms a secondary water-parting between the Buye and the Grupi, which was crossed next day, and which separates Ndoruma's from Palembata's territory. Besides these we had daily to wade through numerous little streams and wooded brooks, often difficult and tedious to cross owing to their marshy banks. The whole country is an uninhabited wilderness.

After passing the night in some abandoned huts near the Grupi, we crossed the Hako, which is the third largest river in the district, and which flows direct to the Werre. It was over three feet deep and thirty-three feet wide, and on its banks we came upon a camp abandoned by Zemio. His present camp lay a little distance farther south, though the rain obliged us to remain for the night in the abandoned huts on the Hako. Here I saw for the first time some small specimens of the elaeis palm, which in the southern and western regions of tropical Africa yields the red palm-oil so highly prized by the natives.

Messengers had been sent forward announcing our approach to Zemio, whereupon he sent me the same evening his greetings, with a still more welcome fowl and some cooked bananas. Next day a two hours' march southwards brought us to his camp, which lay within the territory of Palembata, till recently an independent Zandeh chief. In the western regions the posterity of the formerly potent Zandeh princes had lost much of their importance owing to the general decay of the land through its distribution amongst numerous petty rulers and pretenders. The present rulers all descend either from Mabenge or from Tombo. To distinguish them from the still powerful Zandeh princes, I shall as a rule speak of them merely as "chiefs," though most of them are really sprung from noble blood. Hence the proud and dignified bearing of the true Zandeh race compared with the working classes, most of whom are conquered peoples. The vassal princes, vice-regents, chiefs (Baiki), and sub-chiefs are all exclusively of Zandeh blood. The only exception known to me is chief Kommunda, who holds high rank as a ruler in Ndoruma's territory. Although not of princely blood, he had risen to distinction under Aeso, Ndoruma's father, and had since preserved his exceptional position.

After the invasion of the Bahr el-Ghazal region by the Arab traders and raiders, a number of princes in the northern provinces of Zandeh Land lost their independence. Either driven into exile or slain in battle, they were replaced by dragomans, creatures of the intruding Nubians. Such changes were conditioned by the new relations; but, according to the old Zandeh traditions, none but the princely race distinguished by the leopard skin had any right to be rulers of men.

Palembata's father Balia was descended through Bogua from Yapati, and he again from Mabenge, founder of one of the Zandeh dynasties. As an instance of the family relations amongst these princes, I may mention that Basimbe, being another son of Yapati, was consequently Bogua's brother. But Basimbe was in his turn the founder of another line of rulers, such as Mbio, Malingde, Wando, Ngerria, and Aeso, who were reigning at the time of my expedition to Niam-Niam Land. Aeso again, being Ndoruma's father, Palembata's and Ndoruma's grandfathers were brothers. We thus get the subjoined

GENEALOGICAL TABLE OF THE ZANDEH DYNASTIES.

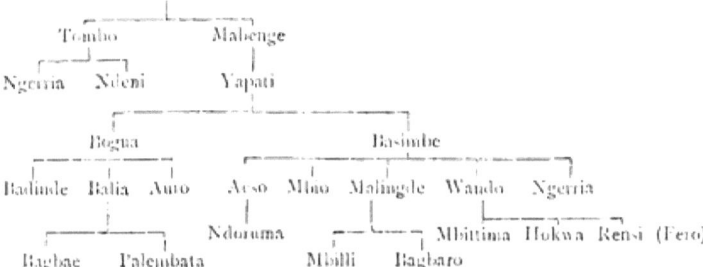

Bagbae was the only brother of Palembata that rose to distinction as a district administrator. North-east of this district, as far as the Werre, the ruling prince was Mbima's neighbour, the already-mentioned Badinde, an uncle of Palembata and brother of Balia, both of whom had been subdued by Zemio the previous year. Their territories lay about midway on the route of his annual expeditions to the southern lands. Besides the ivory here collected for the Government, their reduction had brought other advantages to Zemio, such as feudal service, requisitions, and supplies for his numerous caravans.

I have already mentioned that the ancestral land of Prince Zemio stretches to the north, and that of Prince Zasa to the south of the river Mbomu. Gessi had also given Zasa permission to collect ivory. His yearly expeditions to the south traversed the lands lying more to the west, and he had consequently begun to reduce the region bordering westwards on Badinde's territory. This region, which lay between the Werre and the Welle, had already been broken up into a number of petty chieftaincies. A multitude of princelings, descended from

MEETING WITH ZEMIO. (Drawing by L. H. Fischer.)

Mabenge's brother, Tombo, had already distributed his possessions amongst themselves, and had thus in the third and fourth generations sunk to the position of powerless chiefs. In the region south of the Welle we shall farther on make the acquaintance of those Zandeh princes, also sprung from Tombo, but through his son Ndeni, who till within recent years remained powerful and independent rulers.

Zemio gave me a grand reception. I found the grass had been cleared all along the track from the last rivulet we had crossed to his present settlement; his men—Zandehs with lance and shield in their war-paint—were drawn up under arms, and as we approached two flags were dipped in our honour, while Zemio himself advanced to give us a friendly if somewhat embarrassed welcome.

This vassal of the Egyptian Government is a son of Tikima, and although not more than about thirty years old, is already somewhat corpulent, as many Zandeh princes are later in life. His small uniformly rounded body supports a typical round head with an expression almost of kindliness and benevolence, at least so far as it is possible to draw a conclusion from a Negro's physiognomy as to his inner sentiments. His chubby oval countenance is lit up with the intelligent glance of large piercing eyes. A scanty growth of hair covers chin and upper lip, while the broad nostrils and prominent cheek-bones recall the Niam-Niam type, though his Arab garb with red shoes, tarbush, and cropped hair almost suggested a half-caste Negro. Even at this first interview he gained my sympathy, a sympathy which I was able to retain during long years of friendly intercourse.

At the present juncture the political relations were somewhat unsettled. Palembata had reluctantly yielded him submission, and during Zemio's last expedition through his territory hostilities had again broken out. Palembata had, as was reported, refused to deliver the ivory, and had also failed to furnish sufficient supplies for the caravan, so that corn had to be forcibly seized. But Zemio had taken a lesson in prudence from the Arabs, so that he was at present on his guard against any possible surprise, and had even protected himself by a small fenced encampment.

Within the enclosure a carefully-erected hut stood at my disposal, though I was unable long to enjoy its comfort. For several days Zemio had been awaiting me, and as his supplies were running short, he was anxious to continue his journey southwards. I at once decided to accompany him, and we all started the second day.

Here, as elsewhere, my "curios" excited universal amazement. I presented Zemio with a white cloth, a tarbush, a knife, scissors, and the like; but he seemed most interested in a number of percussion caps, the Government having sent an insufficient supply of the very worst quality of this article.

Palembata, still a young man, had been keeping in the background, fearing the consequences of his sins of omission against Zemio; a little later, however, he came forward somewhat timidly to greet me. I gave him a present, advising him at the same time to accept the situation and submit to the wishes of Zemio, who had come by the order of the Government to collect the ivory from the native chiefs. I added that the powerful Pasha in the Bahr el-Ghazal province had the welfare of the Zandeh people at heart, and required the ivory alone, but no slaves as formerly did the Bahara,[1] so that better times were in store for the people, and he also should patiently trust to the future.

Eastwards the territory of Malingde's son, Mbilli, bordered on Palembata's hunting grounds, where Zemio's people had come into collision with Mbilli's followers. Hence it was now reported that Mbilli, fearing I might join Zemio in a campaign against him, had deserted his settlement and retired to the east bank of the river Gurba. Such is the prevailing credulity of the Negro, everywhere inspiring fear and suspicion, and often causing serious trouble to explorers.

In Palembata's comparatively small territory I had again a good opportunity of observing the motley mixture of broken tribes and scattered populations. For here also in the midst of

---

[1] The current designation of the Nubians, in reference to the *Bahr* or "River," from which they come.

the Zandehs dwell servile peoples, differing from them in speech, habits, and customs. Such are the A-Madi, Bashir (Sere), Augu, and Marango, and in Badinde's district the A-Barmbo and A-Masilli.

Our next goal was the river Welle, on the road to which and even beyond it ivory was to be collected from the chiefs of various local tribes. On August 25th our long procession got under way, a body of men armed with rifles in the van with a trumpeter, the hollow notes of whose five-foot long ivory horn intermingled with the harsh though varied sounds of some iron bells. Then followed Zemio with his personal attendants, and a corps of musketeers, some with heavy old fowling-pieces of Belgian make intended for elephant hunting. The bearers of these were recognized by the little pads used to deaden the recoil, which is often so violent as to break the collar-bone. I fell in with my little company behind this second bodyguard. Farther back came the Zandeh warriors with the national shield and spear, and behind them carriers, servants, slaves, and of course the women, without whom neither Arab nor Negro ever sets out on a journey. The rear was brought up by the dragomans, and there were also some hostages whom Zemio had taken from Palembata as pledges for a further contribution of ivory.

In Palembata's district we passed but few huts, and these stood mostly at some distance from the main highway, which led southwards from the settlement of Palembata's brother, Bagbae. The station stands on the water-parting between the Werre and the Hokko and Gurba affluents of the Welle. Compared with the region hitherto traversed, the land between the smaller water-courses now assumed a somewhat more hilly aspect. For the first time I noticed towards the south-west a distinct crest belonging to the A-Madi uplands south-west of our route.

We encamped near the huts of the A-Madi chief Robia, who lives here under the sway of Palembata with a small colony of his people, driven from their own land by intestine strife. Robia contributed some telebun, followed late in the evening by all kinds of supplies for Zemio's people. Here we were surprised by the arrival of Badinde, ruler of the territory north-west of

Palembata's, with whom he was on bad terms about some disputed lands. Like Palembata, he had at first been hostile to Zemio, who had consequently also taken hostages from him. It was to redeem these that he had now come to the camp with ten pieces of ivory ; but partly through fear, partly through pride of birth, he had not sought a personal interview with Zemio. Many of his subjects, as he told us, had escaped northwards beyond the Werre, fearing that I might join with Zemio in attacking them. I had a long palaver with him, and tried by suitable arguments to convince him of the groundlessness of such fears. Being apparently satisfied he assured me that he also desired peace, and if the Government wanted ivory he could supply it in abundance. The proceedings were witnessed by many of Zemio's people, and ended much to his satisfaction.

But my good offices as a diplomatic agent were not yet over ; for Palembata and his brother Bagbae now also made their appearance, and, jointly with Badinde, asked for my decision in some matters connected with their internal affairs. After the death of Bogua (Bagbawa), father of the already aged Badinde, and ruler of a great part of these western lands, his son and successor, Auro, had been dispossessed by his brother Balia. After Balia's death, four years previously, Bogua's third son, Badinde, and Balia's sons, Palembata and Bagbae, all claimed equal right to the inheritance, and the appeal to the sword ended in the partition of the kingdom. According to the traditional Zandeh right, the eldest son succeeds the father ; but the dismemberment of the state was a sufficient proof that this legitimate custom had long yielded to the law of might over right. Badinde was an aged princely heir, whose calm, sound judgment and whole character pleaded in his favour ; whereas Palembata was a young Zandeh fop, and arrogant withal. Yet he it was who now brought his complaints against Badinde, claiming by prescriptive right the paramount lordship even over Badinde himself. But in my capacity as arbitrator, I now awarded to uncle and nephew equal authority in their respective territories, Bagbae remaining as heretofore subject to his elder brother. At a subsequent interview Badinde put me many other questions in civil and criminal jurisprudence, some of which I found it very difficult to answer; but in many things he himself displayed sound judgment, as well as a sincere desire to act in accordance with right and justice. Some of his difficulties had reference to the victims of the universal belief in witchcraft, and he evidently seemed to fear that perhaps many suffered innocently.

From Robia's to the east bank of the Gurba the road trends first south-east, and then south to the Welle. The above-mentioned A-Madi settlement marks the limit in this direction both of Palembata's territory and of the inhabited land. Beyond it follows a wilderness through which the Pai flows for a day's

VALLEY OF THE RIVER PAI.

journey to its confluence with the Gurba. It was crossed by us at two points, a rising ground north of the second crossing affording an extensive view of its course, which was clearly traced by the dense vegetation fringing its banks through the wilderness.

At the camping-ground on the Gurba, Zemio had provided us with huts, and even enclosures erected by part of his convoy, which had been sent forward a few days previously. In anticipation of a long stay here, the camp had been carefully laid out at a point on the Gurba, beyond which, eastwards to the Mbruole and southwards to the Welle, stretched the territory of the

Mangballe people, with whose chiefs, Nasima and Bangusa, negotiations had to be entered about a contribution of ivory.

We had now left the Zandeh lands behind us, except that

ZANDEH WOMAN.
(*Drawn by Fr. Rheinfelder; from a photograph by R. Buchta.*)

east of the Mangballe people the sons of the Zandeh prince, Malingde, ruled over a territory which stretched still to the south. West of the Gurba a stretch of uninhabited wilderness extended to the Welle, separating the Mangballe from the A-Madi lands. The Mangballe are a branch of the Mangbattu people, whom they resemble in their usages, style of building, arms and utensils; they are also familiar with the Mangbattu language, but speak another amongst themselves. They are not a numerous people, though occupying a wide domain south of the Welle. North of the Welle I met them only in this district; it was not their original home, but had been driven to it by war, and it will be seen farther on that they again left it during my wanderings in those lands. My servant Adatam, a Mangbattu, now took the place of Farag 'Allâh as my interpreter.

Zemio was quick to see that his association with me enhanced his dignity and importance amongst the native princes, and might be useful for the purposes of his expedition. I had on my part recognized in him one of those rare Negroes who, of course speaking relatively, fully justified the confidence placed in them by Gessi Pasha. I was accordingly quite willing to promote his interests, as well as indirectly those of the Government. I could now no longer refuse to be present at the palavers with the local chiefs, especially as Zemio liked to consult me in all weighty matters. He was also well pleased that I clearly explained to these chiefs his own position towards the Government, convinced them of the friendly disposition of the Bahr el-Ghazal authorities, and reminded them of their duties as vassal rulers.

Nasima had arrived with his sub-chiefs, and with his numerous following made a somewhat imposing display of power and authority. Personally he was of insignificant appearance, rather lanky, and adorned with a long thin beard disposed in two tresses. The deliberations were held in a large rekuba, a kind of audience chamber that had been fitted up within the zeriba for the reception of the native chiefs. Nasima gave every assurance of his loyalty, and promised in a few days to produce the ivory. As usual, the proceedings terminated with an exhibition of my marvels, to the great delight of the general public, who were now allowed to join the assembly.

My intercourse with Zemio was greatly facilitated by his knowledge of Arabic. In many things he showed far more interest and intelligence than most other chiefs, and eagerly listened to my statements regarding our European relations, communicating in return much valuable information on his own lands and peoples. With his aid I was able to prepare beforehand a rough map of many districts, although the reports given even by Arabs of countries visited by themselves are mainly meagre and erroneous.

To avoid damaging the Mangbattu plantations our camp had been pitched on the west bank of the Gurba, not far from the settled districts, Nasima promising on his part to supply us with all necessaries. Nevertheless neither the provisions nor the promised ivory made their appearance. Zemio's messengers also brought back far from satisfactory reports, and, in short, I was again to make the experience that the Negro is full of tricks and lies, and not yet nearly developed enough to be treated with strict legality in our sense of the word.

I had spared neither trouble nor patience to convince Nasima and his people of our friendly intentions, and had, on the other hand, made Zemio's followers clearly understand that it was our determination to pass peacefully through the country ; that wherever I set foot, no blood was to be shed, so long as the natives showed a peaceful attitude towards us. Nevertheless Nasima and his brother, Bangusa, were forging other plans, and had already carried them so far that their people were equipped for war. These preparations, however, were aimed not against us, the design being to march with us and induce Zemio to join with them in a plundering expedition against the A-Barmbo tribe south of the Welle.

In the afternoon Nasima himself made his appearance, accompanied by his brother Bangusa, whereupon I severely rebuked them for their bad faith, Nasima especially, who had sent a wretched little elephant's tusk, though claiming to possess a great store of ivory, and further that they were arming against the A-Barmbo, who were as much our friends as were the Mangballe themselves. Nasima had not a word to say in reply, and I returned him a leopard skin which he had brought me. I then withdrew from the assembly, leaving Zemio to continue the discussion. Later Nasima implored me not to leave the Mangballe behind, else he and all his people would be killed by the A-Barmbo; he even promised to bring the ivory the same night,

AFRICAN PYTHON (*P. Sebae*).

but this promise also was broken. I took no further part in the proceedings, and after two days' more palavering Zemio found himself just where he had begun.

The territory of the Mangbattu prince, Mambanga, lay on the

south side of the Welle, where it was conterminous with the eastern tribes of the A-Barmbo nation. From Palembata's Zemio had already sent envoys to Mambanga for the purpose of establishing friendly relations with a view to facilitating the collection of ivory. But these envoys had not yet returned, and there was reason to fear that Mambanga might make common cause with the kindred Mangballe people. To these belonged the boats both on the Mbruole and Welle, which would be needed by us for crossing the Mbruole, and thus reaching the north bank of the Welle. We naturally feared that the boats might be refused if we opposed the wishes of the Mangballe, and we consequently thought it prudent to await the return of the envoys.

Prince Bani, who held the border-land of Ndoruma's kingdom, had accompanied me so far all the way from Palembata's. Before returning he now consulted the oracle on our destiny, and to find out whether Zemio would get the ivory from the Mangballe. The consultation is effected by means of the shrub *baenge*, which yields a red powder, and this powder when mixed with water is given to a fowl. If the bird survives the dose, the omen is good; if not, bad. Ours survived, as did a second supplied by me, whereupon Bani coolly suggested that the poison was bad; obviously he had mentally consigned us to a hard fate.

During these days of patient waiting I again suffered from fever, caused by the constant rain which confined me to my hut. My appetite was also impaired, and at such times my favourite diet was gourds and sweet potatoes. Once Zemio's people killed a huge python (*P. Sebae*) fourteen feet long. This species is not venomous, and is dangerous only from its size, which even exceeds that of our specimen. The skin is beautifully marked with stripes and spots, and is used by the Arabs as a covering for the *sheklik* or girdle worn round the waist as a cartridge-belt.

At last the envoys returned with good news, and even with some of Mambanga's own people. The report of the white man in Zemio's suite had already crossed the Welle, and the envoys assured us that Mambanga eagerly awaited our arrival, though still dreading hostile intentions, as we had not yet sent him any presents as tokens of our friendship. I may here mention that in the eastern parts of Mangbattu Land, first revealed to us by Schweinfurth's visit to the powerful king Munsa, there were some Government stations administered by Arabs. Mambanga had hitherto kept himself independent of these Arabs, but now thinking himself threatened by them, had sent messengers back with Zemio's to seek our protection against this danger. The natives of regions remote from the central administration were quite unable to grasp the idea of a single powerful government to which all Arabs known to the Negroes were compelled to yield obedience. Mambanga, in fact, could not understand that in the present case Zemio himself, as well as the Arabs of those eastern stations, had all alike to carry out the orders of the Bahr el-Ghazal authorities, to pursue the same policy, and not take opposite sides against each other. At the same time it was unfortunately only too true that in many of those remote settlements the Mohammedan officials were inclined to act independently, and neglected to inform the native chiefs of the more friendly intentions of the new administration towards them, as they would have then to renounce their own selfish designs. Thus Mambanga was still under the delusion that Zemio might possibly become his ally; hence he aimed at strengthening this friendship, thus giving events an unexpected turn in our favour.

The Mangballe were now put off with fair words, and forty men at once sent forward to prepare the next encampment. Next day fresh messengers arrived from Mambanga, who informed us that our anxiety about the boats was well grounded. As we had expected, the Mangballe had really removed their boats from the crossing on the Mbruole; but, on the other hand, Mambanga's people had come in their own boats to the neighbouring mouth of the Mbruole, and had ascended to the ferry, so that their boats would have helped us out of the difficulty. The Mangballe also, seeing the uselessness of their manœuvre, now brought back their boats, and meanwhile an envoy from Bagbaro, a son of Malingde, whose district lay to the east of Mangballe Land, had also arrived, obviously in order to gain some knowledge of our intentions. On him, as on all the other envoys, I produced the impression of a being from the other world, for no European had yet visited those remote lands. I generally dismissed them with small presents, and thus sought constantly to open up new relations of a friendly character.

Amongst the numerous envoys now constantly arriving from various quarters were five from Prince Yapati, son of Yango, whose territory lies north of Badinde's district and of the Werre. He is a vassal of Rafai Agha, whose extensive province in the

NASIMA'S PRESENT OF A SLAVE GIRL.

north-west had some years previously been brought under Arab rule by Zibēr and his son, Soliman Bey. Many of the former officials were even still the superintendents of the stations established in that region, and Yapati's messengers now brought complaints against one of these, named Muhammed Hassan. I had again to listen to the usual accounts of outrages, slave-hunting raids, and the grinding oppression of the Nubians, but could do nothing beyond giving a promise to report the state of affairs to Gessi Pasha, and perhaps later visit the province myself.

Nasima, who still withheld the ivory, now sought to curry favour with Zemio by the present of some Mangballe girls. He also sent one to me with the request not to refuse her. Had I done so, it would only have led to fresh discussions; so, pending her future disposal, I placed her in charge of my maid-servant. The value of such gifts is enhanced when they bring some kind of "outfit" with them, and our little maid had some beautiful ivory hairpins, besides a carved stool which she carried in her hand, and a prettily-worked basket, which was suspended on her shoulders by a head-band. It contained everything dear to the heart of a Negress, of course including the box of red powder for dyeing the skin. Two neatly-plaited straw mats completed her equipment.

The false report that a despatch for me had reached Palembata's caused the loss of another day; at last, however, we started for the south on September 5th, and soon came in sight of the Gurba, which lay to the right of our route, just beyond a stony rising ground. Here it flowed through a treeless, grassy depression; but the crossing-place, which was soon reached, was overgrown with a dense vegetation of tall and umbrageous forest growths. Huge trees stretched their wide-spreading branches over and even on the surface, for the banks were here but slightly elevated, and it was now high water with a tolerably rapid current some forty or fifty yards broad. Some of the branches rising above the stream were utilized to construct a bridge of a very primitive type. By its means the carriers with their loads, and Zemio's people, got safely over; but I availed myself of a long dug-out, with which, after much trouble and patience, I managed to land my ass on the other side. Later I saved myself all this labour by simply allowing the animal to swim across even such a wide river as the Welle-Makua, though at times not without some anxiety for its life.

East of the Gurba the huts of the Mangballe lay grouped somewhat closely together in the midst of their banana plantations. We took about half an hour to pass them, while Nasima's residence stood more to the east at some distance from the track. Some of the huts were still of the round style, with pointed conical roofs, as in the north; but amongst them were also some neatly and regularly constructed little houses, with double sloping roof, like those of the Mangbattus beyond the Welle. These symmetrical structures, whose walls are often carefully covered with bark, are provided with large convenient doors, and altogether give an impression of ease and comfort. In front the natives were seated in groups under the shade of their bananas, their weapons leaning against a neighbouring tree.

The road now trended southwards over rising grounds amid the swampy little affluents of the Gurba in Prince Bangusa's territory. By this time we should have come upon the party sent forward a few days before to prepare the camping-ground; but not finding them, Zemio stopped the march and went himself to see what had become of them. He soon sent back orders to resume the march, and in about an hour we reached the new camp, which had also been prepared with great care. Zemio intended to make it his head-quarters during his long negotiations with Mambanga and the Mangballe people about the requisitions of ivory. His return to the north was even made dependent on the result of these negotiations.

But a return was the last thing I now thought of; the long-sought Welle was now distant not more than a good day's journey, and next morning fresh messengers arrived from Mambanga, urging me to visit him. My resolution was soon taken. With the returning messengers I sent my Mangbattu servant Adatam to procure the necessary carriers from Mambanga, undertaking on their arrival to cross the Welle at once and pay him the promised visit. I could then explore the western A-Madi lands, and thus work round back again to Ndoruma's.

The camp lay near the huts of Bangusa's Mangballe people, with whom a lively intercourse was soon opened. The chief himself presently arrived with his followers, bringing corn (eleusine), poultry, sweet potatoes, and roasted bananas. My wonders were of course produced, and quite a furore, mixed

with a certain awe, was created by the matches, from which in an instant was obtained the fire which the natives can kindle only by the laborious process of friction.

One of Zemio's envoys, who was to report on the relations at Mambanga's court, where he had made a long stay, now arrived in camp, bringing all kinds of information regarding the attitude of the Mangbattu prince towards his western neighbours, the A-Barmbo people. These are now divided into innumerable petty states, whose chiefs are at constant warfare with each other. Some were at present on a friendly footing with Mambanga, while others were continually quarrelling with his subjects, some of whom were again reported to have been recently attacked and a few of them killed. Nevertheless Mambanga did not seem at first anxious for Zemio to approach the Welle and make common cause with the Mangballe against the A-Barmbo. The Mangballe, however, were still bent on carrying out this project; hence, no doubt, the arrival of Nasima with his followers on the third day, most of which we spent in palavers with Zemio.

Next day more envoys from Mambanga, and more discussions about the A-Barmbo, to whom Zemio had unfortunately neglected to send messengers. I at last induced him to do so, and his envoy was at the same time to be the bearer of presents from me to their most powerful prince, Buru. Zemio, who showed himself in many respects of a dilatory character, now also decided to start next day for the Welle, and then continue the negotiations, as Mambanga had desired. I had my suspicions as to his real intentions, and later events tended to confirm my impression, that but for the fear of offending me, he might at that time have joined the Mangballe in a raid upon the A-Barmbo.

On September 11th we broke up camp, and continued our southern march, which at first followed the water-parting between the Gurba and the Mbruole. Later we crossed the last affluent of the Gurba, at a point which commanded an extensive prospect of the open, sparsely-wooded savanna, bounded on the distant horizon by the belt of forest fringing the course of the Mbruole. The lower course of this river was crossed next day, on our last march to the Welle. Meanwhile we had unexpectedly taken a wrong turn to the south-west, getting entangled in a swampy district, from which it required tremendous efforts to extricate ourselves. We had scarcely reached firm ground when the threatening rain came on. Sufficient fuel could not be obtained in the neighbourhood, and it was late in the evening before I could get a change of clothes, or the shelter of a wretched little hut where I sat crouching before the fire. Meantime Adatam had returned and followed us hither with the carriers supplied by Mambanga, who also sent me an ivory horn, a *trumbash* (a large Mangbattu knife), some dainty ivory hairpins, and two fowls, accompanying the gifts with the renewed hope of soon seeing me at his residence.

The road we had missed led straight to the north bank of the Welle, at the ferry where it is crossed for Mambanga's. But the Mangballe apparently wanted Zemio to strike the river where it skirts the broad A-Barmbo domain. Next morning Zemio seemed still wavering, and when I wanted to send off the bulk of my effects with Mambanga's carriers under Adatam, he began to feign great concern for my safety, and even attempted forcibly to prevent the despatch of my things. I had not expected such high-handed action, and at once addressed myself to Zemio's people, calling on any to step forward who dared to interfere with my carriers. Saying this I took the lead myself, and after seeing the carriers through the camp and some distance on the road, returned to my hut without taking further notice of Zemio. This brought him round, and he came whining and whimpering to protest that he was half dead with fright. He had no ear for my assurances, and implored me to have my things brought back, as he feared for their loss and my own safety, in which case he would be made responsible by Gessi Pasha. I replied that there was nothing to fear, that in my place Gessi would have acted as I did; that, if he liked, I would give him a written statement exonerating him from all blame, and would not at once follow the carriers, but await and accompany him to the Welle, and even endeavour to induce Mambanga to visit us on this side of the river.

The following night the *ngara*, or great war-drum, was said to have been heard, which was another reason for Zemio to persist in keeping me back. Nevertheless I induced him to send out a party to survey the road, and ascertain whether the boats were ready, which the Mangballe had promised for crossing the Mbruole. The messengers soon returned with the report that much boggy land would have to be crossed towards the southwest where the Mbruole joined the Welle, that the river in that direction could not be crossed, and that the Mangballe had removed their boats thither. Some fresh messengers from Mambanga also reported that there were no boats at the proper ferry, and that they themselves had swum across. They added that the war-drum had been beaten by the Mangballe boatmen, who wanted to pick a quarrel with my carriers, and had refused to take my things over. At last, however, the boats were brought round to the ferry, and a few days after we crossed the Mbruole, and encamped on the banks of the Welle.

The Mbruole, which was now at high-water level, was here about seventy yards wide, with a strong current. South of the river, whose upper course in the north-east I crossed two months later on the return journey to Ndoruma's, the country was occupied by the Mangballe chief Mangalima's subjects, whose huts were passed on our march southwards. But the direction was again suddenly changed, and for about an hour we trended nearly due west to that stretch of the Welle which flows by the A-Barmbo territory.

The new camping-ground lay in the immediate vicinity of the Welle, not far from the Mbruole confluence, in the angle formed by the two converging streams. Here the Welle, a majestic stream some three hundred yards wide, flowed westwards, between banks partly fringed with a single row of tall trees, partly overgrown with dense scrub and woodlands, alternating with open sunny savannas.

Scarcely had the A-Barmbo on the opposite side perceived Zemio's people, when they raised their war-cry, which was answered by the shouts of the Mangballe, who had followed close on our heels, and now gathered from all sides equipped for war. Nasima's lank figure in his fantastic war-paint towered above all, while Bangusa had completely disguised his features with "blippo." The rest of his body being dyed with the same pigment, he presented a perfectly Satanic appearance, armed with lance and shield, with charms and amulets, the skins of small animals and genette tails dangling from his girdle.

As I lingered on the banks of the mysterious stream, whose westerly course was still an unsolved problem, another great war-cry rolled up from the west. Meantime the fully-equipped Mangballe fleet had dropped down from the Mbruole, and a somewhat imposing spectacle was presented by some fifteen boats, propelled by crews of from twenty to forty men, according to their size, all vigorously plying their paddles, churning up the water, yelling and shouting, skilfully manœuvring, dashing forward or returning up stream with surprising velocity. The jubilation of the Mangballe was fully justified, for they had already scored a point by bringing Zemio to the part of the river over against the A-Barmbo territory, and compromising him to such an extent that open hostilities now seemed inevitable. That he should have struck the river at this place instead of opposite Mambanga's district, must have necessarily caused surprise, and in fact soon led to wearisome discussions and misunderstandings, and for me to much worry and anxiety.

Zemio's people already felt that they were on the war-path, and consequently became all the more obtuse to the distinction between *meum* and *tuum*. Ready-made straw roofs and other sections of Mangballe huts were seized, and a spacious camp rapidly constructed, in time to afford shelter from the threatening rain. The little Mangballe huts with their pitched roofs can easily be taken to pieces and re-erected on another site, and such a house was now fitted up for me, which, however, afforded room only for my bed and some basket boxes, so that the work-table had to remain outside. The relations had taken such an unfavourable turn, and the season was now so far advanced, that I had to give up the proposed journey through A-Barmbo Land westwards and then through A-Madi Land northwards to Ndoruma's. Instead of this I hoped to pass later from Mambanga's eastwards, and thence north of the Welle through Wando's district, and so reach my Lacrima station by the beginning of the dry season.

On September 15th fresh messengers arrived from Mambanga, who, as I had expected, expressed his surprise at Zemio's change of route. I had quite determined to start for Mambanga's that very day, when he sent word through another messenger that he would place his people at my service for the war, evidently supposing that the raid against the A-Barmbo had been planned with my knowledge and consent. Presently there arrived hundreds of armed men, who took up a temporary position outside the camp. I was convinced that in thus offering to join in the fray Mambanga was aiming at some personal advantage; but his territory being conterminous with that of the A-Barmbo I now felt that it would be safer for the present to bide with Zemio

MESSENGER WITH UNFAVOURABLE ORACLE.

and watch the course of events from the north side of the Welle. I now despatched Adatam to explain the real state of the case, and meantime experienced a fresh annoyance in the return of my envoys to the A-Barmbo chief, Buru, bringing back the presents which he had refused to accept. Later, when I entered into close relations with this aged prince, the contretemps was explained.

Zemio now openly avowed his intention of fighting the A-Barmbo, and began to make preparations for crossing the river. The air was full of warlike sounds, and a bullet went hissing over our camp, for it appeared that the A-Barmbo were in possession of some fire-arms. But I had now a pleasant surprise in the receipt of despatches from Europe, which had been sent on by Ndoruma. As I opened the package my inquisitive audience kept exclaiming with astonishment: "Kitāb, waranga" (book, paper), Arabic words generally uttered by the natives with a feeling of awe.

Meanwhile messengers came pouring in one after the other from Mambanga, followed at last by his own brother, who in a long oration gave full expression to the prince's suspicions. He seemed to be under the delusion that all measures taken in the camp were directed by me. Hence, in order to ascertain my real intentions, he had consulted the oracle, and as this time the *baenge* got the better of the fowl, the answer was "guilty," that is to say, it confirmed Mambanga's assumption that I was harbouring evil designs against him. When this result was announced to me after a long palaver with Zemio, I lashed the whole assembly with words of withering contempt, that my pledged word was more to be trusted than all their "baenges" and "mapinges" (another kind of oracle), and all their bloodsucking (this last touch was in reference to a process of blood brotherhood that had just been performed between Zemio's and Mambanga's people). Anyhow, I went on to say, there was no need of many more words, for the bird having died, I might die also were I to enter Mambanga's land; so I should simply return without even crossing the river. These last words they had apparently not expected, and all sorts of objections were raised against them; but I was obdurate, and closed the proceedings with the remark that they might henceforth carry on their idiotic baenge with the "Bahara" (Arabs), but not with the "whites," who were quite differently constituted.

From these oracles, for there were several, Mambanga had concluded that I intended crossing the river here and attacking the A-Barmbo, but would perish in the war. Hence he sent me an urgent message warning me against this course, and asking me rather to visit him. And so the mystifications went on, rendering all discussions fruitless, exhausting my patience, and disgusting me with this first visit to the Welle.

I had asked Mambanga to send back some of the things which his carriers had taken over, and which I greatly needed. He had not done so, but sent word to say that he would return them by night, lest his people, and especially the women, should see them, which would cause great fear and alarm. But nothing came, and next day I had another long palaver with Mambanga's brother, in which I had to beg for my own property. I showed him that I lacked oil for my lamp, soap for washing, and many other indispensables; but all in vain, and all I could get was some salt and tobacco, besides some corn and poultry.

We had now been four days on the Welle, and Zemio still hesitated to attack. Hitherto both parties had confined their operations to a war of words, shouting abusive terms at each other across the river. In the still night such wordy strife sounds comical enough, especially as the combatants are never interrupted till they have their say out, so that not a single word of scorn, taunt, or sneer is lost on the hearer.

At last Zemio decided to make an attack, so to say, by way of experiment. A number of men in the Mangballe boats (large dug-outs) approached the opposite bank under cover of the rowers' shields, in order to see how the enemy and the crews themselves would behave under fire. Several A-Barmbo having been reported *hors-de-combat*, the attack was brought to a close, presumably to the satisfaction of Zemio's party.

A landing on the south side had now become more difficult, for the A-Barmbo had not been idle, but wherever the bank was unprotected by trees they had erected regular ramparts of hewn timber and earth, as a protection against the hostile bullets.

Meanwhile I had at last got back two of my boxes, while fresh envoys from Mambanga had brought about a change in the situation. They were the bearers of two tusks in addition to a contribution of ivory already sent in, and they communicated Mambanga's reiterated desire for the camp to be moved up to his side of the river. Zemio agreed to this, and on September 19th we began to retrace our steps, re-crossing the flooded grassy depressions, and then taking a south-easterly direction, which in half an hour brought us again to the north bank of the river, near which a new camp was erected.

On the opposite side of the Welle the little river Akka forms the boundary of Mambanga's territory towards A-Barmbo Land, but the ferry lay still about half an hour's march higher up. In the neighbourhood of our new camp there were also some Mangballe settlements, which, however, were all subject to Mambanga's jurisdiction. Our removal to this place was consequently reported to him by a messenger, and I afterwards learnt that Mambanga himself had also changed his quarters, removing from his old residence, which stood higher up and farther inland, to the place where the river was crossed by the ferry. He again sent greetings to Zemio, with an elephant's tusk and a message announcing his intention of passing the night on the banks of the Welle, in the hope of next morning receiving a visit from me.

The messengers who had brought my last despatches from Ndoruma and Palembata, now returned with letters from me to Bohndorff. The Mangballe, who were still eager to do battle with their A-Barmbo foes, appear to have been induced by Zemio to defer the attack for the present. Meanwhile they continued to send marauding parties round about, though many had doubtless already returned home.

As regards Zemio's action on this occasion, I may here state in palliation of his conduct that later his character appeared in a more favourable light. His apparent vacillation was mainly due to the need of acting unjustly in my presence and according to our ideas of right and wrong, and as the matter would also doubtless be reported by me, he naturally feared to incur the censure of Gessi Pasha. As he afterwards himself confessed to me, he felt himself hampered by these considerations, and but for them his action would doubtless have soon brought on a war with the A-Barmbo. He was, on the other hand, full of suspicion and prejudiced against Mambanga, whence, according to his mode of reasoning, also arose his concern for my safety.

In our new encampment I only passed two more nights. After parting with Zemio at this place, I made a long and half-compulsory stay with Mambanga. This doubtless gave me a fresh opportunity of learning much regarding the social life of the Negro; but my patience was also sorely tried before I was at last able to continue my journey eastwards.

A STOOL.

DIVINING APPARATUS.

CHAPTER VII.

RESIDENCE AT PRINCE MAMBANGA'S, AND JOURNEY EASTWARDS TO TANGASI.

Across the Welle—Meeting with Mambanga—Parting with Zemio—Landscape south of the Welle—Peculiarities and Disposition of the Mangbattu—Mambanga's Effrontery—War Game and Dance—Tattooing and Painting—Head-dresses—Deformation of the Skull in Childhood—Arms—Pottery—Divining Apparatus—Thieving—Lynch Law—Cannibalism—End of my Detention with Mambanga—Junction of my Itinerary with Schweinfurth's—Station on the River Gadda—Changed Political Relations—Tangasi Station—Arab Spies—Projected Southern Journey thwarted—Return to the Gadda.

THE long-expected interview with Mambanga at last took place on September 20th, the morning after our arrival at the new camping-ground on the Welle. I started betimes for the ferry, accompanied only by Farag 'Alláh and Adatam, and felt that I was now plunging into the enemy's camp, for Mambanga, having hitherto closed his land to the Arab expeditions, was regarded by Zemio and his people as hostile to the Government. As we went along they gazed at us in silence, and many doubtless thought me foolhardy and gave me up as a lost man. Zemio himself did not appear, but soon sent us an escort of a dozen men.

Half an hour's march up stream in the direction of the northeast brought us to the crossing-place. Here I quietly but firmly warned the escort not to approach the river, for had they been seen from the other side, Mambanga might have hesitated through fear and mistrust to send over a boat to fetch us. Then I emerged from the tall grass, and stood on the steep bank, here several yards high, whence we descried hundreds of natives on the opposite side. Amongst them Adatam was at once able to single out the prince, who, on seeing us, had also approached nearer to the river. We were soon ferried over, our party consisting, besides myself and two servants, only of one of Zemio's messengers, already known to Mambanga. As we pushed off the escort betrayed signs of fear and alarm, some of them perhaps fancying till then that I was not in earnest. It took scarcely ten minutes to get across, and on landing we were immediately surrounded by hundreds eager to get sight of the wonderful white man.

Curiosity strained to the utmost was stamped on the features of Mambanga, who awaited us close to the shore. I advanced with outstretched arms, an attitude of friendly feeling which is doubtless rightly interpreted in every zone. We ascended the bank hand in hand, and silently approached the neighbouring huts, the pressing throng respectfully parting to right and left as we advanced. But they immediately closed in behind, forming a compact circle round us as we took our seats on one of those daintily-carved benches in the decoration of which the Mangbattus display so much taste and skill.

Mambanga was of tall stature, and at once distinguished by his much lighter bronze complexion from his darker copper-coloured subjects. The careless bearing so often noticed in tall Negroes of the better classes was here betrayed, especially in a decided stoop, which caused him when seated to bend his head well forward. He was still a young man, with almost beardless face, which bore an expression of unbridled sensuousness, heightened by his large, prominent goggle-eyes. In other respects he scarcely differed outwardly from the rest of his tribe, and like them wore the national bark costume, though of better texture, and of light brown cigar colour. His hair was arranged in form of a high chignon, inclined backwards, and surmounted by a basket-shaped hat, which was secured by means of a long ivory pin.

Some chiefs and other distinguished persons were also seated on benches; others were squatted on the ground, but the majority stood in a circle round us, while many swarmed up ant-hills and the nearest trees to see the sight. My interpreter, Adatam, stood by my side, and when I began to speak, silence was called on all sides.

I gave the prince to understand, my words being interpreted sentence by sentence, that I was heartily glad to have at last been able to visit him, which I should have done long ago but for the circumstances known to him. I was sorry he should have doubted my good-will towards him, but in my land people had but *one* tongue, one word, not like the "Fahara" and "Turk" (Arabs and Egyptians). The rejection of my presents by the A-Barmbo was the cause of the delay; but now that I was convinced of his friendship, and relieved by his assurances regarding the peaceful dispositions of the A-Barmbo, I had sought the first opportunity of redeeming my pledged word; it was a great pleasure to see the prince, and personally assure him of my friendship.

My words were listened to in deep silence, and clearly interpreted by Adatam for the audience; they gave general satisfaction, which was expressed by loud applause, after which order was again called. Mambanga replied that, having seen me, his heart felt more at ease, his people also were appeased, and fear would also depart from his women, so that they could sleep in peace.

Thus was the palaver protracted with flattering assurances and fine words, after which the interest of the public seemed to be

MEETING WITH MAMBANGA. (*Drawn by L. H. Fisher.*)

transferred to my personal appearance and belongings. The greatest amazement was created by the mechanism of my rifle and revolver, and much admiration was also bestowed on my laced boots, watch, lucifers, and the like. Meanwhile word was sent, at my request, to the neighbouring A-Barmbo chiefs, announcing my arrival and my desire to see them here. Some came a little later, but they seemed timid and anxious, as if not quite confident of peace. I requested them to inform their people that I intended next day removing to Mambanga's, and at the same time urged them to stop the nightly drum-beating and keep quiet, if they themselves were really desirous of peace.

On returning to camp I allowed the boat to drift a little with the current, and gave myself up to the quiet contemplation of the mighty stream, which rolled away to unknown lands and peoples in the Far West. I was all the more pleased with the turn things had taken, that Mambanga had already promised me the carriers for my eastward journey. But I had once more to learn by bitter experience how little the Negro cares for words and promises.

On September 21st I finally quitted Zemio's camp; he accompanied me part of the way, and many pressed round to take a last farewell. The two asses and all my effects were got safely across in the boats, which, though only dug-outs, are unusually large. The material is furnished by the tall trees of the riverain forests, and they are of very clean build, the Mangbattus being particularly skilful at all kinds of woodwork.

Mambanga was one of the still-surviving representatives of the old Mangbattu dynasty, which had lost much in power and unity since the death of King Munsa, whose court had been visited both by Schweinfurth and Miani. Mambanga was the son of Munsa's brother, Sadi; but owing to the civil discord stirred up by the Nubians, he had been compelled to take refuge with a small band of followers in this district south of the Welle, where he had hitherto maintained his independence, ruling over fragments of the Mangballe and A-Barmbo tribes as well as some scattered Zandeh and Bissanga groups.

The last-mentioned are themselves distant relations of the

Mangbattu, although speaking a distinct language and forming a widespread nation. In the districts east from Mambanga's, I met their representatives only in small isolated communities, whereas south of the river Bomokandi I frequently hired them as porters jointly with the local A-Barmbo. The Embatas, some of whom dwell in Mambanga's territory on the banks of the Welle, are also akin to the Mangbattu, though speaking a different dialect. They occupy the banks and islands of the Welle far to the west and are the exclusive owners of all the river craft.

A march of scarcely an hour brought us to the residence of the territorial chief. Yet in this short space the botanical aspect of the land had undergone a distinct change. Here, south of the Welle, extensive banana groves make their appearance, imparting in some places a different aspect to the scenery. The cultivated species (*Musa sapientium*) certainly occurs in the northern districts, and is even common in the southern and western parts of the Zandeh territory, but only in small patches; we shall see farther on that the Arabs penetrating southwards have successfully replaced it by cereals, especially maize and sorghum, which undoubtedly yield better returns.

In many places the oil-palm (*Elaeis guineensis*) also plays its part in producing the changed appearance of the landscape, which is further modified by the character of the streams, no longer flowing in deep troughs with terraced forest growths, but in shallow beds where the vegetation spreads out more on both sides. In the cultivated districts I everywhere noticed huge trunks of trees, which often lay, just as they had been felled, right across the narrow track, obliging us either to scramble over or walk round them.

Mambanga's residence also presented some novel features, the group of huts and other structures forming a regular stronghold, such as is rarely seen in non-Mohammedan Negro districts. The whole place, some 600 or 800 yards in diameter, was encircled by a trench several yards deep with vertical sides, and further strengthened by a palisade on its inner side. Yet the whole stockade lay in the midst of a dense thicket, where the enclosure was fringed by great forest-trees, everywhere affording excellent cover for an attacking party. On the other hand, all the timber had been carefully felled within the enclosure, where the earth excavated from the trench had been thrown up in irregular heaps, and not utilized for the construction of an inner rampart.

A bridge on the west side (see plan, *a*) formed the only approach leading to the place of assembly, which occupied a

MAMBANGA'S STRONGHOLD.

central position on a carefully-levelled and well-kept piece of ground. It comprised a kind of arbour (*i*) tastefully constructed with branches and foliage for the prince and his women, besides two long crescent-shaped passages (*f*) diverging right and left from the arbour; each of these was about seventy yards long, open on the sides, and covered with a horizontal awning of banana leaves, which rested on four rows of posts. Mambanga's private huts, with those of his chief wives, occupied a special enclosure (*b*), not far from another group of enclosed huts (*c*), which had been placed at my disposal, and which included one very large structure of the typical round form, serving in wet weather for small gatherings, and for Mambanga's evening entertainments. Behind the arbour stood a very pretty little structure (*h*), whither Mambanga doubtless withdrew at intervals during long assemblies.

The four walls of the Mangbattu huts, with their pitched roofs, may be taken to pieces, like the houses which children build with a pack of cards. Each wall is formed of successive layers of banana leaves, pressed together between thin boards like the laths used in plastering. All the boards correspond on both sides, and are firmly stitched together. The roof is prepared in the same way in separate sections, which are adjusted at the proper angle to form the ridge. The Mangbattus have an eye for regularity and symmetry, such as I have met amongst no other Negro people.

Another spacious structure (*d*) was set apart for a peculiar kind of divination practised only by the Mangbattus. But, besides these larger buildings, interspersed amid the numerous little earth heaps, were dozens of huts, some isolated, some disposed in groups, all with conic roofs, and occupied chiefly by Mambanga's women and slaves. The defensive works were planned not so much against hostile Negro tribes as against the Nubians, whose sudden attacks the natives had only too much reason to dread.

My arrival was awaited by hundreds of people, whose demeanour was quite different from what I had hitherto been accustomed to amongst pagan Negro populations. The women enjoyed many privileges, such as the right to take part with the men at public gatherings. Hence, unlike their Zandeh sisters, they betrayed little shyness even towards me, and even brought forward their little children to see how the youngsters would behave in my presence, their indications of fear or alarm causing general shouts of laughter. Later their boldness and importunity increased to such an extent that it was very late before I could get rid of my inquisitive visitors. Nor did they leave me long to myself, for at the break of day, almost before I could wash the sleep from my eyes, I was again beset, especially by the women, who of course brought their babies and their beautifully-carved stools, making themselves perfectly at home in my "private apartments." I showed them all sorts of curious things, and had also to ride-a-cock-horse with a very dusky little "olive branch," to the great delight of an admiring audience. No European child could have acted more becomingly, tugging at my beard, grasping my shirt-studs or any other bright object within reach.

Altogether I had a better opportunity amongst the Mangbattus than elsewhere to study the sociable aspect of the Negro character, whose tender side is often unjustly called in question. They may doubtless now and then lack a genial temperament, as is too often the case with civilized peoples; but it would be premature to deny such qualities in the untutored children of nature. At all events, I satisfied myself that the Negro takes pleasure in his little ones; he kisses their dumpy little hands, and the women fondle them without reserve in the presence of the men, which, however, I noticed more frequently amongst the Mangbattus than others.

In other respects also, and especially in their higher artistic faculty, the Mangbattus show a marked superiority over many other Negro peoples; yet they otherwise stand at the lowest stage of culture—at least, if cannibalism is decisive on that point. This practice is more widespread amongst them even than amongst the Niam-Niams. But it cannot serve as a final test in estimating the relative position of uncultured races, as determined by their general capacity and mental qualities.

Why some of these more highly-gifted races should be addicted to anthropophagy remains an unsolved riddle, but the fact is beyond dispute. The inhabitants of the equatorial region within the Congo basin are also more or less cannibals; yet they take a high position amongst the riverain populations in respect of their intellectual faculties. The same impression was produced on me in comparing the various races in the regions comprised within the sphere of my explorations. Thus the Bari of the Bahr el-Jebel can hardly be compared, from the intellectual standpoint, either with the Zandehs or the Mangbattus; yet, like all other Negroes dwelling in the eastern and northern provinces, they hold human flesh in abomination. The practice earned for the Zandehs the nickname of "Niam-Niam," just as their easternmost tribes, the Idio and Bomba, are known as "Makaraka," both terms having the same meaning of "man-eaters."

Mambanga gave us a supply of durra, a grain which I had not expected to meet in this district, though it is extensively cultivated by the A-Barmbo farther west. The variety here produced is very similar to, if not the same, as the red kind raised in the north. But I was still more agreeably surprised by the gift of a fine black buck-goat, one of the few found in the country. They come, in fact, from the Far East, for the Mangbattus themselves are not stock-breeders. Mambanga, who had reached the station soon after our arrival, received in return various gifts, besides a dagger, sundry pieces of cloth, and scissors, which I had already sent him. I now gave him some white and coloured cloth, a turban, a scarf, a Russian peasant's costume, beads, and other trifles. He was soon strutting about in his new suit, and doubtless found everything so far excellent; but somehow he was not quite satisfied, for he still aspired to the possession of a rifle. I explained, however, that the two he saw in my possession were all I had, and of course I could not trust myself in the wilderness with one alone.

Now he seemed quite appeased, and even sent me something for my ethnographic collection. Hence my surprise and indignation were all the greater at his sudden change of manner a few days later. He came as usual with some of his "cabinet ministers," but behaved in an offensive, insolent way, hoping thus to browbeat me. On entering my hut, he planted himself, not on the chair, as hitherto, but on the ground, and when I requested him to take the chair, he answered gruffly that he was angry because he had not yet received any fine present meaning a rifle, the attendants nodding approval.

This was nearly too much for my equanimity, so I shouted

MANGBATTU WAR-GAME. (*Drawn by L. H. Fischer.*)

for Farag 'Alláh, so that he as well as Adatam might hear my reply. It was to the effect that I was neither a Nubian nor an "Abu Turk," nor one of his kindred, with lies always on their tongue. I had already told him I had only two guns, both indispensable for my protection, and for hunting, so they might kill me before I parted with either of them; but if he thought he could claim a gun for the knife he had sent me, he might have his knife back again, saying which I ordered the *trumbash* to be placed before him. And, I continued, as I saw what his professions of friendship meant, I should return that very day to Zemio's.

My vehement speech produced the desired effect. Mambanga yielded the point, promising never again to speak of the rifle, and begging me not to return to Zemio's, and also to keep his presents. I graciously acquiesced, warning him, however, that nothing could be extorted from me by threats, but that he should have more presents, amongst others some percussion-caps for a dozen old muskets in his possession. This was an unexpected and welcome offer, and so the subject of the rifle was dropped.

My ordinary work was now much interrupted by the inquisitive crowds prying about at all hours. Envoys were also continually arriving from the A-Barmbo chief Buru, reporting his desire to visit me after Zemio's departure. On the other hand, Mambanga lived in constant dread of the Egyptian officials in the eastern parts of Mangbattu Land. At his request I sent messengers to ascertain the state of affairs in those parts, and report my approaching arrival there.

Meanwhile Mambanga entertained me with the spectacle of a sham fight, winding up with a dance in which several of the notables, and even the prince himself, took part. The surrounding inhabitants were summoned to the feast by much horn-blowing and drum-beating. Most of them brought their light benches and took their seats in rows along the semi-circular passages of the trysting-place. The open space between these was the scene of the war-game, at which Mambanga looked on from his arbour, surrounded by a number of his women. Here also, I took up my position seated on my own chair.

Then the warriors, armed with shield and spear, advanced in groups and began their characteristic and highly-entertaining sham fight against the invisible foe. Rushing furiously from Mambanga's arbour into the open space, they hurled their spears into the air, vying with each other in their efforts to throw them as far as possible, and holding the shield with a few reserve spears in their left hand. While standing or advancing they endeavoured to protect themselves from the hostile darts by various rapid manœuvres, springing to one side, starting back, crouching behind their shields, and continually moving the shields themselves in all directions. After the first group had exhausted its round of tactics, it was succeeded by a second, and so the game was kept up for hours together, being varied now and then by interludes of imaginary single combats.

Later a small but select group of dancers assembled in the open space near my huts. But instead of all joining in a numerous band, as is usual amongst other Negro peoples, the more distinguished or more accomplished members of the company went through the performance alone. Mambanga was again surrounded by a circle of his women, painted either a black or bright red colour, and seated on their little stools by his side. As I entered the dance had already begun, and was kept up with little intermission by a number of performers succeeding one another as each became exhausted. Then the prince's brother, Yodi, executed a *pas seul* to the accompaniment of several drums, varied now and then with a kind of rattle made of wickerwork and filled with pebbles, not unlike those in use amongst our children. At intervals the dancers were encouraged by a chorus of singers, the burden of whose chant was "long drawn out," and really harmonious, reminding one of the swelling notes of the Russian peasant songs.

But the spectacle of the evening was yet to come, when the prince himself stepped forward to exhibit his terpsichorean skill. In order to heighten the effect, he had been freshly greased and painted while his brother Yodi was performing, the folds of his rokko smoothed down, and a finishing touch given to his toilet by a tall hat and enormous feather planted on his already-elevated chignon. But the most important and indispensable adornment was a number of wild cats' tails which were attached in bunches both to the left upper arm and to the abdomen. Decorated in this fashion, Mambanga capered down a row of women, who applauded with hand-clapping and bending of their heads from side to side, thus keeping time to the tam-tamming and vocal music. The dancing was thus kept

MAMBANGA'S DANCE.

up, the prince filling up the few short intervals with speeches, in which he referred to current topics, such as my arrival, the universal joy caused by the event, and so on.

About this time I had an opportunity of making some interesting observations on the complexion of the Negroes. During my previous excursions I had already been struck by their endless gradations of colour, and in these districts south of the Welle my attention was drawn to the same phenomenon.

It confirmed my own impression, and that of other travellers, that the colour of the skin is an absolutely unreliable criterion for tribal distinctions. I, of course, here exclude the extreme cases of peoples separated by great distances, as, for instance, the intensely-dark Shilluks compared with the much lighter Mangbattus and Wagandas, who may doubtless be grouped according to colour. But amongst kindred tribes, such as the dark Zandehs, I have met people with very light, almost yellow, leather skins; and, on the other hand, very dark people amongst the Mangbattus and other southern tribes. But assuming a more extensive intermingling of races in this region, we should expect to find such great diversity in the complexion. In the direction from the Nile westwards, the general tendency appears to be from dark to light, though the numerous displacements and migrations have given rise to many exceptions in the more westerly districts, and the same law holds good for the regions stretching from the north towards the equator.

The Negro colour-scale is, in fact, endlessly diversified, ranging from the rarely-occurring deep black to a dark iron-gray, dark chocolate or roasted coffee-berry, light cigar, the yellow-brown of dressed leather, *café-au-lait*, and, in exceptional cases, even the fair colour of the Malays. But the intermediate shadings are the commonest, and these may be reproduced with tolerable accuracy by mixtures of sepia, Indian-ink, red, and Vandyke-brown, and especially with raw or burnt sienna earth. Albinoism is as rare as amongst Caucasic peoples. I met altogether from six to eight cases amongst children and adults; their hair was kinky or curly, and the colour of flax or tow, the skin of a light washed-out leather yellow. Like all Albinos, they avoided the light, screening their eyes with the fore-arm, as with us. Red hair occurs both amongst dark and light peoples, and, by a peculiar sport of Nature, the dark pigment is occasionally absent in various parts of the body. This feature is met even amongst the lighter Nubian tribes, the individuals so affected presenting various types of piebald skins. They reminded me of the hairless, dappled American greyhounds; but the phenomenon is not always congenital, being sometimes the result of diseased or distempered conditions, causing partial loss of the black pigment.

Tattooing, especially on the chest and stomach, rarely on the face, is practised by many of the southern populations visited by me. The designs are often extremely varied, and take years to execute, fat being rubbed in after each operation to reduce the inflammation. As amongst the Zandehs, the Mangbattus, and many other tribes south of the Welle, also paint themselves with the dark sap of the blippo (*gardenia*), and with the red powder of brazilwood, either dry or mixed with fat. Two pots of blippo and red are the most indispensable articles of the Mangbattu ladies' toilet. The favourites of the chiefs, in fact, have little else to do but have themselves painted over from head to foot by professional painters of both sexes.

Both men and women also devote much attention to the *coiffure*, which, when completed, remains untouched for days and even weeks together. A part of the head-dress peculiar to the Mangbattu and kindred tribes, as well as to the A-Barmbo and the A-Madi dwelling within the great bend of the Welle west of Mambanga's,

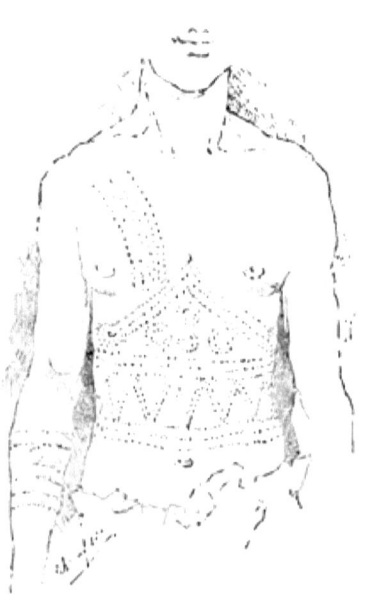

TATTOOING.

is a fillet made of numerous black threads about the thickness of knitting-needles, and from two to four inches wide, which covers the whole forehead from the glabella above the root of the nose upwards. The threads, which are brought close together, converge on both sides about the region of the temples, forming behind the ears and back of the head-gear two broad superimposed twists which run out in strings, by means of which the whole superstructure is made fast to the head. Such fillets are also used as bandages round infants' heads, whereby the form of the skull becomes considerably modified. Hence, amongst the Mangbattu children, I noticed a striking deformation of the cranium, which, owing to the continued pressure, assumed an abnormal pointed form upwards and backwards. Amongst adults, also, many such abnormally pointed skulls are doubtless concealed beneath the towering chignon, on which the men wear a high straw-hat.

Experience, however, shows that the mental faculties are in no way impaired by such artificial deformation, at least so long as the brain-pan and its contents are allowed free development in a given direction. Thus the Mangbattus themselves stand undoubtedly at a higher level of culture than many Negro peoples to whom such practices are unknown. They excel the Zandehs, for instance, in their oratorical powers, which in parliamentary and judicial proceedings are developed to a perfectly amazing degree of fluency.

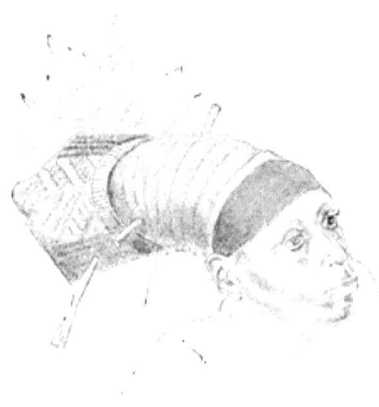

SON OF THE MANGBATTU KING, MUNSA.
(From a drawing by Schweinfurth.)

The prince assists in his arbour at their frequently-recurring trials of rhetorical skill, his chiefs and lieges occupying the semicircular passages on both sides. When the discussion turns on a point of law, the plaintiff does not address himself directly to the prince, but, advancing a few steps from the passage, pours out a torrent of eloquence on his antagonist, who is often seated from fifty to seventy yards off, and in this way the whole assembly becomes cognizant of the matter in dispute. His figurative and elevated flow of language is accompanied by confirmatory and theatrical gesticulations, by an expressive play of features, a nicely-balanced intonation, sudden studied pauses, and even pantomimic illustrations, enforcing the argument, for instance, and making numerical statements clear by bits of sticks or reeds or leaves thrown forward one by one. Such displays of eloquence occasionally verge on the ludicrous, exciting the hilarity of his audience, by whom, however, he is never interrupted until his speech is concluded, and the defendant rises to reply.

On one occasion a man brought a complaint against the wooer of his daughter, that he had not yet paid over the customary number of spear heads. After listening for a mortal hour to the aggrieved father's exposition of the case, I left the assembly, for the deliberations threatened to be interminable. In such contests the contending parties vie with each other in volubility, the man who holds out longest remaining master of the situation, and doubtless usually wins his case. Still the prince has the last say, and from his decision there is no appeal. The Mangbattus are equally long-winded in their ordinary intercourse. Every question or announcement is followed by a cloud of words, rendering all dealings with the natives extremely dilatory, and often obscuring the point at issue.

During my stay at Mambanga's, I could not but recall the name of Miani, for the Italian traveller presumably traversed this district at the time of his visit to Prince Bakangai in the summer of 1872. But owing to the uncertainty of the few data collected by him, and embodied in the map issued by the Italian Geographical Society in 1875, I was now anxious to procure some further particulars regarding the route followed by him in company with an Arab trading caravan. To my surprise, however, I was able to get very little information, for the simple reason that, as I afterwards discovered, his route lay considerably more to the south. But all accounts agreed that Miani died at King Munsa's, and not north of the Welle, as had been supposed, and as appeared from the map.

My previously-arranged six days' visit to Mambanga was more than completed on September 28th, when I asked for the carriers to continue my journey to the east. The supplies hitherto sent us by Mambanga also began to fall off. Still he would not hear of my departure, at least until I had used my influence to induce Zemio to break up camp and return home. The negotiations were also impeded by the absence of my interpreter, Adatam, who, on one pretext or another, was now constantly kept at a distance. I stormed, and even threatened to start without my effects, which could afterwards be brought away by the soldiers from the eastern stations. This startled him, and he seemed more accommodating, though still putting me off till "the day after to-morrow."

Meanwhile messengers fortunately arrived from the Nubians stationed in the eastern districts, bringing a Remington cartridge as a token of recognition, and declaring that they were instructed to await my departure. But Mambanga now discovered that the route was crossed by a deep river, which would have to be bridged over, and a camp constructed for me. Although suffering in health from the monotonous diet, and subjected to other annoyances, such as the pilfering of knives and other articles, I felt that resistance would be useless, and that I must still possess my soul in patience. The Nubian envoys also had again quitted Mambanga's territory, apparently through fear, as they belonged to the unfriendly A-Mazilli tribe.

On October 3rd it rained all day long, a somewhat rare phenomenon in tropical Africa, where even in the wet season the thunderstorms and downpours are usually of short duration, though recurring constantly after the midday heats.

Amongst the customs which I noticed during these days of enforced idleness was a peculiar game which is very popular with the children and even with adults, and which is played in the following manner. Two of the party squat down on a straw mat with a pile of twenty or thirty pebbles between them. Each then takes a handful in turn without counting them, and gives either all or some to his partner, or else restores them to the heap. The action is repeated with a rapidity that reminds you of the performances of a conjurer, and when the whole heap has passed to one of the players, he wins the game. The little tufts of feathers worn by every Mangbattu in his hat serve as stakes.

The relatively high position taken by Mangbattu women was shown, amongst other incidents, by the fact that they were able now and then to act as my interpreters. One of Mambanga's wives, who understood the Zandeh language, displayed much intelligence in this capacity during the frequent absence of Adatam. Amongst other tribes I often received unintelligible answers from my own female attendants, who would then turn aside, as if to conceal their confusion. Not so the Mangbattu women, who approached me without the least fear or embarrassment, and often paid me long visits seated on their stools.

They were usually painted in a highly artistic style, with alternate broad and narrow black lines converging on a central line in such a way as to inclose square patches of the natural skin which are coloured a light bronze with the red pigment and grease. Across the face is drawn from ear to ear a band two fingers wide, which is also coloured with blippo.

Unlike the men, the Mangbattu women wear no hat or other covering on their heads, or rather their chignons. But, like them, they

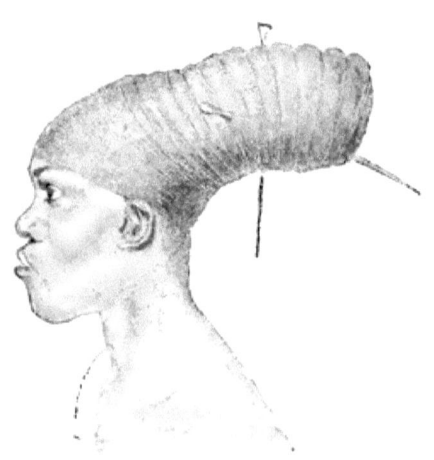

MANGBATTU WOMAN.
(*From a drawing by Schweinfurth.*)

have their long curly hair elaborately arranged in a long superstructure inclined backwards and kept together by means of long ivory hairpins, the ends of the hair being turned inwards to line the toupee as in a nest. Hence the great demand for these pretty hairpins, varying in size and form, which also serve as combs, and which are worn by both sexes. Like the Zandehs, the Mangbattus use for the same purpose long, slender iron pins, the heads of which present a great variety of designs.

But the artistic faculty of this nation culminates in the

preparation of iron weapons, amongst which specially noteworthy is the sickle-shaped *trumbash*, a kind of knife unsurpassed for the beauty and originality of its numerous forms. Their spearheads also present an amazing variety of types in the size and shape of the barbs, teeth, and tips. The bow and arrow are less common, though some are procured from the kindred Maedye tribe, or obtained by barter, or taken in battle from the Momsu, Maigo, and other hostile peoples.

The large wooden shields are made of a single piece of wood, and are often ornamented with light iron and even copper studs and bosses. Copper has not yet been discovered in any of these regions, but being in great demand has long been introduced by the Khartum traders. Like the Zandehs, the Mangbattus use it for making bracelets and anklets, and various other ornaments, besides spear-heads and blades for the trumbashes, and such-like costly arms. The Mangbattus also display surprising technical skill in the artistic treatment of diverse wooden utensils and earthenware vessels, which, as in all these Negro lands, are turned out without the aid of the potter's wheel.

Beside the *baenge*, or divination by birds, the Mangbattus practise a more comprehensive oracular system known as *mapinge*, for which regular temples are erected, administered by priests, and equipped with all manner of apparatus. At Mambanga's, the *mapinge* was a spacious house with pitched roof, like the Sudanese *dahr-et-tor*. As it stood near my huts, I was daily entertained with the noisy performances and awe-inspiring utterances of these African augurs. The apparatus consists of a smoothly-barked banana-stem, several yards long, resting horizontally on low pedestals. On this the priests very carefully arrange numerous highly-polished little rods, about the length and thickness of a cigar; they are disposed in threes at certain intervals, so that, according to the length of the stem, there may be from twenty-five to thirty-five of these nicely-balanced little piles.

The number of such apparatus varies, and at Mambanga's there were as many as five, usually attended by two priests. When any one desires to consult the oracle, these augurs place the little rods in rows along the banana-stem (see illustration, p. 224), and then set up a sufficient commotion to cause some of the rods to fall to the ground. The more that thus topple over, the worse the response; and should a large number be displaced, it is regarded as highly unfavourable. Thus if any one lies under suspicion of a crime, his guilt will be established beyond question if the majority of the rods tumble down. During the commotion caused by their shouting, singing, and hand-clapping, the performers keep jumping in a crouched attitude up and down the banana-stems, but must not actually touch the rods.

It was now the 5th of October, but not a word about the bridge that was to be erected for my convenience. To my energetic remonstrances, Mambanga now replied that he would send a boat to cross the deep river, and as soon as it was ready I might really set out. Meantime, I had been informed of another serious difficulty, for it now appeared that his subjects flatly refused to carry my loads through the extensive wilderness stretching eastward to the Government stations. To meet this opposition, I proposed that all but a few indispensable things might be forwarded in the boat up the Welle, under Farag 'Alláh's charge. This suggestion was gladly accepted by Mambanga, who promised that everything should be at once got ready for the start.

About this time we were much tormented by a little winged pest scarcely visible to the eye, which, strange to say, I met at this season only in Mambanga's district, where it swarmed in myriads about dusk. Its sting left a strong irritation on the back of the hand, though it was some time before I was able to trace the effect to its real cause.

As the pilferings still went on, I now threatened in a loud voice to protect myself with my gun, Mambanga being evidently powerless to prevent the depredations. He replied that he had no objection to my shooting the offenders; but at a private interview I explained that I should never think of firing on his subjects, and had spoken thus only to frighten them. At the same time, if things did not mend, I should certainly shoot myself, as was customary in our country when people were driven mad by their tormentors. This I said in a highly theatrical manner, and with all the suitable gesticulations, at which I had already become quite an adept. I even went so far as to thrust the muzzle of the revolver into my mouth, adding that this had all been previously arranged between myself and my brother, the Pasha, who would thus understand the kind of treatment I had met with wherever I happened to blow my brains out. I may here remark that the threat was all the more startling that suicide, an outcome of our Western civilization, is extremely rare amongst Negro populations. All my inquiries on the subject brought to light only a solitary instance, that of a girl accused of witchcraft, who, to escape a worse fate, had hanged herself.

Mambanga, being seriously alarmed, now suddenly discovered that the boat was quite ready, and that the things should be at once brought down to the Welle, which was scarcely half a mile off. Then I could myself start next day by the land route.

But a violent storm caused a further delay, during which I acquired some experience of the extreme cannibalism of these populations dwelling south of the Welle, who even eat members of their own tribe, as well as everybody condemned to death. According to the universal belief, nobody dies a natural death, but the *mapinge* soon discovers the author of the crime; so that amongst the Mangbattus there is an unfailing supply of human flesh. A kinsman of Mambanga's having just died, the oracle denounced as the criminals two young men, one of whom escaped in time to the A-Barmbos, while the other fell a victim to the popular superstition.

Although the proceedings had taken place in my immediate vicinity, I had no suspicion of the occurrence until informed by Farag 'Alláh that the youth, who wanted to take refuge with me, had been gagged and then led away to execution, after which he would be eaten by the people. In the hope of rescuing him, I at once sent Farag 'Alláh, laden with gifts, to the prince, who promised to bring him round in the morning. I soon learnt, however, that he had been lynched on the way to the place of execution, and that some female slaves were now preparing the porridge for the cannibal feast. Thus the gruesome deed was performed while the thunder rattled and the blue-black clouds discharged a tropical deluge.

That morning the rolling of drums and blowing of horns, repeated at intervals for hours together, summoned the whole of Mambanga's warriors to parade before me. Under other circumstances I should have felt a lively interest in the gay spectacle; but in my impatience to get away, I now looked on at the barbaric scene almost with indifference. The day was well advanced before all the chiefs had led their bands from every quarter of the compass to the central rallying-place, where some arrived at quick march, some went through their war-game and other manœuvres, while the various groups took up their position round about. Mambanga's women, freshly painted and greased, sat on their little stools two or three rows deep on either side of the arbour, where Mambanga himself appeared in princely state with a huge straw-hat towering above his head.

His rokko of bark fibre was of the favourite light-brown cigar colour; the shades of this national garment pass to a deep red-brown, while the cheaper kinds closely resemble thick gray blotting-paper. Some of the exceptionally large specimens, such as are worn by a few Zandeh princes, consist of several pieces, not artistically sewed together with banana-thread as amongst the Wanyoro and Waganda peoples, but glued one over the other to a finger's depth by means of fresh white caoutchouc sap.

FOLDINGS OF THE ROKKO.

When all were mustered they numbered probably several thousand, including representatives of many kindred tribes subject to Mambanga—A-Barmbos, Mangballes, and even some Zandehs and A-Bissangas. The few retainers of Mambanga who were armed with guns took part in the manœuvres, which were varied with dancing and long harangues by the prince, always received with rapturous applause.

Zemio, who still lay encamped on the opposite side of the river, had meanwhile made peace with the A-Barmbo, and even contracted blood-brotherhood with their chief, Buru.

On October 8th, Farag 'Alláh was at last able to start with the loads for the boat, though even for this short distance we could not procure a sufficient number of carriers. It also presently appeared that the boat itself had not yet reached the appointed landing-place, and much haggling about more glass beads had to be got through before a start could be made.

I was now reduced to a few of the most indispensable things, and had even to do my own cooking, for the little Saida supplied nothing but the kisra and cooked bananas. Besides Adatam, I retained Morjan and a young Zandeh, who had recently joined our party.

October 9th at last brought my redemption, after my proposed six days' visit to Mambanga had expanded to fully a month. Even now there were not sufficient carriers for my few personal effects and the provisions for the uninhabited wilderness we should have to traverse during the next few days. It was significant of his little influence over his own subjects that Mambanga was obliged to procure me a few extra hands from amongst the Zandeh retainers of Mbittima, who, after the capture of his father, Wando, by the Arabs, had taken refuge with Mambanga. As it was, I was obliged still to leave several things behind, such as the plank for crossing swampy places, a Mangbattu angareb (couch), presented to me by Mambanga, and some of my reserved stock of provisions. But some of these things were brought on afterwards by the prince himself, while a few beads procured me a fresh supply of sweet potatoes and yams on the frontier.

Notwithstanding all the troubles and annoyances I had endured at Mambanga's, I was able to make allowance for the shortcomings of the Negro character, and we parted good friends. I now followed the carriers with a light heart until we began to plunge into the intricacies of an exceedingly difficult route, everywhere beset with felled timber and swampy tracts, soon followed by stretches of laterite. A two hours' march brought us to chief Bali's, the last settlement in Mambanga's territory.

Here a delay was caused by Adatam, who had the misfortune to get bitten in the foot by a snake while passing through the tall grass. The usual symptoms of poisoning soon set in, and having nothing better at hand, I gave him a double dose of quinine, which threw him into a long and deep sleep. On awaking he felt much better, and next day was well enough to continue the march with us. Here also walking was very toilsome over some ground freshly reclaimed for planting bananas. Beyond it the narrow track entered the uninhabited wilderness, trending this day and the next in an east-south-east direction at a short distance from the Welle.

After a long day's march we encamped beyond the river Kliwa, the seventh we had crossed, all swollen by the rains and flowing through swampy land to the Welle. The ground between these rivers is but slightly undulating, and the reddish laterite formation everywhere crops out amid the sparsely-wooded savanna, while the river banks are fringed to a considerable depth by tall and dense forest growths. In one of these thickets we met a number of people, who at sight of us took to their heels, and were followed by my carriers. But we soon discovered that they were also some of Mambanga's subjects who were bringing bark and the fruit of the oil-palm from the river Kliwa. They had made off because they had taken us for some of the still independent and warlike A-Bissanga tribe, who dwell to the south on the water-parting between the Welle and Bomokandi basins.

The Kliwa was the formidable stream over which Mambanga had spoken of throwing a bridge. But it was now forded by the carriers, while I scrambled over by means of a huge snag and some smaller branches and foliage. The flooded banks were everywhere so beset with thorny scrub, snags, roots, and felled timber, that a boat could have scarcely got through.

Although we were now in the inhospitable wilderness south of the Welle, it was here in the Kliwa valley that I first met the stately oil-palm (*Elæis guinensis*) growing in large patches. The bunches of fruit, which grow to a length of two feet, and

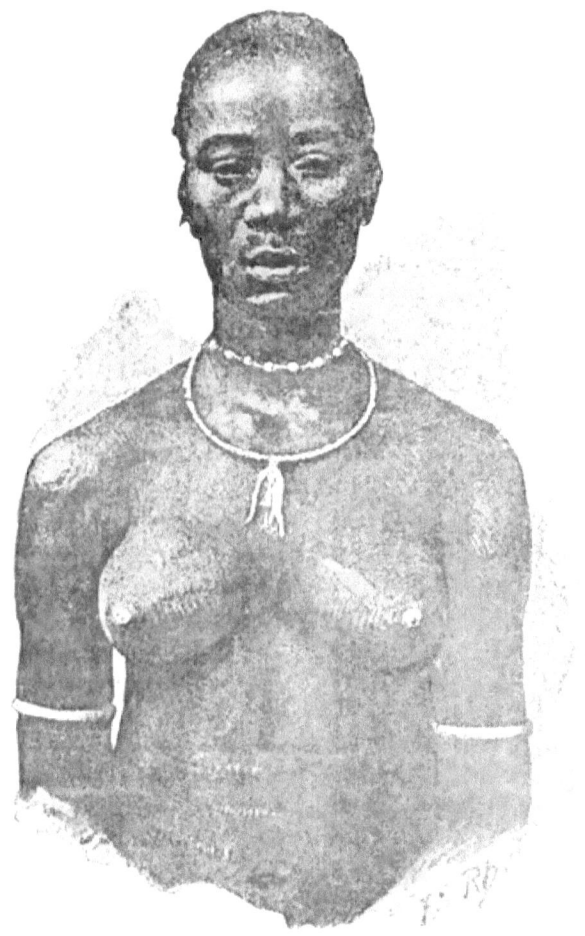

MANGBATTU WOMAN. (*Drawn by Fr. Rheinfelder; from a photograph by K. Buchta.*)

yield the deep red palm-oil of commerce, consist of innumerable clusters of berries about the size of a plum, naturally round, but reduced to a somewhat irregular, angular form by mutual pressure. The disproportionately large kernel is embedded in a mass of cinnabar-red pulp, which, when chewed, has a decided taste of fat.

The next day's route also traversed a flat country in the broad depression of the Welle, where a few rising grounds afforded glimpses of the riverain vegetation; but the aspect of the land remained otherwise unchanged. Although the selvage of fluvial avenues is missing along these shallow water-courses, the vegetation itself is quite as exuberant and even more varied than in the north. The luxuriant plant life greatly increases the difficulties of the march, especially in marshy and flooded districts.

After crossing eight finely-wooded river valleys, of which the Wawua was the most important, we reached the first settlements beyond the uninhabited wilderness. Having been drenched to the skin by a heavy downpour, I was glad to accept the hospitable welcome of the friendly Mangballe people, whose huts were here scattered over the banana groves of the plains watered by the Welle. They formed a recently-founded colony under Dsumbe, brother of Nasima and Bangusa, and they recognized the jurisdiction of the small Government station on the south bank of the Gadda at its confluence with the Kibali, whither I was next bound.

We were here detained by the incessant rains, and next day I received a visit from Ali, administrator of the station, with whom we continued our journey on October 14th. The route, which trended mainly to the east, crossed six streams near their mouths, and in some the current was so strong that boats were required to get over. Here the river banks are so thickly peopled that small groups of huts were passed every twenty or thirty minutes.

From the Mangballe territory the settlements of the Dai people are soon reached. Although a branch of the Mangbattu nation, the Dai speak a peculiar dialect. They keep entirely to river banks, and are the fishers and boatmen along these eastern reaches of the Welle, as are the Embatta people farther down west of Mambanga's. Near the station on the Gadda, besides the Mangbattu half-breeds, there are some colonies of the Niapu tribe, whom we shall again frequently meet in other districts. They are widely separated from the Mangbattus, being related to the A-Madi, who dwell in the western region north of the Welle.

The last march brought me to a district that had already been explored, so that after long wanderings I was again able to make use of my maps. Dr. Schweinfurth had been the first European to cross the river both west and east of the station on the Gadda, on March 19th and April 13th, 1870. To him we are consequently indebted for the first definite account of the great river traversing this part of tropical Africa, as well as of the peoples dwelling on its southern banks. Under the escort of the ivory trader, Abd es-Sammat, he at that time reached the court of King Munsa, sole monarch of the Mangbattu nation.[1]

Scarcely ten years had passed since Schweinfurth's visit, but what profound changes had taken place in that short interval. King Munsa, with many other members of his dynasty, had been slain by the Arabs, and the A-Bangba, a tribe akin to the Mangbattus, had come to the front, so that at the time of my expedition the A-Bangba chief Niangara was ruling over Munsa's personal estate. It may here be further mentioned that the Mangbattu lands were now also included in Gessi Pasha's province.

Mula Effendi, a relation of Jussuf es-Shellali and his successor in the Rôl province, had, during my stay in Jur Ghattas, been entrusted by the Pasha with the mission of restoring order in these lands. For this purpose he was to make a tour of inspection in Mangbattu Land, and I fully expected to meet him here. Unfortunately I was disappointed, and my hopes of continuing my explorations in this region under a regular Government were thwarted, for I found the state of affairs even worse than could have been foreseen. I may add that Mula never came at all, which, as it turned out, was all the better for the people, as

---

[1] Schweinfurth always writes "Monbuttu," but to my ear the word always sounded "Mangbattu." In the same way I write "A-Bangba" for "A-Banga."

he proved to be a ne'er-do-well, and had later, at Emin Bey's instance, to answer for his misdeeds in Khartum. Emin himself had meanwhile been made independent of Gessi Pasha as governor of the Hat el-Estiva (Equatorial Province), and his jurisdiction was extended to Mangbattu Land, which had formerly been included in the Rôl province. Thus it happened that no orderly administration was established in the Mangbattu territory till the year after my first residence in the region south of the Welle, when Emin sent his officials thither. Hence I had still to experience all the vexations of arbitrary native rule, and consequently resolved to make my stay as short as possible.

The few Nubians at Ali's zeriba were a thoroughly corrupt and beggarly lot. I had scarcely arrived when they beset me with all kinds of begging requests. Ali alone showed some kind of moderation, and even provided in a friendly way all my wants.

Farag 'Allâh had made the trip up the Welle without accident, and I found all my effects intact at the station. This place, which was distant only a few minutes from the Gadda, had been recently founded after Abdu'lallahi's war with Prince Wando. The chief settlement of the Government officials, which I was next to visit, lay farther south. After vanquishing Wando, Abdu'lallahi had been charged by Mula Effendi to look after Mangbattu Land, and had already started on a tour of inspection—in other words, a plundering expedition—to the eastern districts; but I hoped before returning northwards again to meet him, for I had already made his acquaintance during my first journey, when we travelled together from Jur Ghattas to the Rôl.

On October 17th, after discharging Adatam, who had become very troublesome and apparently wished to remain with his Mangbattu friends, we started south-eastwards for Tangasi, the chief Nubian station south of the Welle. We encamped for the night about half-way, at chief Bongwa's, and I found all the streams so far flowing north-east to the Gadda. Beyond the Anakaba, which has a sandy bed ten yards wide, the ground rises perceptibly to a broken, hilly district, which, beyond the third stream, merges in gneiss and granite rocks of slight elevation. As a rule, however, the broad-ridged plateaux between these little water-courses present the usual laterite formation.

Abd el-Min, former administrator of the Tangasi station, but now superseded by a certain Muhammed weled Abdu, had come as far as Bongwa to meet me, with a raggedy rabble of Nubians, mostly from Dongola, and a large number of natives.

NATIVE UNDER THE NUBIAN LASH.

But the rascals had not come to do me honour, as they would fain have me believe, but, as soon became evident, to place me under a kind of surveillance, and prevent all intercourse with the natives. All their tactics were aimed at this one object, for they greatly feared that some of the people might bring me complaints of their shameful misrule. At Bongwa itself, a native, who had of his own accord accompanied me from Ali's station, rendering me many little services on the way, had been, unknown to me, so severely thrashed by order of Abd el-Min, that some days later he was still unable to proceed farther.

The illustration will best show how this terrible punishment is inflicted with a lash made of hippopotamus hide. This is the most general mode of chastisement throughout Egyptian Sudan and Negro land, wherever the Nubians have penetrated. It is occasionally varied with the bastinado on the soles of the feet, and then the victim is held in a somewhat different position. Many even of the native chiefs under Egyptian control have already adopted the practice; nor will I deny that, applied in moderation, it is the most effective means of putting down crime and maintaining order amongst the Negro populations, destitute as they are of all sense of personal dignity. It may even be regretted that the lash has been altogether removed from the penal code in certain colonies on the west coast of Africa.

Next day we entered Tangasi, after crossing six streams, of which the first four alone flowed to the Gadda. Then followed a broad-ridged water-parting between the Gadda and the Bomokandi, largest southern affluent of the Welle; to it were tributary the last two streams which we forded before reaching the station. The land between all these brooks and watercourses gradually acquires a more undulating and hilly aspect, while the streams are concealed from view by their high, wooded banks. But any attempt to describe the luxuriance and variety of this fluvial vegetation must fall short of the reality.

In the river valleys impenetrable thickets are formed by the raphia-palm, parts of which are used by the southern populations for making their comfortable and extremely light benches. Its foliage also plays an important part in the construction of the symmetrical Mangbattu huts and spacious assembly-halls, which are here grouped on the wooded slopes, surrounded by plantations of various cultivated plants, and embowered in the soft green of banana groves. Above all towers the oil-palm, whose sap, besides oil, yields also an effervescing and intoxicating drink. Here, also, are everywhere seen well-tilled fields of manioc (*Manihot utilissima*), sweet potatoes, gourds, maize, besides small patches under tobacco.

But no increase in the number of settlements was noticed till we reached the region south of chief Bongwa's station, where at that time were dwelling Mangbattu people with colonies of Niapus and fragments of other tribes, all under the rule of the A-Bangbas. At one point we seemed, as it were, to enter historical land—King Munsa's district and residence visited by Schweinfurth, which lay beyond the Duto rivulet on a gently

MUNSA, FORMER KING OF MANGBATTU LAND. (*From a drawing by Schweinfurth.*)

sloping rising ground, not far from our route. But no vestiges were any longer to be seen of a royal capital; even the large assembly-hall described by Schweinfurth had vanished, and my glance wandered in vain over the grassy surface in search of some slight traces of this former busy centre of Mangbattu power. Miani's grave also lies on the slope, for he died alone and after much suffering, at Munsa's court. Munsa himself was shot by a Nubian soldier while endeavouring to seek shelter in the woods from the northern invaders.

At Tangasi I was received by Muhammed with the customary round of musketry, and the throng of curious spectators was soon joined by the local prince, Niangara, with his chiefs and followers. My relations with the Arabs were thus of a friendly character; nor did they omit the usual rights of hospitality, sending us supplies of maize, poultry, and even tomatoes, which were successfully introduced some years ago by the Nubians.

But next morning already brought a change in their demeanour. Muhammed came to my hut and asked to see my papers with a haste to which I had never before been subjected. The notary, a fellow of sinister, gallows-looking aspect, also appeared, and spent some time poring over the documents. Thereupon Muhammed declared in a scornful tone that the paper signed by Saati Bey, Mudir of the Bahr el-Ghazal province, was invalid, because Mangbattu Land belonged to the Rôl province; Gessi's letters also were addressed to "the above-mentioned," by which words Mula was doubtless indicated.

A greater impression was produced by the firman from Cairo, apparently more on account of the ministerial seal than the contents, for these half-educated Sudanese notaries are not always able to decipher the script of the Egyptian divan. The firman from Khartum also was handled with a certain degree of respect, though these Sudanese officials, with the "hokuma" (Government administration) constantly on their lips, as a rule trouble themselves little about that remote centre of authority.

Later, when I paid a visit to Prince Niangara, whose residence stood on a neighbouring eminence, I was still followed by a crowd of Nubians, with Muhammed at their head. This strange conduct was opposed to the customs of the Arabs themselves, and I therefore requested the people quietly but firmly to stand back. Thereupon all but a few of the more importunate withdrew; but at Niangara's Muhammed again presented himself with his whole rabble. He took the prince aside, and, as I afterwards learnt, reproved him in a threatening tone for having occasioned my visit.

I thus remained under the constant surveillance of these jail-birds, many of whom had fought under the rebel Soliman Ziber and had then escaped to these parts from the arm of justice. Under the circumstances, I was glad that I had not brought all my effects with me, for everything would assuredly have been devoured by these needy and greedy officials and their retainers.

Being determined never to return to this district, I collected as much information as possible about the surrounding lands. From Niangara's women, who also visited me, I gathered some particulars regarding Prince Sanga, whose territory lies south of the river Bomokandi. Like Mambanga, he had hitherto maintained his independence, and kept out the Nubians; but he would have gladly received a visit from me, and have even sent me carriers, as Niangara's people assured me with bated breath. I accordingly at once decided, despite my incomplete equipment, to continue my journey to Sanga's, and return by another route to the Welle.

But this plan also was frustrated by Muhammed, who, on my asking for a few carriers, assured me that Sanga's lay ten or fifteen days off. Happening casually to remark that I should also like to make the acquaintance of the little Akka people, this accomplished hypocrite suddenly asked, with an air of friendly interest, whether I should not also like to bring one away. Scarcely had I unguardedly answered Yes, when he turned round and asked in a peremptory tone whether I was not aware that this was forbidden? adding that he would require to be paid for the carriers. Now it was my turn to lose patience, so I plainly told him I had had enough of him, and withdrew to my huts.

Meanwhile Farag 'Allâh had delivered my message to Niangara that I intended, under the circumstances, marching back next day. In the evening, as I sat before my hut, the Arabs again swarmed round, Niangara being also present. After an interval of silence, Muhammed asked whether and why I had sent Farag 'Allâh to Niangara's that day. I replied, to pay my respects to the local prince, as I intended returning northwards next day, he having sent me word that the carriers were engaged. Muhammed doubted whether that was the real reason, adding that Farag 'Allâh was heard to say that I was enraged with the

MARCH BACK FROM TANGASI. (*Drawn by L. H. Fisher.*)

Arabs, and wanted to get back in order to induce Gessi to despatch troops to Gurguru (Mangbattu Land). He still insisted on the carriers being paid, insolently remarking that he was there to protect the interests of the "hokuma." I made a long reply, concluding with a demand for a written statement of the charge for the carriers, which should be paid forthwith, although it was made in direct contravention of the firman. The speech was not without effect, and Muhammed himself came later to my hut, offering me, amongst other things, a young Akka. This offer I declined, at least "for the present," leaving them under the prevailing impression that I might make them another visit from Ndoruma's, which they seemed to desire, but which I had no intention of doing.

Despite all Muhammed's efforts to prevent any communications with the natives, many secret complaints reached me on the lawless rule of the Arabs, and from Niangara himself I gathered much information on the subject indirectly through Farag 'Allâh. There could evidently be no question of any further exploration of this district, and I was heartily glad to get away on October 22nd. I had effected nothing in Tangasi, and my urgent expostulations had even failed to mitigate the hard fate of Mbittima, eldest son of Wando, who was still kept in fetters at the station.

Equally useless were my objections to a contemplated expedition against Mambanga, though I was destined later to play an active part in this business. The Arabs were evidently much relieved at my sudden departure, and made no offer to accompany me beyond the station. On the other hand, I was escorted a long way by the unhappy natives, who were reluctant to let me go, and implored me to return. It was pitiful to see the women, especially, showing by pantomimic action the cruel scourgings to which they were subjected, all the while stumbling over ploughed ground and stubble-fields along the track. I tried to console them with the prospect of my return, at which they broke into shouts of delight. Many, especially of the young, wanted to come away with me altogether.

Light attacks of fever and the desire to gather all the

information possible regarding the region, on which I had been obliged to turn my back, detained me a few days at the station on the Gadda. On hearing how I had fared at Tangasi, the aged administrator Ali was all the more friendly, and did everything in his power to please me. The other Arabs were also more civil than before, fearing I might report them to the Pasha. Ali even asked me for a written certificate that he had not acted like Muhammed, but had shown himself obliging in all respects. In exchange for sundry presents of scissors, needles, beads, mirrors, and the like, I here received a supply of maize, flour, and a buffalo ham, which was speedily converted into "sharmut" or jerked beef. These things were intended chiefly for my followers, who thrived on their coarse regular fare, often reminding me of the saying that "the lion starves where the ass grows fat."

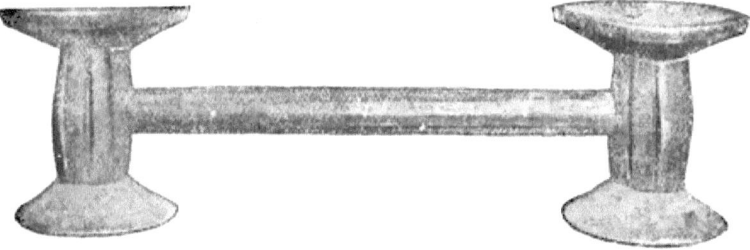

MANGBATTU DOUBLE STOOL.

A HYÆNA'S NOCTURNAL VISIT.

CHAPTER VIII.

FROM THE WELLE BACK TO NDORUMA'S AND LAST STAY IN LACRIMA.

Gadda and Kibali Rivers—In the Wilderness—More Hostilities—Supplies fall short—Muhammed Kher's Station—Aspect of the Land—Meeting with Hokwa—Zandeh cultivated plants—Arrival of Fero—Upper Course of the Mbruole—Peace Negotiations with Wando—Mbio's Hostile Attitude—Locust Diet—Ngerria's Territory—War Rumours—Binsa's Arrival—Ndoruma to the Rescue—Upper Course of the Gurba—Arrival in Lacrima—Horticultural Results—Bohndorff's Departure with Kipa—Projected War against Mbio—Insect Plague—Meteorological Relations—My dog "Lady"—Christmas, 1880.

LEAVING Ali's station on October 27th, I crossed the Gadda and encamped for the night on the Kibali. Both rivers converge a little farther west, the united stream taking the name of Welle. At this time they had reached their highest level, which varies, according to the seasons, about twenty feet between vertical banks. The Gadda was here seventy-five and the Kibali over one hundred and fifty yards wide,[1] and both were fringed with mighty forest growths widely overshadowing the stream.

The flat peninsula at their confluence is inhabited by the A-Bangba branch of the A-Baginso tribe. These are the boatmen and fishers of the district, and they also acted as my carriers for two days in the uninhabited steppe stretching north of the Kibali. Although I had passed the last few weeks close to the Welle, I could get nothing except now and then some smoked cat-fish. This was due to the fact that the natives use nothing but traps, for which low water is most suited, so that scarcely any captures are made during the floods. Hence at this time you can get nothing but what is caught and cured in the fishing season.

On the Kibali we had a nocturnal scare from a prowling hyæna, from which my buck-goat had a narrow escape. Our repose for the rest of the night was destroyed by a marauding expedition of ants, which regularly invaded the camp. We defended ourselves with brands, destroying millions and putting the rest to flight, thus gaining the victory, but losing our sleep.

On October 28th we crossed the swollen Kibali in boats, leaving Mangbattu Land behind us, and again plunging for two days into the uninhabited wilderness. During the first day's march the route trended north-eastwards through a fluvial depression, with little timber but much tall reedy grass, with laterite cropping out here and there, but no rising ground of any kind. While crossing this flooded tract I was overtaken by a severe attack of fever, which so exhausted me that I was quite prostrate when we reached the little river Bua, where we passed the night.

However, I soon rallied, and next day was able to continue the march, which still followed in a north-easterly direction through an uninhabited wilderness. But the broad riverain depression of the Kibali was now succeeded by a wooded savanna with much low bush and stunted growths. Here the tall grass had already

---

[1] Schweinfurth, who crossed them farther east, gives 155 Rhenish feet for the Gadda, and 325 for the Kibali.

been fired in many places, and the ground quite cleared round about the settlements, which we reached towards sunset. During the march we crossed no less than eight streams, the last of which, called the Kapili, was the largest, receiving all the others and itself flowing to the Kibali. Although for the most part merely wooded rivulets, they had almost without exception broad swampy banks. The shallow channels of the slightly undulating land favour the development of these riverain swamps, which are often filled with a gray mud, or laterite in process of formation.

After our two days' journey through the wilderness, we gladly

FLOODED STEPPE.

greeted the scattered settlements of the Zandeh chief Ngerria, son of Tombo, who is not to be confounded with Prince Ngerria, son of Basimbe (Basinde). Yet fresh vexations here awaited me, for the carriers had to be changed at this station, and it presently appeared that nearly all the adult male population, including some A-Baginsos and A-Madis, as well as Zandehs, had been summoned to the war in the north. It was therefore necessary to re-engage the present carriers, who, however, bolted to a man during the night, thus causing me a delay of several days, till fresh hands could be procured from the north. In this direction a new station, which was my next goal, had been founded after Abdullahi's expedition and during the hostilities with Wando; so I at once despatched messengers to the local administrator for more carriers.

That the people had all gone on the war-path was owing to the still unsettled differences between the rebellious Hokwa and his aged father, Wando, whose former territory we had entered on reaching Ngerria's inhabited district. The land assigned to Wando's eldest son, Mbittima, extended from this point eastwards along the lower course of the Kibali and Duru. The middle course of the same rivers, which lay farther north, Wando had ceded to Hokwa, while he had himself retained at least nominal possession of the northernmost section with his youngest son Rensi, or Fero. But since the captivity of Mbittima and the occupation of his share by Hokwa, Wando found himself hard pressed, and even at times compelled to seek safety in flight, though not yet conquered by Hokwa and his Arab allies. (See Genealogical Table, p. 194.)

Such were the relations when I entered this region, and fresh measures were now being taken to reduce Wando; hence the muster of Ngerria's people, though no actual conflict had yet taken place. I learnt all this from some of Wando's subjects, who also told me that negotiations were still pending between Wando and the Nubians. One of Wando's men, who had been sent to Mangbattu Land for some *baenge* with which to consult the oracle, now remained with me, having received instructions to act as a guide to Wando, who was anxiously looking forward to a visit from me.

Meanwhile our supplies were running short. There was, to be sure, an abundance of provisions in the numerous settlements scattered round about; but in the absence of the chief nothing could be had, the women especially protesting that they were powerless in the matter. We managed, however, to capture a few guineafowl, and Farag 'Allâh obtained some sweet potatoes and manioc.

Fortunately the messengers returned, on November 1st, with the carriers, and we were able to resume our march next day. This time I had even a superabundance of hands, and utilized some of them to get me through the swampy tracts.

The route ran, not to the north as I had expected, but eastwards, and even south-eastwards; but during the last stage of the day's march it trended round to the north-east, having passed numerous settlements, chiefly of the A-Bangba people. We had to cross no less than twelve marshy rivulets, besides the Gongo, which might be called a river, being some ten yards wide and four feet deep. All the streams crossed on this and the next day flowed south-eastwards to the Duru, which, like the

MY ASS IN THE SWAMP.

Kapili, flows independent to the Welle. It is the fourth northern affluent of that river, going from Ndoruma's up stream eastwards, the others being the Gurba, Mbruole, and Kapili, of which the first two are by far the most important.

We passed the night at chief Ndoruma's, though the ants and mosquitoes, with an interlude of another visit from a hyæna, prevented me from getting any sleep. November 3rd brought us to the new station in Hokwa's territory, the route trending north-east through numerous settlements chiefly of the Embomu (Zandeh) tribe, who differ in no respects from the kindred Idio and Bombeh groups in the north-west.

The aspect of the land also remained unchanged, everywhere presenting a gently undulating surface without any deep fluvial beds and fringing avenues, though the broad, marshy river banks were overgrown with a rich tropical vegetation. Wherever these swampy tracts prevail, the path itself often disappears, and even shifts its course with the seasons. In some places the wayfarer sinks to the hips; but so far as my experience goes there are no very deep or dangerous quagmires, the tangled roots of the forest growths generally presenting a safe footing against the bottomless swampy ground.

On the march to the station we had again to cross eleven such boggy river valleys, in one of which we had a little mishap with an ass, from whom they had neglected to remove the saddle. The girth getting torn, everything turned over and got thoroughly saturated with muddy water and slush.

Here, also, some of Hokwa's people had been marched off; but Muhammed Kher, administrator of the station, had made every provision for our reception. This little post in a hostile district was defended by a double row of stakes, the inner enclosure containing about a dozen huts for the Nubians, the outer and stronger leaving ample space for the huts of the Negro troops. In talking over the present political relations, Muhammed Kher displayed an exceptional degree of intelligence. He was a native of Kassala, and had been only a few years in Negro land, where, as he emphatically remarked, he had nothing to do with the infamous slave-dealers.

In former years, and at the time of Schweinfurth's visit, Wando's territory had been limited north and east by the districts of several petty Zandeh chiefs, all of whom had already been reduced to a state of vassalage by the Khartum ivory-trader, Abd es-Sammat, during his expeditions to Mangbattu Land. Some strong Nubian stations had even been founded in the country, though they had fallen to decay after Abd es-Sammat's death. Since then Mangbattu Land had been visited by representatives of Jussuf es-Shellali, Mudir of the Rôl province, by routes which took a more easterly course through Abaka Land. Recently, however, Jussuf's successor, Mula, had re-opened the old routes, after Hokwa had rebelled against Wando, and sought the alliance of the Nubians.

Hokwa had thus possessed himself of Mbittima's district, accepting the position of a vassal chief under the Arabs, as he was now hankering after the land of his younger brother, Rensi, and even aimed at the expulsion of his aged father, Wando. I now learnt that after I had left Ndoruma's Wando had sent me his ivory at that station, thus acting in contravention to the official regulations. He at the same time again protested that he would have nothing to do with the stations, which in fact had been founded in the district for the very purpose of collecting the ivory; for a second station, which I was next to visit, had just been erected two days farther north in the district of Rensi, who had taken refuge with his father, Wando.

When my arrival in the country became known, all negotiations and hostilities were suspended, and envoys from both sides daily despatched to me. Wando sent me word that on my arrival in the northern station he would like to come and visit me, but was afraid that Hokwa might capture him, as he had captured Mbittima.

I all the more willingly complied with Muhammed Kher's request to stay a few days at the station that he kept a good table. At our departure, on November 7th, he also sent some provisions for the journey, including a basket of gourd-seeds, which, when ground and cooked, make an excellent accompaniment to the native porridge. When eaten raw the seeds of the pumpkin (*Cucurbita maxima*) may be dangerous for the stomach, though taken as a remedy against worms.

Muhammed Kher also showed me a practical method of dyeing the white Dongolan *damur* cloth a brown-red, a process apparently first introduced into this part of Africa by Sir Samuel Baker. We started late, and made a march of only three hours, accompanied by Muhammed Kher. For several days our route now trended north-north-westwards to Wando's temporary station. After leaving Hokwa's zeriba on our right, we crossed a few streams, which here also flow east to the Duru, but which are fringed by a less exuberant vegetation than the more southerly water-courses.

During our first night's encampment all our carriers made off, and before their place could be supplied the unexpected news arrived that Hokwa with his men was approaching. He arrived about noon on November 8th, accompanied by Bibi, the future Arab head of the northern station. After some discussion on the state of affairs, in which I aimed at reconciling all parties, we all continued our northern journey next day, crossing in succession the three last sluggish affluents of the Duru and the scarcely-perceptible water-parting between that river and the head-streams of the Kapili. Then the Kapili itself was forded at a point where its sandy bed was ten yards wide and three feet deep.

Farther on only one tributary of this river was met, after which another uninhabited tract was traversed before reaching our night quarters. The main upper course both of the Duru and Kapili, which we had now left behind us, flows from the east, while their source lies in a hilly district culminating in Mount Baginse with its southern offshoots, Banduppo, Nagongo, and Yambeli.

In this region maize is everywhere grown, though in insufficient quantities for general consumption. Durra and dukhn (*Sorghum* and *Penicillaria* or *Pennisetum*) are almost unknown, their places being taken by telebun (*Eleusine coracana*). From the whole meal of this corn is made a dark chocolate-coloured porridge and kisra of like appearance, which is very gritty to the taste. Here are also cultivated sweet potatoes and various kinds of gourds, and, to a less extent, yams, bananas, and manioc. Of the last-mentioned there are two varieties in Zandeh Land: the sweet, which whether boiled or roasted is harmless, and the bitter, which, owing to the presence of prussic acid, has to be steeped for a whole day in running water before being ground and cooked. But even this manioc-flour may be greatly improved and made palatable to Europeans by mixing it in due proportion with other meal. The Zandehs also grow sesame, using it, like the gourd-seeds, as an accompaniment to their porridge, and they have a variety of *Colocasia* (*C. antiquorum*), greatly superior in flavour and much whiter than the Egyptian variety. I was also agreeably surprised again to meet the bamia

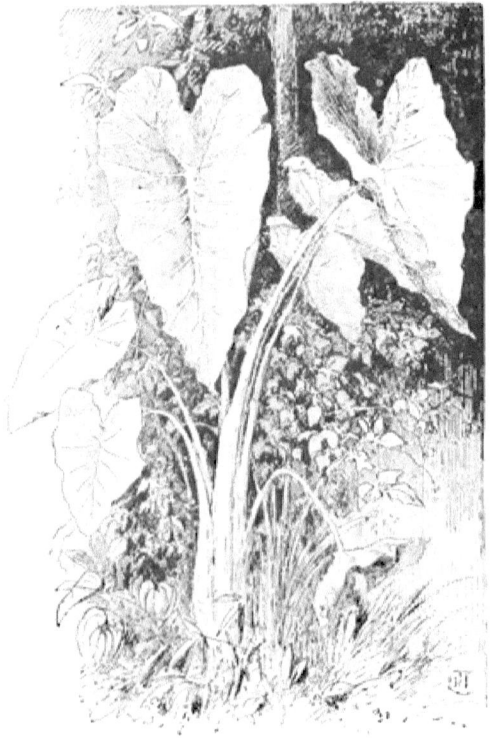

COLOCASIA ANTIQUORUM.

(*Hibiscus esculentus*), which here grows to a much larger size than in the Nubian lands.

Poultry is reared in all the Negro lands visited by me; but the fowls are everywhere very small, except one variety found in a region far to the south of the Welle. The plumage is as varied as with our domestic species, though the eggs, which are never eaten by the natives, are comparatively smaller. Most of the birds are reserved for divining purposes, but occasionally also eaten.

In this district my fowling-piece yielded a more plentiful supply of guinea-fowl than elsewhere. They are boiled down with gourds or sweet potatoes to the consistency of a thick soup, which I found much improved by adding a slice from the breast.

For the successful issue of my arbitration between the contending parties, it was important that I should have an interview with Wando and Fero apart from Hokwa and the Arabs. I accordingly remained behind with chief Bendi, and when the rest had moved forward to the new station, still an hour's march distant, I sent at once for Fero, who presented himself on November 10th, and stated that Wando was too fat to walk any great distance, but that my route to Ndoruma's passed near his residence, where he would await me. He assured me that he yearned for peace, but that Hokwa had for years been hostile to him.

HEAD OF A ZANDEH COCK.
(From a drawing by Schweinfurth.)

At this interview I again discovered that much of the trouble was due to Fero's failing to understand the nature of the altered political relations. The native chiefs residing in remote districts still supposed that there existed, as formerly, various independent trading companies; and that, for instance, Abdu'lallahi, Osman Bedawi, and others were engaged in the ivory business on their own account. On the other hand, Fero and Wando were aware that Ndoruma sent his ivory straight to the Pasha, hence was exempt from the presence of the hated Nubian soldiery, and received arms, ammunition, and other things from the Government.

So Fero had concluded that it would be best for him to send his ivory to Ndoruma. But I now explained the true situation, pointing out how foolish this would be, as Ndoruma could give him no compensation, whereas he would receive beads, cloth, copper, and the like at the station. I also laid stress on the fact that henceforth the Government would tolerate no strife or discord, and no longer desired any slaves, like the former companies, but only ivory, caoutchouc, and such things.

I wanted soon after to resume the journey, but a delay was caused by the unexpected arrival of Hokwa with Bibi and Muhammed Kher. Then began fresh deliberations, Hokwa and Fero pledging themselves in future to preserve the peace, and to regard the river Kapili as the boundary between their territories. The proceedings concluded with an exchange of presents and the usual blood-brotherhood to cement the reconciliation of both parties.

Our route on November 11th led by chief Bendi's huts nearly due north to Wando's, where we arrived late in the afternoon. On the road we crossed the upper course of the Mbruole, which, like the Kapili and Duru, comes from the east, and lower down flows partly through Ngerria's, partly through the districts of Malingde's sons; its lower course in Mangballe Land has already been described.

On this march the last stream crossed by us belongs to the Jubbo, consequently to the Nile basin, for the Jubbo flows north to the Sueh, which is the lower course of the Jur, and this again, after its junction with the Wau, falls into the Bahr el-Ghazal. As we approached Wando's the settlements became more numerous, so that from each successive group of huts the next was visible. Neither the Zandehs nor the inhabitants of the other districts we had passed form villages or communes, but the families live apart, distributed in small groups over the territory of their respective chiefs.

At one of these groups of huts were several hundred Zandehs, amongst whom I was at once able to single out the aged Wando by his corpulent figure. Like all members of the old Zandeh dynasty, he despised princely adornments, and even his rokko was no better than those of his surrounding followers. His hand also grasped, not a warlike assegai, but a peaceful fly-fan! Our friendship was soon sealed, though he remained for some time absorbed in thought, which perhaps was natural enough, seeing that facing him sat his rebellious son, Hokwa. Wando's resentment was doubtless fully justified; still I was interested in bringing about a better state of feeling with as little delay as possible. After a turn at the music-box, which was now everywhere in constant requisition, I exhorted Wando to let bygones be bygones, as Hokwa had at last come to him in a repentant mood without waiting for Wando at the Arab station. I told him of the satisfactory conclusion of negotiations between Fero and the opposite side, and now invited him to declare his wishes, so that everything might be peacefully arranged.

The traitorous Hokwa was doubtless little edified at my remarks, for he was evidently aiming at the supreme power over the whole land, and would have gladly seen father and brother annihilated on the spot. But Wando replied in a long speech that he had nothing more to say; he was now old, and had left his land to his three sons, claiming for himself and his retainers only a little plot of ground, where he could live in peace, and not be compelled every moment to escape to the desert from night attacks and sudden surprises. When his sons were thoroughly reconciled, and the relations established on a footing of permanent peace, he would also return to his former residence on the Duru.

I had certainly not expected a thorough reconciliation between father and son, but at least so much was effected that a few friendly words passed between them on this and the following day, when Hokwa took his departure.

I stayed several days with Wando, awaiting the return of the messengers sent to Ngerria and Binsa, through whose districts lay the road to Ndoruma's. They had also taken letters for

Bohndorff, announcing my approach. The temptation was certainly great to attempt a visit from this place to Prince Mbio, whose territory stretched north of the river Yubbo. Both Wando and Fero also held out some hope that Mbio might receive me, so I at once sent messengers to his court. But every effort to open relations with this last absolutely independent Zandeh

LOCUST GATHERING.

ruler proved futile, for his answer was not only a refusal, but a threat to attack and kill us on the road to Ndoruma's. However I might despise his menaces, it was still necessary to take precautions, and the western route through Binsa's now seemed the safer.

Wando, who passed much time in my hut, showing great interest in my belongings, received several gifts of blue cloth, scissors, knives, mirrors, beads, and the like. The Zandeh women also gradually overcame their shyness, and often went away rejoicing in their glass beads. Wando much appreciated a few glasses of sherry and the empty bottle, the only one I possessed, and sent in return some of their favourite "batossi," a beer brewed from telebun (*Eleusine coracana*). Compared with the merissa prepared from durra, it comes much nearer to our European beer, and though often cloudy, is both strong, very palatable, and nourishing.

Wando and Fero kept us on such short commons that my people were glad to join the natives of an evening, when they went with lighted torches locust gathering. This was done not through any absolute want of food, but because of their prefer-

FIKO SHOT BY ORDER OF FERO.

ence both for locusts and termites, which, however, do not by any means form a common article of their diet. In Central Africa I only once saw a large harvest, though in Tunis it was of frequent occurrence. I soon overcame my repugnance to such fare, which, in fact, I found very palatable. The insects were very fat, and when roasted without wings and legs, looked like little fish or shrimps.

Meanwhile the messengers had returned from Prince Ngerria, who sent word that he not only expected me, but would later himself accompany me to Binsa's. I had been now a week at Wando's, from the 12th to the 18th of November, and therefore urgently pressed for the carriers. But, in the evening, while the people were again collecting locusts, the report was suddenly spread that Mbio and his warriors were approaching. I did not credit the rumour, and Fero, who had come back with some soldiers from the station, went some distance north to ascertain the truth, and returned with the news that it was a false alarm.

Next day Fero promised to go himself and procure some carriers, but I soon found that he had a very different object in

A-MADI COLONY.

view. He marched off with the men from the station, not, as I supposed, to collect provisions, but to compass the destruction of his vassal chief, Biko, who had deserted him and gone over to Hokwa's side. Fero now fell suddenly on his huts, carried off everything movable, the women included, and brought back Biko himself in fetters. The unhappy chief was prevented by his guards from escaping to me, and in the evening I heard some firing in the neighbourhood, after which Farag 'Allāh came to say that Fero had just had Biko shot.

After all this I was right glad to get away on November 20th.

The route, which had hitherto run northwards, now trended almost due west. Within Fero's district, which extended still a day's march and a half in the same direction, we crossed a number of streamlets, all flowing north to the Yubbo. The land was here also thickly peopled, numerous A-Madi colonies being settled amongst the Zandehs. Many of these, on whom chief Biko had levied contributions, had gone southwards, but had since returned, and their huts were now picturesquely grouped on the flat reed-grown banks of a sluggish stream. Here and there this broad valley was broken by rising grounds, and even hilly formations, often commanding an uninterrupted view towards the north, where the smoke visible on the distant horizon was said to rise within the limits of Mbio's territory. These A-Madi, now under Fero's rule, had migrated hither owing to the civil strife prevailing in their distant western homes.

The western frontier districts of Fero's territory, which we were now traversing, were even more broken than the plains hitherto passed, presenting in some places continuous chains of hills, which culminated in Mount Saba, with a relative altitude of scarcely six hundred feet. The water-courses also assumed another aspect, for here the deep troughs fringed with forest growths again prevailed.

Besides Zandehs, the border-lands are occupied by some A-Madi settlements. These border-lands between Fero's and Ngerria's territories also form the parting-line between the tributaries of the Yubbo and the streams flowing south-west to the Mbruole. I consequently here again crossed the Nile-Congo divide, as for several of the following days the rivers met along our route all belonged to the Mbruole (Congo) system. Farther on this common political and hydrographic parting-line took a south-westerly course to our first camping-ground at chief Makaru's, in Ngerria's territory.

Here another day, November 22nd, was lost for lack of carriers, although Makaru did his best to procure fresh hands. There were plenty of loafers about, but they were attracted solely by curiosity to see the white man; so after an expenditure of much useless eloquence, I fetched one of the louts within reach a sound box on the ear, and told the lot to be off. Then they offered to lend a hand, but I scornfully declined their proffered aid, adding that their prince, who had invited me to visit him, would also provide me with carriers. I had, in fact, already applied to Ngerria, with the result that the same evening a number of men arrived in camp.

Our route next day still lay mainly to the west, though often deflected to the right or left by the numerous settlements which here lined nearly all the water-courses. Between these water-courses the surface was broken by broad-ridged eminences, one

MOUNT SABA.

of which afforded a distant prospect towards the south, where a long line of tall trees marked the course of the Mbruole.

Soon after noon we reached Ngerria's mbanga, where the prince with a numerous company awaited me in a spacious gable-roofed open hall. Ngerria, brother of Wando, Mbio, and Malingde, resembled Wando, but was younger and less corpulent. In the mbanga messengers had already arrived from Binsa, to say that he expected me to visit him. Then Ngerria accompanied me to the huts which had been specially built for us, and which were of unusually large size. Here also I had to produce my raree-shows, for the talismanic words *kundi* ("music") and *kitab* ("book") had already preceded us hither.

Ngerria's subjects were in the habit of daily assembling at his mbanga, which had long stood in the same favourable position, undisturbed even by the early trading or plundering expeditions of the Nubians. Hence, unlike the temporary places of assembly of Ndoruma, Wando, and Fero, Ngerria's residence presented the stamp of the old traditional usages of the Zandeh nation. A large open space carefully cleared of grass lay a little apart from the huts, and in the centre stood a wide-branching tree, under whose shade the meetings took place. Near it was the hall, which, however, was little used except in bad weather.

Specially noteworthy are the frameworks of timber, usually set up on two sides of the mbanga, and consisting of posts connected by horizontal spars, which are disposed at regular intervals one above the other. Thus is formed a kind of large-meshed latticed structure, on which the visitors hang up their shields and rest their spears. As the Zandehs mostly go about with their arms, such places assume a peculiarly characteristic aspect, especially at large gatherings.

The Mangbattus, scorning to sit on the ground, bring their stools and benches with them; but amongst the Zandehs the *Bia* (prince) alone sits on a stool, while his subjects squat on the ground round about, the chiefs on their antelope skins or mats, the rest on foliage or a piece of wood from the neighbouring thicket.

Ngerria showed much interest in my curiosities, and was specially pleased with the gift of a blue-enamelled metal jug for drinking merissa. Only he had great difficulty in understanding that between the outer blue and inner white enamel there was an iron body, until I convinced him of the fact by pointing to some damaged parts.

Besides their large earthen vessels for water and merissa, the Zandehs make others of somewhat similar form, but smaller, some no bigger than a small coffee-cup. These, with the various wooden porringers, complete their stock of household utensils.

MGEKRIA'S MBANGA (TRYSTING-PLACE). (*Drawn by L. H. Fischer.*)

The upper rim, especially in those of medium or smaller size, often projects upwards, and is outwardly carved, so that the vessel, when filled with eatables, may be covered over with a few large leaves.

In the houses of the chiefs there are also found clay drinking vessels in great variety of form, used especially for beer. The accompanying illustration shows one of these beer-pots, about eighteen inches high, which is remarkable for its double neck.

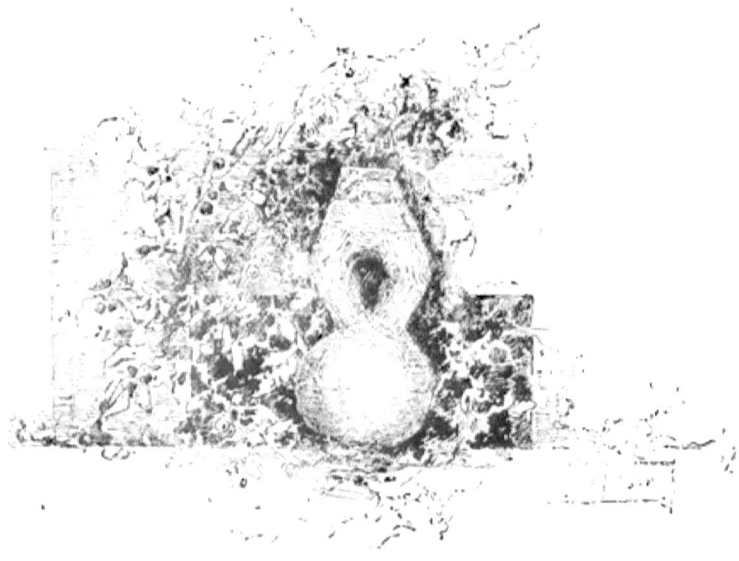

ZANDEH BEER-POT.

Less frequent are the small earthen water-bottles, in shape and size exactly like our flat, bulging decanters used for sherry and port. It serves to offer the chief a drink of water, and in after years I used it for keeping liquid honey or cheese-milk.

I was detained at Ngerria's some time, partly by lying reports, amongst others that Mbio had sent a bundle of spears to Binsa. This is the Zandeh method of inviting a neighbouring prince to an offensive alliance against a third party, which, in the present instance, of course meant myself. Although fresh messengers from Binsa denied the report, it had all the same to be threshed out in a long palaver, and after all Ngerria still remained suspicious. Then came the rumour that Binsa was coming in a friendly way to bring me away, which caused a fresh delay to await his arrival. Another postponement was caused by the surprising tidings from Bohndorff that (the report of hostilities having also reached Ndoruma) that prince wanted to march to my assistance.

All this made Ngerria undecided how to act, while I kept urging him to despatch messengers to stop Ndoruma's "armed intervention." At last this was done, the messengers being instructed, in case Ndoruma had already set out, to request him to return, as Ngerria would himself escort me, not, however, through the territory of Binsa, against whom he continued to harbour suspicions, but by another route. Other false rumours, that I had been completely plundered at Mambanga's and even thrown into prison, and so forth, had got about, and as I afterwards learnt, had even reached Khartum, and thus found their way to the European newspapers.

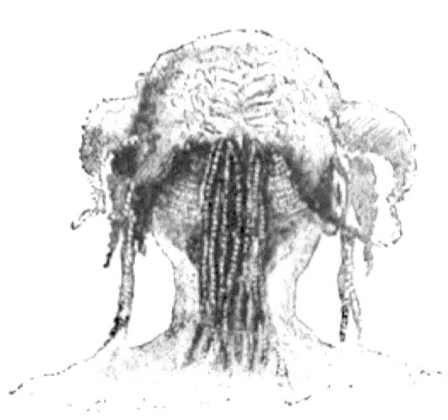

ZANDEH COIFFURE.
(From a drawing by Schweinfurth.)

Amid these constant vexations I managed as a rule to keep my equanimity; but at times the strain was too much for my nerves, and then Ngerria could think of nothing better than his own panacea, merissa, which he plied me with liberally. He also presented me with two large and four small tusks, which, however, were useless to me, ivory being a Government monopoly; so, for lack of carriers, I simply left them behind when we at last made a start for Ndoruma's on November 28th.

Here the route again changed, sweeping in a great bend round to the north, through an undulating wooded savanna, poorer in running waters than the region hitherto traversed. In fact, we crossed only one stream, an affluent of the Tau, which, however, was a respectable river some ten yards broad and seven feet deep. A huge tree lying athwart the swirling current served as a primitive bridge; but, as was so often the case, I found it impossible to keep the unruly carriers in order. They scrambled over anyhow, and then started off in different directions; but to the honour of the Zandehs be it said, I never on such occasions lost a single load.

Ngerria, who had lingered behind, overtook us next morning in the camp, where Binsa was again reported to be approaching, though with friendly intentions. His district lay to the north-west of the camp, whereas Ngerria proposed conducting me by a different road from this point straight to Ndoruma's. This time the rumour proved true, Binsa presenting himself before we could get away, and thereby obliging me to take the route through his district. Now came the news that Ndoruma had

A ZANDEH FOP.
(*From a drawing by Schweinfurth.*)

pitched his camp on the north frontier of his territory, where he awaited me. I at once again sent him envoys, in order as far as possible to clear up this comedy of errors, and avoid hostilities on the frontier.

Binsa, son of Malingde, was still a young man, but lacked the dignity of the elder Zandeh rulers, and was in fact the prototype of the genuine Zandeh dandy of the rising generation. Many of these lordlings apply a large assortment of native products to the embellishment of their person.

The hair especially is treated with amazing care, and, at an expenditure of much time, built up in a great variety of head-dresses. The triumphs of our European dames in this respect are far surpassed by the rich diversity of these elaborate coiffures. The towering toupees, or the arrangement of narrow tresses clinging close to the head and falling in wreaths down to the shoulders, are often decked with cowrie shells, glass beads, little copper plates, and other trinkets. A favourite adornment of the forehead is a string of dogs' teeth or of small wild animals', while the neck is encircled by diverse fine copper, iron, or bead rings, and the like. But the most costly and highly-prized is an ivory ornament falling low down on the breast, and consisting of thirty or forty cylinders from one and a half to two and a half inches long, strung together according to their size, and terminating in a point downwards. The cylinders are supposed to represent the teeth of predatory animals, especially lions, which are very difficult to procure. Throughout the Zandeh lands the lion compared to the leopard is very rare, whereas in those regions where lions are numerous, leopards are seldom seen. These ivory ornaments, whose preparation with their primitive tools involves an amazing display of skill and patience, belong properly to an earlier, one might almost say a classical, period of native art, and are now possessed only by a privileged few.

The toilet of the Zandeh fop is not complete without the little straw hat, which, as far as the form of the chignon allows, is set jauntily on the crown, and decked with a tuft of cock's feathers slit up through the quills to let them wave more lightly on the breeze. The whole effect is also often heightened by smearing the body with powdered red dyewood, or painting it with the juice of gardenia.

The route to our next encampment on the Tau led north-west to the Makussa, which, after joining the Tau, goes to feed the Mbruole. But Ngerria's inhabited domain is limited by the

Makussa, beyond which river a desolate wilderness stretches away to the west. It took several hours to reach the first settlements of Binsa's people, and next morning, November 30th, we entered his station. Here the country was uniformly flat, but intersected by a large number of rivulets, all flowing to the Makussa. The rains had long ceased, and the grass on the more elevated ground was already burnt up by the sun. Crowds gathered to see us and to gaze in astonishment on the ass, a phenomenon unknown in those parts.

On the road I was met by two of Ndoruma's chiefs, who at sight of me at once returned to report that they had seen me in the flesh, some doubts being still entertained of my existence. They left word that the warriors would be all sent back, and that Ndoruma with a few of his lieges would come and meet me at Binsa's.

To understand what follows, it should be remembered that Osman Bedawi, leader of the Nubians, had left some of his people and ivory at Binsa's on his way southwards to Bakangai. Complaints had already been made regarding the high-handed doings of Malingde's son; but Osman Bedawi, who had in the meantime returned home with the ivory, had nevertheless left with Binsa a few Negro soldiers with fire-arms and several loads of goods, especially beads, for next year's expedition southwards. Later Binsa had deprived the soldiers of their fire-arms, ostensibly because of their disorderly conduct and plunderings, whereupon they had gone off with their complaints to Ndoruma. Binsa was also reported to have appropriated the goods left with him by Osman Bedawi.

All this I had learnt before my interview with Binsa, and it was chiefly owing to these events that neither Ndoruma nor Ngerria had any faith in the peace made with Binsa, and even feared for my safety. At our first meeting I had shown him my displeasure, without, however, touching on these events. But at the mbanga Binsa himself soon referred to them for the purpose of justifying himself, and even asked me to take charge of the fire-arms taken from the soldiers, which, however, I firmly refused to do. Binsa denied that Osman Bedawi had left any goods with him, and this in the teeth of the strongest evidence, his own women being bedizened with beads and copper rings to an extent that I had never seen before or since.

In the evening I was agreeably surprised by the arrival of my faithful Mangbattu servant, Dsumbe, who had been left behind invalided at Lacrima. He entertained me with a detailed account of the occurrences at Lacrima during my absence, culminating with an adventure which had nearly cost him his life, and of which he was not a little proud. One evening, as he was strolling along the Werre with the Mauser rifle, a magnificent buffalo suddenly emerged from the thicket. Dsumbe was struck dumb with fright, but somehow the rifle, without even being aimed, went off of its own accord, and the animal fell dead at his feet.

On December 1st, a twelvemonth since my departure from Cairo, I renewed acquaintance with Ndoruma, who arrived early in the morning at Binsa's, and was visibly rejoiced to find me alive. Then an assembly was held at Binsa's mbanga, where he again vowed that his intentions had never been hostile, and also that the charge of making common cause with Mbio was a gross calumny. He persuaded Ndoruma to take over the rifles and forty cartridges, and so once more all ended happily.

In the evening my little cook, Saida, having also arrived from Lacrima, we prepared a sumptuous repast for Ndoruma. To do honour to such a successful issue of serious complications, I uncorked the only bottle of brandy I had brought with me on this journey, leaving, however, the lion's share to Ndoruma, who shared a little with his lieges. The empty bottle went to Binsa, who had bid for it.

Binsa's residence stood on the scarcely-perceptible water-parting between the Gurba and the Mbruole, whose affluents we had just left behind us. Nine tributaries of the Gurba were crossed before the Gurba itself was reached on our last day's journey. But they presented few such difficulties as we had met on the rivers farther south. For weeks no rain had fallen, and we found many swamps already dried up.

The route to the Lacrima station now ran north, with a point

ISUMBE'S LUCKY SHOT. (*Drawn by Fr. Rheinfelder.*)

to the west, first through an inhabited tract, then across a dreary steppe, and again on the border of Binsa's district through some cultivated land. Shortly before reaching this district we crossed the shallow, sandy bed of the Buole, which was here ten yards wide. Beyond this largest affluent of the Gurba we encamped for the last time at the last settlements in Binsa's territory. For our evening meal we luckily captured a harnessed antelope, which I enjoyed all the more that it was accompanied by some of the produce of our garden. The thoughtful Saida, besides preparing some of the excellent tomatoes for future use, had brought a few to the camp, and these made a delicious relish with our roast antelope. I had also to thank Bohndorff for some cigars, which helped to gladden the last evenings of this journey.

Meantime we had been overtaken by one of Osman Bedawi's men, who had recovered from an illness which had detained him at Binsa's. He told us that during our stay at that place he had been watched, evidently to prevent him from revealing anything about the beads. He now confirmed the charge of misappropriation brought against Binsa. After our departure he managed to escape, and remained the following months in my service.

More rejoicings were occasioned the last evening by the feast of the new moon, which, according to Mohammedan usage, was greeted with a round of musketry. As in the whole of the Moslem and a great part of the Negro world, all eyes were strained to catch a glimpse of the scarcely-perceptible silver crescent in the firmament; with it begins the new month for all followers of the Prophet.

During the dry season the temperature falls considerably in these latitudes. Soon after sunset the glass stands at about 62° F., and the body being no longer accustomed to such a moderate degree of heat, an uncomfortable chilly feeling sets in, so that at night I often shivered under my woollen coverlet.

After an absence of nearly four months, I re-entered my station at Lacrima on December 3rd. During the march we had traversed an extensive, uninhabited, frontier wilderness, a monotonous, slightly undulating, steppe region, where we were again much impeded by the tall, dry herbage. Ndoruma had issued special orders that the grass, which afforded cover for the game on his preserves, was not to be fired till later in the season.

About noon we crossed the sandy bed of the Gurba, here twelve yards wide and still eighteen inches deep. Although the umbrageous fringing vegetation invited to repose, after the sun-burnt steppe, we pushed forward, all being eager, and I not the least, to reach their homes. Along the rest of the route through the steppe we met nothing but a swampy stream, flowing from the north to the Gurba, after which followed the water-parting between the Gurba and Werre basins. I had thus so far determined the upper course of the Werre, though its farthest sources lay more to the east in an extensive frontier steppe land on the water-parting which here separates it from the rivulets flowing to the Yubbo, that is, to the Nile system. But the Gurba-Werre water-parting crossed by our present route lay entirely within the territory of Ndoruma, whose first settlements were now soon reached.

Meanwhile our van had arrived at the station of chief Helwa, who was already known to me, and who had made all preparations for our reception, even entertaining our hungry people with porridge and merissa. Then, after a short rest, the several groups hastened forward to their own huts, while we had still to cross the last swampy streamlet, the only one which in this district flows north to the Werre. This brought us near the station by the road which four months before had led us to Palembata's. Here I got a glimpse of our buildings at Lacrima, which I entered the same afternoon with mingled feelings of relief and proud self-consciousness.

Bohndorff, now in good health, had come forward to welcome us, and in the station I found everything in the best order, the only cause of regret being the death of our ass from Khartum. I was at once attracted to the garden, where I saw with delight, and also learnt from Bohndorff's further communications, that the labour bestowed on this horticultural experiment had not been in vain. The evening was passed in pleasant conversation over a bottle of wine, followed by the luxury of a comfortable night's rest on my Sudanese angareb. On the journey I had used a narrow iron camp-bedstead, so lightly constructed that its thin iron laths often sank in the loose soil, and the thing had to be "shored up" before I could get any sleep.

Next day, December 4th, I was again in the garden, where much agreeable time was now constantly passed in reaping the fruits of our former sowing. In fact, the harvest season was already well advanced, as Bohndorff had only managed to keep a few things growing against my return. But two months before the ground had been clothed with a bright vesture of ripe vegetables, although everything had not succeeded equally well. Thus of the many varieties of maize, for which the site was very unfavourable, only a few had ripened, and even those scarcely recalled the fine cobs grown at Erfurth. The different kinds of cucumbers also, after efflorescence, fell off during the rainy season, though I had still the pleasure of raising a few in December. The cauliflowers had run up to some height without forming a head; but, on the other hand, both beans and peas had yielded excellent returns, supplying Bohndorff's table for weeks together. I found a quantity still on hand in the dried state.

The tomatoes continued to ripen even in December, while the curly endive still filled some beds, and when cut down went on sprouting vigorously during the dry season, so that it was daily cooked as a vegetable for the servants. The still surviving cabbage-stumps had already run to seed, but this did not prevent me from sending some to keep the pot boiling. The radishes were over-ripe, and had grown to a monstrous size, hence were naturally hard; yet when cooked were quite palatable. As long as my stock of oil and vinegar held out, the beet-root supplied an unfailing ingredient for an excellent salad. I also found red cabbages, swedes, and other things still growing, so that we were able to draw supplies from our garden during the rest of my stay at Ndoruma's, that is, to the end of December. Although some of the vegetables were over-ripe, old and woody, consequently, according to European notions, tasteless, I valued everything too highly as a relief from the endless monotony of batatas, yams, and bananas, that I would have nothing lost or wasted. Even the turnip, radish, and coarse lettuce-leaves were often cooked as vegetables, and a fresh supply was thus constantly available for the household.

Anyhow my vegetables had thriven during my absence better than some of my servants. Immediately after I had set out, two of Bohndorff's assistants had gone off, and he now informed

LEOPARD IN THE SPRINGE.

me that, owing to her obstinacy, he had been obliged to dispense with the services of Saida, and do his own cooking. Later, however, Osman Bedawi, when passing through from Ngattua's, had visited Lacrima and left him another servant, the Moru negress, Halima. Saida had also taken other liberties, appropriating Farag 'Allāh's mosquito-net, which she exchanged for tobacco and merissa; she had even managed to become possessed of two female slaves, so that I now found the household increased by three new maid-servants. In my presence Saida still continued to show herself willing and industrious; nevertheless I took her seriously to task, threatened on the next occasion to dismiss her, and at once sent off the two girls purchased by her. Halima, however, remained in the station and continued for years in my service.

About this time we managed to take a leopard with our large iron springe. The beast had killed a native in the vicinity of the station, whereupon Bohndorff had the snare set up on the same spot, using as a bait the arm of the victim. So next evening, when the leopard returned, he was caught in the springe, which had been secured by a heavy chain. Here he was found and despatched by some of our people next morning, though not without damaging the skin.

The smaller gins had also proved useful, capturing several rodents for my collection. Bohndorff had also explored the surrounding district for birds, and with the aid of the servants had filled many of my spirit flasks with all kinds of insects. But he complained of the difficulty he had in preserving the large specimens, whose skins, instead of being stretched and dried, had been sewn up like bellows, whereby the skin of the large chimpanzee was quite ruined.

My journey with Zemio had become widely known throughout Zandeh Land, and since then all the chiefs and rulers wanted me to visit their states. The first to announce himself was Prince Zassa, whose ancestral land lay south of the Mbomu. As already stated, his attitude towards the Government was similar to that of Zemio, and as Zemio had done with Palembata and Badinde, he had in recent times endeavoured to secure for himself the position of a vassal amongst a number of powerless chiefs, between the middle course of the Werre and the Welle. Meanwhile, to safeguard his interests, he had stationed a younger brother, Kipa, in that western district; Kipa was also now instructed to visit me at Ndoruma's, and invite me to his territory, where my influence over refractory chiefs might be very useful to him.

Thus it was that on my return I found Kipa and his people already awaiting me at Lacrima. Zassa himself was just then with Gessi Pasha about some differences between himself and

Rafai's officials. Finding from my personal experiences that the relations were not favourable for a long stay in Mangbattu Land, I had already made up my mind to shift my headquarters from Ndoruma's to the residence of the powerful Zandeh prince, Bakangai. Years before the Nubian trading expeditions had penetrated to his domain; but although willing to exchange his ivory for their wares, Bakangai had never permitted them to found any settlement in his country.

The rapid growth of his power had, so to say, become proverbial, and I hoped to receive a friendly welcome from him. Hence my plan was, despite the difficulty of procuring carriers, to remove after December with most of my effects, and all my people, temporarily to A-Madi Land. So there now remained only a few weeks for rest, for sifting and arranging the results of my previous expeditions, and for many urgent personal matters. Hence I was fain to decline Kipa's invitation, but arranged to substitute Bohndorff, in order to open up new relations, and collect further particulars about those lands. Before moving southwards I intended also leaving in some safe place a part of my effects as a reserve against unforeseen contingencies.

Kipa had the ten required carriers ready, so that Bohndorff could start at once and be back again by the end of the month. He set out on December 7th, and as he took a few of the servants with him, it was now very quiet at the station. All the more busy was I, taking stock of the goods, and especially inspecting such things as were likely to suffer damage during the rainy season. Leather ware is most liable to injury; hence it is always best to stow away these things loosely, so that they may be easily unpacked, examined, exposed to sun and air, and cleansed. Thanks to my constant care, I found everything in good condition; even the blocks of salt, which easily crumble away in damp weather, were perfectly dry, thanks to the precaution of wrapping them in straw and then sewing them up in canvas before stowing them away in boxes.

From my trip I had brought back a choice collection of native products, amongst which Ndoruma specially admired the fine

Mangbattu knives. He would have given anything for one of these objects, but I was all the more obdurate, that he again gave me reason to complain of his conduct. During the rumours of threatening troubles with Binsa and of my imprisonment, Bohndorff had yielded to his urgent request for a loan of some of our fire-arms, and a hundred bullets with powder. But no ammunition had been expended, except as Ndoruma pretended, against buffaloes; so I demanded at least half of the bullets back, but could recover only about forty, after much higgling and the threat of my serious displeasure.

I could not waive my claim, partly because I was myself short of supplies, partly because it is always best to act on the principle of leaving as little powder and shot as possible in the hands of the natives. The Nubians were wise enough always to act on this principle in Egyptian Sudan, and there were also standing orders against the introduction of fire-arms and ammunition for trading purposes in the Arab lands.

As the time for leave-taking approached, I was anxious in a substantial way to testify my gratitude to Ndoruma for his undoubtedly valuable support. To twenty-five of his chiefs chosen by himself, I promised as many costumes, which in the eyes of the natives have as much value as perhaps twice the quantity of material required to make them. The Negro soldiers and the servants of the Nubians soon learn to sew; I therefore fitted up a regular tailor's workshop, where in a few weeks they turned out about a hundred complete suits. So I was able to keep my word with the chiefs, giving them also some sewing-thread with needles of various sizes for stitching their bast cloth.

Ndoruma received a finer costume with a bright-coloured scarf, fez, and turban, further a Russian peasant's dress, some plain cloth (*tirga* and *trumba*), a European shirt and stockings, red slippers, a dagger, and other trifles. In return he supplied me, off and on, with eleusine corn, a little maize, occasionally bananas, more termites and sesame, which was now ripe, and from which I had some oil extracted for my lamp and the cuisine.

It was now the hunting season, and Ndoruma soon sent me a buffalo's leg, while Farag 'Alláh brought in a harnessed antelope and guinea-fowl; the old birds were sent to the stock-pot; the young, stuffed with rice, were excellent roasted. The tough buffalo flesh I passed through the mincing-machine, and then made into large meat dumplings, which were occasionally served with genuine truffle-sauce. Saida's art did not reach the level of this *recherché* cuisine, so I had to play the chef myself. We even got milk again, our little flock of goats having been increased by a kid during my absence.

Thanks to this nourishing diet and my comfortable quarters at the station, I rapidly recovered my full strength, and even the stoutness which I had partly lost on the journey. A young chimpanzee captured about this time greatly interested me. At the capture he had been wounded with a spear in the hand and head; but the wounds gradually healed, with the loss of the little finger. He mostly remained in my immediate vicinity, and his human, childish ways were often really affecting. He watched me at work with the curiosity of a child, and whenever a box was opened he toddled up, peeped in, smelt and tasted the various contents. Then at other times he would sit still, contemplating his wounded hand, with the other brushing away the flies with a perfectly human gesture, and with his index finger-nail removing the pus and the insects from the sore.

But one day he suddenly disappeared, presumably reminded irresistibly of his native woodlands by the dense vegetation of the Werre. Here began the search, and here he was soon descried in the fork of a tree. The hue and cry was now raised; a number of people swarmed up the tree, hanging like apes from the pendant boughs. At last he was again captured, and brought in triumph back to the station. To punish him and make a second escape more difficult, I had a stick tied round his neck; in fact a milder form of the "shebba," a yoke used in Sudan to prevent slaves from escaping. Nevertheless he soon made a second attempt, making for the station, and every now and then anxiously looking round to see that he was not observed. As he could not get along very fast, I quietly

CAPTURE OF THE RUNAWAY CHIMPANZEE. (*Drawn by L. H. Fischer.*)

watched him for some time, and then had him brought back, pretending to be very angry and striking at him with my handkerchief. For a moment he seemed ashamed, then raised his hand screaming against me, but presently crept back and remained quite still.

Another distraction was afforded by an Arab mendicant monk, apparently from Mecca, who had come to Ndoruma's

THE CHIMPANZEE'S SECOND ATTEMPT TO ESCAPE.

shortly before my return, and often accompanied him on his visits to me. He knew by little conjuring tricks how to play on the superstition of the natives to his own advantage, and Ndoruma himself was sufficiently afraid to yield to the holy man's demands for slaves. The "miracles," which he attributed to the assistance of Allah, were accompanied with the distribution of certain consecrated remedies. For instance, he pretended to extract drops of water from the point of a knife, and wanted to press this upon me, as well as some oil and cotton, as an efficacious imbrication against all kinds of affections. Through special respect for me he was also willing to sell me a bead from his rosary. To strengthen the people's faith in his miraculous powers, he had recourse to such simple yet persuasive devices as the undoing of nine firmly tied knots.

But these essays of the miracle-monger interested me less than some samples of wild rice (*Oryza punctata*) which came from Bellanda. The wild rice, which in north tropical Africa has a wide range, reaching as far as Senegambia, scarcely differs specifically from the cultivated varieties. In those northern regions it springs up abundantly during the rainy season; yet the natives are unable to make any use of it. The specimen shown me was of a dirty gray colour, and we failed to boil it quite soft, though it tasted well enough.

No fresh news had arrived about Mbio, whose threats brought to Wando's had not been carried out. No attack was made on us along the route to Ndoruma's, which was traversed without any disturbance. On the other hand, a report came from the Mudir Saati Bey in the Bahr el-Ghazal province (Gessi Pasha had already started on his disastrous voyage down the Nile to Khartum) that the project was being seriously entertained of an attack on Mbio with Government troops. Ndoruma himself was to come to the Mudiriyeh, and at the same time provide a store of corn for the soldiers. Ndoruma, however, still dreading an invasion of Mbio's people, thought of only sending his brother Mbima to Saati Bey.

Meanwhile Bohndorff wrote me that Kipa's territory was much farther off than we had supposed, so that he could not get back till after the New Year. This decided me to hasten my departure, and march with all my effects towards Bohndorff in the direction of Ndoruma's south-westerly border-lands. I could not afford to lose the favourable dry season; and on the other hand I was afraid, after the arrival of the soldiers for the war against Mbio, of getting entangled in fresh complications, and finding great difficulty in procuring carriers.

Ndoruma, who now looked forward to the realization of his cherished hope of breaking Mbio's power, made no objection to my departure, and even promised me carriers as far as Palembata's.

On December 16th I expected a lunar eclipse; but when the moon rose above the trees, the phenomenon was nearly over. I continued to record the meteorological observations to the end of the month. In the dry season, and especially in December, east and north-east winds prevailed during the day, being followed by calms in the evening. The temperature rose at noon to 90° or 91° F. in the shade, falling at night, and especially before dawn, down to 59° F. At night heavy dews often fall; but dense mists were rare, though on December 8th the morning was so foggy that I could not see thirty yards ahead.

At this season the sunsets were indescribably beautiful, and I would often gaze in rapture on the glorious scene till the glowing firmament was veiled in the shades of night. I would then retire late to my evening meal, where I was awaited more or less impatiently by the company. This consisted of the chimpanzee and my dog "Lady," who during the following years proved herself the dearest and truest companion of my solitary hours. The little thing was a cross between a European and a native breed, which I had picked up in Khartum as they were about to throw her into the dust-heap. On my return from the circular journey I did not expect to be recognized by my little friend, being so young when I set out. But she welcomed me back with a delight which was really touching. She was now two feet high and quite strong, with somewhat woolly black hair, white on breast and brown on lower part of the legs. Her fame spread far beyond Ndoruma's frontiers, and many would like to have had her, for the Zandehs are very fond of dogs, not merely because often partial to their flesh, but also platonically for their own sake. Their own smooth, ruddy-brown breed, with short curly tail and pointed nose (see p. 150), are all of medium size, thick-set build, and inclined to put on fat.

Hence my slim, long-legged, black-haired pet naturally excited lively interest, and later many chiefs bid hard for her possession. But we could not part company, and she seldom left my presence. At table also she was well-behaved, far different from the unmannerly chimpanzee, whose forwardness and greed were irrepressible. His relations with my Negro people were always somewhat strained, raising a plaintive cry at their approach, and even pursuing them with uplifted arms, so that the young servants generally gave him a wide berth.

Towards Christmas about a hundred loads, all repacked, were ready to be sent off, and others followed during the next few days. But the last twelvemonth had made a considerable inroad on my stock. The numerous loads of corn from Dem Bekir, the Khartum biscuits, the heavily-weighing sugar and many other things had been used up, so that I now required fewer carriers than hitherto. Most of the loads I sent on straight to Mbima's, intending to proceed thither later by a roundabout route through Ndoruma's north-western districts.

On Christmas Eve Ndoruma paid me a visit, and I was induced to treat him to another bottle of cognac. He had enjoyed the "fire," as he called it, at Binsa's, and he and his suite now soon disposed of this second bottle. For myself this evening differed from others in that my thoughts turned more frequently homewards. I also indulged in a light novel, with a bottle of red wine, followed by a midnight meal of cold meat, Dutch cheese, dates, and English biscuits.

On Christmas Day, to give my household some idea of what a merry feast it is at home, I distributed a liberal allowance of rice, macaroni, and the like, to which were added three fowls stuffed with rice, finely sliced dates (instead of raisins), and ground nuts (instead of almonds). This choice and varied fare, served in the evening, was certainly the most sumptuous repast ever placed before them.

On December 29th the carriers started with the reserve loads, under the escort of some native chiefs. With them I also sent two of my maid-servants, and Farag 'Alláh, with instructions and an inventory of the goods for Bohndorff. Ndoruma's orders were that the things were to be taken without change of carriers straight to Bani, the frontier chief in his territory. I was so rejoiced at seeing the bulk of my effects at last on the road, that in my overflowing gratitude I presented Ndoruma with sundry other gifts, such as a large folding-chair, the buck-goat, a cock, and so on.

But my generosity was somewhat premature, for the very next day I was disgusted at the sight of many of the carriers, who had taken their loads no farther than Gangura. Ndoruma himself was enraged, and went out to arrest the refractory carriers. He brought back fifteen of them with two chiefs, and had the *shebba* (yoke) immediately placed on the necks of five, whom he intended sending to the Mudiriyeh in the Bahr el-Ghazal province for further punishment. I may here mention that Mbima's proposed journey to the Mudiriyeh was put off, Ndoruma having decided after my departure to proceed thither himself. At my request he now promised to take the prisoners only as far as Bellanda, and there dismiss them.

The last day of the year 1880 was spent in writing letters to far-off friends, for with the new year I was to leave Ndoruma's, and again plunge into the unknown wilds of Central Africa.

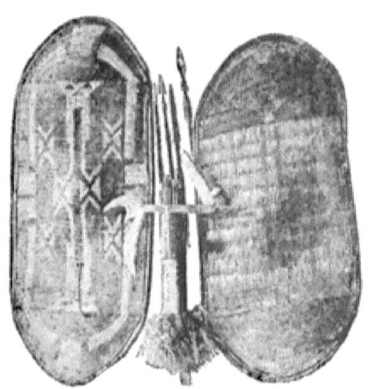

ZANDEH SHIELD.

MAID-SERVANT NARROWLY ESCAPES DROWNING.

CHAPTER IX.

FROM NDORUMA'S THROUGH A-MADI LAND TO THE A-BARMBOS AND BACK TO THE A-MADI.

Zassa's Arrival—Through Toto's, Yambo's, and Yabikumballo's to Mbima's—Bohndorff's Return and Departure for the North with the Reserved Stores—Second Trip to Palembata's—Death of the Chimpanzee—Envoys and Presents from Mambanga—To A-Madi Land—Chief Masinde—Historical—Malingde—Ascent of Mount Lingua—The Embatas on the Welle—Shelterless in the Wilderness—With the Zandeh chief Mambanga in A-Barmbo Land—Trip to Bakangai frustrated—Critical Situation—Strange Growth of Mushrooms—Termite Gathering—Arrival of Bohndorff—Desperate Position—Secret Message to Zassa—Reports of our Murder—Tremendous Tropical Thunderstorm—Zassa's Arrival at the Welle—Increased Alarms—Sleepless Nights—Eventual Escape—In Zassa's Camp—Parting from Zassa and Bohndorff.

MY intended departure from Ndoruma's on January 1st, 1881, was delayed by the unexpected arrival of Prince Zassa from the Mudiriyeh. He had been induced to return by the report of Bohndorff's and Kipa's movements, and he now hastened still farther west in order personally to arrange matters in his vassal lands. Zassa, brother of Zemio's father, Tikima, had for years maintained active relations with the Nubians, was familiar with Arabic, and, like Zemio, had adopted the Arabo-Nubian dress, so that his features alone recalled his Zandeh nationality. He was considerably older than Zemio, had a dignified carriage, and inspired confidence by his outward appearance and courteous manners.

I was all the more pleased to meet him now that it was still my intention to leave my reserve stores in charge of Kipa in Zassa's territory, at which he seemed well pleased. I gave him a friendly welcome, and placed Bohndorff's quarters at his disposal for the night. He took much interest in many things, admired the garden, and gathered some seeds with his own hand. Both Bohndorff and myself had already collected considerable quantities of various kinds, especially that of teosinthe, an American plant, said to make excellent fodder for cattle. I proudly presented Zassa with a huge pumpkin and a few radishes that still lingered on.

Next morning Zassa was off betimes, making straight for Mbima's. I soon followed, but in a north-westerly direction, to the district of Ndoruma's brother, Toto. Ndoruma saw me some distance on the way, and then we parted the best of friends. I did not at that time foresee that I should have again to traverse his territory almost as a fugitive.

Just before leaving Lacrima, I also received tidings from Ngettua about Mbio, who was reported to be mustering his men for the purpose of invading Ndoruma's territory; but this now troubled me little, and I was more affected at the thought of our beloved station, the fruit of so much toil and anxiety, which would now rapidly revert to a state of nature.

The road to Toto's lay a little to the west of that which I had followed from Kommunda's to Ndoruma's. The Bikki, which forms the boundary between Ndoruma's personal domain and Toto's district, was crossed nearer to its source; here the eye was again gladdened by the sight of some small banana groves, as well as fields of durra, a cereal so little cultivated in the more southerly Zandeh lands. Few streams were met, though this district is the source of some large rivers, such as the Mbomu in the north-west, the Bikki in the south, and in the west the Duma, largest affluent of the Werre. Toto's settlement lay just on the water-parting between the Bikki, which belongs to the Nile basin, and some northern tributaries of the Werre; but during the following days all the streams crossed by us flowed to the Werre.

From Toto's we struck south-west to Baliagi's, and for the last two days due south to Mbima's. A good day's march brought us from Toto's to chief Yango's, whence Baliagi's was reached next day, January 5th. The second half of the route lay through a broken, well-watered tract, where swamps alternated with limpid wooded streams. At Baliagi's I unexpectedly met my servant, Dsumbe, who had been sent forward by Bohndorff from Badinde with unfavourable reports for my future plans. The territory nominally under Zassa's rule lay far to the west, where the numerous petty chiefs had meanwhile disowned the authority of his lieutenant, Kipa. Dsumbe further reported that only a part of the loads had been brought from Ndoruma's to Mbima's, that much was still on the road, where the carriers were causing much trouble to Farag 'Allâh. These tidings induced me to hasten straight to Mbima's, without visiting Ndoruma's brother, Mbellebil, as I had intended.

Dsumbe was accompanied by a native, who, in accordance with the Zandeh penal code, had lost all ten fingers for seducing a woman. Such punishments were formerly far more frequent; but several instances of similar mutilations were from time to time brought under my notice. Theft is so punished, with the result that it is of rare occurrence; I myself never lost anything in Zandeh Land, but did not escape pilfering amongst the Mangbattu and A-Barmbo peoples. Though the chopping off of fingers is the commonest form of mutilation, the ears also as well as the nose, and even the lips, are occasionally cut away either as a punishment or through revenge.

A short march through Yango's district between Toto's and Mbellebil's brought us to Baliagi's, whence, on January 6th, we reached Yabikumballo's. Next day, after an hour's march southwards, we struck the Werre, a mere rivulet at Lacrima, but here a considerable stream about fifteen yards wide and a few feet deep. At one point, in fact, it was deep enough to have drowned one of my female servants, had not a carrier come to the rescue.

South of the Werre followed an extensive uninhabited tract with long, stony rising grounds, which, however, nowhere developed into hills. Thus the land continued to maintain its characteristic undulating appearance, and the whole region was everywhere far less thickly peopled than Wando's and Ngerria's territories. The streamlets crossed during this last day's march to Mbima's flowed through swamps and depressions north-west to the Werre.

Yabikumballo's carriers returned about half-way, but were immediately replaced by fresh hands for the rest of the route to Mbima's. In this respect I had no cause to complain throughout Ndoruma's domain, though some of them had carried their loads of reserved wares somewhat wildly up and down the land. A part of these things were still missing, and Bohndorff himself had gone from Mbima's to Peru's to collect the scattered loads. He got back with everything on January 8th, and his verbal account of his experiences with Kipa confirmed my resolution not to send the thirty reserved loads to Kipa's, but to some northern station, either Raffai's or Zassa's, south of the Mbomu.

The road thither led from Badinde's through Yapati's territory northwards; with both I had entered into friendly relations, either personally or through envoys, and therefore expected there would be no difficulty in forwarding the things through their districts. But it was arranged that Bohndorff would see to this, while I adhered to my original plan of proceeding with most of the effects to Bakangai's, where Bohndorff could join me after carrying out his part of the programme. I had instructed him in surveying work, so that the routes followed by him alone might be made available in the construction of maps.

Bohndorff's excursion to Kipa's led from Zemio's first camp in Palembata's, marching for eight days in a southern bend farther west to the Werre. I thus became aware at that time that this river could not possibly reach the Welle-Makua anywhere east of 26° E. long. of Greenwich; but the more accurate determination of the confluence had to await a later expedition to the Makua. Bohndorff's route crossed streams mostly flowing from the south to the Werre, though its southernmost section also crossed some direct tributaries of the Welle-Makua. The water-parting presented several continuous ranges of hills, and of the numerous Zandeh chiefs, mostly living at feud with each other, I will here mention the names only of Sirro, Remundua, and Farielle.

Ndoruma having already set out for the Mudiriyeh, the troops destined for the war against Mbio might soon arrive; while, on the other hand, Mbio himself might take the offensive at any moment. In either case Mbima would have at once to march eastwards, whereby my further movements would be long delayed for want of carriers. Hence I was all the more anxious to get away, and meanwhile sent off messengers to Palembata and Badinde with presents and a statement of my plans. At a meeting of Mbima's chiefs, the number of carriers to be supplied by each was agreed to, and it was settled that Bohndorff should first set out with forty loads and my servants, Dsumbe and Morjan. But many days still passed before he got away.

Then came my turn, but so many hands were needed that with the best intentions Mbima and his chiefs found it impossible to get them together. I threatened to go off and leave everything behind, in which case the Government soldiers would come and fetch the things, and I should also report the matter to the Mudir.

Dsumbe had started for Badinde's on January 14th, with thirty loads, and Bohndorff on the 17th with the rest. The same afternoon my servant Belâl left for Palembata's with twenty loads. During this delay at Mbima's we had made a considerable inroad on our own provisions; but some, such as the macaroni and Khartum biscuits, were getting damaged, while plenty of supplies could now be had on the spot, the crops after the rainy season having already been garnered. Amongst them was *Hyptis spicigera*, an oleaginous plant resembling our poppy, which grows two or three feet high, and is much cultivated by the Zandehs for culinary purposes.

The nights were already cool enough to require a second coverlet on our beds. It is amazing how susceptible northerners are to these changes of temperature in hot climates, though all are not uniformly affected. The water kept cool in the leather bottles produced the same effect on my hands as iced water in Europe; the skin immediately turned red as a boiled crab, and this was often followed by a burning irritation like that of nettle-fever.

Now came the false report that the aged Prince Malingde, with his sons and also Ngerria, wanted to take sides with Mbio in the war against the Government troops and Ndoruma. However, my plans were not disturbed by these rumours, and on January 19th I was able to send off thirty loads, following myself with the rest two days after for Palembata's. I was attended on this journey by Farag 'Alláh, a newly-engaged Zandeh named Rensi, the little Dinka, Farag, and Belál, who had joined me at Binsa's. We followed the same route to Palembata's as in August the year before; but I again surveyed the ground, and was pleased to find that both results harmonized.

Our little chimpanzee had been ailing with a bad cough, just like that of a human being. My instructions to protect him in his basket with some matting from the rays of the sun had been neglected, and he died on the second day's march. The same day I had the mortification to find that some of the men had left their loads in the wilderness and bolted, conduct of which the Zandehs are rarely guilty. The things were soon missed and recovered; but to prevent a recurrence of the mishap, I formed the convoy in closer order, made a great show of loading the fire-arms, and threatened mercilessly to shoot the first man who attempted to make off. That told, and all went smooth as an oiled wheel for the rest of the journey.

At Zemio's first camp in Palembata's we diverged from the road followed on the former occasion. From this point Bohndorff had taken a westerly course to Badinde, while I now struck south to reach Palembata's residence. Along this last stretch all the rivulets flow to the Hako tributary of the Werre, whereas those met on the route to the A-Madi went straight to the

Welle. Thus Palembata's present residence lay on the water-parting between the Werre and the Welle-Makua.

I reached the camp in a somewhat sorry plight. My ass having suddenly stuck in a bog, I had hastened to his aid and was trying to get a fore-leg out, when he completely extricated himself with a single strenuous effort. Being unprepared for such a display of energy, I was thrown backwards into the slush before there was time to get out of the way.

Meanwhile my departure from Ndoruma's had been bruited about, and envoys from distant chiefs already awaited me at Palembata's. Yapati's messengers were again full of complaints against Rafai's officials; the A-Madi chief also, whom I intended next to visit, had sent to complain of internal troubles, urging me to come without delay.

But the greatest surprise was an embassy from Mambanga, headed by my former interpreter, Adatam, bringing rich offerings, such as a bundle of twelve new and choice Mangbattu spears, four finely-wrought trumbashes, a shield richly ornamented with copper, a gray parrot, and so on. Mambanga wanted me back again, for he was still, not without good reason, haunted by his dread of the Nubians. Though unable to accede to his request, I sent him numerous return gifts with the promise again to communicate with him from Bakangai's.

But while so highly honoured from without, I found myself sadly neglected by my host, Palembata, who had made little provision for my reception. The accommodation in the little huts was wretched, and the second day passed without any supplies. He pretended he had no corn on hand, and it was only after a sound rating that the young fop sent some telebun and sweet potatoes.

While still smarting under the indignity of this inhospitable welcome, I had already ordered the nugara (big drum) to be beaten to summon the carriers; presently the whole neighbourhood was alive with the ringing of bells and trumpet-blowing, which soon brought Palembata on his knees. His dejection lasted long enough for me to get the greater part of the loads sent off on January 24th and 25th to A-Madi Land. Belâl

ENVOYS WITH PRESENTS FROM MAMBANGA. (*Drawn by L. H. Fisher.*)

again conducted the first convoy, and the leader of each following convoy was supplied with a bundle of rods corresponding with the number of loads entrusted to him. In this way everything was controlled and verified at the end of the journey.

Before I could start myself the news came that Mbio had really invaded Ngettua's district, and that Mbima had already marched eastwards. He had heard of Mambanga's presents to me, and now wanted me to let him have five of the spears, which I flatly refused.

At last, on January 30th, I started for A-Madi Land, and after two good days' march towards the south-south-west, reached chief Masinde's. The district traversed differed little from the northern region, but was here and there more undulating and even hilly. Some isolated low mountains were visible on both sides of the route, though the eye was chiefly arrested by the more elevated crests rising on the southern horizon in the A-Madi country.

The whole district was well watered, the first rivulets beyond the Werre-Welle water-parting flowing to the Siri, which runs in a rocky bed eight yards wide eastwards to the Gurba; others follow a south-easterly course straight to the Welle. The last head-streams, met on the second day, go partly to form the Hekke, which flows south-west and west also to the Welle. Although the country itself is uninhabited, there was at that time a colony of Sheres (Bashirs) settled a few hours' south of Palembata's residence, so that I again met in the Far South a fragment of that people who are so widely scattered over the north. Their settlement marks the western terminus of Osman Bedawi's expedition to the A-Madi, and some traces of his last encampment were still visible.

With Masinde's district began the highly-favoured domain of the A-Madi, a distinct ethnical group differing in speech as well as in usages from the surrounding Zandehs, Mangbattus, and A-Barmbos. Their territory is bounded east, south, and west by the Welle, which, under the twenty-seventh meridian east of Greenwich, describes a vast bend to the south. The land is mountainous and copiously watered, with a productive soil yielding an abundance of valuable plants, which elsewhere occur only south of the Welle, and even then only in certain limited districts.

All these advantages must have long attracted the envy of foreign peoples, so that the history of A-Madi Land is a record of incessant wars and forays. Here the evils of war were intensified by the partition of the country from time immemorial into a number of petty states, whose chiefs were always fighting with each other, thereby giving more easy access to foreign enemies. Thus it was that several districts were now possessed by Zandeh and A-Barmbo princes; the Nubians also preferred to follow the A-Madi Land route on their southern expeditions, while Osman Bedawi had even founded a small station there garrisoned by ten Negro soldiers of the Bongo tribe under the Nubian, Mahmud.

A few years previously the A-Madi had been hard pressed by Zassi, who had stationed his dragomans at the residences of some of the southern chiefs for the purpose of collecting ivory. These powerless chiefs, always at feud with their neighbours, were often glad enough to have a few foreign muskets at hand with which to fall at the right moment on their rivals.

Owing to these internal dissensions, whole tribes of the A-Madi nation had either voluntarily migrated elsewhere or been forcibly expelled from their lands. Thus we found the Niapu living under the protection of the Mangbattus, while others had founded new homes amongst the eastern Zandehs ruled by Wando. At the time of my visit the most distinguished A-Madi chiefs were Mbittima (not to be confounded with Wando's son of that name) and Masinde, who, however, was a Zandeh by birth, brother in fact of Badinde. He had reduced to a state of vassalage the northern A-Madi about Mount Malingde, while Mbittima ruled over another branch of the nation in the central district of Mount Lingua; in the southern districts were other independent chiefs at enmity with Masinde and Mbittima.

After Osman Bedawi's departure these two princes also fell out, and at the time of my arrival they were ready to come to

PANORAMIC VIEW OF MOUNT MALINGDE. (*Drawn by L. H. Fischer.*)

blows. Hence endless palavers, at which I was entertained with their mutual wrongs and grievances. Masinde also endeavoured to prevent me from going south, describing the route as very unsafe. But to this I paid no heed, but at once sent Belâl and Farag 'Allâh to Bedawi's agent, Mahmud, at Mbittima's. Thereupon Mahmud came to see me with his dragomans under the guidance of my servants, for they would not have now ventured alone into Masinde's district, where I was meanwhile amusing the public in the usual way with my " stock-in-trade."

From Mahmud I learnt, what most concerned me, that the southern route was open, and that south of the Welle I should doubtless have no difficulty in getting carriers for the journey to Bakangai. A brother of Mbittima had come with Mahmud, and later followed another interminable palaver with Masinde on their internal affairs. I admonished all to keep the peace, warning them that, should hostilities break out, Osman Bedawi would soon return and punish the delinquents. I had especially to restrain Masinde, who was indulging in some warm language; but his intelligence and frank disposition otherwise enlisted my sympathies, and I was later brought into close and lasting relations with him.

On February 2nd a few heavy showers warned us of the approaching close of the dry season. Soon after I ascended Mount Malingde, the summit of which was reached by a circuitous route in about an hour. Although Malingde and Lingua are the highest eminences in the country, neither of them attains the relative altitude of one thousand feet. About half-way up we came upon a broad plateau marking the upper limit of the laterite formation, which in A-Madi Land is specially characterized by an intense yellow-red colour. Strata of a very hard reddish sandstone must here somewhere crop out, for although none was visible, I often noticed large slabs of this rock used as grindstones. I do not, however, pretend to determine the exact nature of the formation, for such rocks, apparently belonging to the sandstone group, also occur between deposits of real gneiss.

The upper part of the mountain consists of gneiss and granite masses of a blackish brown colour, presenting a great diversity of outlines caused by much weathering. Amid these rocks is a broad sedge-grown depression, where the A-Madi were wont to take refuge from sudden attacks of the enemy. The weather, which had been cloudy during the ascent, now cleared up, affording distinct views of the glassy waters of the Welle at three widely separated points towards the south-south-east, the south-west, and west-north-west. I had thus ocular demonstration of the already-mentioned great semi-circular bend here described by this river.

Southwards, at about two hours' distance, the gaze fell on Mount Lingua, and beyond it, but a little to the east, I detected far off Mount Angba; south of the narrow but still visible thread of the Welle the horizon was bounded by Mount Majanu in A-Barmbo Land, while to the right of Lingua another eminence could be descried in the extreme distance. But specially characteristic of an African landscape was the rolling and hilly tract extending from our immediate vicinity away to Mount Lingua. Here the broad undulating valley, stretching from mountain to mountain, was intersected by narrow belts of dark green vegetation, marking the winding courses of rivers and rivulets.

The broader patches of woodlands at the head of these long fringing avenues indicated the sources of streams and brooks which here take their rise. From the summit of Malingde the observer thus obtains a clear view of a highly-intricate hydrographic system, and marvels at the abundance of running waters increasing southwards in this favoured region. Here, also, I enjoyed the pleasant picture of peaceful life in a fertile and cultivated part of Negroland. At the very foot of the Malingde slopes, the habitations of the natives were embowered in the rich foliage of banana groves varied with clumps and even thickets of the stately oil-palm.

After taking my topographic observations on Malingde's breezy crest, I returned by a more easterly road, passing several A-Madi dwellings, some with pitched roofs and gables like those of the Mangbattus, others merely straw huts with conic roofs.

But the settlements were everywhere enclosed by luxuriant banana plantations, showing that this valuable plant supplies the A-Madi with their staple food.

On February 4th I continued my journey to Mahmud's station, which was only two hours' distant. The route trended southwards through a valley enclosed on the east by the spurs of Malingde, on the west by a line of low hills. Half an hour's march brought us clear of the mountainous district proper, though beyond it followed hill after hill, which, in the neighbourhood of the Lingua group, again merged in ridges of considerable elevation. Here the road lay over hill and dale, opening up wide prospects now in one, now in another, direction. Even the difficult swampy tracts along the wooded banks of the streams and in the bottom-lands were now and then relieved by open sunny stretches of wooded savannas.

Masinde's carriers, a somewhat unruly though harmless gang, had stopped half-way, as had been arranged, and now Belâl hastened forward to fetch fresh hands from Mbittima's station. Here we were overtaken by Farag 'Allâh with the rest of the loads; but I missed an iron stand, which is stuck in the ground and used for hanging clothes, hats, guns, and the like. It is a very serviceable article, much in vogue with the Nubians on their journeys through Negroland, and at each halting-place mine was always set up close to my chair. Not wishing to lose it, I quietly took from the last carriers five spears as a pledge for its return; by this stroke

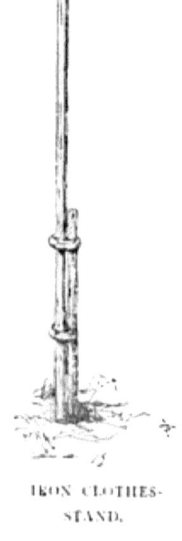

IRON CLOTHES-STAND.

I recovered it in a few days, and then Masinde got back his spears. The new hands arriving late in the afternoon, it was dark before we entered Mahmud's (Mbittima's) little station.

Several of the dragomans at this place had taken part in the

previous expedition to Bakangai's, and from them I got a detailed account of the route. On that occasion Osman Bedawi had employed Bongo carriers from the north, and in two good days' marches had covered the distance from the Welle southwards to the Bomokandi, beyond which river Bakangai's territory begins. But I had to depend on the A-Barmbos, and in order to get carriers would have to traverse the inhabited districts. Hence my route lay more to the west, where I was also informed that about a day's march west of the Welle a Zandeh colony was settled under a chief Mambanga, not to be confused with the Mangbattu prince of that name. From him I was most likely to get carriers, as he presumably held the surrounding A-Barmbos in subjection.

I should have gladly sent envoys from this station to Bakangai, but the people were too much afraid of the A-Barmbos dwelling south of the Welle. A few of their chiefs on this side of the river were subject to Mbittima, and they gave me hopes of obtaining men for the journey to the Zandeh chief, Mambanga. I had little trust in their assurances, and wanted first to go alone to Mambanga's without any baggage; but they made me all kinds of promises, and at last I yielded, trusting to my luck to pull me through. Thus, in a few days, after arranging with the Embata boatmen for crossing the river, I started with all my effects for the Welle.

From the local chiefs I had received supplies of bananas, poultry, palm-oil, batatas, manioc, a little telebun and maize. I made several successful experiments with the bananas; the green, unripe fruit may be treated in various ways like our potatoes. Sliced and roasted in all stages of maturity, they make an excellent dish. But they may be also grated in the raw state, and then fried in batter like pancakes, and so on. The natives prepare a banana-flour, which, however, is greatly improved when mixed with grated tubers or with various kinds of corn-flour. The Zandehs call the banana *hira*, the A-Madi *a'buggo;* but there are so many varieties that several different words are required to express them. The *badingo* of the Mangbattus, that is, ripe bananas dried over the fire or in the sun, will keep for months together, and when sliced and cooked in palm-oil make a savoury dish.

Palm-oil itself I soon got accustomed to, so that it gradually entered into the preparation of nearly all kinds of food. In these parts the natives have an original method of packing and carrying it. The jar when filled is lightly covered with strips of fresh banana leaves, from which the raised mid-rib has been removed. Over this is placed a second covering of long strips

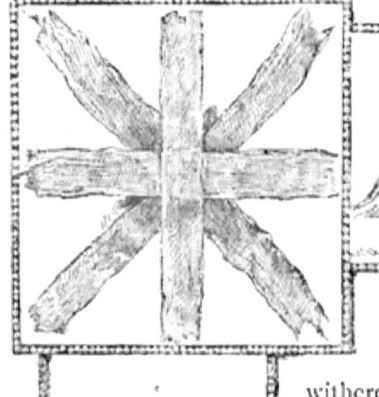

PACKING PALM-OIL.

made from the outer dry bark of banana-stalks, which, when withered, are as firm as bast; thus several layers of such strips crossed one over the other form a hermetical covering. The vessel is then tilted over and wrapped round its sides with the long, over-hanging ends of the strips, and this envelopment gathered together in a bunch at the bottom of the jar; a plaited loop of the same material is now passed through the bunch to serve as a handle, by means of which the vessel is slung on the shoulder and carried mouth downwards.

On February 8th I ascended Mount Lingua; owing to the rugged character of its craggy western slope, it must be approached from the north side, at whose foot the little river Oggae flows in a deep wooded bed. Amid the banana and oil-palm groves were scattered the dwellings of the A-Madi, who, in accordance with national usage, brought us the produce of their soil, and even laid some spears respectfully at our feet. The highly-cultivated ground extended some distance up, and from the point where all cultivation ceased it took us still half an hour to reach the upper plateau, from which the supreme rocky cone rose to a height of about eighty feet. This fissured crag could be scaled only on the north side, and on top presented room for scarcely a dozen men. Here some overhanging ledges formed little caverns, and one far-projecting rock when struck with a stone loudly reverberated like a huge gong.

Although the prospect was clouded, we could still descry the Welle at several points, while Mount Angba was more conspicuous than when seen from Malingde. South-eastwards Lingua is separated by a broad saddleback from the slightly more elevated Balimassango, whose rocky walls fall in some places precipitously southwards. Balimassango is itself connected with a third eminence, Mount Girro, so that the whole system forms a continuous range.

Towards the north Malingde masked the view, which in this direction was confined to the broad valley extending between the mountain groups and to the northern hills visible from Lingua. But on either side a wide prospect was commanded of the distant prairie, where my followers detected a dark line of men crossing the distant plane. These proved later to be the people of a remote chief who were coming to welcome me.

The steep southern flank of Lingua led down to Mbittima's settlements, beyond which the track wound along the foot of the mountain through some brushwood, where the natives had laid some snares for genettes. These consisted of long, low enclosures of cane-stakes, interrupted at intervals by passages scarcely a foot wide, but seven or eight feet long, which were fenced by double rows of similar stakes. Over the passages were lightly poised heavy beams to fall upon and crush the animals as they crept through.

In Mahmud's station two Bongo dragomans had died during the last week. So the others fancied they also might be bewitched by the A-Madi, and consequently wanted to be allowed to return home. I pointed out the folly of such superstition, and thus induced them to remain.

The loads were now again forwarded in batches to the Welle, which river I reached on February 10th. The route ran for several hours south-westwards through Mbittima's territory, then westwards through the district of the A-Bangbaras, an

SNARES FOR GENETTES (*Viverra genetta*).

A-Barmbo tribe. The land was again uniformly undulating, without any chains of hills or mountains, which are confined to the northern part of A-Madi Land. Soon after leaving the station we crossed the Oggae, which, like all others within the bend of the Welle, is an unimportant stream; rising in the enclosed tract, they have necessarily a short course to the

Welle. Nevertheless, in the rainy season they are swollen by the mountain torrents, and become themselves impetuous mountain streams, rushing through gorges and deeply excavated channels.

The Welle, whose swollen stream had excited my admiration on the journey with Zemio, was now at low-water mark, and many rocky ledges appeared above the surface. Its bed, about eight hundred and thirty feet wide, was confined between steep banks, and very deep towards the south side. Here a pole twenty feet long failed to reach the bottom, although the water had subsided fully to that extent and even more, for during the floods it overflows its highest margin.

The section of the Welle here visible, a stretch of about two and a half miles, had a northerly trend. My position on the river was for the moment all the more critical that I could get no news of the Zandeh chief, Mambanga, who, the reader will remember, had been represented to me as ruling over a section of the A-Barmbo nation. A person had also presented himself at Mahmud's station, pretending to have come from Mambanga, who wanted to know why we delayed our visit to him so long.

At the time I believed all this; but now that I had reached the Welle, and not a soul was to be seen on the opposite side, my suspicions were again awakened, and I at once despatched Farag 'Allàh to the Zandeh chief. To be sure the Embata people suggested that perhaps the A-Barmbos had not arrived because they lived a long way from the river.

As a relief from my brooding thoughts, I occupied myself with the Embata fishing-folk, for whose methods of capture the low state of the river offered favourable conditions. I tried my hand at the primitive process, but with little success. The use of nets being unknown, they set up strong traps along the banks and amongst the ledges of rock in mid-stream. But though little is taken in this way, the Welle undoubtedly abounds in fish, and should have many surprises for the specialist. I obtained from the Embatas some cat-fish, and another peculiar fish about a foot long, distinguished by a fleshy underlip four inches long.

Meantime Mahmud and Mbittima arrived with the last loads,

while Farag 'Allâh returned with far from satisfactory tidings of Mambanga. From his report it became evident that all the statements made about this Zandeh chief were false, and that he had not so much as heard of me, much less of our intended visit. Regarding his person, I learnt that he was doubtless sprung of a princely Zandeh line, which had formerly ruled over all the A-Barmbo tribes, but that at present he had only a few adherents, and was powerless in the land. He would, however, have some huts erected for us, and expressed himself very eager to see us as soon as possible, though unfortunately he had no carriers for so many things, and I would have to forward the loads by the A-Barmbos. In support of this invitation he had sent a few of his people with Farag 'Allâh.

I had already secured the good-will of the Embatas by presents, and it was now all-important to induce them to act as carriers. But while I was treating with Senu, one of their local chiefs, about getting my things across the river to the nearest A-Barmbo huts, Bassansa, an A-Barmbo chief from beyond the Welle, presented himself, and volunteered to forward the loads to Mambanga. In reply to my question whether he had sufficient carriers, he laughed, and with his hands made the usual gesture signifying "many."

In their calculations the native scarcely gets beyond 10, and even then has often recourse to gesture language. He expresses 10 by raising both hands; for 15, if standing, he grasps the right leg, if seated, the foot with both hands, by which he means to add 5 toes to the 10 fingers. For 20 he grasps a leg or a foot with each hand, thereby expressing 10 fingers *plus* 10 toes = 20. To indicate the intermediate numerals, he first of all expresses by pantomimic action the basal numbers, 5, 10, 15, 20, and then supplies the required digits by grasping a corresponding number of left fingers with the right hand. Forty is indicated by placing the hands twice on the thighs; 60 by touching the legs three times, which makes 20 + 20 + 20, and so on. The numeral 100 already implies a scarcely-intelligible quantity, involving the concept "many," "multitude," at which his mental efforts and powers of calculation begin to flag;

hence he has recourse to rapid and frequent clapping of hands on legs, thus giving expression to an indefinite number, something for him unlimited.

As this was Bassansa's pantomimic reply to my question, I was fain to conclude that he had sufficient hands at his disposal, all the more that he offered to have them ready next morning. I thereupon unsuspiciously sent over one hundred loads across to the south side the same evening. As there were no huts to house them, I had them carefully covered and left in charge of three of Mahmud's Bongo dragomans.

We followed next day with asses, goats, and the rest of the things. But it was hours before we got over, for the Embatas had removed their boats, and their attitude now pointed at extortion. In all this Senu professed to desire nothing more from me; but he had unquestionably instigated his people and those of another Embata chief, Bamadsi, to clamour for more, so that many pressed round and had to be "tipped" before they would take us across.

But this was not all. Many others, who had followed with their wives and children in boats, now became very importunate, while I began at once to distribute the loads, regardless of their obstreperous conduct: for Bassansa had presented himself, though with only forty-five carriers, but assuring me that the rest would follow without delay. Then occurred an incident which had well-nigh ended in a disaster. One of my maid-servants detecting a theft, hailed me just as the pilferer was making for his boat with a small load of salt. Enraged at the sight, and also in order to overawe the mob, I seized my rifle and advanced a few steps in a threatening attitude. Thereupon the whole rabble took to their heels, rushing helter-skelter down the steep bank to their boats, many women, children, and others tumbling into the water. Perceiving the danger, I at once stepped back to allay the panic, while Senu restored confidence.

Soon after Belâl went off with Bassansa and forty-five loads; later I sent forward a few more A-Barmbo chiefs with convoys of ten and fifteen loads, but had myself to remain behind with nearly half of my effects. I parted from Senu and his boatmen

EMBATA CHIEFERS. (*Drawn by L. H. Fischer.*)

on friendly terms, informing them of Bohndorff's approaching arrival.

In the evening some Embatas, chiefly women, came over to collect termites, which were now expected to take wing with the beginning of the rainy season. But I had to face a shelterless night in an African wilderness, for no sign of human habitations was visible far and wide. After vainly awaiting the promised carriers, I placed the loads by a small ant-hill, where my few people, Farag 'Alláh, the young Dinka (Farag), and the maid-servants, encamped for the night. A frugal meal was soon consumed, and twilight was quickly followed by darkness, the nearly full moon being concealed for the first hours by the banking-up rain-clouds.

Presently, as I was seated moodily on my angareb, my little dog began to give tongue, darting round the ant-hill, where some loads were also heaped up. After some more yelping "Lady" trotted quietly back, and I, without suspecting anything wrong, ascended the hill and then took the road leading from the river southwards. I had gone a few steps when I stood still, more mechanically than for the purpose of prying about. In the immediate vicinity some fresh grass had sprung up in the midst of the withered herbage, and just where the track reached this spot my gaze fell upon a shadow; but, at that moment, the moon, which had shone out later in the evening, again disappeared behind the rain-clouds. I now approached a little nearer, when a figure suddenly started up scarcely ten paces from where I stood, and beat a hasty retreat in a stooping attitude. I thought it might be one of the women engaged in collecting the termites, but who had been scared by the barking of the dog. So I told Farag 'Alláh, who had hastened up, to call out and disalarm the fleeing shadow. But I was soon disabused of this idea, for on searching the grass we found one of my boxes on the spot where the figure had been crouching.

Being convinced that we were surrounded by thieves, I took extra precautions, and for the rest of the night mounted guard on the ant-hill armed with two rifles. But nothing further occurred, and next morning Belál brought the unpleasant news that a box was missing from the things sent off the day before. Similar reports came in later, whereupon the Embata carriers were charged with stealing. Meanwhile, other A-Barmbo chiefs presented themselves with more men, and as there was no alternative, I had to accept them, taking the usual precaution to note their names.

I now opened negotiations with the Embata, temporizing with Senu, well knowing him to be accessory to the pilferings. I had induced him to come over by the offer of various presents, promising many more on his recovering the stolen goods for me. Thereupon he went straight up the river, returning in a couple of hours with a tin box which had been forced open, and from which Bohndorff's clothes and linen were now missing. The thieves, however, had left the boots and shoes and other things useless to them, but indispensable to Bohndorff.

On the promise of more presents, Senu soon brought back another box, mostly containing objects used by Bohndorff in collecting specimens. Thus passed the second day with the dismal prospect of spending another shelterless night on the inhospitable shores of the Welle. In the evening the firmament became overcast, dense masses of vapour and black clouds gathering from all quarters, and at last discharging a heavy and continuous downpour, which left us in a miserable plight.

Next morning the sun refused to shine, and we remained shivering for hours in our wet clothes. But towards noon Mambanga arrived with about twenty-five men of his tribe, and fifteen loads were at once sent forward. But the others refused to lend a hand, until the rain coming on again they consented to take up the loads, and so we at last got away from our dreary camping-ground on the Welle.

The route ran westwards through a slightly rolling district, leading in an hour's march to the first A-Barmbo huts. Their settlements now followed in quick succession at intervals of fifteen or twenty minutes along the track. We were beset with swarms of yelling women and children, but few of the loafers about the huts were willing to relieve our Zandeh carriers. By sunset we reached our goal, an isolated group of wretched cabins standing at some considerable distance from Mambanga's residence. Here, again, the first tidings were about more pilferings; but I was too weary to interest myself in anything, and sank supperless and exhausted on my couch.

Next morning an inspection showed a load of salt and some ammunition missing, while from a box that had been forced they had abstracted our whole stock of arsenic required for preserving skins, besides the metal handle of the large barrel-organ. The rascals had also by sheer force raised the thin lids

SHELTERLESS ON THE WELLE.

of several of the Berlin tin boxes, and thus without breaking the locks taken out linen, clothes, cloth—in fact, whatever could be hastily abstracted.

The original home of the A-Barmbo people is inclosed by the Welle and Bomokandi rivers, though even south of the Bomokandi A-Barmbo tribes are found as far west and east as the Makongo and Pokko rivers respectively. On the south bank of the Welle they are conterminous eastwards with the territory of the Mangbattu prince, Mambanga. They are a numerous nation, whose strength has been frittered away by the chronic state of strife prevailing amongst their countless petty chiefs. Thus they were reduced to a condition of vassalage by the Zandehs, and the A-Barmbo tribes south of the Bomokandi were now subject to Prince Bakangai, while the northern groups had again asserted their independence.

But the Zandeh colonies, which were still settled under their own chiefs north of the Bomokandi, had migrated thither at the time when the Zandeh prince, Kipa, Bakangai's father, ruled over the whole A-Barmbo nation. Thus the Zandeh prince, Mambanga himself, was the son of Ingimma and grandson of Kipa. He had managed to maintain his independence amid the numerous little A-Barmbo chiefs, but possessed no power over them, and lived, as he himself confessed, in constant fear of his life.

Similar relations prevailed amongst the Zandeh colonies which were settled in the western parts of A-Barmbo Land. They were ruled by Bandia, Bangatelli, Nbasso, Baggi, and Kamsa, either sons or more distant kinsmen of Kipa. But none of them displayed any power except Kamsa, whose residence lay near the Bomokandi-Welle confluence.

My mistrust of the A-Barmbos was now sedulously fostered by the young and inexperienced Mambanga, who informed me that the surrounding A-Medio, A-Badunga, and A-Bukunda tribes, who were chiefly professional carriers, had been guilty of the recent pilferings. It may be mentioned that our nearest neighbours were the A-Bangele, while farther east were many other tribes, including the A-Mesima, through whose territory lay Osman Bedawi's line of march to Bakangai's.

But Mambanga also warned me about my next journey to Bakangai's, and pretended to know that the A-Barmbo intended to plunder me on the two days' march through the wilderness to the Bomokandi. He even feared I might be poisoned, and cautioned me especially against drinking merissa. However, my mistrust did not go so far; nor did I care to deprive my household of this nourishing beverage. So to remove their fears I would myself take a glass with them.

Prudence, however, warned me to await the arrival of Bohndorff, with whom our further plans could be more easily carried out. Hence I anticipated a lengthy stay at this place, and as the two huts assigned to us afforded insufficient accommodation, I provided for better shelter. In this I had the ready aid of Mambanga's people, while the A-Bangele lounged about without moving a finger to help us. I should have sent messengers to Bakangai, but for the fears entertained by the people, and I only too soon became cognizant of other reasons which prompted Mambanga to oppose the expedition.

The sullen attitude of Bassansa and the other A-Barmbo chiefs naturally surprised me, and awakened the suspicion that they really harboured some sinister designs against me. So the days went by in constant care and watchfulness, while the Zandehs themselves seemed to have struck work; the huts remained unfinished, and my things, goats and asses, and guards at night, continued without shelter against the weather.

On February 20th, five days after our arrival, the report was spread that a stranger had arrived at the Welle, but the Embatas refused to supply the boats to cross over. Thinking it was Bohndorff, I sent off Farag 'Allâh, who reported that the news was false, but that the stolen things would be returned. At last one of the A-Bangele chiefs called on me, and I left nothing unsaid to show him how foolish it was of the natives to hold aloof.

About the same time there arrived an ostensible envoy from Basingebanno, an A-Mesima chief, announcing that Bakangai had been inquiring of him about us. The same person soon after presented himself again, requesting to know whether Basingebanno might send messengers to Bakangai in my name. Though giving no credit to all this, I still wished no chance to be lost, so sent presents also to this Basingebanno. Later I learnt that those messages were all lies and inventions.

Now Mambanga gave out that he had heard from a female slave that the A-Barmbos wanted to kill me; hence, fearing for his own life also, he besought me not to associate with the people unarmed, and to forbid too numerous visits at the same time. But I had my own suspicions of Mambanga's motives, and in the meantime sent Farag 'Allâh and Belâl with presents to the surrounding chiefs, in the hope of opening up friendly relations with them. It now appeared that my suspicions were not groundless, and that Mambanga was really scheming to keep the A-Barmbos alienated from me. They thought I intended supporting his pretensions to sovereignty over them, as he had himself declared that my soldiers would soon be here. Nor could I even later dispel this fear, for it was assiduously fostered by the Zandeh chief.

All the greater was my surprise when one day a bundle of clothes reached me, which, as I was now told, had been abstracted from the boxes by the A-Badungas. Many were soiled by the red laterite earth, but otherwise intact, except the metal buttons, which had all been cut off from the trousers. The restitution was very welcome, as showing that the numerous designs against my life and property were all phantoms of Mambanga's brain, and based on his own fears.

The huts being at last finished, I took possession of my new home on February 25th. About this time I noticed a most remarkable natural phenomenon. One morning on leaving my hut I saw a somewhat yellowish white mass thrown up like little mole-hills in many places that had been cleared of the grass. When examined it was found greatly to resemble fresh whey-cheese passed through a sieve, but contained some hard round white grains like tapioca. The whole was the product of a species of termite, and I even found a few little insects embedded in the white substance. Whether the grains were eggs, as seemed probable, I must leave undecided, for then the question would arise, why they should have been brought to the surface and thus exposed to destruction. Or could this be taken as an instance of "cussedness" in nature?

Meantime my servants had enclosed the places with bits of stick and covered them with foliage, assuring me that something good to eat would soon appear. Then followed the most singular phase in this puzzling process. The upper surface of the little heaps, which had been steadily enlarged by accumulations from within, appeared in a few hours overgrown with tiny white mushrooms, distinctly formed, though scarcely a millimetre, say the twenty-sixth part of an inch, in size. These little fungi now began to shoot up on graceful slender stems, and next day

TERMITE HARVEST.

were already from one to two inches high, and were then eaten as dainty morsels by the natives, ever on the look-out for eatables. I had a dish of them prepared for myself, and found them excellent. After their removal the little heaps began to shrink, and at last crumbled away to dust.

I have already remarked that with the commencement of the rainy season, the natives also begin to gather certain species of termites. Weeks before the "harvest," the people mark off those nests which seem most suitable for their purpose. Here they dig a round hole a foot wide and several feet deep, whereby the place is at the same time set apart for a certain person and left untouched by the others. Like everybody else, my servants had done this, and also prepared a quantity of long bundles of dry grass, which here take the place of the resinous torches elsewhere in use.

Rainy days and excessive moisture are unfavourable conditions for the appearance of the termites, which may be safely expected on fine evenings following sunny days. Then the people may everywhere be seen with their flaming brands squatting down each at the hole which he had dug at the foot of the hill reserved for him. The female termites creeping out go straight to the fire without actually rising on the wing; others soar into the air, but also partly wheel round towards the light, while the rest fly away. Those approaching the hole are all swept in with tufts of foliage. Many lose their wings, and most of them are in a dazed state, so that they are afterwards easily transferred to baskets, sacks, or pots. The termites for the most part take wing during several successive days, or else at intervals in bad weather.

To my great relief, Bohndorff's anxiously-awaited arrival took place on February 27th. "Lady" was the first, late one evening, to announce his approach by a friendly whimper, while he was still a long way off. Presently Dsumbe entered and told me they had crossed the Welle without accident, and readily found carriers for their few effects. Bohndorff remained for the night on the way, while Dsumbe hastened forward to report the news, which caused great rejoicings amongst our people. Early next morning he returned with Farag 'Alláh and Belál to Bohndorff, who soon after made his appearance in excellent health, and with the glad tidings that his mission had proved successful.

I will not here touch upon the geographical results of his expedition, as I had later to visit the same northern region myself. I may state, however, that he carefully surveyed the route, and the working up of his materials occupied several hours of my time during the following weeks. He had gone, as arranged, from Badinde across the Werre and through Yapati's district to the Deleb zeriba, the chief Nubian settlement in Rafai's domain. But Rafai himself was absent, and his people were too mistrustful to take charge of my things, so that Bohndorff, according to arrangement against this contingency, pushed on three days farther west to Zassa's, and consigned the reserved loads to his care. Thereafter Bohndorff returned by a more westerly route southwards to the Werre, and so on to the Welle through Zassa's vassal lands, where his present itinerary was connected with that of his previous expedition to Kipa's. The next stretch brought him eastwards to A-Madi Land, where exaggerated reports of my losses by pilferings induced him to hasten forward to our trysting-place.

Hitherto no change had taken place in our relations with the A-Barmbos. Hearing nothing further from the A-Mesima people or from Basingebanno, on March 3rd I sent thither Dsumbe and Belāl with more presents. Their report confirmed my suspicions that Basingebanno had never sent us any messengers. My servants were also badly received, the A-Mesima threatening even to put them to death should they ever again venture to show themselves there. Thus vanished my last hope of perhaps getting through with a few loads to Bakangai's by the aid of the A-Mesima. I was also frustrated in my intention first to send most of the things back to the station in A-Madi Land. Yet some place of safety had to be found for the loads before I could carry out any other plans.

Mambanga himself now began to betray his real motives. He openly complained of my wishing to return, his main hope being that help would after all come from the north, and that perhaps men with fire-arms might be stationed with him, in which case he would make short work of the A-Barmbos. At the same time he regretted, while wishing to keep me, that he had not sufficient supplies for all of us, suggesting, however, that I might send the A-Barmbo chiefs as many rods as I wanted bunches of bananas from each, that being the way paramount lords dealt with their vassals. Such a step, which in any case would have had no result, I of course declined to take, being particularly anxious to avoid everything that might cause offence to the A-Barmbos.

Yet, at this juncture, my sorest trouble was undoubtedly the food question. Bohndorff had replaced the servants who had run off at Ndoruma's, with three other lads, so that we had now nine servants and five girls to provide for. There was still a good store of dried bananas, and sweet potatoes were also procurable. Every day the girls also gathered some of the wild meluchia (*Corchorus olitorius*), the boiled leaves of which form a favourite accompaniment to the native porridge. I preferred the wild meluchia (pimpernel, or "Jews' mallow") even to the variety cultivated by the Nubians; it also grows to a much larger size, especially in moist depressions, and might serve as a valuable article of the export trade. But we were running short of our staple food—corn—so that I could only allow a little maize and telebun to be baked every other day for myself and Bohndorff.

Meanwhile our people had erected another hut for Bohndorff and a few smaller ones for themselves, and I also had a spacious verandah constructed for my work. But all was open to the wilderness, at some distance from any settlements, plantations, or banana groves, and close to our huts the prairie grass was now already several feet high. The absence of any enclosures produced an uncomfortable feeling of insecurity, although the traveller gradually learns to regard with indifference what may at first have seemed dangerous.

There was some justification for Mambanga's assumption that help must come from the north, and I was myself driven to look in that direction for aid, after all my efforts had failed to bring relief. There was a probability of Osman Bedawi's passing this way on his expedition to Bakangai's; but many months might pass before that happened. On the other hand, Zassa was soon to visit his vassal states, when he would come to the Welle. Hence I relied exclusively on Zassa and his people to

OUR HUTS AT THE ZANZEH CHIEF MAMBANGA'S. (*Drawn by L. H. Fischer.*)

rescue us from the snare into which we had fallen. But he also might postpone his expedition, unless informed of our critical position, and I therefore decided at once to send him messengers. I despatched Dsumbe for one of his dragomans stationed with the A-Barmbos north of the Welle, and on his arrival I learnt that but for Zassa's support the Embatas would cause me much trouble. This was another reason for communicating with Zassa, so the dragoman went back on March 9th, accompanied by Dsumbe. I kept the matter secret, and gave out that Dsumbe was gone to fetch a long-expected postal despatch from A-Madi Land.

By a lucky coincidence what was stated merely as a pretext proved a reality, for Dsumbe actually brought some letters from Europe when he returned on March 12th, with several dragomans from Mbittima's station. Since September of the previous year, when I was encamped with Zemio on the Welle, no home news had reached me; but the feelings awakened by such incidents are of too personal a nature entirely to enlist the reader's sympathies.

A despatch from Gessi caused some anxiety, for it brought the first news of the terrible disaster on the Bahr el-Ghazal, with the certainty that the work begun by him would have to be continued by other hands. I learnt at the same time that the administration of Mangbattu Land had been transferred from Gessi to Emin Bey, governor of the Equatorial province. Dsumbe further reported that my dragoman had continued his journey from Mahmud's station to Zassa's. Still, according to every calculation, it would take at least a month before the expected aid could reach me.

Meanwhile our commissariat difficulties increased. The attempts to purchase supplies failed chiefly because the natives had no standard whereby to determine the value of their produce, hence made such absurd demands that our enraged servants mostly returned empty-handed. Having too large a household for present requirements, I sent off four boys and two girls with Farag 'Allâh to Mahmud's station. They were followed later by my cook, Saida, whose intolerable attitude towards the natives had often annoyed me, and who was now a confirmed invalid.

So passed weeks of weary expectation, their monotony broken only by fresh rumours and diverse trifling episodes. Repeated reports came of Zassa's arrival at the Welle, where, however, he could get no boats from the Embatas to cross over. The A-Barmbos doubtless suspected that I was expecting his arrival, as on former occasions also he had reached the Welle.

Once Dsumbe fired at an antelope, whereupon all the Zandehs ushed up fully equipped for war, supposing we had already

A FALSE ALARM.

come to blows with the A-Barmbos. Amongst the A-Madi it was even given out that we had already been "eaten up," the rumour circumstantially adding that I had been simultaneously pierced by four assegais. Farag 'Allâh, who at the time was staying at Mahmud's, was terribly startled, and at once hastened with four dragomans to the river, whither he was to be followed by Mbittima, and even by Masinde, to take the field against the A-Barmbos. Later he learnt that it was all lies, and on March 21st came to tell me all about the scare.

As I have already remarked, the rainy season begins in these southern lands much earlier than in the north. Here a short interval of several fine days in the first half of March was followed by frequent and heavy thunder-showers. Such tropical storms as I often witnessed in A-Barmbo Land seemed to me overwhelmingly grand, for Nature here revealed herself in her full might and majesty. The massed clouds, ranging from gray-blue to deep black, roll up menacingly, and are often preceded by a light foggy wall of dense vapour, which seems to press sheer upon the spectator; and this lighter mass of haze drives incessantly before the storm Fury, whose approach is heralded by a wild roar. Then, without an instant's delay, I would call upon our people to quench the camp-fires; for my long experience in tropical lands had taught me how urgent was the danger, and how easily at these times the huts may be enveloped in flames.

But the gale, nearly always from the east, has already rent the light volumes of vapour, and then fall the first heavy raindrops, or else the tempest rolls away to the west without discharging any rain. But soon the whole firmament is again overcast with the darkness of night, the hurricane whirls round, streaks of lightning resembling strings of pearls flash from every quarter, the storm rolls back, the peals of thunder grow louder, and at last the lowering welkin discharges a torrential downpour.

During the last days of March the chase yielded us an abundant supply of meat. Farag 'Allâh and Dsumbe had taken to hunting, and one day returned late, with the aid of some natives, dragging along sundry parts of a young buffalo. The capture had nearly cost Dsumbe his life, for the beast had knocked him over in the tall grass of a depression, and was about to make for him again, when a lucky shot from Farag 'Allâh arrested its career. A part of the spoils had been given to the A-Barmbo in return for their help, though this did not prevent them from stealing more on the way back in the darkness. Still there remained a good supply, of which I reserved for myself the brain, the tongue, and the feet. Some was also bartered on reasonable terms for corn, the natives evidently estimating flesh at a higher rate than my wares.

In case Zassa should come to the rescue with carriers, I intended to send most of the things with Bohndorff back to Zassa's, and then await the arrival of Osman Bedawi in A-Madi Land, in the hope of still reaching Bakangai's under his escort. In the hope of getting tidings of Osman and Zassa I again sent Dsumbe to the A-Madi; but all he brought back was the unpleasant threat made him by the A-Barmbos to cut off our road to the river.

THUNDERSTORM IN A-BARMBO LAND.

Thus our troubles were daily increased, my own people adding to my worries. Even Farag 'Alláh disappointed me, though he had been years in my service. I had given him Saida as a wife at their joint request, and conferred many privileges upon him; yet he was often so troublesome that I had even threatened to discharge him.

For a change I seized the opportunity of trying to throw out a feeler in the direction of the south. One day Mambanga introduced a person ostensibly as an envoy from Bakangai. I may incidentally mention how this Zandeh lordling attempted to maintain his dignity on the occasion of this visit. I had on principle for some time back discontinued offering him a chair; so one of his lieges had to serve the purpose with his lap, on which Mambanga gravely took his seat. The envoy now represented that Bakangai knew nothing of our being here. Thereupon I showed him some of my things, remarking that many were intended for his prince; I even gave him a few trifles for Bakangai, although attaching little credence to his statements. Anyhow this last attempt to open communication with the south was no more successful than the others.

At last, on April 10th, came the welcome news from Mahmud's station that Zassa had reached the Welle. But my anxiety was at first rather increased, for what I dreaded had actually happened. On the one hand, the Embatas refused Zassa's people the boats to cross over; on the other we were threatened by the A-Barmbos, who feared that Zassa intended invading their territory. Their ill-feeling was at first directed against my servants, whom I had at once sent off to bring about concerted action with Zassa. They blocked the way to the Welle, and were so menacing that my men had to return in all haste, although escorted by some of Mambanga's Zandehs.

Mambanga himself was highly delighted at Zassa's arrival, hoping that all his ambitious plans would now be realized. Thus we stood between two, or rather three, fires, and we felt that our rescue depended entirely on a wise and resolute action on the part of Zassa. Any rash movement, such as an attempt to force the passage of the river, might have the consequence of exposing us to the full fury of the A-Barmbos. I trusted, however, that their well-known dread of our rifles and revolvers, a common topic of conversation amongst the people, would prevent them from openly attacking us. All available fire-arms were now produced and kept loaded for any emergency, and on inspection I found that we had over one hundred and twenty shots at our command to meet a sudden onslaught.

While I was meditating a personal visit to Zassa, two

messengers unexpectedly arrived from him. They had been allowed to pass through without molestation, whereas it was reported beyond the river that my servants had been killed. I immediately sent back the messengers to warn Zassa against any rash step, and not to cross the Welle without the consent of the A-Barmbos. Fresh envoys now arrived from the river, amongst them the son of Senu, with whom Zassa had meantime made blood-brotherhood. They wanted to know whether Senu was to ferry over Zassa's people or not. This was, of course, merely a way of asking for presents, which they received with instructions on their return to explain to the A-Barmbos that Zassa's people were coming only to bring away my effects, and would not cross the river against their wish. Zassa himself, however, secretly asked for a supply of percussion-caps, which I sent him, so that he might be ready for any contingency.

Fresh alarms were now started by Mambanga, who pretended to have positive information that the A-Barmbos, who had been watching Zassa's movements from their side of the river, had withdrawn with the intention of falling upon us. Consequently, we all kept vigilant watch throughout the night of April 13th, which, however, passed without any disturbance.

Next day more messengers from Zassa brought us some bananas, as it had been reported to him that we were in great straits for food. On Zassa's arrival at the Welle, the Embatas had crossed with their boats to the opposite side, and Senu's son alone plied to and fro in a small boat as intermediary between both parties. It was evident that the Embatas were acting in concert with the A-Barmbos. But a decided change for the better occurred on April 14th, when another messenger from Zassa arrived, in company with many Embatas and Senu himself, who reported that the A-Barmbos were now willing to convey my loads to the Welle. But I demurred, having already been warned by Zassa against this course. I spoke very firmly, pointing out that my life might be sacrificed, but the A-Barmbos should understand that Osman Bedawi would soon arrive, and also that a brother of mine was on the way down stream, and then they would all be ruthlessly destroyed. This last pill

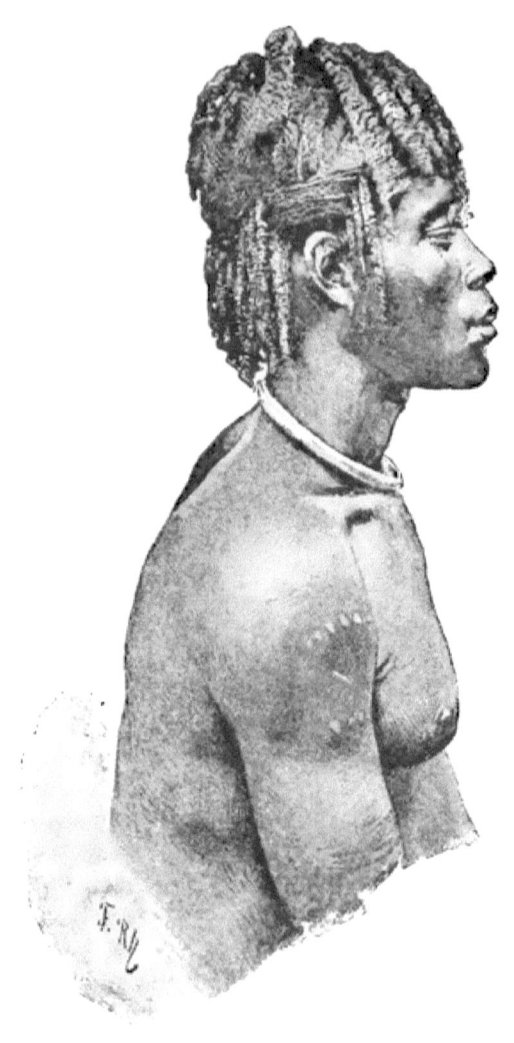

A ZANDEH. (*Drawn by Fr. Rheinfelder, from a photograph by R. Buchta.*)

was aimed specially at the Embatas, who were somewhat over-confident in the possession of their boats.

Meanwhile, Zassa had ventured to send me thirty of his carriers accompanied by a party of Embatas, all of whom passed through unmolested by the A-Barmbos. A day or two after their arrival, Bohndorff got away with a first convoy of thirty loads, returning next day from Zassa's camp. After they had started, many A-Barmbos came and also offered to act as carriers to the river. But I again flatly declined their services, and in a long speech made their mouths water at all the fine things they had lost by obstinately avoiding me, either through senseless fear or evil intentions.

Then out came all the musical instruments, but only a few tantalizing notes were doled out from each, while I kept up a running commentary on what they had missed, particularly in the way of presents which I had brought specially for them, but were now forfeited through their ill-advised action. Then I told them how amongst other Negro peoples even the women approached me fearlessly, how their children sat on my knee and received shiny beads; this was for the benefit of a number of A-Badungas who had gathered round with their wives and children, while I was holding forth.

The somewhat crestfallen people now began to collect from all quarters, even swarming up the trees to get a sight of me. Many assured me that had they known and heard all this before, they should certainly have visited me; nor did they harbour any hostile intentions at all, but on the contrary were rather afraid of me. Next day more came squatting round, making themselves comfortable while satisfying their curiosity with all the wonderful sights.

On April 17th I managed to send off another batch of fifty-two loads, and this was for me the pleasantest way of celebrating the feast of Easter. Two days later more carriers from Zassa enabled me to forward all that remained. But at this peaceful issue Mambanga presented a doleful picture; for him it meant the shipwreck of his amicable views with regard to his A-Barmbo neighbours, and he could now only hope that perhaps Zassa might be persuaded by me to leave him the protection of a few soldiers.

April 20th saw my final release; yet it was with mingled feelings that I quitted the inhospitable place, where I had passed over two months in a kind of imprisonment. It was pleasant enough to get away from these frail huts, which threatened to collapse with every storm, and leave behind me all cares and troubles about our daily bread and even our very lives. But, on the other hand, it was bitter to reflect that this enforced retreat thrust further and further into the background my cherished hopes of visiting Bakangai. During this very retreat the A-Barmbo still held aloof, only a few here and there venturing a stealthy glance as we passed. Yet a time was coming when we were destined to become better friends, and till then a detailed account of this people may be deferred.

The aspect of the Welle had much changed since February. The flat rocky ledges at that time showing above the surface had now vanished beneath the swollen stream, which during the last few days had risen ten feet. I crossed rapidly over and rejoined Bohndorff in Zassa's camp, where I now gave myself up to the repose so much needed after the strain of late events. The very star-lit sky seemed brighter, and Bohndorff seemed to think that the air was really better than in A-Barmbo Land.

My servants, who had been temporarily stationed with Mahmud, were already returned. I now learnt that Morjan, who had all along caused so much trouble, had abstracted several things, such as knives, scissors, and presents for the chiefs, all of which were hidden away at the station in A-Madi Land. As a warning to others he got a sound thrashing, and, to prevent his bolting, a yoke was placed on his neck until Zassa could hand him over to the authorities at Dem Soliman.

Saida, being quite incapacitated for further work, received a grant of money with recommendations to Khartum. But having later recovered her health, she preferred remaining in the Bahr el-Ghazal province, where, thanks to her culinary skill, she obtained a good appointment. Some arrangement had also to be made with Farag 'Alláh, who had been heedless of repeated warnings, and who, as a married man, aspired to the ambition of founding a home amongst his Mondu kindred in Makaraka Land. So he received his discharge with one hundred and fifty-two dollars, and I at the same time dismissed Belâl, thus reducing my establishment to the Mangbattu (Dsumbe), the Dinka (Farag), and the Zandeh (Rensi), besides my maid-servant Halima.

All the other young persons of both sexes accompanied Bohndorff to Zassa's land, where he was to found such another station as that at Ndoruma's. I still adhered to my plan of waiting in A-Madi Land for a favourable opportunity of visiting the southern regions. Farag 'Allâh and Belâl, who wanted to make their way through Ndoruma's to the Bahr el-Ghazal, continued with me as far as A-Madi Land.

I was grieved to part with Farag 'Allâh; but here again I saw how loose after all were the ties by which the Negro was bound to the white man; how easily he loses his balance, if prematurely advanced to a position of trust above his fellows. I was later informed that Farag 'Allâh bitterly regretted his rejection of the conditions on which I would have consented to retain his services. He had learnt the cares of housekeeping. Nor did he even long enjoy the sweets of freedom. Instead of going to Makaraka Land, he remained in the Bahr

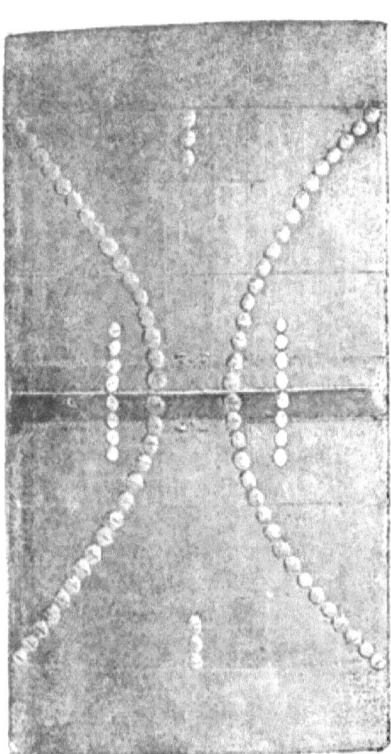

WOODEN SHIELD OF THE MANGBATTU, A-BARMBO, AND A-MADI TRIBES.

el-Ghazal province, where two years later he perished with so many others at one of the stations surprised by the rebels during the Dinka revolt.

Zassa had full claim to my gratitude; but for his aid we could not have escaped, and I now rewarded him with diverse gifts. At his request I also willingly made some presents to the followers of the new vassal chiefs, Berissango and Ngabia, who had accompanied him.

With Bohndorff I made all necessary arrangements for a long separation, and left in his charge the greater part of the loads, retaining only about fifteen for myself. On April 24th I continued the return journey to A-Madi Land, while Bohndorff and Zassa a few days later struck northwards for Berissango's.

Towards the end the Embatas avoided us, and Senu, who had not shown himself when I crossed over, could not be persuaded to visit me. I did not then foresee that I should be again brought into contact with these people, and should later even recover some of the stolen things.

MADOQUA ANTELOPE.

CHAPTER X.

RESIDENCE WITH THE A-MADIS AND JOURNEY TO HAWASH STATION.

Mahmud's Station—Intercourse with the Natives—Mbittima's Jealousy—Removal to Mazradeh's—Intercourse with him—Ancient History of the A-Madis—Harvest time and produce of the country—Chimpanzee hunt—Oracle apparatus—Dancing of A-Madi Women—Comparison of A-Madis with other Tribes—Letter from Casati—Journey to Hawash Station—Eastern A-Madi Territory—Welle Scenery—Arrival at Hawash Station.

AFTER parting with Zassa and Bohndorff, I arrived at Mahmud's station on April 24th by the road traversed the previous February. I was in good spirits, having got rid of my chief worry—the forwarding of my bulky baggage. This was purchased at the sacrifice of every comfort, and I certainly did not foresee that I should be sixteen months without my things. My business for the moment was to wait, in order not to miss

Osman Bedawi's expedition to the A-Madis. So I waited and waited in vain for months, until it appeared, to my no small disgust, that on account of recent occurrences no expedition would be sent that year to Bakangai. I made arrangements for a prolonged stay at the station, and hoped to obtain news of Osman Bedawi through messengers; but the timid Bongos, whom this zeriba life had made very lazy, refused to go to Ndoruma. Farag 'Allâh and Belâl also remained for weeks at the station for want of travelling companions. For me a period of stagnation set in, though by no means one of quiet, the screaming of the babies rocked on the knees of their affectionate Bongo fathers, and the quarrelling amongst the people made itself painfully evident. The few soldiers in the station were always grumbling at the stay amongst the A-Madis and under Mahmud, of whom they often complained to me, though they themselves were constantly getting into mischief. They set fire to the dwellings of the intimidated and defenceless chiefs for the merest trifles, and even carried off their wives and children, who were kept as slaves to the Bongos if not released at a high ransom.

The number of our soldiers was increased by one whom Zassa had left with Mambanga-Zandeh at his earnest request, and who speedily took refuge with us for fear he might be murdered by the A-Barmbos, some of the dragomans quartered with different A-Barmbo chiefs north of the Welle to look after Zassa's interests having lost their lives. Yango, Mangu, and others of the southern A-Madi chiefs, who had formerly endeavoured to maintain their independence against Mbittima, also came to me and provided me abundantly with the produce of their district—for instance, maize, which being sown early in the damp valleys, was already ripe, and the first gourds. So many guinea-fowls were shot near our camp that Mahmud and Mbittima got some of them, not to speak of my own people. A buffalo, which had been shot by Dsumbeh, and found later, formed a further addition to our larder, and its dried flesh kept a long time.

Mazindeh, whose relations with Mbittima continued strained, had sent me honey and other provisions, and offered to despatch a messenger to Osman Bedawi. This strengthened my resolution to quit Mahmud's station and await the still-expected arrival of Osman with Mazindeh, for the disorders in Mbittima's district soon disgusted me. My attitude to him was once for all cool, and my friendly intercourse with all his rivals aroused his jealousy. When sufficiently well provided, it was a pleasure to entertain the chiefs who had come to me from a distance, a hospitality which the pride of the Nubians towards the natives forbids them to exercise. Consequently the chiefs considered it a distinction, and greatly appreciated it. On such occasions I sometimes went so far as to sacrifice a box of sardines, or such like, that they might taste our dainties, and such an event became the current topic of conversation throughout the district, especially as the favoured ones often asked to take some to show their wives and others.

About this time Zemio appeared again on the Welle, and even crossed it, staying in the territory of Buru, the friendship with whom he had strengthened. Hearing the uncertain reports of my sojourn with the A-Madis, he sent a messenger to me. He returned again to the north, after arranging his affairs with the A-Barmbos, but this time the business did not go off without a skirmish; Zemio assisted in an attack on some of the tribes at enmity with Buru, many of whom took refuge with the A-Madis.

The 7th of May was a memorable day in the monotony of my life; it transported me to my home, where I took part in spirit in a family festival; it was also the occasion of a happy event close at hand, the appearance of two fawn-coloured kids, followed the next day by a second pair. Unluckily an ass trod on one of our nurslings and killed it, but the other three got on famously; and later I got milk from the goats, a welcome change in my unvarying diet. Every morning for the next month I enjoyed the veritable luxury of a glass of hot milk over a dish of lugma or Kisra bread.

A great dispute arose with the chief, Nangu, before I left Mbittima's, brought about by a frequent cause of hostilities amongst the natives, a "Rape of the Sabines." Mbittima was the aggressor, and Nangu asked me to mediate. Whilst the one was making up his story the other attacked him. There was great excitement at the station, and no means of shutting out the tumult and noise. I kept myself out of it though, especially as the first raid was unsuccessful. But soon the dragomans sallied forth again, returning at night laden with spoil, and relating with loud cries that some of the natives had been shot. The bandits had kidnapped some children and driven them bound together to the station, and they had brought away whatever they could carry—maize, spears, knives, small benches, and other household utensils, even nets for trapping game. When I gave vent to my indignation, Mahmud contented himself with remarking that the persecuted negroes were, as a matter of fact, *nas batalin*, a bad lot.

Disgusted at this spectacle, I determined to go over to Mazindeh, who had often sent me provisions, and who was delighted that I was now to be his guest.

OIL-PALM (*Elaïs*).

Mbittima and the people at the station did everything they could to keep me back, but in vain. My few possessions were soon packed, and the 21st of May, on the arrival of Mazindeh's carriers, I set out in spite of the pouring rain.

Although it had rained frequently in A-Madi territory during the last few months, we were spared a soaking on this day, and I arrived at Mount Malingde by the old road; this time, however, going round its eastern side to Mazindeh's instead of taking the shorter road west of it. So we were obliged to spend the night at the foot of its southern slope, and went round the mountain next day, through the thickly-populated country of the North A-Madis, who are mostly subject to Mazindeh. Rich cultivated tracts, banana thickets, and oil-palms, which I had noticed from the mountain heights, surrounded the huts of the natives in this district. I was now able closely to inspect these leafy retreats, for our way led us from one enclosure to another, situated often on a slope at the edge of a precipice, or bordering a noisy forest brook which runs round the hill for some way in a deep ravine to the right. I found Mazindeh's huts transplanted ten minutes' walk further away on the north bank of the Hekka stream. He came a long way to meet me, and I took up a temporary abode with him, having determined to superintend the construction of the new huts myself. Mahmud had accompanied me by Mazindeh's desire, to inspect the ivory collected for Osman Bedawi; this business led to another long discussion, for the Zandeh chief had fresh complaints to lodge against Mbittima's subjects. A shield pierced by a spear was produced as *corpus delicti*, and a man appeared who had been surprised on the boundary of the two rival chiefs by Mbittima's people and wounded in the shoulder.

The new settlement of Mazindeh and his relatives was situated on the gentle slopes descending to the Hekka, and there I also found a suitable place for building my huts near some shady trees and thickets, not far from the thickly-woven fringing wall of river vegetation. Everything needful was already at hand, and soon busy hands were at work under Mazindeh's personal superintendence, and in a few days I, with my people and animals, were established under a roof of our own. The troublesome work of an enclosure was omitted, for I was always hoping that Osman Bedawi would arrive and our journey continued, but the space in front of the huts was cleared of high grass, and all around lay the new fields of the A-Zandehs, extending to the edge of the river. Near my hut was a small thicket, out of which I cut with my axe a natural arbour, a pleasant retreat from the sun's rays, in which I spent many a delightful hour alone. I found here three elephants' tusks, which Mazindeh had hidden. The chiefs often conceal their ivory in this way to keep it safe in case of attack, and also because they prefer bartering it piece by piece to parting with it all at once to the Nubians passing through. When they want to make quite sure they bury it in marshy spots.

It soon spread to the western and northern territories under the chiefs subject to Zassa that I had taken up my quarters with Mazindeh. They were all dissatisfied with Zassa's government, and the two chiefs, Zirro to the north-west and Berissango on the west bank of the Welle, sent envoys to me. The former offered me ivory, and the latter proposed leaving his territory to emancipate himself from Zassa's jurisdiction. Thus these petty chiefs still laboured under the delusion that the object of the collection of ivory was to pay for the caravans passing through. If the ivory had been all, they would gladly have borne Zassa's rule, but all such expeditions were occupied with their own individual interests, and although Zassa and Zemio made their excursions independently of the Nubians, they were invariably the occasion of lawless acts of violence, the natives being robbed or even carried away, for Zassa also was quite alive to the value of acquired slaves. In short, it fell to my share to explain more fully to these messengers, and to others from different provinces who applied to me for protection, the administration of the Bahr el-Ghazal province, and to comfort them with the prospect of better times. Of course I did not in any instance accept of the ivory offered to me.

At this time I received tidings of Bohndorff. He had reached his destination in safety with his luggage, and was engaged in laying out the station and a kitchen garden. Zemio had in the meantime quitted the Welle, and was staying with Palembata. Finally, Mazindeh sent messengers thither and further on to Ndoruma and Osman Bedawi, for there were rumours that Osman Bedawi was taking part in the war against Mbio; as to whether this scheme was put into execution and what happened

OUR DWELLINGS AT MAZINDEH'S.

further I heard many contradictory stories, but nothing certain. My late servants accompanied the messengers to Ndoruma, though Farag 'Allâh repented of his obstinacy on arriving at Palembata's, and would willingly have returned to me unconditionally, as I was afterwards informed by Zemio. Dsumbe gave me every satisfaction, although he had only been in service a year; he did his work far more carefully than Farag 'Allâh.

At this time, though without my knowledge, recourse was had again to the fowl oracle, and on my behalf. Mazindeh had an irresistible desire to gain in this manner unquestionable certainty as to my future fate. So the *benge* was administered to a hen who carried her malevolence towards me so far as to depart this life. Mazindeh was inconsolable, and hesitatingly informed me that my fate was sealed, and it was unfortunately beyond all doubt that I should lose my life whilst with him, though, as the oracle had testified, not by the hand of his people, but through Zirro's or Berissango's. He and all his kin were bewildered when I made fun of this solemn warning and their superstition, and asked them rather to make me a present of their hen than to put life in danger at my cost, and then I should at least be sure not to die of hunger whilst with them.

Many apes of different species made their home in the wood bordering the Hekke, baboons, Cercopithecus, and the Colobus Guereza; one kind, with a blue face and white hair on its nose and cheeks, was very prettily marked. From my hut I often watched them springing from bough to bough in merry parties, or making daring inroads on the adjoining maize fields. The Negro boys would try to scare them with shouts, but there were always several who had managed to fill their pouches with the corn.

As soon as I had, with the aid of my followers, comfortably established myself in the new home at Mazindeh's, I supplied my servants with regular and useful employment. I showed Dsumbe how to prepare skeletons, and after a time we successfully mounted, not only specimens of small mammals, but also of the larger species of tropical birds. I endeavoured, too, to preserve the skins of mammals, though I had to be very sparing in the use of sodium arsenite, having had the greater part stolen by the A-Barmbos. So the skins were carefully cleansed from any remains of fat, and rubbed for hours with porous stone. I sent my followers out insect and butterfly hunting, and got together a good collection. Alas, the work and trouble were lost, for of all these things nothing reached Europe.

Mazindeh often came to see me. He showed much interest

on all subjects, and I used to tell him stories of civilized lands.
His pertinent inquiry as to why we wanted all the ivory led to
my telling him how the "Turk" Government the Egyptian
Government is called "Turk" here) sold all the ivory to western
lands, where it was made into all kinds of things; and I showed
him small articles made of ivory and horn, knife-handles, fittings
of a workbox, &c. He was delighted with these valuable results
of our industries, especially with my small collection of different
knives, in the bright blades of which he could see his reflection.
On such occasions I always gave him something to keep, thereby repaying the gifts of my newly-acquired black friend. I
also taught him other things within his comprehension, the way
we till the soil, and that with us nearly the whole land is under
cultivation, and that stones, roots, and weeds are carefully removed from the fields; that in our woods no trees are felled
without a purpose, and further explained to him the hunting and
fishing regulations. Mazindeh listened to all this with the
greatest interest, and often by his questions opened the way to
the discussion of other points. I also endeavoured to extend my
knowledge of the land and people, helped by Mazindeh and the
A-Madi chief Buru, who must not be confused with the
A-Barmbo chief of the same name. He was a rival of Mazindeh's, only nominally subject to him. The relations between
them were very strained, and Buru often complained of the
government of a stranger. Mazindeh was feared rather than
beloved by all the A-Madis, and soon after I left his rule in this
part of the country came to an end.

Buru often visited me, and I learned from him the following
details of the former history of the country. The most ancient
supreme ruler over the A-Madis of whom there was any account
was Zilabi. He was followed by his son, Batinnepaleh, who was
succeeded by Dundaleh, the contemporary of Bazimbeh, the
grandfather of Ndoruma, it was by Dundaleh that the A-Madis
were brought under the foreign rule of the A-Zandehs. The
Mangbattus also attacked the little country at this time, and
through internal dissensions a part of it became subject to the
A-Madi chief Runsa. This man was still living in my time,

though very old, but Kanninga had wrested the government from him; and after that the internal feuds went on without intercession, while the inroads of aliens became a yearly visitation. But this belongs to more modern history, and has already been related by me. Let it suffice here to note that Buru was a son of Kanninga's. Two sons of Runsa, Ngurra and Bani, and a few other chiefs were still living in some state, but they stood like Buru, in a vacillating subjection to Mazindeh. The A-Madis, like the A-Barmbos, are sub-divided into a number of septs, which are often only distinguishable by their names.

Thus passed the month of May. In the first days of June a tedious congress took place to decide the degree of punishment to be inflicted on an A-Madi for seducing a woman. The formalities of the government officials of the criminal court were unenders. Mazindeh wished to punish the man according to A-Zandeh law, by cutting off a finger; but Buru and the others appealed to me against this decision, and I decreed, as the superior court, that a number of spear-heads should be delivered to the owner of the woman, which atonement was willingly accepted. Just at this time I saw a man who had been punished a year previously by the loss of his finger and of another important member. I examined the wounds and found only small scars—nature had proved a good healer, the sole remedy used having been hot water. The maimed man, who belonged to the territory ruled by the sons of the A-Zandeh prince, Malingdeh, told me he knew about twenty men who had been similarly punished.

Shortly after this trial, I was myself the innocent cause of a punishment customary in the country. Mazindeh came to me one day in a great state of excitement, and declared himself in anxiety for my safety, as there was a magician in the neighbourhood who bore me ill-will, but that he would have him found and put to death, for the monster had laid a spell on one of his women and seduced her. Before long this terrible wizard was discovered in the person of a wretched youth, hardly past boyhood. He hastened to me asking for my protection and protesting his innocence. Of course I took his part, and even threatened Mazindeh, but the youth lived in constant terror, and finally fled from the country.

One of the most remarkable customs still practised among the A-Madis and the Mangbattus living on the Welle, is that of circumcision. My informant, Buru, could give no reason for it, and said that they had inherited it from their fathers. This custom is not observed by the A-Zandehs and the other northern negroes.

These monotonous and uneventful days afforded me leisure for writing and sketching maps; and I also sent letters to Europe, but my despatch from A-Madi Land of over one hundred pages was lost on the way.

The one excitement was the false reports of all kinds which sometimes told of war. Occasionally the nugara was heard in the distance, but the enemies were mostly imaginary, or a quarrel had broken out, and after some noise among the men, was favourably settled. One night we were awakened by loud cries in the neighbouring huts. It was said that a leopard had broken in amongst the people. But it soon appeared that there was nothing more alarming than a family dispute in which some blows were given. The cry was raised on one occasion that the A-Barmbos from the Welle were marching against Mazindeh, and that some of them had been seen in the neighbouring wilderness. The war-drum was beat to collect the fighting population, who then marched about in Mazindeh's mbanga with many war-hoops. I had to be prepared, and passed the night fully dressed on my bed holding the instrument of death in readiness. At daybreak a few A-Barmbos of the A-Boddo tribe made their appearance certainly, but they were terrified fugitives who had concealed themselves in the wilderness, and now besought shelter. They brought us confused rumours of an inroad on Prince Mambanga, who had been attacked by the Nubians in the eastern stations. Further they told us that the rest of their tribe had marched to Mambanga's aid, that they had refused to go with them, and that the A-Boddo women and children were now left defenceless. This was quite enough for Mazindeh; he declared that the A-Boddos had kidnapped some

MAZINDEH INTRODUCES THE KIDNAPPED WOMEN.   (*Drawn by L. H. Fischer.*)

of his relatives some time before, and marched with his troops that very day to make a raid on them.

His departure enabled me to see something of his wives. These ladies lived in great awe of their lord, but as soon as his back was turned they came and settled themselves near me, at the same time assuring me that the chief killed any man with whom they were found. As a matter of fact, many an A-Zandeh pays not only with his finger but with his life for a trivial remark to the wife of a chief.

Under the circumstances Mazindeh's raid was naturally very profitable, and the men returned next day with full hands. This success was celebrated in the chief's mbanga with a great merry-making and dance. I must confess that I had my share of the blood-stained booty. Mazindeh knew my passion for collecting, and that I used to bargain for skulls of the natives. He therefore had some of the heads of the A-Boddos who were killed in the onslaught prepared, and they were added to my collection of typical skulls, but I accepted only those about the origin of which there could be no doubt. I was not always successful in such quests, and the skull of a man who was lynched for a murder escaped me, his corpse being quickly disposed of by his relatives. The chief fruits of the raid were girls and women with their children. Mazindeh sent me about twenty of them next day, thinking I should be greatly delighted with a present of a very light-coloured Barmbo girl. Her skin was the shade of dark leather, which made the dirt on it the more perceptible. I kept the poor creature with my woman servant a few days to avoid mortifying my patron, but afterwards sent her back.

Among those petty tribes of the black race which belong to no large community, such raids are innumerable; and afford the best proof of the value of large states. They show also that kidnapping is not only practised by the Nubians, but that the catching and enslaving of their fellows is an old and deeply-rooted custom of the blacks. In such districts as have come permanently under their jurisdiction, the Nubian Arabs have exercised a good influence; and, in their own interest, put an end to one of the chief miseries of Central Africa. In the centres inhabited by them, they have compelled the half-exterminated native tribes to live at peace with each other. In Makaraka, for instance, such deeds of violence on the part of a single chief are unknown. Naturally the kidnapping of the women and their frequent voluntary flight are the chief subjects of discussion in the mbanga, and the occasion of endless strife and quarrels. Buru often complained of Mazindeh in this respect, and at the same time made similar raids himself on the pretence of recovering runaway women.

June had passed without bringing tidings of Osman Bedawi. The rainy months had brought all kinds of field produce to perfection; and afforded a variation in the monotonous banana diet of the Negroes. The maize (called mbaya by the A-Zandehs, a'bundo by the A-Madis, and endo by the Mangbattus) was nearly all ripe and gathered in; being sown in different months, the time of harvest, seventy days after seed-time, varies. I often had half-ripe maize boiled and crushed, and then made into flat cakes of bread, which were thus rendered light and delicious. The sheaves of ripe maize are bound together with the outer leaves and hung in rows on large frames, thus forming high walls, which, being exposed to the air and sun, are thoroughly dried and protected from white ants. Smaller quantities of maize are hung in bundles on high trees and kept there to provide grain for the next sowing. In these parts the inhabitants appear only to cultivate one small species of maize; the cobs are different sizes, sometimes streaked and sometimes entirely red. To the south of the Welle we shall find a tribe which cultivates a species of maize equal to our largest and best.

Maize is one of the staple foods in the rainy months, and the *Eleusine coracana*, the other grain chiefly cultivated in the southern lands (the telebun of the Sudan Arabs, monlu of the A-Zandehs, a'girro of the A-Madis, nyetyimbo of the Mangbattus) is sown in July, and cut after the rainy season with small iron rings, fitting the top of the right hand thumb and sharpened on one side. The durra (*Sorghum vulgare*) and dukhn (*Penicillaria* or better *Pennisetum typhoideum*) of the northerly and easterly districts, are not cultivated by the A-Madis. Hence, after the chief harvest, when the improvident Negroes have consumed the *Eleusine* corn, a period of famine sets in, until the new rains provide other nourishment. The chief resource then is the banana, which ripens more or less all the year round. There are other substitutes for corn—sweet potatoes, manioc (the a'bangbe and bavra of the A-Zandehs), and pumpkins. Three kinds of the latter are cultivated for food. The seeds of three other kinds are freed from husks and crushed to be eaten with the porridge. The smallest and one of the nicest kinds (A-Zandeh, bisanda) closely resembles our small rough melon, the pulp is of an orange colour, sweet, and when boiled mealy, not watery as in the larger kinds (bokko and nbellibo), which somewhat resemble our water-melons.[1] The pumpkins all ripened in the rainy season, and the A-Madis had them in June or earlier. Though not so wholesome as vegetables, I learned to value them highly, as they were not repugnant to me when I was poorly or had lost my appetite, and they agreed with me, whereas bananas often caused flatulency. I generally had these pumpkins cut in thin slices and fried in fat, or stewed with chicken, guinea-fowl, or meat, or crushed and mixed with chopped meat, which was then made into rissoles and fried. My attempt to preserve pumpkins like the Julienne vegetables, by cutting them into small pieces and then drying them, was only partially successful. The preparation was fit for food, but not palatable. The other three kinds of pumpkins (detiro, bogumbe, and pago in the Zandeh dialect) were left in the fields till the seeds were collected sometime after the rainy season; the seeds are sometimes large, with a rough gray husk; sometimes small, smooth, and of a whitey-yellow tint. It takes a long time to free even a small quantity from the husks; the women do this with their finger-

---

[1] It may be mentioned that the genuine water-melon (*Citrullus vulgaris*) grows wild in several parts of tropical and South Africa, though the fruit is poor. Dr. Schweinfurth met with a gourd allied to the water-melon, cultivated in banana thickets by the A-Zandehs and Mangbattus, the *Cucumeropsis edulis* vega. which is also found on the Niger and in Upper and Lower Guinea. Schweinfurth describes the fruit as sometimes oval, sometimes round, and as large as two fists. It is of a pale leather colour or quite white when ripe, with a smooth thin hard rind. The white pulp is tasteless but not bitter. The seeds when mixed with tobacco are said to produce stupefaction when smoked.

nails. Besides the kinds already mentioned, there are in all districts other gourds of every shape which are made into household utensils. Sesame (nbigpalla, of the Zandehs) is in this latitude sown in June, is in the blade in July, and is harvested after the rains. The A-Madis also cultivate ground-nuts (*Arachis hypogæa*, in Zandeh, wanda), and another kind of earth-bean (*Voandzeia subterranea*, in Zandeh, a'bondu), which, however, is not so tender and palatable, and does not yield any oil. Here and there the lofty bamia (*Hibiscus esculentus*, A-Zandeh, mboyo) was cultivated, and this vegetable of the Hindoos and Arabs is indigenous to most districts of tropical Africa; at least it has not recently been introduced by the Nubians. The oil-fruit, *Hyptis spicigera* (A-Zandeh, ndakka), and the wild melochia[1] (molumbidda, *Corchorus olitorius* and *C. capsularis*) should also be mentioned. The *Helmia bulbifera* (A-Zandeh, menne) is a creeper which clings to the tree trunks. The tuberous roots and large air-balls attached to the base of the leaves are edible, and in taste and structure resemble our potatoes. The thick yams (*Dioscorea alata*, A-Zandeh, mbarra) are also grown here, and the A-Madis distinguish them by different names according to their white or red colour. The bulbs and young leaves of the *Colocasia* are eaten. The *Portulaca oleracea* (Arab, rijel; A-Madi, asesera) grows wild like the *Corchorus olitorius* (Arab, melochia), and I often enjoyed it as a vegetable.

The pulse variety most cultivated here is the *Vigna sinensis* (Nubian, lubia; A-Zandeh, a'bagpa). This dwarf-bean has thin pods, four inches long, with small round gray-green seeds. The young pods can be prepared like kidney beans, and I ate them whenever I could get them. The lubia, so much cultivated in Egypt, varies but little from the tropical variety. Other beans are grown and distinguished by the A-Zandeh as a'manzenzi, a'urro, and a'bangwa. The first two grow in low bushes and have russet and black beans; the third (*Phaseolus lunatus*), with black beans, is a creeper. The sugar-cane also grows in A-Madi

---

[1] It may here be mentioned that one of the commonest marsh plants of tropical Africa, *Melochia corchorifolia*, belonging to the *Sterculiaceæ*, was chosen by Linné as the type of a genus, and the name may give rise to some confusion.

Land. The hard covering is peeled off, and small pieces bitten from the inner part are sucked. The wax, with the white larvæ often still in the cells, is eaten by the natives with the honey. I got some from the A-Madis in this state, and the honey had a bitter taste after it was boiled and cleansed.

We come now to the tobacco plant (*Nicotiana tabacum*, A-Zandeh, gundo). All the Negro races known to me cultivate tobacco more or less, though not all of them smoke. Only about a dozen plants are grown with great care in raised beds close to the huts. Large fields are not laid out, as the cultivation entails constant watching and great trouble, yet it is so highly prized that often before they are ripe single leaves are broken off, dried at the fire and smoked, generally with a mixture of charcoal. Thus, in these parts, one seldom finds a store of tobacco, whereas the people on the Rol, in Kalika, Latuka, and especially in Unyoro and Uganda, cultivate it largely. There it served as an article of barter, and sufficed to supply the Egyptian stations. During my sojourn among the A-Barmbos the tobacco I had brought with me dwindled down to the small quantity kept among my reserve stores. I had mixed the last of it with Negro tobacco, and from this time there was no other source from which I could procure the needful luxury.

During my stay in the mountains with the A-Madis, I noticed amongst other things a frequently-recurring detonation, a long single report like the firing of a cannon, for which I found no explanation. Livingstone also remarks on this. The natives knew nothing about it, and, during my stay among the A-Barmbos, they attributed it to the report of my gun. They innocently believe that a shot can be heard several days' journey off; Zemio's people, for instance, insisted that they had heard the shots in Soliman's war with Gessi at a distance of eight days' journey. This acoustic phenomenon invariably occurred at sunset, when the sky was clear and no thunder-clouds were about; the bare stone of the mountains often showed clefts, which appeared to have been made suddenly, and not to have been formed gradually, and the rapid change of temperature and sudden cooling of the stone may account for this and explain these detonations. This naturally brings to mind another sounding stone in Africa, the statue of Memnon.

The dark river forests of A-Madi Land are inhabited by the chimpanzee also. I persuaded Mazindeh to get up a hunting party to catch the young ones alive with the help of nets, and after two days' search traces were found of a colony of eight or ten chimpanzees. The men laid nets all round the spot and then withdrew and beat the nugara drum in the distance. The apes took fright at this, and climbing down from the trees, took to

YOUNG CHIMPANZEE NURSED BY A GOAT.

flight. They were clever enough to raise the nets and slip under them; and almost all escaped in this manner. One old female alone left a young one close to the net; she came back for it, but at the approach of the men fled to her nest in a tree, and Dsumbe and Mazindeh, who sent some dozen shots after her in vain, declared that she was bewitched. The young one, a male, was handed over to me; he was only a few days old. The proportions of the body were those of a human fœtus of six months; the features like those of a very old man, a peculiarity of young chimpanzees. The hair was much thicker on the head than on the body, and the breast and stomach quite bare. The little thing kept stretching its limbs to find its mother and seeking for nourishment. When held in my arms it was quiet enough, but whined and cried the moment it was put down. I tried to rear it with one of my goats, and it soon took greedily to her milk, and afterwards would sleep day and night wrapped up in a cloak in a basket. Little Tom, as I called him, took plenty of milk, so that I hoped to rear him; but he died in the second week. As the last work of affection, I with my own hand prepared his skeleton for the collection.

I now resolved myself to watch the chimpanzees in their hiding-places, and sent out scouts to discover their new retreat. Next day, receiving satisfactory intelligence, I set out immediately with the guides for the place, which lay to the north. After following a narrow footpath for an hour, we turned off to pursue the course of a stream through the pathless underwood of a lofty forest. The luxuriance and strangeness of some parts of this wilderness defy description; it is quite different from the ordinary primitive river forest. In some places, for instance, the high growing trees entirely disappear, or the forest is replaced by thicket and bush, out of which single giant trees rise here and there, such spots being covered with a thick impenetrable web of creepers. This mass of vegetation stretches out horizontally, in large waves occasioned by the varying height of the bushes and trees, a labyrinth of green hills and moist valleys. This wide, continuous, half-hanging carpet of Nature's weaving stretches from the crown of a tree over the undergrowth to the ground, rising again in a wavy line to the next bush, falling once more to climb by the help of undergrowth and rotten tree trunks until it covers even lofty trees. Only single threads of this wonderful carpet reach the crowns of the forest giants, from which isolated creepers appear to strive literally to reach the sky. One may lie down on this hammock without any fear of its giving way; its elasticity and durability are proved by the difficulty of breaking through it on the march. It only spreads in the open damp spots on the bank of the river; in the eternal twilight under high trees standing close together, it lacks the light necessary for its growth. Here, also, strange types of vegetation like thick ropes

CHIMPANZEE.

climb to the high tree tops and approach to the light, but with offshoots or foliage, until, in the air and sun, they gather strength to cover the boughs with a dense green mantle. These small arbours in the tree-tops are the favourite resorts of the chimpanzees. Lower classes of animal life also divert themselves in these airy heights. Many kinds of ants climb to the very tops of the trees, and their nests, skilfully constructed of clay or of leaves and lime, and looking like imitations of small barrels, hang on the boughs in all sizes.

Passing on under the high trees and through the brushwood and undergrowth of this river forest, we at length arrived at the last halting-place of the chimpanzees. But they had already made their escape, although the men had surrounded them during the night with watch-fires; only one old male had hidden himself in a natural arbour in the tree-tops and could hardly be seen. However, with a happy shot I brought him down several yards, but he caught hold of the lower branches, trying to hide again, and was only brought to the ground after several shots, the last having pierced his heart. The nests of the chimpanzees are woven of broken branches and foliage in the tops of the highest trees in spots sheltered from the rain, from which it may be concluded that they are not covered in at the top. A favourite food of the chimpanzee is the round brown fruit, as large as a head, of an enormous tree of the bread-fruit species (*Treculia*, A-Zandeh, pusso). It contains one thousand seeds the size of a bean, and the apes carry it on their heads walking upright. The men had not succeeded in finding the escaped animals, and so I hastened back before nightfall. The specimen we shot was a full-grown male, a very old one, as could be seen by the grizzled hair on the lower part of the back; only the head was still quite black. The colour of the hair enables us to tell the age of the animals, but it doubtless accounts for the native idea that there are white chimpanzees. When dissecting him I was struck by the extraordinary size of the gall-bladder. The flesh taken from the bones was consumed in Mazindeh's mbanga, but I preserved the skin and skeleton.

Towards the middle of July some messengers came to me from the leader of a government expedition south of the Welle, who had heard that I was staying with the A-Madis. I asked him to send men who understood Arabic, that I might hear more about the expedition, and on the 23rd of July these arrived with a numerous following. I now heard of all that had been going on in Mangbattu Land during the past months. I will merely mention here that war had been made on the Mangbattu chief Mambanga, and that Hawash Effendi, an Egyptian officer, had, with the regulars from Makaraka, founded a station close to the A-Barmbo chief, Buru. The campaign against Mambanga was not yet concluded, and knowing my relations with the chief, Hawash asked me to come and use my influence with him. I was told further of the arrival in Mangbattu of the Italian traveller, Captain Casati, and of the rumours that an expedition was coming up from the south, and on its way making war on the Akkas. Hawash's embassy consisted of a dozen armed dragomans and forty A-Barmbo soldiers, led by a certain Nezim. Its approach having been previously announced to me, I asked the chiefs to have provisions in readiness for these guests. The excitement in A-Madi Land was naturally great, and the distrust still greater. This, however, soon gave way to curiosity, and when the messengers made their ceremonious entry, the elders of the A-Madi were present with their kin, and Mazindeh paraded his entire armed force, himself leading his little band, which marched several times in a circle round the guests. Then followed a great assembly with addresses and national songs, each party trying its best in friendly rivalry to outdo the others in screaming. The songs of the A-Barmbos were solemn and melodious, and whilst singing, one would spring to another, giving him a brotherly hand-shake.

I could not accede to Hawash Effendi's request that I should join his people forthwith, for I was still hoping for the return of the messengers despatched to Osman Bedawi. In the meantime I sent him word that I should probably visit the station later. During this visit there were often tedious discussions with Mahmud and Mazindeh about the station at Mbittima's. The Bongo dragomans were continually bringing some fresh accusation against the chief, many of which were doubtless to be ascribed to foolish fear, suspicion, and superstition; but the people were kept breathless with unfounded reports of planned attacks, quarrels, poisoned drinking-water, disputes about stolen and runaway women, &c. &c. Mazindeh fanned the flame against Mbittima, and urged Mahmud to remove the station to

DIVINING APPARATUS.

him, partly to oblige Osman Bedawi, and still more to get the control of the A-Madis into his own hands; however, finally things remained as they were.

I must here say something about the way in which justice is

administered here. First of all, an explanation of the *Benge* poison so often mentioned, by means of which fate was questioned. Whilst with Mazindeh I saw the experiment of giving the *Benge* to the person suspected of witchcraft instead of to a hen. He died of it, and was found guilty in accordance with the popular belief; if he had lived it would have freed him from the imputed crime. The accompanying cut shows the apparatus which, despite its harmless appearance, holds the balance between life and death. It resembles a plaything of our children, in which a number of small wooden bars cross one another in such a manner that by pressing two of them together, the length of the whole is increased. The bars of this portentous plaything of the Niam-Niams are attached to each other by threads, so that it is never steady, but when held perpendicularly, inclines to one side or the other. An imperceptible movement of the hand suffices to give this small wooden trellis the wished-for inclination towards the right or left; and on this depends the sentence of fate, "guilty" or "not guilty." The A-Zandehs call this apparatus "Bagara muyeh" (Come, little wood). The rascal who manages this instrument pretends that he incites it with this appeal; it is astonishing that there should be faith in this hocus pocus, the fraud being so clumsy and palpable. Another divining apparatus of the A-Zandehs and the A-Madis, the Ifna, consists of two pieces of wood; the upper, having a handle, is rubbed on the lower, which is shaped like a small bench. The surfaces are planed very carefully, and the sentence of the accused depends on whether they are made to adhere or not by rubbing them together and pressing out the intervening air.

The July rains were now over, and the end of the month was so far satisfactory that it brought me fresh tidings of Bohndorff, and with his letter a dispatch from Khartum and Europe—the third since I had left Khartum. But I waited in vain for news of Osman Bedawi that would enable me to make my journey to Lakangai. Remaining for a long time at one place may be fatal to a traveller; for it weakens his energy and injures his health. Most of my attacks of fever and illness have occurred in the pauses between the journeys; whilst on the march I was generally well and in good spirits. Protracted spells of idleness in one place make one prone to useless brooding and fancies; at such times my mind would be haunted by the most paltry trifles and my brain would follow out every foolish detail. Memory sometimes took me back to the earliest years of childhood, and even in sleep my brain busied itself with things that never before occurred to me.

Meanwhile they had been at work in the fields, and later in Mazindeh's mbanga. New ground was prepared for cultivation close to the old, many of the subjects taking part in this work according to custom. And these tasks completed, the ruler invited his people to the usual merry-making, in which dancing and singing with much feasting and more merissa-drinking were

GOLUNDA BARBARA.
(*From a drawing by Schweinfurth.*)

kept up for several days. The women busied themselves brewing the ever-popular Negro beer from telebun malt; the men went hunting to provide meat, if it might be, for the feast. The hunt, with nets laid in the high grass, was certainly not very successful, but a few of the small yellow antelopes (*Antilope madoqua*) were brought back, and in the absence of anything better, many other kinds of meat, more easily obtained and of questionable origin, found their way to the pot of the careful housewife. I do not positively assert that the merry-makers were rejoiced by partaking of *homo sapiens* (though the A-Madis are cannibals on occasion), but there were certainly any number of small monkeys in the neighbouring wood, and rat and mouse catching is a favourite and profitable pastime of the masculine youth. The boys employ for this purpose small ingenious traps, which are in use far around. They are about a foot long, with large meshes, the opening being the size of a mouse's hole and gradually diminishing to a point. Small thorny twigs are set on the inner side of this funnel, the thorns being pointed towards the thick end. The mouse runs in without hurting itself, but cannot get back as the thorns stick into its skin. A small rodent of wide range, the *Golunda barbara*, occurs here also. It abounds chiefly in the Atlas, and seems to have spread from Kordofan, where Brehm discovered it, over the Nile region and to Central Africa. The trunk is four inches long, the tail about four and a half, the beautiful skin of a golden brown colour with regular stripes of a deep brown running the whole length. I collected a large number of these field-mice, stretching their skins on small boards to dry.

The festivities in Mazindeh's mbanga lasted several days, and the last was celebrated with special solemnity, several chiefs from a distance being present. I contributed by making all sorts of small presents to Mazindeh and his followers. The dancers, among whom women and children mingled, were the centre of the merry-making. The dances of the A-Zandehs differ in rhythm from those of the A-Madis, so that they were executed alternately and in separate groups. What most struck me in the dancing of the A-Madi girls, which consists merely in tripping round in a circle, was the way they threw their heads backwards and forwards by turns, the muscles of the neck being entirely relaxed, and this with such rapidity and zest that I was astonished alike at the suppleness of their necks and that the girls did not fall down from giddiness. The heads of the A-Madi women have certainly more to do in the dance than the legs. Some old women certainly contented themselves by keeping time with their feet, but the young ones rivalled each other in madly twisting their necks about. The old gentlemen sat round meanwhile in groups and ladled the quickening draught out of an enormous earthenware bowl with small calabashes. This bowl was replenished from time to time from peculiar reservoirs which seemed to contain an inexhaustible fountain. These wonderful beer-troughs, over a yard high and considerably exceeding half a yard in diameter, would hold their own with barrels of stately proportions, and yet were made merely of a piece of bark with a wooden bottom, and looked not unlike hollow tree stumps. The join of this large bark cylinder is sewn, and the bottom is attached in the same way, the crevices being stopped up with pitch. These large vessels have to be filled and emptied where they stand to prevent their falling to pieces. The natives make similar objects in all sizes and with lids to them, reminding one of the bark snuff-boxes of the peasants of northern lands. They serve instead of chests and drawers, and are used as travelling trunks by the chiefs. I had some of them in my African menage.

As time brings the different races more into communication, the more striking differences in their manners and customs disappear, and the wars and nomad tendencies help to do away with any contrasts among the black races. Despite their different origin, their way of thinking and feeling and the instinct of self-preservation are almost identical, so that any differences are rubbed down and only few individual traits remain to distinguish the various tribes. This is the case with the A-Madis. Outwardly they are in many respects the same as the surrounding tribes, and in build and colour are akin to the A-Zandehs, but lack the strong muscles of their northern neighbours. The A-Barmbos are a shade darker. The manners and customs of the A-Madis are influenced by the A-Zandehs on the one hand and the Mangbattus on the other. I have already pointed out that their huts are built with conical roofs and with gables. Many of them wear the head-circlet of the Mangbattus, whose weapons and armour, especially the large wooden shields, are also used, together with the simpler weapons of the A-Zandehs. The A-Madi wood and ironwork is certainly inferior to the Mangbattu, but this is accounted for by their having been constantly at war. Thus, in a few generations, the A-Madis have lost most of their individual traits, and often the colour, build, expression, mode of dressing the hair, and even the shape of the skull are insufficient to distinguish the races. Their dialect is the most trustworthy guide in classifying them correctly; it shows the degree of relationship between the different races. There is one other token which often suffices to characterize a race when other distinguishing features have disappeared, namely, the national ditties, which are retained longer by a people than any other peculiarity; and these also afford a good standpoint from which to determine and classify the black races. The native ditties of the Africans are certainly far from being songs in the ordinary sense, but the few constantly-recurring and often melodious strains, the recitative rhythm and cadence, are so distinctive, that the difference in the ditties of separate races strikes the ear. This individuality is often stamped on the Negro dances also. At the first glance the dances of different races seem often much the same, but closer observation shows that they differ much in rhythm and beat, and in the attitudes and motions of the limbs. Thus a comparison of the races in question, A-Zandehs, Mangbattus, A-Barmbos, and A-Madis, shows that in these respects the differences are considerable.

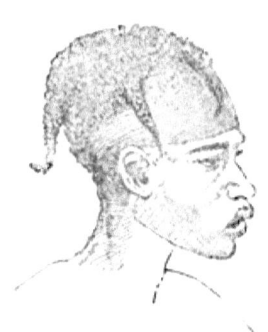

A-MADI. (*From a drawing by Schweinfurth.*)

Mazindeh had at this time been making raids on some A-Barmbo tribes living near the Welle. Ever eager for gain, he took advantage of every loophole, and was always ready with what he considered a sufficient pretext. For instance, on hearing that the Embata chief, Bamadsi, was wearing a coat that had previously been stolen from me, and that a locked tin box of mine was also in his possession, Mazindeh was anxious to march against him, but I prevented this. The chief used to do as seemed good in his own eyes, and afterwards try to justify these expeditions to me. But he was open-handed, and distributed the booty and the captured women and girls amongst his subjects and the dependent chiefs. This is customary, and the men are therefore ready to take part in these marches. A raid of this kind was undertaken in the second half of August, and the spoil of women, girls, and children was divided in a general assembly. Here again I emphatically assert that such acts are committed here and elsewhere without any incitement from the Arabs and Nubians, and that the common idea that the Arabs alone practise slave-stealing is mistaken, and can only arise from an ignorance of the state of things in Central Africa. To attack this undeniably sad state of affairs with the weapons recommended of late by those at a distance, and unfortunately adopted by credulous philanthropists, is a grave error, and impedes the civilization of Africa. It is quite clear that a custom which has been deeply-rooted in the black races for centuries is not to be done away with in a moment by fire and sword. Although at present the Arab element is the only one attacked, it will be found in executing the scheme that it is impossible to keep it separate from the African, since both are alike guilty. The blow will fall most heavily on the Negro, who is incapable of comprehending sudden innovations, such as the abolition of slavery. He will require considerable education before he can see that under happier conditions he may lead a more comfortable and worthy existence by abstaining from enslaving others. Until he is more familiar with European culture, these hasty measures will only awaken his distrust and increase the distance between him and the white man. To pave the way to such improvements, it will be necessary first to occupy the land permanently with military stations belonging to civilized states, such as those of the Congo State, and meanwhile to permit house-slavery and make vassalage compulsory. Of course I am not advocating the export trade in slaves, the suppression of which would gradually put an end to house-slavery. In a word, the bought slave should be confiscated, but the relations of the natives to their chiefs should not be interfered with, and work should be compulsory in Africa as military service is in other lands. Complete freedom ought, as I think, to be the crowning of the work of culture in Africa, and granted to the Negro only after he has passed through an intermediate educational stage. Every experienced African traveller will say the same.

My comfort had not been increased by the departure of my

Khartum cook, Saida, and I ceased to look for culinary works of art. Halima, who now held my fate in her hands, showed more good-will than knowledge of the noble art of cookery. So I had to give her lectures in gastronomy and illustrate these with experiments, sometimes taking an active hand in the preparation of dishes, and thus in time she came to be a modest substitute for the incomparable Saida. In one matter only she was a born genius, she knew how to make excellent flat bread cakes (kisra), and this was always the foundation of my table. This kisra bread tasted especially good among the A-Madis, as I ate it soaked in hot milk early in the morning.

The prospect of proceeding with my journey had become more hopeful. The messengers I had despatched to Bedawi had not returned, and I had received no news of him from any other source, and had at length sent Dsumbe with fresh messengers to Ndoruma, where he was, who were also to bring tidings as to how the war against Mbio had been proceeding. But a few days after his departure more envoys came from Hawash Effendi, bringing a letter from Captain Casati, who was in Tangasi, and who expressed the hope of meeting me at Hawash Station. This decided me to depart, the more so as Hawash pressed me to come, and the messengers said that Mambanga was still at war with the garrison; besides, I had given up hoping in Osman Bedawi's journey to Bakangai for that year. Dsumbe was to follow us on his return, and Hawash's messengers, a soldier named Dembeh-Dembeh, who accompanied me on some of my journeys later, and some of Buru's A-Barmbos, remained with me till I set out. Of course Mazindeh and the A-Madis bewailed my determination, for I had become for them a supreme tribunal and an umpire to whom they brought their small differences for settlement. The chiefs would often come to me and ask for "a good saying" and "sweet words," and then listen eagerly to my advice and carry out my injunctions. At my instance the main roads in the district were cleared of high grass, and intercourse was made easier for the people. They feared that when I had left fresh disagreements would arise with Mbittima, and even that Zassa, who had formerly made war on them, might attack them again. I calmed their fears with the promise that I would return, and left some things in Mazindeh's charge, part of my collection, bleached skulls, bones, and skeletons, ethnographic objects, and seeds of indigenous plants. The beetles and butterflies I took with me to keep them aired. My pair of goats I entrusted to Mazindeh, and was obliged to take farewell of my ass from Sawákin for ever. He was worn to a skeleton and devoured by vermin, and so perished. I had him washed with tar-soap and even shaved in vain. As a rule asses are not attacked by vermin, and are free from the ticks which infest dogs and attach themselves to the hairless parts of goats. Possibly the mischief was caused by poorness of blood, resulting from unsuitable food; he had served a long time under conditions foreign to his nature.

My small amount of baggage was soon in readiness, and on the 28th of August, 1881, I took my departure after three months' residence with Mazindeh, taking on this occasion a south-easterly route that I might see the eastern part of A-Madi Land. I touched on the Welle several times, and made acquaintance with the A-Barmbo tribes situated north and east of it. Some of their chiefs were on friendly terms with Mazindeh, and had heard of my journey. Our goal, Hawash Station, lay due east of Mazindeh's; but a direct route would have led me through large tracts of uninhabited country, whereas the circuit towards the south took me through cultivated land.

After leaving the familiar ground on the southern slope of the Malingde mountain, we passed through the territory of a number of small chiefs, and reached our halting-place at the A-Madi elder's, Bakkara, in the afternoon. In our march we crossed the upper part of the Tong, probably the most important stream in A-Madi Land, and its confluent, the Ha. Although it was some distance from their confluence with the Welle, they were ten yards broad and very high owing to the rainy season.

Mazindeh and the A-Madi chief, Buru, accompanied me to Bakkara's, who had recently been a vassal chief of Mbittima, but nevertheless now swore allegiance to Mazindeh's standard. At

Mazindeh's request I remained the following day, to allow his new subjects time to give us greeting, his chief anxiety being that I should strengthen his new authority by showing him distinction, and praising his powers and virtues in the presence of his subjects. I gratified him, thus lengthening my stay by several days. The men were at variance, too, as to our further route, but an end was put to this by the arrival of the A-Barmbo elder, Manda, of the A-Mangli tribe, on the Welle, who gave me an invitation, and so I asked to take my leave. But first the high grass on the path had to be cleared away, and so my departure did not take place till the 1st of September.

Bakkari's district lay on the border of A-Madi Land, and our way to the next halting-place at the A-Mangli chief's, Bau, lay through a wilderness, which surrounds the A-Madis with a broad girdle and separates them from the A-Barmbos who live on the Welle, where it makes a bend to the north, the A-Madis confining themselves to the hilly centre of the territory. Gradually the ground assumed the character of the broad undulating plain through which the water flows south-west towards the Tong. Mount Lingua vanished from our sight, and Mount Angba to the south became more distinct. The streaming rain drenched me to the skin, and we had to wade breast high through a brook that had overflowed its banks, so that on arriving at Bau the rest of the day was spent in drying our clothes.

Curiosity brought many visitors next day; and I made an excursion with Manda to his district, although it took me out of my way, and I had to come back to Bau again. But I was repaid for my trouble, for I saw a magnificent river landscape, such as one seldom meets in Central Africa. An hour and a half's march southwards brought us to Manda's huts. The river district is thickly populated by the A-Mangli division of the A-Barmbos, and many people joined our march. I thought of the miserable, solitary life I had led in the midst of the East A-Barmbos; but their conscience did not trouble them, and after the first diffidence had worn off, I saw more of them than I cared for on this journey.

On the further side of Manda's huts the ground rises consider-

VIEW OF TOTA ISLAND IN THE WELLE. (*Drawn by L. H. Fisher.*)

ably until, close to the Welle, it falls precipitously at an angle of 45°. The precipitous banks are here surrounded by a girdle of lofty trees, and the thicket and brushwood extend down to the foot of the cliffs, which rise 150 feet above the water and afford a fine view. The stately river flows towards the south-west, and the islands in its course make its breadth considerable. The largest island visible from here, called Tota, is in the middle of the stream, and from above one can see the Welle beyond its southern bank. The second island, Paali, joins it on the south-west, and another small one extends from Tota towards the north-east. These islands rise like emeralds above the silver surface of the magnificent stream, the further bank of which was also bordered with stately trees. Various shades of green shimmered in the shrubs and groups of trees on Tota and Paali, the bananas with their large and beautiful leaves being lightest, and cottages and huts showed picturesquely amid the dense verdure. A sunny heath stretched over the A-Mubanga district on the other side of the river, the monotony of it being relieved by the winding lines of vegetation bordering the brooks and small streams. The view was closed in the south by the tabular mountain Madyanu, and the distant A-Barmbo Land, which disappeared in the horizon. The view to the east and west was shut in by the trees of the precipice, which made a picturesque frame for the sunny prospect which long held me enraptured. The islands and banks of the Welle are populated by the Embatas, and one of their elders, Erruka, governs Paali. Some A-Mazillis also live on the banks and have boats. Erruka left his isle of paradise on my arrival and crossed over to me. The interview took place near Manda's huts, and I obtained a good deal of information about this part of the country. The absorbing topic of the day was the newly-founded Government station, and Erruka had sent messengers to Hawash Effendi to intimate his friendly disposition.

It may here be mentioned that the high shooting bamia (*Hibiscus esculentus*) is largely planted here, and I had a considerable quantity of it collected whilst staying with Manda, another proof that this vegetable is cultivated in districts not subject to Arab influence. The people also brought me presents of tobacco, sesame, &c.

Heavy rains surprised us on the return march to the Bau, and the forest morasses and dripping trees did their part towards drenching us; but on the excursion I had found good points for taking angular measurements of the mountains lying behind, and these data had been of practical value in constructing the maps.

The A-Manglis offered to clear our further route of grass, so I decided to lengthen my stay at Bau, especially as the daily rains prevented the roads and grass from drying. I had a visit from another chief from the " Islands of the Blessed," as I am tempted to call them, for the inhabitants of the Welle islands are happy above others, and as safe as a mouse in its hole. Few besides themselves possess boats, so that they are in little danger of being attacked, and are protected even from the wild animals. The narrow limits of their home keeps them more united than the tribes on the mainland; they can shut themselves in and lead a life free of care. This makes them arrogant to their neighbours on the mainland. I learned from the island chief, Nyeki, that between Bau, whose huts were at some distance from the river, and Erruka, there was another group of inhabited islands, Kisakeddi, Bugge, and Manziggo, and that there were no other islands further up the stream except Mabangi, the little one to the north, at the place where I had twice crossed the Welle.

Whilst thus extending my knowledge of geography, my thoughts often flew northwards; for the last papers had announced that the third International Geographical Congress at Venice was to be opened in those first days of September, and I longed more than ever to be in the cradle of transmarine enterprise, where so many of my friends and colleagues were now assembled.

The continuous rains delayed our departure from Bau till the 6th September at midday, when we took our course towards the north-east. Now and again we caught glimpses of the Welle, until we finally lost sight of it, together with the last A-Mangli habitations. We now came to the dwellings and cultivated land of the A-Boddo division of the A-Barmbos, but many of their huts were forsaken, having been plundered shortly before by Mazindeh, as the reader will remember. The small streams we crossed were all tributaries of the Welle; we encamped on the last of these, the Burwa, in the ruined huts of the A-Boddos. I stopped in the open, as was my habit when we spent the night near dirty, tumbled-down huts, for as soon as the natives leave them all kinds of vermin take up their abode there, and sometimes serpents make their nests in the roofs. Only the rain drove me under cover. I never used a tent in Equatorial Africa, as a solitary traveller can always make friends with the natives and use their huts at night. There is plenty of building material too, so that huts can at any time be made more easily than in other parts of the continent. A well-made Negro hut is preferable to the best tent, the straw-roof affording greater protection against both rain and heat.

News from Hawash of a fresh attack on the station by Mambanga, which was repulsed with a heavy loss among the natives, caused me to hasten my march in the hope of inducing Mambanga to make peace. We reached the Welle next morning, but the owners of the boats had fled owing to the troubled times, and we could not cross till Erruka's men, who happened to be near, lent us their boats. We had great difficulty in getting my ass across; the boat and the animal swimming close to it were both driven to another difficult landing-place. Then we had to wait for the porters, and finally starting again, we had a tiring piece of work to get across the floods left by the Welle in the midst of a thick wood, where our path was hemmed by old tree stumps, roots, and branches.

Hawash Station lies due east of the river. The more direct way led through unfriendly independent tribes, so that I was obliged to make a great detour to the north, following a bend of the Welle through the A-Bondus, A-Bangos, A-Megos, and other tribes already subject to the station. In this thickly-populated district the dwellings were close to the road, and often large and well constructed, with gables like the Mangbattu huts. The news of my approach preceded me everywhere like a beacon; the people streamed together and accompanied me from one homestead to another. I spent the night and the next day at Nieballo's, instructing the assembled crowd in their duties to the new Government, and exhorting them to keep peace and to devote themselves to agriculture. Some Arabs and soldiers came from the station to meet me, and I reached my temporary goal on the 9th of September, without any foreboding that the course of events would detain me there. From Nieballo's our way lay to the north-east. The streams were inconsiderable, but the last but one crossed before we reached the station boasted a small waterfall. Then followed a treeless grassy tract, where was an old earthwork of Zemio's, who had a few months before been besieged by the A-Barmbos, and being cut off from water, had caused a deep ditch to be cut to collect rain-water. Buru rules over a large portion of this territory, and Zemio and Hawash Effendi had made friends with him. Buru was a man of mark among his equals, many of the A-Barmbo tribes having recognized him as their leader; and I remembered having exchanged presents with him when at Mambanga's. He now sent his forces to meet me with tokens of submission, and at the head of this numerous company I reached the station, the crescent banner waving a greeting to me from the flag-staff.

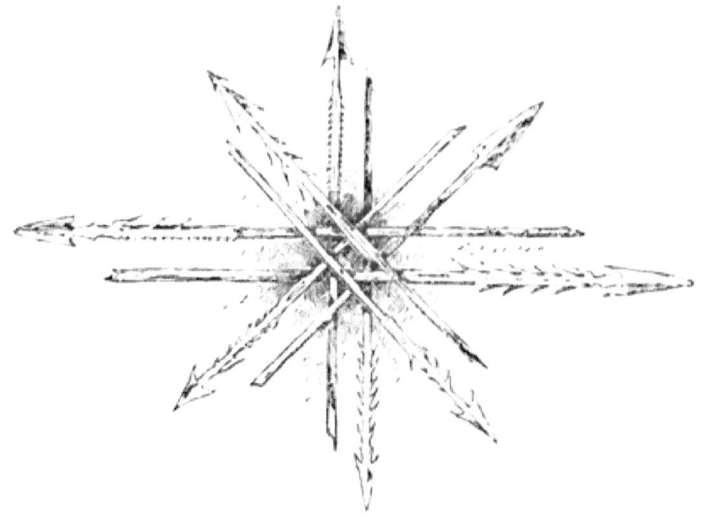

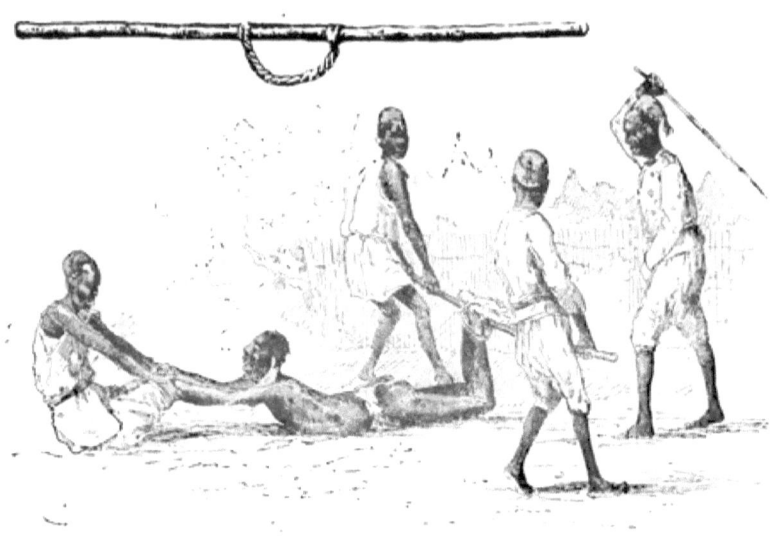

THE BASTINADO.

CHAPTER XI.

NEGOTIATIONS FOR PEACE WITH MAMBANGA AND STAY AT HAWASH STATION.

Reception at the Station—War with Mambanga—Hawash Effendi—Situation of the Station—Meeting with Mambanga—Return to Station—At Mambanga's Assembly—"Mapinge"—A-Barmbo chief, Bobeli—Casati's Arrival—Negotiations unsuccessful—Return to Station—Dsumbe's news and letter from Emin Bey—Casati leaves—Further negotiations with Mambanga—The Vulture Guineafowl—The Flattermaki—Mazindeh's Arrival—Mambanga declines Peace—Bahit Bey's Arrival—Mambanga's Flight—Entry of Troops—Preparations to leave Hawash.

I WAS received at the station with great honours; the soldiers stood to arms, salutes were fired, and the curious of the neighbourhood waited just outside the settlement. After the first greetings, I was soon seated in the reception-hall, drinking honey water with abreh (dried kisra in water or water sweetened with honey is always offered by the Nubian Arabs to a traveller on his arrival), and once more enjoying sweet coffee. The hearty reception and clean, well-arranged station made a favourable impression on me, and I was glad to speak once more without an interpreter. Important events had taken place meanwhile in this tiny corner of Mangbattu which interested me more than any political revolutions in the civilized world. The story was as follows:—

After my departure from Tangasi, the authorities in the Mangbattu zeribas had, in spite of my warnings, made preparations for war and attacked Mambanga. The war had not yet broken out when Mambanga sent messengers and presents to me at Palembata's, but his spies had probably informed him of the intentions of the Arabs. Shortly afterwards Mambanga was attacked and driven from his barricade, where the administrators Abd-el-Min and Abd Allah established themselves. Elated by their victory, they soon made a sally and were struck down at the head of their men by Mambanga's troops. Only a few regained the barricade, and Nezim, the dragoman whom Hawash had sent to me at Mazindeh's, led them under cover of night back to Tangasi. Mambanga had captured about forty guns, and the Government had lost others in an attack on the Momfus in the East. The governor, Emin Bey, in whose jurisdiction the province Mangbattu had been for a year, now sent Captain Hawash Effendi to restore order with full authority and forty regulars. Hawash Effendi Montasir was an Egyptian officer, who had lived for years in the Negro lands, and was well up in all the matters of the Upper Nile, the Rol, and Makaraka Land. His orders were to recover the guns taken by Mambanga and to bring him into subjection to Egypt. Mambanga, however, managed to evade him, and in following him up Hawash came into A-Barmbo territory and even as far as Mount Madyanu, soon after I had, with Zassa's help, left the western district. Then came dissensions among the leaders, and some of the troops returned to Tangasi, but the A-Barmbo chief, Buru, had already been won over to the Government. A station was founded at his residence, and some of the A-Barmbos brought into subjection. As at this time those western districts were nominally also under Emin Bey's jurisdiction, Zemio received warning from Hawash that he was not to extend his expeditions beyond the Welle, which was probably looked upon for the time as the boundary line for the raids of the Bahr el-Ghazal and the Hat el-Estiva (Emin's equatorial province) governments, though there were no official instructions. The mistakes which naturally arose often led to arbitrary measures on the part of the officials, who frequently had to act without directions. But after Zemio left, the Mangballes, whom the reader will remember from my first journey to the Welle, retained their friendly disposition to Hawash. Their boats were of great service in establishing communications by water with Ali Station at the confluence of the Gadda and the Kibali, for Mambanga had in the meantime returned to his territory and cut off land communication with the eastern stations. He was well supported by the A-Barmbo tribes allied with him, amongst whom the chief Bobeli, a rival of Buru's, held a prominent position. Buru had removed with his men to the immediate neighbourhood of the station for safety. Many A-Barmbos lived there in wide-spreading villages, and joined in the attacks made by the soldiers at the station, the women and children with their goods and chattels taking refuge on such occasions behind the barricade. All this time Hawash limited his action to the defensive, his object being to come to a friendly understanding with the A-Barmbos, and in this he had in a measure been successful. But many of the tribes were influenced by Bobeli and held with him to Mambanga. Matters remained thus until, a few days before my arrival, Mambanga, with Bobeli and about fifteen smaller A-Barmbo tribes, made his attack upon the station. The enemy made many charges of a varied character with great boldness during the day. Some tried to get close to the station with firebrands, others dragged up a heavy wooden hook with a rope attached to it, hoping to find a favourable moment for pulling down the barricade with this instrument. I found this product of Negro ingenuity preserved as a trophy. Some incidents connected with Mambanga related to me showed a strange mixture of feeling and brutality. Shortly after I had left him in the previous year a boy with a very light skin was born to him and was called Hawaja ("Stranger," or better "trader," the common designation for all Europeans in Egypt and the Sudan), because I had often been so called by the Nubian Arabs and my servants. This boy was Mambanga's favourite child, and he was so unwilling to have him out of sight, that in the last attack he had the child carried by his side exposed to the balls of the soldiers, so that at the worst he might die with his own flesh and blood. Less feeling is displayed in the following act. After the massacre of the governors of the station, he sent Abd el-Min's head to the independent Mangbattu chief, Sanga, south of the Bomokandi, and one of his hands to the chief Niangara, to mark his triumph and as a proof of his having completely cleared the land of the detested Arabs. His attack on the station was not successful, and although the foolhardy men ventured in numbers close to the barricade, they withdrew in the evening. During the day 1800 cartridges were fired from only forty Remingtons, without counting muzzle-loaders. The guns in the hands of Mambanga's people had not much effect, as the Negroes did not understand how to use them and had no shot, so that the soldiers had few wounded, whilst the enemy lost over 200 warriors. The women and children from Buru's camp had been completely protected in the station during the fight. Some of the killed were dragged away, and others devoured by Buru's force in accordance with the custom of the country, proof enough that the A-Barmbos also are cannibals on occasion.

The relations to Mambanga remained unchanged after the attack. There had been no fresh onsets, but peace was still a long way off, and it seemed to me useless to attempt negotiations through messengers. So I formed the plan of myself seeking out Mambanga on the strength of my friendly relations with him, and of the faith he had already expressed in my ability to help him. I did not think there was any danger for me personally, though under the changed circumstances that was not impossible. Hawash consented to my scheme. The conditions to be offered to Mambanga were agreed upon, and a messenger found to carry my presents to the chief, and ask if he would confer with me. In that case I would come half-way to

MEETING WITH MAMBANGA. (*Drawn by L. H. Fischer.*)

his camp to meet him accompanied by one servant and an interpreter.

Whilst awaiting his answer, I settled down for a long stay at the station, and in unpacking distributed among my neighbours many useful little articles. I even rejoiced them with some palm-oil, which in default of butter is, with sesame-oil, greatly prized by the Arab officials. The elais palm, which yields it, is only found in East Mangbattu Land; it was scarce in Mambanga's territory, and only occurs here and there further west. For this reason the palm-oil is sometimes imported carefully packed, and I had brought some from A-Madi Land to give to Hawash Effendi and others.

I now also closely inspected the station. It was carefully planned and solidly carried out, standing on a broad flat height and surrounded by a strong palisade. At the four corners were projecting towers which commanded the sides. High covered balconies over the gates, east and west, served as posts for the sentinels. The ammunition was protected from fire in a ditch covered with hides and sheltered from the rain by a light straw roof which could easily be removed in case of fire. In the middle of the station was a large, well-constructed building for the daily meetings of the men. Buru and the A-Barmbo chiefs used to bring their benches thither to hear what Hawash had to say and receive his commands. He was very patient in his intercourse with the natives, and though a strict ruler, he knew how to gain their confidence. The space round the hall was free, and from it the soldiers' quarters extended to the palisade. The slopes outside the station were cleared of wood, and thus could be covered by fire from the walls. The weakest point was to the south-west, but here the temporary huts of Buru's men were erected at a distance of 200 yards. A lively and varied picture was offered by the small dirty huts closely huddled together, surrounded by the silent forest, which in places branches out from the river belt to some distance south of the Welle. Clearings have to be made in this wood for the huts and fields, and those made by Buru's A-Barmbos extended some distance. The wood shut out the more distant view from the hill; I could only see the mountains of A-Madi Land, but not the Welle, which flowed by, two miles to the north, at the very spot where I had first seen it on the journey with Zemio.

The messengers to Mambanga returned next day, the 12th September, the chief sending with them some of his men, amongst them my former servant Adatam, who had brought me his presents to Palembata's. Mambanga sent me a trumbash as greeting, with the message that he would come half-way to meet me as I had proposed. I sent my assent immediately, appointing the desert between two streams as the rendezvous. Adatam and the messengers remained to accompany me next day. Many voices were now raised to warn me of my certain destruction at the meeting with Mambanga. Buru had questioned his oracle, the "mapinge," and the answer was unfavourable to me. Even Hawash expressed his fears for my safety and tried to delay the meeting. I would not listen to any of them, and was ready at the hour appointed. It was very lively in the station. Hawash held long audiences every day, and after my arrival the crowd pressing to his assemblies was even greater, for everybody wanted to stare at me and my wonders. Buru and his colleagues gave expression to their joy at my arrival in the usual long-winded speeches, and in games and wild rejoicings.

On the day of the meeting the looked-for messenger made his appearance and announced that Mambanga was on his way. The excitement was great, the people standing in hundreds on the hillside, but not a sound was heard as we marched off towards the east, and soon disappeared from their view. A messenger went on in front to tell Mambanga that I had started. His vanguards met me on the way, but turned back at once, evidently to tell their master that they had seen me advancing with their own eyes without any escort to speak of, and that there was no danger in approaching. At last I saw Mambanga's escort marching towards me in a long winding line. As soon as I reached them they lined the way, and I proceeded through their ranks greeted with demonstrations of joy. I noticed, however, that a number of the men went further, probably to see that no ambush was lurking near. Many an old acquaintance greeted me from the thick ranks of spears, and at last I stood before the dread ruler himself. I greeted him as an old friend, but he seemed ill at ease at first. It is difficult to say what he was thinking, but he at once expressed his surprise at my coming, and indeed, under existing circumstances, it was probably entirely beyond his comprehension. We sat down on the roadside, his escort surrounding us in a circle, with the guns taken from the Arabs bristling high above their heads. But the sun was already setting, and I proposed that we should spend the night there together. Mambanga would have preferred taking me to his hut, but he consented to my proposal, and preparations for camping there were made whilst I sent to the station for bread and a blanket. But now Mambanga had a fresh fit of distrust and wanted to return to his hut. I represented to him how undignified his conduct was, and said : " Very well, he would not see me again ; " and shutting up my chair turned to leave, in spite of the heavy clouds and the thunder already grumbling in the distance. Then he gave in, and even went the length of sending all but a hundred of his men back to guard those left behind. Now the critical moment was over for me, and I looked on in peace at the men working at the temporary huts of banana leaves.

Such a shelter was soon put up, and fully answers as a protection from the rain. First the framework of a gabled hut is made of small trees. The rafters going lengthways are supplied by the tendrils of creepers, and cross ones are unnecessary. The banana leaves have to be arranged like tiles, so that the rain may run over them. A diagonal cut is made in the lower third of the leaf, and they are by this means hung sideways, one over the other on the liana lines, beginning with the lowest, the leaves thus filling up the space between one line and the next above it, the bottom third of the leaves on each line overlapping the tops of those beneath. At the top of the gabled roof the leaves are bent in the middle so as to hang down on either side, and the loose leaves are kept from blowing away by liana lines stretched over them.

Once safely under cover, the discussion with Mambanga as to

HUT WITH ROOF OF BANANA LEAVES.

recent events began. I tried to make him understand the advantages of combination with the Government. I showed him how great the change for the better had been in recent times in the provinces, that the Nubians would stop plundering, that the Government would look after the interests of the natives, and that Hawash Effendi had been sent to see that there should be fair play. I laid particular stress upon the condition that Mambanga would not be punished for the death of Abd el-Min and Abd Allah, but would continue to rule in his territory, and that his power and influence would be increased, as with the help of the Government he could bring under his sway many of the A-Bisanga and A-Barmbo tribes at present independent. To all this Mambanga replied again and again there was nothing he so ardently desired as peace, and that he would willingly deliver up the fire-arms and submit to the new Government, but—and to this he always came back—his fear and distrust was too great. He was afraid he would one day be assassinated, like so many of his relations, or that he would be kept in confinement like Wando's son, Mbittima, who, however, had already been freed by Hawash and was now staying with him.

The innate distrust of the Negro had in Mambanga's case been kept alive by frequent breaches of faith on the part of the Nubian Arabs, so that it was vain to hope that I could allay his fears in a few hours, though I left no means untried. The chief point was to persuade him to visit the station. I even offered to remain with his people as hostage during his absence. Then I proposed that we should enter into blood-friendship according to the native custom, and this certainly was hailed with enthusiasm. These negotiations went on until late in the night; then Mambanga went to sleep, while his men kept watch by turns. I spent an almost sleepless night on my chair tormented by a burning thirst, after the five hours' discussion, for no one had provided water.

My first meeting with Mambanga was so far successful that he promised to go with me to the station later, on condition that I remained with him first for some days to allay the fears of his wives, as he said. Though laying little weight on his promise, I would not destroy this faint hope, and consented to his terms, first returning for one night to the station to make the necessary preparations. The extent of Mambanga's timidity and cunning may be seen from his having, on some pretext, sent messengers to the station on the night of our meeting to keep watch lest an attack should be made on him. Before parting, my friendship with Mambanga was sealed with the ceremony of blood-brotherhood. The chief sat opposite me. One of the men made a scratch on each of our chests near the heart, and squeezed out a drop of blood. We wiped this off one another with a piece of sugar-cane which we then chewed, afterwards blowing the fibres partly over the wound, partly down the neck, each at the same time repeating the points which led him to contract the blood-friendship, and which were to be kept sacred. At the end of each clause we solemnly repeated, "If thou dost not hold to this, may my blood destroy thee;" a third person giving additional strength to this utterance by beating on some object with a stone. Mambanga spoke first, making a long string of conditions, after which I came to mine. My chief point was that neither Mambanga nor his people should make any fresh attack on the station.

CEREMONY OF BLOOD-BROTHERHOOD.

The extraordinary formalities of friendship with a vein of diplomacy were carried out with fitting solemnity, and proved to me that the Negro is capable of theory, though his practice hardly carries it out. The conditions made were by no means of a material nature, but touched more or less on the ideal. But I felt the temptation to flavour all this earnestness with a touch of humour, and raising my voice, I spoke my last condition: "Great ruler, if I am to be content when I come to you to-morrow, grant my request for a basket of tobacco; if you do not do this, well—you will be but a poor friend." My words were received with acclamation, for the unexpected turn from serious demands to a trifling request highly delighted the people. No further concessions could be expected from Mambanga for the present, so I returned to the station, where the men who had witnessed my departure in fear and silence received me with loud expressions of joy. Curiosity brought hundreds to see me; many of them pressed round me, and old Buru's face shone with delight as he pressed my hand. I ordered the A-Barmbos to go at once and clear some of the road of high grass for the next day.

As I was relating my interview with Mambanga to Hawash, the signal which sounds for war was suddenly heard at the place where the men were clearing the way. It is made by uttering a cry and at the same time tapping with the fingers against the opened mouth. The remaining A-Barmbos hastily stormed down the hill with their shields and spears, whilst the soldiers were called out and posted in front of the station. I angrily commanded the men to be quiet, and declared it was a false alarm, bringing one of the busybodies who ran to announce an attack to reason with a sound box on the ears. The A-Barmbos soon returned laughing, and told us that Buru had raised the war-cry in order to effectually bring up the idlers who had loitered behind to help in clearing the way.

I sent information of the peace that was being negotiated to the eastern stations, so that no untimely measures might be taken, and enclosed a letter for Captain Casati. This despatch was sent later from Mambanga's to Ali Station by road.

On my setting out to return to Mambanga, the people were seized with a fresh panic, and Buru again foretold a catastrophe, having consulted his "mapinge," which maintained its ominous views as to my end. I went to meet my fate with a very small escort. My servant Dsumbe had not returned from Ndoruma, Farag and Halima the cook were suffering with swollen legs, a common and tedious complaint amongst the Negroes, and were disabled for weeks. But a small A-Madi, named Binza, had accompanied us on the last journey. The boy showed aptitude for his work, and accompanied me in all my journeys until I reached Zanzibar. H. M. Stanley took him with him from Zanzibar on the Emin Pasha Relief Expedition, with which he returned afterwards to the coast. Renzi and Binza were my only servants at that time, and Dembeh-Dembeh, who had often come to me at Mazindeh's with messages from Hawash, acted as interpreter at Mambanga's.

This chief had now established himself about four hours' march south-east of the station, and three hours' march south of his settlement in the previous year. We crossed three brooks on the way, the dwellings of his subjects beginning on the further side of the last. Mambanga came to meet us, and offered me another beautifully-worked trumbash by way of welcome. I spent the night in a small gable-roofed hut, but the following days with the chief, mostly in an open hall. And now the endless negotiations began again, the same old story in different words. Mambanga hardly spoke of anything but the doings of the hated Arabs, and gave small attention to my earnest warnings. He did not positively refuse any proposal, but would at first make no definite statements, and the question dragged on from day to day, while he pursued the veritable Negro policy, which does not know what it is aiming at. He often interrupted the discussion to speak of the most trivial matters or ask me for presents. Then I would tell him in plain words that his conduct was undignified and threaten him with the gravest consequences, but made some allowance for his bragging and recklessness and did not press him beyond a certain point. When he raised too many objections I would propose that we should divert ourselves, and after he had aroused the enthusiastic plaudits of his subjects by his grotesque springs as an accomplished cancan dancer, and I had joined in the flattering cries of "Mokua viviiiiii...!" (Great and mighty Ruler) matters would go on smoothly once more.

But he would renew his old requests, which were often foolish and utterly undignified. For instance, he had, in the last attack on the station, seen an Egyptian with a very light skin, which the people looked upon as something highly remarkable. This

MEETING OF MAMBANGA'S ALLIES. (*Drawn by L. H. Fisher.*)

man's name was Omar, he had been punished for all kinds of offences, had served as a soldier, and was now a clerk. Mambanga insisted on entering into blood-friendship with him. In vain I represented to him that this was entirely beneath him, and that, as a prince, he ought to enter into blood-friendship with Hawash Effendi only; he stuck to the point, and I finally sent to the station to appease his longing. This instance is proof that the native looks upon a white as a being of a superior nature. I was repeatedly asked to show them my feet and legs, and on this occasion I yielded to Mambanga so far as to allow the men to touch the soles of my feet, which appeared to them of such marvellous whiteness.

The private hut of the chief lay hidden in the wood, at the edge of which a circle was formed by about twenty huts for his wives. Within this was the council hall, and the games were held close by. Mambanga generally disappeared into his hiding-place at sunset, and I remained for some time by the fire in the hall talking to his subjects, and learned in that way that he still retained a little son of Abd el-Min's, some female slaves, an angareb with covers and cushions, and other things as spoils of war. One evening some of Mambanga's wives and his sister came and sat with me round the fire. Some of them had been slaves among the Nubians and spoke a little Arabic. It is a custom of the Mangbattu rulers to keep one of their sisters constantly by them, who remains unmarried and looks after her brother's interests. That evening we laughed and chatted and the women clumsily smoked some cigarettes I rolled for them, listening now and again for fear of being surprised by their stern lord. Suddenly Mambanga's long figure appeared in the dusk and he gave the woman nearest him a slight blow on the shoulder. In a moment they had all disappeared, followed by Mambanga. Only his sister remained, saying that in such matters her brother had no authority over her. I prepared myself for a scene and the jealous reproaches of an aggrieved husband; but Mambanga soon came back, saying he was only angry with his wives because he had sent three times for his dinner and not got anything. Whether he wished to conceal jealousy or fear of my growing

influence, I do not know. In any case the men are strictly
forbidden to speak to the wives of their chief, and he once half
laughingly reproved me when I ventured to address them at a
feast. Thereupon I described to him how at home we whirl the
wives of others round in a dance, walk arm in arm with
them, &c., illustrating it, to the great delight of the people, by
taking the arm of the mighty ruler himself.

To push matters on, I got Mambanga to convoke a great
assembly of his subjects and the A-Barmbos allied with him.
Horns and drums were sounding on the 18th of September from
an early hour, and soon the troops began to appear. It was past
midday when the last of the A-Bisangas and A-Barmbos from a
distance arrived; and until then the chief was invisible, having
himself decorated and his hair dressed. On ordinary days this
operation sometimes took place in my presence, he meanwhile
stretching himself full length on a bank, whilst several women
worked in turns at his wool with long ivory sticks.

In the meantime those who had arrived collected branches
and grass to make arbours or shady roofs, which formed together a wide circle, and with the thousands of warriors presented
a bright and curious picture. The proceedings were of the same
nature as I have already described, only on this occasion there
were more long-winded speeches than processions and games.
Bobeli, the dread chief of the A-Barmbos and Buru's rival, was
also present, a long gaunt form, light in colour for an A-Barmbo,
with a gray wrinkled face.

By Mambanga's desire I made the first speech, standing on
the clear space in front of the arbour, and uttering one sentence
at a time, which was then immediately translated in a loud and
distinct voice by Dembeh-Dembeh. I described my efforts to
bring about peace, and represented the advantage of friendly
relations between the natives and the Government. Then I
invited them to come in peace and confidence to Hawash
Station, assuring them that no one would be called to account
for what had already occurred.

Before the last words were out of my mouth, Mambanga had
placed himself at my side and begun to demonstrate his side of

the question. A long-winded story about Munza's time and how he with his brothers and relations had fallen in war with the "Dongolawi" (Dongolans, a common name for all Nubian Arabs) and "Bahara," and many had been murdered; he never wearied giving vent to his bitterness against the intruders, at the same time declaring that he did not wish for further hostilities, but that Hawash had allied himself with Buru, who was now his slave. The one definite request he made was that the station should be removed to his territory; all the rest was nothing but empty phrases to fill up the time. If, notwithstanding, his speech interested me, it was owing to the comic setting. All the time he was speaking a policeman sprang with the agility of an ape all over the place, commanding silence, though not a mouse was stirring, sometimes gabbling parrot-like the last words of a long sentence, or giving weight to the utterances of this illustrious Demosthenes by a grunt. Other servile auxiliaries busied themselves unceasingly about their ruler, overwhelming him with small attentions. In the pauses of the speech were heard the far-sounding signal-horns, made of elephants' tusks, artificially lengthened to about three yards, and the cracked booming of large iron bells.

Then some other chiefs spoke, Bobeli emphatically denying that the hostilities were any fault of his, and declaring likewise that he wanted no more war. The speeches were followed by war dances, in which Mambanga took part, hurling spears at an invisible foe amid the acclamations of his people. The sham fight with the guns was still more effective and very comical. The men threw and caught the guns like sticks, pretending to fire now with the left hand and now with the right, and when some of the guns were really shot off, a dozen men near them fell flat on their faces, evidently in involuntary recollection of the bullets with which they had recently become acquainted in front of the station. I could not help laughing outright, and Mambanga stormed not a little at the cowardice of his people. War games, dancing, and speech-making thus continued alternately till the evening. Then a closing conclave of the chiefs took place in the obscurity of the wood near Mambanga's huts, at the spot dedicated to the "mapinge" oracle. I was also called to this special meeting, but my hopes that at last something was to be settled were not realized. The only point on which they were unanimous was that they would not continue warfare or make further attacks on the station. This was something gained, if they only kept word, for Hawash was short of ammunition; but I made a strong effort to persuade them all, especially the morose Bobeli, to come to the station.

Meanwhile my messenger returned from Hawash, bringing word that he would contract blood-friendship with Mambanga instead of Omar, and meet the chief half-way for this purpose, as I had done. But the Negro prince could not overcome his distrust, so nothing came of it. I was vexed, and pressed him for some definite decision, as I wanted to leave, and was tired of sacrificing, for his sake, everything I required, and forcing myself to eat the same food as his people, which I often had to beg for into the bargain. He was disconcerted and tried to keep me back, promising that he would then accompany me to the station. I asked him to give me pieces of wood to denote the exact number of days I should have to wait, and when he hesitated I broke off the discussion and left him. This brought him up to the mark, and he sent me two bits of wood, but I was sure when the time came he would break his word.

On the 19th of September I was surprised by the intelligence that Captain Casati was in a boat, on the way from Ali Station to Mambanga's. He had heard that I was staying with the chief, and was coming to see me there. I at once requested Mambanga to send carriers to bring him from the landing-place, and in a discontented mood delayed my journey; for this was the first day I had spent in Africa without anything to smoke. Tobacco was a necessity, for it often served as a substitute for food, or at least stilled my hunger. In the evening one of Mambanga's wives took pity on me and brought me some tobacco leaves, which I immediately dried over the fire, and then drew in the delicious fumes whilst waiting for my guest in the great hall. It was late at night before he arrived, accompanied by Mambanga.

Captain Casati is an Italian, and was for a long time with the Bersaglieri in Sicily and Calabria. Shortly before returning to Khartum, Gessi Pasha had asked him to the Bahr el-Ghazal, and he had soon after made his way to Mangbattu through the Rol province and Abaka Land. We heartily greeted one another as fellows in sympathy and suffering. I soon found him to be a brave and open-hearted man, entirely unassuming, unselfish, just,

MEETING WITH CAPTAIN G. CASATI.

and fearless. He had been ill a long time among the Abakas, and had taken too much quinine whilst unconscious from fever. He had recovered at Mangbattu, and was now quite well. We sat talking late into the night, though my Italian was rusty for want of practice, and I involuntarily mixed up Arabic words with it. I learned that Mambanga's men had already robbed him on the march; his servants' beads had disappeared. I at once raised a hue and cry about this, and did not rest until the chief restored the stolen treasures. Bohndorff was brought to my recollection by his two runaway boys who were in Casati's train, having joined him in the Bahr el-Ghazal province on his journey to Mangbattu. He had another relic of Gessi Pasha, a small bright little Dinka boy; this small "Wekil" (administrator) afterwards enjoyed an important position; and was treated by his master like an adopted son. Casati was soon informed of how matters stood with Mambanga, and he endeavoured in his turn to win over the suspicious chief to the Government. But Mambanga was on the look-out for valuable presents from his new guest; above all he coveted the Vetterli gun, and did not scruple to say that he would exchange the ass he had taken from Abd el-Min for "much" powder, and this in the midst of our endeavours to conclude peace. He quite overlooked having repeatedly promised, without any express demand on my part, to restore to the station the guns he had taken. I took him to task severely for his double-dealing and his shameful behaviour in general, which he actually carried to the point of leaving me without tobacco. And I stuck so steadily to the tobacco that finally Mambanga went himself to order that a basketful should be gathered for me.

So the latest day for departure arrived, and Casati said he would go with me to Hawash Station. Of course Mambanga now brought his heaviest guns into play to detain us, promising to consult the "mapinge" next day, and that we should witness with our own eyes the revelation made by the oracle. That certainly was a great temptation, so I stayed to look on at this fraud once more. Next day everything was in readiness, and I heard that one of the problems to be solved was whether I was really friendly to Mambanga. This time fate showed discretion, and the oracle fell out well for me, *i.e.* none of the bits of wood moved, and the long row was not disarranged. The other part of the apparatus was to pronounce whether it would be safe for the ruler to go to Hawash Station. Here too the bits of wood lay in an orderly row, the augurs began their clapping, yelling, and jumping, and lo, one of the little heaps fell down, at which the deceitful soothsayer jumped as if a snake had bitten him.

And as if this fearful omen were insufficient, the pieces of wood from another block began tumbling about to corroborate the untoward prophecy. Of course I was powerless against the "mapinge." I longed to get away from this idiotic business, and warned Mambanga once more to take my advice before it was too late, or I should not be able to guard him from war and certain ruin. I was really sorry for the poor prince who shrouded himself in this mantle of distrust, for a great part of the blame rested on his people, who were constantly misleading him with their nonsense. He confessed as much, and said that for the present he would keep up frequent communications with the station and later come himself.

My seven days' stay with Mambanga had brought me closer to him and his people; and I could at least rely on their not attacking the station so long as I was in it. On the 22nd of September Casati and I reached the station. During my absence Dsumbe had returned from Ndoruma, and he gave me the latest intelligence of the northern provinces. What concerned me most nearly was the certainty that Osman Bedawi was not going to Bakangai this year, being engaged in the war against Mbio. To my astonishment he had not yet commenced operations, and was only just collecting the troops for that purpose. He had been conducting some Government property from Meshra er-Rèq, and the messengers sent from Mazindeh's had followed him thither, hence their long absence. Dsumbe told me further that Ndoruma was expecting a box for me from the north, and would forward it directly it arrived.

We were received at the station with all honours. The garrison stood to arms, and Buru was also present with his men, though I chaffed him by saying his "mapinge" was no good, for I was still pretty much alive. Hawash had also been in some anxiety on my account, as it had been rumoured that my servant Renzi had been killed by Mambanga's men. The general rejoicing at my return was unfortunately interrupted by a sad accident. I had not yet entered my hut, and was standing outside telling Hawash about our stay at Mambanga's, when a shot fell close to us, and immediately afterwards we heard that a woman had been killed through carelessness. I was much grieved when I heard that my gun had caused the accident. Dsumbe had taken it with him on his journey to Ndoruma; on his return Hawash Effendi had wished to look at it, and it had been laid, whilst still loaded, in the hut on my box. Renzi had probably been meddling with it, and it had gone off, and after piercing several straw fences had first gone through the woman's breast, and then through a boy's hand. To all appearances my consternation was greater than that of the woman's master, a soldier, who was evidently very well satisfied when I gave him some stuff to make good his loss, and Hawash promised to find another wife for him. The boy's hand soon healed, again showing how easily the Negro recovers from wounds when nothing unfavourable intervenes.

Amongst other matters of interest awaiting me was news from Ladó, a letter from Emin Pasha, which delighted me the more as he gave the prospect of a speedy journey to Mangbattu. But he also sent me the sad tidings of Gessi Pasha's death. Thanks to his wiry frame and strong will, he had got as far as Suez after his severe accident in the Bahr el-Ghazal, but there his fate overtook him, and he died alone, without seeing the dear ones for whom this resolute man had shed tears of longing. I recollected him with mingled affection and regret; all the happy associations of our frequent intercourse during many years were awakened, never to be effaced from my memory.

I passed many pleasant hours with Casati, in which we bore one another company in visits to our respective homes, and this brought us closer together. Some good Gedaref tobacco had been sent to him in a packet from Khartum, and this comfort enhanced the enjoyment of the agreeable time we spent together.

The men who had escorted us to the station returned to Mambanga's on the following day, but I persuaded Hawash first to let them see the garrison at drill, that they might carry to their ruler a vivid description of the readiness of the soldiers and their superiority to the natives. Thereupon followed a kind of national feast, in which the A-Barmbos took part with their war games, dances, and songs; and a dragoman went so far as to dance the favourite *pas seul* of the Mangbattus with much skill; speeches referring to the peace were not wanting, and all of this the messengers were to relate to Mambanga.

Casati's luggage had been left behind at Tangasi, so his stay with us was but a short one. His departure was fixed for the 25th of September. But the course of events necessitated my prolonging my stay at the station for an indefinite period. The chief reason was the universal dread and discontent which manifested itself in the garrison. The soldiers expressed themselves so strongly on passing events that Hawash sent them to me, whereupon they complained of Casati's departure and expressed the fear that I should leave too. This was very flattering for us, but I was angry nevertheless at their conduct, which was nothing less than a punishable demonstration, culminating in the avowal that as soon as I left they too would forsake the station and the enemy's country. Of course I reprimanded them severely, and told them that if they had dared to behave thus in our country, every fifth or tenth man of them would have been executed without grace, for that they stood in open insubordination to their commander Hawash; if they wished me to remain in the station they should have refrained from threats, for these would certainly not keep me longer than I meant to stay. They withdrew discomforted, and Hawash told me that they had long been discontented and wished to return to Makaraka; for there were no meat rations among the A-Barmbos, only banana flour, and they did not dare to leave the station on the small foraging expeditions so dear to them. They feared, too, that if I left, Mambanga would attack them again, and there were but three thousand Remington cartridges remaining, and an insufficient supply of percussion-caps. I had already distributed one hundred of these from my private stores. So, to ward off the possible catastrophe, I decided to remain at the station until either Emin Bey or reinforcements of men and ammunition arrived, and informed Emin and the soldiers of my resolution. Casati, however, left us, and we saw on this occasion how little ready the friendly A-Barmbos really were to do any one a service, for though Buru and his men idled away hours at the station, we

could not find five carriers even for Casati, and Hawash had the
few light bundles taken to the Welle by his own men. We often
had renegades from the hostile A-Barmbos. They longed for
order to be established that they might return to their huts and
fields; but nevertheless hung about in the wilderness. The most
obstinate was Bobeli, who thus led the others astray. Communication with Mambanga was for a time after my return maintained by delegates. Dembeh-Dembeh was first sent to him,
and afterwards others. If by any chance the messengers
remained away for a few days, the wildest fears were again
entertained, to be again allayed by the return of the courier with
presents from Mambanga to Hawash.

In their manners and customs the A-Barmbos most resemble
the Mangbattus, but the difference in their dialect is very marked.
Their implements, both for war and household use, were often the
same, but the industries, like those of the A-Madis, were of a
lower order. The union of small states under one ruler endured
longest in Mangbattu, and this gave them a good start in the
protection of their arts. In general, industry declines with the
breaking up of large states into smaller ones, and in this respect
Mangbattu has now also passed its prime. A few more decades,
and in the struggle for existence, the beautiful, carefully-executed
original art pottery in these lands will have given place to the
production of bare necessaries. Among the peculiarities of the
A-Barmbos, their women denote mourning for their lord and
master by a thick bast-rope wound several times round their
aprons. Other tribes have other signs; in Makaraka they
bestrew themselves with earth and ashes, and throw off their
garments. The Mangbattu women, with whom the hair is an
important ornament, cut it off close when their master dies, until
they have another suitor; and this sacrifice of hair is widely
practised as a mark of grief and mourning for the dead in other
parts of Africa. Fashion, too, is keeping pace with the times
among these children of nature—for instance, during the war
with Mambanga, the brass cases of the discharged Remington
cartridges were soon in great demand as articles of fashion and
barter; and the native dandies would certainly have had diffi-

culty in finding a more suitable ornament for the round holes in their ears than these bright metal coverings. The aristocratic fashion of long finger-nails is also in observance among the A-Barmbos, amongst whom I often saw nails two inches long; indeed, Mambanga's sister wore a rare necklace of long finger-nails threaded on a string.

During the last week of September, heavy thunderstorms were of daily occurrence, and on the 29th we had the first hailstorm I experienced during my second journey in Central Africa.

I had sent messengers to Mazindeh to look out for the box promised by Dsumbe, but they turned back, because a rumour was afloat in the Welle district that war had broken out again in A-Madi Land, and Mazindeh's huts had been burnt. I received this with the same incredulity as all rumours, and sent the men back with Dembeh-Dembeh to reconnoitre, and of course the intelligence proved to be false and exaggerated.

October was introduced in the station by festivities to celebrate the newly-formed alliance between the chief Bobeli and Hawash. On such occasions, as in all cases where natives assembled in large numbers, the precaution was taken of not admitting every one to the station, and those who entered had to give up their arms while within the walls. In times of peace many Mangbattus replace their lances with long prettily-patterned sticks. Old Buru supported himself on one of these in his daily visit to the station. He was a pleasant sociable old man, with enough youthful vigour left to wield a spear with good effect. His long gray beard had assumed a ruddy tinge from the red paint on his hands and body. It was remarkable how many old people I met at this place. Buru's father, an aged shrivelled-up mannikin, often made us merry with his humorous gestures and imitations of dances. It is probably a matter of chance that the A-Barmbos live to so great an age, for in general the Negroes in these parts lose their life in their best years.

As usual the progress of the peace negotiations was hindered by the endless gossip and lying rumours of Mambanga's hostile intentions. The A-Bisingas were said to have told the Mangballas that Mambanga had only contracted the blood-friendship with me out of policy to put us off our guard, and that he intended to descend unexpectedly on the station, massacre everybody, and then fly over the Bomokandi to Sanga. Such reports always found many among the Arabs and black soldiers to give them credence, especially as the half-breeds, who are fast held in the toils of their own superstitions, gladly adopt those of the Negro, including the "mapinge" and "benga." They imagined that I also must have some method of divination, and pressed me to show them my "mapinge." They often interpret our writing and printed matter or manuscripts as an oracle, or divining apparatus.

But Mambanga did nothing to conciliate them. He certainly sent delegates occasionally to Hawash with protestations of his friendship, but always the same men, and never any of those nearly connected with him, as he had expressly promised. Besides, his demands were often childish and silly, so that they could but serve to arouse dissatisfaction on our side. For instance, he requested Hawash to send him a good gun and powder, though he said not a word of giving up those he had taken from the Arabs, as had been agreed. And yet on every occasion I sent serious warnings by Adatam. Soon there came another report, to the effect that Mambanga intended to flee over the Welle northwards to Malingde's, and so the Mangbattus had to keep watch on the river. Fresh renegades joined us, among them the A-Zandehs who had previously fled to Mambanga when Mbittima was taken prisoner by the Arabs. They went back to their old master in the neighbourhood of the station.

I was glad to turn from these political events to the zoological discoveries which I made from time to time. I saw for the first time a new kind of guinea-fowl, the existence of which in these parts had been unknown to me. Its beautifully-marked plumage resembles that of the vulture guinea-fowl (*Numida vulturina*). I had already noticed the beautiful purple-black feathers, spotted or striped with white, in the caps of the Negroes. It was Dsumbe who brought me a pair of these birds, the plumage of which, shot in parts with ultramarine, confirmed the existence in Central Africa either of the vulture guinea-fowl hitherto only met with on the coast of East Africa (?), or of some other bird closely resembling it. A ruffle of black velvety quills goes round the neck from ear to ear, and gives the head of the fowl that faint resemblance in which its name originates. I met with single specimens afterwards in my Welle journeys to the Far West, chiefly on trees in the shady river forests. The A-Zandehs call

VULTURE GUINEA-FOWL.
(*Numida vulturina.*)

it timbombo, the Mangbattus kinge, the name for the ordinary guinea-fowl being Korandya.

Among the A-Barmbos I obtained another animal, little known as yet, the Flattermaki (*Galeopithecus*), a kind of furred flying creature, of which I had already procured a few skins. It is about the size of a small cat, and is distinguished by a wing membrane extending from the neck to the fore-legs, back-legs and tail, which serves as a parachute, and by means of which it flutters from tree to tree. The skin consists of two layers, which can be divided from one another; the upper disappearing into the skin at the back and upper side of the tail is covered with thick gray hair, the lower running down the middle line of the breast and stomach to the lower side of the tail, is bare at the edges and covered with light gray hair in the middle. The whole skin is fawn-coloured, very silky and soft, by far the most beautiful fur I ever met with in Africa. One peculiarity is a small bare place about two inches long on the under side of the tail near the root, covered with a kind of scales, which shows that it often comes in contact with branches, so that probably the tail helps to support it in some of its movements. The toes are armed with small sharp hooked claws; the eyes are large and brown. It is very difficult to catch this animal alive without damaging its skin, for it lives during the day in the trunks of hollow trees, and only comes out at night uttering a wailing cry. Its hiding-place has often an opening top and bottom, and the natives take advantage of this in catching the animal, by stopping the upper hole with basket-work and making a fire in the lower. The heat and smoke finally drive the terrified creature into the basket, but its feet and skin are often singed in the process, and in one case some of the claws dropped off, which, however, did not prevent the animal from fighting hard and biting one of my servants severely in the hand with its sharp long brown teeth. The native names for the Flattermaki are: A-Zandeh, nguyu; A-Madi, andupa; Mangbattu, nambuma. I carefully prepared the skeleton and beautiful skin. My collections of insects and butterflies were greatly increased at this time by the boys. I availed myself of part of this tedious leisure to make a fair copy of a map of A-Madi Land.

On the 14th of October the station was greatly enlivened by the arrival of Mazindeh from A-Madi with his A-Zandeh followers. The messengers despatched thither returned with him, but without the package I was awaiting, which had not yet reached Mazindeh's; however, messengers were on the way to Palembata to see about it. And Mazindeh by no means came empty-handed; he brought three elephant tusks for Hawash Effendi in addition to fowls and palm-oil. My black friend soon won over the Egyptian and his men by his lively and intelligent conversation, and Hawash laughingly acknowledged the effect of my four months' stay in A-Madi Land, for Mazindeh endeavoured to prove himself a good servant of the State. It was great fun to hear him in his picturesque manner setting forth to the A-Barmbos at their great festival next day their duties to the "Hokuma" (Government). I heard my own oft-repeated injunctions retailed word for word from his lips. It may here be remarked that the princes and chiefs of the A-Zandehs in general, once won, are more loyal vassals than the other black tribes, as may be seen from Zemio, Zassa, and the Makarakas; and short as was the time that Ndoruma had been subject to the Government, I am convinced that he, as well as Badinda, Japati, Mazindeh, and others, would have been powerful supports under a good rule. It is evident that the bold scheme of trying to persuade the people of Central Africa to acknowledge a settled and ordered Government is not everywhere so difficult and impossible of execution as might at first sight appear.

Mazindeh came with the ambitious idea of attaining, with Hawash's help, to a firm and important position, probably the sole rule of A-Madi Land. But his immediate object was to lodge all kinds of complaints, especially one of fresh inroads on the part of the South A-Madi chiefs into the country of his allies, the A-Manglis. He also hoped, by Hawash's intervention, to regain some of his daughters and female slaves, that had been taken from him in former raids of the A-Barmbos settled in the neighbourhood. His most ardent desire, however, was to obtain a few of the soldiers in the station to give support to his ambitious aspirations.

During the discussion as to whether this request could be legally complied with, the main question of the boundary line cropped up. Did A-Madi Land belong to Emin Bey's province or to the Bahr el-Ghazal? This vexed question, which had hitherto never been raised, led to misunderstandings harmful alike to the Government and to the natives. A-Madi is the best example of this. On the one hand Osman Bedawi had stationed his men there, and they demanded not only ivory, but other things in their own private interests, and, to call a spade a spade, made excursions for the purpose of robbery. On the other hand were Zassa's dragomans, who were by no means behind the others in arbitrary measures, and now the small territory was to be inflicted with a third category of leeches. In territories thus violently taken possession of by different authorities, who for the most part consider that they have a right to unlimited plunder, misunderstandings and differences are inevitable. Hawash Effendi had forbidden Zemio to extend his expeditions south of the Welle in future, but he himself had probably no authority to extend his jurisdiction over the A-Madi territory, at all events so long as the Bahr el-Ghazal administration was represented there. This evil was aggravated by the prevailing rivalry between the high officials and commanders of the stations to procure the largest quantities of ivory and to extend their field for plundering expeditions. In the former case they gained the acknowledgments of their superior officers and of the governor of the province, and the extension of their hunting-ground by increasing their power added to their personal interests. Personally I should have been pleased to see Mazindeh's tributary rule strengthened and supported, for it promised to be of service to the Government; but I could not in justice approve Hawash Effendi's acceding to Mazindeh's request by handing over the soldiers to the chief whom he made answerable to himself, thereby increasing the rivalry between the A-Madis, and adding a fresh cause of dissension to those already in existence, without bringing about a better and more enduring state of affairs. For if the commanders were in doubt as to the boundary line between the two great administrations, and I also was in the dark, it was of course impossible for the chiefs to tell to which flag they owed allegiance. And thus it happened that rulers to the north of the Welle, who had previously delivered their ivory to Osman Bedawi, now declared themselves under tribute to Hawash Effendi, and sent him ivory. This was done even by the old chief Malingde. This was of course encroaching on the rights of the Bahr el-Ghazal officials, whilst in other districts the matter was reversed. These remarks are not intended to convey a reproach to the officials, but only to confirm the fact that up to that time no one had thought of providing each chief with a kind of certificate to which he might attach some importance, and which would have had effect in his hands. And finally neither Hawash Effendi nor his colleagues were entrusted with articles of value to provide the customary return offerings for the presents sent to him by the vassal chiefs. Thus it became the ruling principle that the end justifies the means. Hawash took freely in order to give more freely. A shield, a spear, a knife, or some other native article, either presented to him or otherwise procured, would serve his turn as a complimentary present.

The A-Madi chief, Mbittima, would not be behind Mazindeh, and so arrived in his turn at the station to take part in the political squabble over this little land. In this case again, overhasty measures were decided upon which could not be carried into effect. I did not conceal my opinion, but beyond this I would have nothing to do in the matter. Hawash Effendi was certainly obstinate, and often took excessive and arbitrary measures, a tendency which, as he acknowledged, often drew upon him the censure of his superiors, and was the cause of his afterwards temporarily incurring Emin Bey's displeasure. But his untiring energy and tact in dealing with the natives were merits which placed him far above many of his colleagues in office. The Sudan official must be measured by a special standard, and being much sinned against, must be pardoned many transgressions. All of them are culpable, and this was just the difficulty that Gordon, Gessi, Emin Bey, and Lupton had to contend with: they had to entrust the execution of their instructions to officials who would not restrain their inherent corrupt tendencies.

Hawash's name will often occur in the history of the next few years; he proved himself under the circumstances a good serviceable officer, and later reached the coast and Egypt with Emin Pasha.

The new alliance with Mazindeh gave rise to the thought, on

the part of Hawash, of again attacking Mambanga with the help of the A-Madi; and for this purpose the A-Zandeh chief was to return later to the station with his men. I could not consent to this scheme either. It did not come to anything, the plan being thwarted by a rumour from Tangasi that Bahit Bey was on his way with soldiers from Makaraka, to re-open the war with Mambanga. On the 22nd of October a letter from him put the matter beyond all doubt. The reader will remember Bahit Bey as Mudir of Makaraka, from my first journey; Gessi Pasha had since suspended him from office, and now he was again reinstated in Makaraka by Emin Bey. Bahit announced his arrival from Hokwa's (Wando's son) together with Abd Allah Abu Sed, the administrator of Rimo in Makaraka, and a numerous troop; and desired that as large a number of boats as possible should be in readiness at the confluence of the Kibbali and the Gadda. Mambanga had without doubt also been informed by spies of the approach of his enemy, for we soon heard that he was preparing for flight.

The news of the arrival of the troops was so far satisfactory to me that it would enable me soon to continue my journey without let or hindrance; but at the same time it annoyed me that Mambanga, having rejected all my advice, should be hunted in the wilderness and probably finally perish there. It may be easily understood that I should gladly have seen the obstinacy of the chief yield to peaceable measures, and should have been glad for Hawash to have had the satisfaction of recovering the guns before Bahit Bey's arrival.

At this hour of Mambanga's greatest need, I determined to make one last attempt to save him, and in conjunction with Hawash, sent envoys to him. They took him a present from me, warned him of the approaching danger, and were instructed to earnestly enjoin him to come to the station and deliver up the guns. I sent word that I would even go so far as to meet him next day, but that he must hesitate no longer, for the danger was near at hand. If he came and delivered up the guns, Hawash would at once send him a bugler and ten soldiers to guard him from hostilities on the part of the troops from the east.

The next twenty-four hours passed in great suspense, for Mambanga's fate hung on his answer. It came on the 23rd of October, and destroyed every hope of a peaceful issue. His message was full of contradictions; the only one thing clear was the old story of distrust and fanaticism. Hawash's intentions were certainly not favourable to him, he said, or he would have sent envoys more frequently; but if his welfare was really of consequence to me, I was to come to him and remain with him. My proposal that he should meet me in the neighbourhood appeared to him a snare: he himself knew no fear, but his people considered that his life would be endangered. The messenger informed me privately that Mambanga wished for hostilities, and said that he would wage war on the Turk for years to come, for he had many brave warriors and allies in reserve. I was distressed at his blindness, but could not really be angry with him, for he was only defending his hereditary rights, his own and his people's hearth and country. The suspicion he nourished against me personally certainly vexed and wounded me. A large number of A-Barmbos and the chief Zurunga, formerly an ally of Mambanga's, with his men, were present when the message arrived. Zurunga had that very morning visited the station for the first time, and other chiefs afterwards followed his example; they assured us that they would not quit their dwellings at the approach of the soldiers. But the headstrong Bobeli and others held to Mambanga. So I had my answer translated by the interpreter in loud and decided tones that no one could fail to understand; this had been my last attempt to save Mambanga from certain destruction, and now my part as protector was at an end, and he must look after himself. I had repeatedly advised him and held out to him a saving hand in vain, but I had no intention whatever of complying with his useless summons to join him. He would now lose his home and country, and be hunted in the wilderness like a wild animal. And this was in fact my last message to Mambanga, for the terrible events I had foretold were only too soon to overtake him.

But efforts in another quarter had been successful. Buru with some fire-arms undertook a sally to the west, and brought back thirty A-Barmbos as hostages. As frequently happens in such cases, their kinsmen came to ransom them, and this invariably affords the best opportunity for disarming their ill-will. These, too, became tributary.

Hawash had a number of huts put up for the expedition from Makaraka, and with the aid of the A-Barmbos a considerable village soon sprung up at the foot of the eastern slope.

On the 26th of October we heard suppressed nugarra tones from the south-east, the direction of Mambanga's settlement ; all sorts of conjectures were raised, and it was even whispered that Mambanga was about to attack the station. The soldiers were enjoined to keep a strict watch, the number of sentinels was increased, and Buru's men were sent out to scout at night ; but the enemy kept at a distance, the anxiety subsided and gave place to gaiety, which Buru's people carried so far as to organize a dancing festival outside the station. On this occasion four fantastically-clad prophets distinguished themselves by a wild dance, in the pauses of which they prophesied the future fate of some of the spectators—exactly the same performance I had already witnessed at Ndoruma's. At all such festivals among the Mangbattus and A-Barmbos the jester plays an important part. His office was originally to keep the flies off the chief; he is the court dwarf, or "merry councillor"; but at popular festivals the comical little fellow is the wag of the whole throng. It was really highly diverting to watch him pursuing imaginary flies, pretending to catch them with great ease, dashing them angrily to the ground, and then in great triumph at his successful chase proceeding to kill them with the air of a conquering hero. To whom does this not recall the similar feats of heroism performed by the circus clown ! But in these lands the fly catchers are held in far higher esteem than among us ; they alone are privileged to mingle with the grandees and to accompany them into their dwellings. One of these Jack Puddings would frequently follow me also like my own shadow, waving his fly-catcher in the air.

The communication with the eastern stations had until now been maintained only by the boats of the Mangballas. Their chiefs, Nazima and Banguza, whose acquaintance I had made on my journey with Zemio, had been unfortunate in Mambanga's war with the Arabs; Banguza had fallen, and Nazima had been shot in the foot. The Mangballas assisted in the transport of Bahit Bey's troops over the Welle, and on the 29th of October the last of the men from Ali Station were conveyed to the south bank. The first to bring us certain tidings was Nezim, the same man who, three months previously, had come to me at the A-Madi station as Hawash's messenger. He had then been despatched to Emin Bey at Ladó, and was now returning with the expedition.

A few minor events at the station may here be recorded. First of all the attempt to transport six cows, which were waiting to be conveyed from the north bank of the Welle to the soldiers at Tangasi Station, where for six months nothing had been killed. This attempt was unsuccessful, for the district inhabited by Malingde's sons lay far inland, and there were no roads near the river. Then there was an elephant hunt, to which the A-Barmbos were summoned *en masse*. A herd of these animals had unexpectedly made their appearance in the neighbourhood of the settlement; but the pachyderms soon saw that something was wrong, made their way to the Welle, and simply swam across. Then messengers arrived again for Hawash from Mazindeh, with six elephants' tusks and a young chimpanzee. And then, by way of variety, there were further tedious discussions with the A-Madi chief, Mbittima, who was still at the station, and the weal and woes of the little mountain country always had its place on the orders for the day.

I was able also to make new studies of the punishment by flogging. Having already described how it is carried out in the Nubian and Negro lands of this district, I will here say a word of another method, the bastinado. This mode of punishment was up to the last few years much practised in Egypt, but was only inflicted in exceptional cases by the Egyptian officials in the Sudan. To keep the feet fast, a long thick stick is used, to the middle of which a loop for the feet is attached. The culprit, lies flat on his face, with his legs bent upwards from the knees, so that the soles of the feet are uppermost. Then the feet are secured in the loop and two men hold the ends of the stick, twisting it so that the loop is drawn up and the feet pressed close together. Then the heavy whip of hippopotamus hide comes into play with such serious effect as often to cause death. The flexible whip frequently curls round the foot so that the thin skin of the instep and the bones near the surface suffer most, and inflammation and dangerous mortification often set in. I once saw a boy, the skin of whose instep had been entirely destroyed, perish after months of suffering. In Egypt there certainly are people who can bear an astonishing number of blows on their soles without detriment to their health. But there the bastinado is carried out with a leather strap two inches broad, instead of the whip of hippopotamus hide.

I seized every opportunity of obtaining information as to the features of these southern districts, of which I always made a rough map. Later I travelled through the district and was able to revise these first impressions. But long before I myself visited the northern portion of this immeasurable forest, which has since been traversed and described throughout its entire breadth by H. M. Stanley, I had heard of it, and learned that it was inhabited towards the west by the large tribe of the A-Babuas, who cover their heads with clay.

So October came to an end amidst new plans and hopes, and the 1st of November brought round the great Arab festival "Id-el-kebir." Quite early in the morning the buglers were already on their round from hut to hut, with the customary request for a small present. Every one possessing holiday attire donned it for the occasion, but the best part of the festival to the people was wanting, namely, the feast, for it was not possible to kill a sheep or goat for the occasion in accordance with the Arab custom.

Day after day we awaited the arrival of the expedition, but as it happened, Bahit Bey had first turned off to Tangasi, and November had half gone before he appeared. Hawash Effendi was by no means overjoyed at the prospect of a superior officer in his neighbourhood, and often gave vent to his discontent in foolish and unwarrantable terms. It vexed him to play second fiddle, to be under orders to another, and to see both his prestige and gainings curtailed. For this reason he tried once more, of course in vain, to effect a reconciliation with Mambanga. But from Tangasi Bahit Bey had already put himself into communication with the chief, and sent back one of his sons, who had previously been taken by the Arabs. Thereupon the chief reciprocated by sending some of the guns so frequently mentioned, but Bahit's advances had no further result. On the contrary, Hawash's spies announced that Mambanga had sent on his wives and all his goods and chattels into Bobeli's territory, though he himself still kept near the huts with his troops, in order to provide for his people. Thereupon a raid on Bobeli's camp to capture the women was undertaken by our A-Barmbos, the Mangballes, and dragomans of the station; they hoped to take Bobeli by surprise, for his A-Barmbos had to make long excursions to procure provisions. But this cunning scheme was not successful, for they were unable to find the camp.

At last positive tidings came from Bahit Bey that the expedition would start during the next few days in several divisions, so as to prevent Mambanga's escape. Abd Allah and the administrator Bashir were to take a southern route from Tangasi through the chief Bauli's territory to cut off Mambanga's flight in this direction, whilst the dragoman, Mabub, with his contingent, was to go down the stream from Ali Station and prevent the chief crossing the river, and Bahit Bey intended to march into the enemy's country by the direct road.

Mazindeh and Mahmud arrived from Osman Bedawi's station at the same time as this intelligence, and were ordered by Hawash to turn back and see that, on the approach of the expedition westwards, the A-Barmbos did not escape along the north bank of the Welle to the A-Madis.

On the 15th of November it was announced that the three divisions of the expedition had left Tangasi. Mambanga had learned this from his spies sooner than we did, for he too left his territory with his warriors, though the Mudir's march was so rapid that, on the 17th of November, the first messengers sent by Bahit Bey from Mambanga's territory arrived at the station, bringing the news of the chief's flight and the possession of the huts by the troops. A permanent station was to be founded there, from which Hawash rashly concluded that Bahit would himself conduct the pursuit of Mambanga from that spot. This, in addition to the jealousies and scandal of all kinds to which Hawash gave his ear, incited him to further unwarrantable outbursts against Bahit Bey. He was at the same time unpopular with his troops, both on account of his severity and because he was unable to accede to their often unreasonable requests. I saw that evening to what all this would lead, for the news of Bahit's arrival at Mambanga's gave rise to a scene such as is only possible among the undisciplined soldiery of those countries. A sergeant forced the gate of the station that evening after it had been closed for the night, and armed with his gun rushed swearing into the dark to lodge a complaint with Bahit Bey against Hawash Effendi. As soon as it was known, pursuit was given, but he had already disappeared. The remarkable thing was that instead of being punished for this offence by Bahit, the culprit openly boasted of his impudent act. Over-severity and misplaced indulgence were exercised alternately according to the momentary situation, and this of course was bound to bring its punishment in its train. I always treated such conduct very seriously, and once when a sergeant spoke disrespectfully to me, I insisted on his being punished, and he was put in the pillory and only released when I interceded for him.

In Mambanga's territory, where Bashir Saleh's contingent had joined Bahit's forces, a strong settlement was founded with sixty soldiers; the former ruler, who, as has been said, had fled to the south, was deposed, his lands forfeited, and Wando's son Mbittima put in his place. He continued to rule there with his A-Zandehs after the return of some of Mambanga's subjects, who came back later.

In the meantime, before taking steps to pursue the fugitives, Bahit Bey came alone to the station, and was greeted by me as an old acquaintance. Years before I had made the journeys from Ladó to Makaraka and back as well as in the Bahr el-Ghazal province in his company, so there was plenty we could talk about in common. The intercourse between the two

ENTRY OF BAHT BEY'S TROOPS. (*Drawn by L. H. Fischr.*)

representatives of the Government was less friendly. Bahit and Hawash made mutual recriminations, both true and untrue, and their discussions were often conducted with the utmost violence to the detriment of the matter in hand. These battles of words were witnessed by many of the men, who might thus have taken example from their leaders. I kept myself out of it as much as possible, but often had to witness these scenes. Bahit's demeanour was certainly quieter and more sensible; Hawash's temper was almost beyond his control. The only thing that I could approve of in all this tumult was the address in which Bahit energetically represented to the troops the impropriety of their behaviour and demands. Not until they had given full vent to their anger did they go on to the chief matter in question, the pursuit of Mambanga and the acquisition of the A-Barmbo territory further westward for the Government.

The troops made their formal entry into the station on November 21st. Hundreds of A-Barmbos had assembled to witness this spectacle and to wonder at the forces which kept coming up from the distance. The officers walked at the head of their men with waving banners to the sound of the nugarra, the blowing of signal horns, and the rattle of all kinds of sound-instruments. On coming up to the station they made the circuit of it, drawing up for a short time in front of the awning erected for us, and were finally directed to their quarters on the slope of the hill. First came the regular troops with about fifty Remington guns, under the command of a black Sudan officer; then the garrison of Rimo Station in Makaraka, led by Abd Allah Agas Abu Zed, who was also well known to me during my travels in Kalika; further, over a hundred auxiliaries with the notorious Bashir Saleh, of whom I shall have more to say later, at their head; Niangara, Munza's successor, with his Mangbattus; A-Bangba, Niapu, and other warriors armed with spear and shield, or bow and arrows; the A-Zandeh chief Bauli, from the Bomakandi in the south-west, with his forces; and bringing up the rear of the endless procession, my black friend Ringio, from Kabayendi in Makaraka, whom the reader will also recollect in my first journey. He led up his sturdy Bombehs and Makarakas with great confidence to the clear sound of bells and the blare of long ivory horns to receive Bahit Bey's instructions with the others. The number of these different contingents was further increased considerably by carriers, women, servants, and slaves; for, in addition to the ammunition required and the personal effects of the officials, Government property had also been conveyed.

Another animated picture was soon afforded by the construction of huts for this mass of people, those erected by the A-Barmbos being quite inadequate for their accommodation. The life in the station was also active; the officials and clerks had work enough, for the loads were unpacked, the property given over and entered, and the greater part of it distributed at once among the soldiers and officials and debited against their allowance. Stuffs, tarbushes, shoes, soap, provisions, &c., were to be had in such abundance that many discontented spirits felt overwhelmed with earthly possessions. Active hands were busied at the quern and in the kitchen, making ready to entertain the guest and to meet the demands of many hungry mouths.

The greatest interest was aroused in the station by the new equipment which had been decided upon in Cairo for the Sudan army. Thousands of these uniforms had been sent to Khartum, and several dozens now found their way to this remote corner of the world. The uniform consisted of white knickerbockers, long white gaiters with innumerable fastenings, a full blouse of a kind of gray calico, and a large turban of the same, which was worn over the tarbush and secured with thick cords like those of the Bedouins. It was certainly very imposing. Unfortunately most of these things are only an encumbrance to the soldier in Negro countries. The assembled A-Barmbos were certainly greatly impressed by a parade of the men in their bran-new masquerade, but the soldiers were as little at home as a yokel in evening dress. The turbans were soon put to a practical use as aprons, and probably the sapient business was but of short duration, at least I do not remember seeing any such uniform in use at the stations later.

The chief matter for me was a despatch from Emin Bey. He wrote again that he was coming shortly to Mangbattu, and a box with which he surprised me was full of all kinds of things for my use and enjoyment, which he had selected with careful forethought for my bodily and mental comfort; lentils, coffee, soap, candles, matches, sardines, &c., a packet of the "Neue Freie Presse," even two bottles of Chartreuse, mixed pickles, and a box of golden Turkish tobacco. In my delight I gladly sacrificed some of these as a contribution to the public supper given by Hawash Effendi. The bottle of Chartreuse made the round several times and found great favour among the less scrupulous followers of Mohammed.

Halima and my Dinka man, Farag, were obliged to remain behind on my departure from the station on account of their swollen legs, but another girl was given to me as cook, and I still had Dembeh-Dembeh as dragoman. This time letters and tidings for Europe were sent by Ladó, in company with a temporary map of those southern districts I had made for Emin Bey. I had awaited in vain a despatch from Ndoruma, which reached my hands later. I received many visits from old Makaraka acquaintances, and Ringio had much that was interesting to tell me. It only remains for me to mention a *prima ballerina* such as I had never seen before. She was an A-Barmbo virago, a masculine giantess, who enjoyed the reputation of being the best soothsayer, and who danced one of the Mangbattu men's dances with such remarkable vigour and gestures as to impress even me.

The weather was now favourable for our setting out. During the first week in November there had been daily rains, which had become less and less frequent, until finally a short rainless season set in even in this latitude. So, on the 25th of November, the combined march began, led by Bahit and Hawash. A garrison with seventy fire-arms remained at the station, but our ranks were increased by a numerous train of A-Barmbos. Mabub descended the river at the same time with thirty boats with Mangballes under Nazima, and twenty boats with armed forces.

HIPPOPOTAMUS HUNTING.

CHAPTER XII.

JOURNEY TO THE CHIEF BAKANGAI FROM HAWASH STATION.

Mount Madyanu—At Magaragare—Landscape on the Welle—Mambanga pursued—His Troops dispersed—Spoils of War—Partition of A-Barmbo Land—Remarkable Giant Beetle—Rainy Season—Ringio—Parting of the Expedition—Amongst the Thievish A-Barmbos—Arab Raiding System—Vandalism—Negotiations with the A-Barmbos—Lynch Law—My Stolen Effects Recovered—Recall of the Expedition—Envoy to Bakangai—Parting from Hawash—Stormy Night in the Wilderness—Scenery on the Bomokandi—We enter the Great Forest—Reception by the Prince—At the Goal.

BAHIT BEY had greatly facilitated my journey by providing me with fifteen Makaraka carriers, who, being well drilled in their duties, took up their burdens with a will and without any of the noise and disturbance to which I had for months been subjected. We set out several thousand strong, but were continually brought to a stop during the first hour until the disordered mass formed itself in the usual single file. These delays and irregularities on the march interfered greatly with our advance, for every stoppage and variation in the rate of progress had to be taken into account and noted down.

For the first two days, and until we had left Mount Madyanu behind us, we proceeded in a south-westerly direction. The wide undulating country was covered here also with low woods interspersed with grass reaching to the neck, and sometimes already turning quite yellowish.

We now left Buru's territory and entered that of the

KALA ANTELOPE. (*A. leucotis.*)

A-Banya branch of the A-Barmbos, the A-Mayalas lying to the east of our route. All the huts—even those of Bobeli—were deserted, and the fields abandoned to be pillaged by our advancing hordes. Towards noon we crossed the river Kibongo, twenty yards wide and very full of water, and shortly afterwards pitched our camp on the further side of the Konsala brook about half an hour's march from the Welle, on a level elevation gently sloping down to the river. Once more camp life with so large a company, to which I had long been unaccustomed, exercised its charms upon me; and in the day-time the sight of hundreds of busy hands working at the huts riveted my attention, and in the evening countless camp-fires throwing up flames between the huts reawakened in me the old feeling of comfort. I was, moreover, just in the state of mind for such feelings, and once more new districts and new experiences lay before me. In a more material sense, too, my journey opened well, for a Kala antelope (*Antilope leucotis*) had fallen into the men's hands, and the more highly-favoured amongst us were able to have some meat, for it is the custom to bring all game captured to the leader of the expedition, who can divide it as he pleases.

The following day we had a hard march southwards, past Mount Madyanu, and made considerable progress. At first we encountered only low grass on the steppe, so that the multitude could march several columns abreast until this was prevented by the high grass and the difficulties presented by the ground. The chief body of water crossed on that day was the Tota, twenty yards broad and four feet deep, which bears the same name as the island under Erruka's sway, situated just before its confluence with the Welle, from the northern bank of which I had previously seen it. It was now, however, out of sight, as the Welle had been since our first encampment. It took us over an hour to cross this rapid river, and it required all my exertions as well as those of Bahit Bey to preserve order and prevent accidents. The women and children were carried and supported by the men. South of the river lay the land of the A-Bondus, and beyond them came the A-Mazungas, whilst the A-Mubangas dwelt on the hilly land at the foot of Mount Madyanu. During the latter half of our march we passed over undulating and even hilly land, stretching all round Mount Madyanu and far away to the south, characterizing this part of A-Barmbo Land for several leagues round. Madyanu forms indeed the still distinctly prominent southern spur of a pre-existing mountain range running from south-east to north-west, as still most clearly evidenced by the mountain group of Angba, Lingua, and Malingdeh in A-Madi Land; and the hilly south of Mount Madyanu points probably to other southern offshoots of this once great mountain chain. As to the east, so to the west of Mount Madyanu, the hilly character of the land, gradually vanishing after several leagues, gives place to the predominant formation of the country.

In the immediate proximity to the mountain we crossed the Sano, a river fifteen yards wide, and so deep that, besides placing a tree-trunk athwart the stream, we were forced, on account of our large numbers, to erect a temporary bridge higher up. On the opposite side extended the cultivated fields and huts of the A-Barmbos, which, however, were likewise deserted and left to their fate. The order to encamp there for the night being given, each man looked to his own wants, and all kinds of food were soon brought in, besides whole huts, roofs, wood, grass, cooking utensils, pots, and gourd dishes of all sizes. The main body of the expedition was to remain in this neighbourhood for some days whilst hunting out Mambanga, for here, thanks to the well-cultivated fields, means of subsistence were plentiful. But a still more advantageous spot was found, and the camp moved thither next morning, the 27th of November; here we were situated on a hill, surrounded by the chief Magaragare's huts. Although the site had not been chosen from any æsthetic considerations—for neither Arabs nor Negroes are susceptible to the charms of Nature—yet in all the surrounding country I could hardly have found a more delightful spot, with the sole exception of Mount Madyanu itself. The view from Mount Magaragare over the country to the north was quite an African piece of scenery, no less than that landscape, Erruka's "Isles of the Blessed," which I have attempted to describe. A mile away flowed the majestic river, winding down the valley in a curve slightly turned towards us, while here and there on its bosom reposed inhabited islands. From its southern end, lying nearest me, three islands were visible between the lofty stems of the forest bordering its banks. Their lord was the chief Goggi.

To the east the Welle was hidden for a short distance, soon, however, again appearing in the north, to disappear eventually behind the spurs of Mount Madyanu, where, hidden away from me now, were Erruka's islands. The western part of this small curve stretched away to the north-west for a mile or two in a broad sheet of water, where it likewise encircled a long island of irregular shape called Apuka (the tenth important island down stream), belonging to the Embata chief, Nendika. Far behind, the Welle curves round to the west, and is lost to view. There, however, lies the group of islands belonging to the chief Kaimba. Behind the visible portion of this western reach, forming a background, are the A-Madi mountains, and nearest the spectator Mount Angba. To the east of it is situated Mount Lingua, and still further to the east Mount Malingde shuts off the horizon. A small peak visible in the bluest distance must lie in the wild tract extending to the north of A-Madi Land. The country immediately to the north of the Welle is hilly, and there, too, a rich vegetation followed the course of the small streams.

Moreover, the view from Mount Magaragare enabled me to take important angular measurements, which afforded me a new basis for the triangulation of A-Madi Land. To the south, at the water-parting of the Welle and Bomokandi, lay the country of the A-Zandeh chief Gansi, a son of Kipa. Ever since the more prosperous times of his father he had held some of the A-Barmbo tribes (A-Nguyas, A-Meferres, &c.) under his sway, just as the Zandeh prince Mambanga did in the west, and also Bangatelli, Kamsa, and other sons and relations of Kipa.

Suddenly news came from Gansi telling us that Prince Mambanga and his followers were in the neighbourhood, and asking us to come with all speed. Accordingly, on the 25th November, Abd Allah and Bashir with about one hundred and sixty soldiers and Ringio with his Bombeh's, as well as Bauli's people, were despatched to look for Mambanga, whilst I remained behind in the camp with Bahit Bey, Hawash, and about an equal number of armed men, besides the A-Barmbos and Niangara's men, and all the women, servants, and carriers. Meanwhile the

VIEW OF THE WELLE FROM MAGARAGARE. (*Drawn by L. H. Fischer.*)

Mangballes under Mabub had been sacking and burning on their journey up stream, and I saw the flying Embatas making their escape in boats. It was said they had lost about forty boats and several men, and that Erruka's islands had unfortunately been also looted, whilst the chief himself had taken refuge with his father, Kaimba, and that all the islands in sight had been deserted beforehand by their inhabitants. We then received the news from the opposite bank that Mazindeh had carried out Hawash's commands, and was actually keeping a look-out. In the camp all went merrily, for articles of many kinds were brought in without much trouble. The telebun-corn was not yet fully ripe, it is true; but when beaten and ground it could be winnowed, and many then prefer it to bananas. We could also obtain manioc, sweet potatoes, and small quantities of maize, sesame, tobacco, &c. As to the red durra, I may remark that it is grown here, though only in small quantities, as I had already noticed when with Prince Mambanga.

Of course all sorts of utensils were also picked up by our men, and they were well pleased to find the Rokko-tree growing near all the settlements, and even pieces of the dry, peeled-off bark lying ready to hand in the huts, so that many of them could without more ado change their old Rokko rags for a fine new garment. But first of all, of course, it had to be "woven," *i.e.* the piece of bark had to be metamorphosed into a web-like material, a process which was accomplished with proportional rapidity. Far into the night one could hear on all sides the noise of the hammers busily at work upon the Rokko bark. For this purpose the natives of the district make use of antelope horns attached to small elephant tusks, about a foot in length, a net-work of deep grooves being then cut into the cross section, which has a circumference of one or two inches. The damp bark is then placed on a block of wood and stamped and beaten until the fibres are separated and the mass made thin and flexible. At a pinch, however, this can also be managed with round stones, and the Wagandas and Wanyoros use large well-made mallets for the same purpose.

The Embata chiefs soon came into the camp, and foremost among them Erruka himself, followed by Kaimba and the rest, bringing all kinds of provisions, including baskets of fowls, as a token of submission. They were told to collect their people and return without fear to their homes, and to submit peaceably henceforth to the commands of the Government. Many received a long red cotton shirt as a mark of their subjection.

Many and well-founded were the complaints raised on this occasion—as had often happened before—by Bahit Bey and Hawash as to their lack of presents and peace-offerings for the Negroes, and of sufficient quantities of objects to barter in exchange for ivory. For this reason it was indeed often very difficult to form a lasting bond between the Government and the natives, whose reconciliation might really be effected at so small a cost. Only a small portion of the value of the ivory delivered was returned in the shape of merchandise, hardly enough to meet the requirements of the officials.

On the evening of the 29th of November, news was received by a letter from the Secretary of the success of the expedition sent against Mambanga; his forces had been dispersed, and a great deal of booty taken, but the chief and Bobeli had again made their escape. On the 3rd of December, another letter announced that the expedition would return on the following day. I then received further details from Ringio—that Mambanga had been relying on help from the Zandeh chief Gansi, who had, however, betrayed the fugitive's retreat to Bahit Bey. When our men advanced, Gansi's A-Zandehs and Ringio with his Bombehs composed the vanguard, and were therefore not recognized by Mambanga's people as enemies until the Nubian Arabs, the soldiers armed with rifles, and the colours came in sight. Then ensued a general panic, and many, to run the better, threw away their large wooden shields and even, as is the wont of Negroes, their Rokkos, which might have impeded their flight. Quantities of these shields were afterwards thrown on the camp-fires, for the warriors found more valuable booty in the numerous other discarded weapons, and the Bombehs did in fact return with a fine assortment of Mangbattu knives (trumbashes), lances, &c.

Ringio and Gansi pursued the enemy nearly as far as the Bomokandi, where tracks at length diverged in so many directions that the right one was lost. Meanwhile Abd Allah and Bashir established themselves in Mambanga's deserted camp, where they feasted off many of their slain enemies. Some of Mambanga's personal property reached our camp, besides about a hundred women, two of his sons, and little blonde Hawaja and the mother of Mambanga's sons, who were brought in as prisoners of war.

Mambanga and Bobeli had escaped with most of their men; but each day many deserters came in, and on one occasion two of Bobeli's grown-up sons, with a few hundred of their A-Barmbos. One hundred and fifty lances and seventy-five shields were taken from them as being legally due to the victor, and they returned to their homes as Buru's men. What most disgusted me in the whole of our dealings with Mambanga was the treachery of the Negroes. He had been betrayed, not only by Gansi, who thought to increase his importance by keeping away from him, but even Bobeli's sons made most eager offers to betray their ally, pledging themselves to lure him into the desert with nugara cries, and then bring him in as a prisoner. This dishonourable plan was, however, unsuccessful, for the hunted chieftain found means to escape by secret paths, eventually, with a few of his comrades, reaching the independent Mangbattu chief, Sanga Popo, to the south of the Bomokandi. He was not indeed spared the tragic fate of his predecessors; but further details on this point belong to a later period.

The neighbouring A-Barmbo chiefs and Magaragare having now returned and sent in their submission, we were able to make a further advance; and Hawash Effendi resolved, with the help of the Government troops, to bring the whole of A-Barmbo Land by degrees under the dominion of Kipa's successors, the A-Zandeh chiefs, who were already settled in the district. I acknowledge having supported this plan, for it was the best means of consolidating the numerous small A-Barmbo tribes; Buru, of course, continuing even later to hold sway over the eastern district. As to Bobeli, he wandered about for a long time even after this, with a few faithful followers, until at length fate overtook him also. Gansi, on the other hand, was entrusted with the central portion of the A-Barmbo territory, and soon afterwards a station was founded on Mount Magaragare. The next step was to gain possession for the purposes of the Government of the western district also, if possible as far as the confines of the Zandeh chief Kamsa, where the Bomokandi flows into the Welle. I of course pursued my peaceful avocations apart from these warlike occurrences. Mabub, who had just returned with some Mangballe and soldiers from a reconnoitring expedition down the river, informed me that there were about ten more inhabited islands on this side of the Embatas, whom I had previously visited. At Magaragare I also had the great satisfaction of enriching my collection with a rare creature. It is true it was only a beetle, but of such a size that in sober earnest it would have been more appropriate to that period when our earth was still like some fabled world, inhabited by giant beasts. Just as we are accustomed to look upon the elephant as a descendant of far larger pachyderms, so also my A-Barmbo beetle resembles one of the giants surviving among the coleoptera. When the creature whizzed over our heads, for the moment I really took it for a bird; but recognizing my mistake the next moment, with the help of my men began an exciting chase. The beetle luckily settled on a tree close by, and

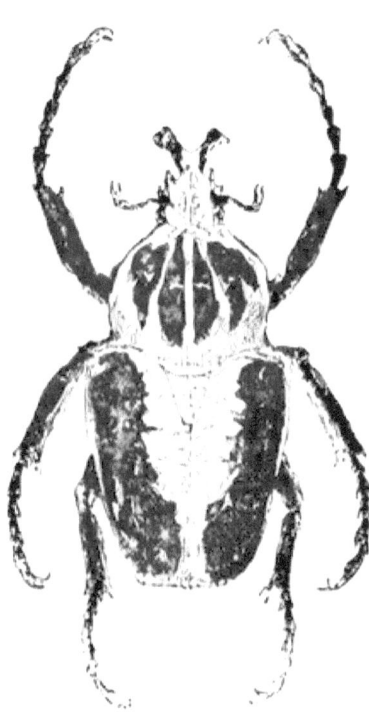

GIANT BEETLE. (*Goliathus Atlas.*)

was then easily captured. The wing-cases were brown, and on the black thorax there were broad white bands converging towards the head, while the sides of the abdomen and the legs were of a dark olive green colour. The body was ten cm. long by four and a half wide. Unfortunately this specimen of *Goliathus Atlas* was lost with the rest of my collections. The accompanying copy, about two-thirds natural size, is taken from a specimen in the Imperial Natural History Museum at Vienna. At Magaragare I also obtained the skin and skeleton of a young otter for my collection, besides a curious bracelet made of a number of thoraces of large weevils strung together, and some queerly-constructed wooden amulets. These wonder-working pieces of wood are worn by the A-Zandehs, as well as by many other Negro tribes, as a safeguard in battle or to invite or prevent rain.

The rainy season meanwhile had really come to an end in the second half of November, but we had thunderstorms from the east nearly every day, and some showers even in December. It may be remembered that the rains began in February with the western A-Barmbos, so that in that latitude the rainy period lasts nearly ten months, and, as will soon be seen, I myself experienced some heavy showers on the Bomokandi even at the end of December. But there the vast forest commences which stretches away to the south. This heavy rainfall, extending through the greater part of the year, is one of the chief factors in causing the fertility of the soil. As at the commencement of the rainy season, the wind during the last month blew pretty strongly from the north-west between the hours of eleven and four. I had foretold an eclipse of the moon for the 4th of December, and when it occurred the greatest surprise at my omniscience was expressed.

At this time I received frequent visits from Ringio, who had been in the service of the Arabs and the Government for nearly a quarter of a century, and had a better knowledge of the radical abuses than any one else. He was chief dragoman to the Makarakas and Bombehs, of whom the greatest services were required as being the most reliable amongst the tributary tribes, and in this official position he was the first to suffer from the unwarranted demands made on his people. In former times he had often complained to me of the state of affairs, and now assured me once more that there was no improvement, the people were disaffected, and so his position as intermediary between them and the Government was most onerous. Having spent his whole life with the Nubian Arabs, he was thoroughly imbued with their manners and customs, repeating his prayers daily as they did, and he always impressed me as a true and faithful servant of the Government, although as intermediator it was perhaps not always possible for him to fulfil the heavy obligations imposed on his people. I have noted my opinion of him quite impartially in this place, because it was here that I saw him for the last time, and I shall briefly relate his ultimate fate in due course.

About this time I was again reminded of that infamous impostor who made my stay at Tangasi so disagreeable. While returning from the Rol this scoundrel was lately caught in possession of some slaves, whom he had passed off as the property of sixteen Arabs in Mangbattu Land. Emin Bey now ordered all of those inculpated in this slave traffic to be sent to Lado. This will serve to show how all were in principle still devoted to the slave trade. Exportation to the north had become much more difficult, but the slave traffic was carried on all the more vigorously at home.

Unfortunately there was no improvement in the state of feeling between Hawash Effendi and Bahit Bey, and this was probably the reason why the former suddenly changed his mind and retreated with half the men—to wit, the Makarakas—nominally to continue the search for Mambanga. I then joined Hawash and Bashir, and, following the original plan, we resumed our journey on the 9th of December. We were reinforced by Gansi with his men and many A-Barmbos from the new district; Buru, on the other hand, returning home with his people. We still had a considerable force collected at the foot of Mount Magaragare, and, the order being given, marched forward with closed ranks, for it was reported that the western A-Barmbos were going to attack us. Leaving the territory of the A-Mubangas with its noticeable mountainous character already described, we found a narrow stretch of desolate country, and then passing the A-Balas, encamped in the land of the A-Gandas. During the first few days we made a devious course westwards away from the Welle. Here, too, and farther on, the natives had fled, but did not venture to attack us.

The second day we crossed the Warra river, about twenty yards wide and five feet deep, and were forced to use tree trunks for the passage. We concluded from the many dwellings and extensive fields that there was a considerable population, though here again the populated tracts were small in comparison to the whole district, and are always separated by the desert country and found only near the river; while the water-parting of the Welle and Bomokandi is almost entirely uninhabited. It was a good time of year for the march of a large number of men, for the telebun corn was mostly cut and gathered into the granaries. Our men, unfortunately, were not content with stealing what they required for food, but the numerous camp-followers carried their vandalism so far as to set fire to many of the corn stores.

Leaving the territory of the A-Gandas, we passed through another short stretch of desert and reached the A-Mezimas, where we caught sight of the Welle once more, about twenty minutes' walk from our second night's encampment. Between Kaimba and the A-Mezimas the islands for the most part lie in groups.

My black friends, Bamadsi and Senu, the thieves and receivers of stolen goods who had treated me so badly, were in hiding further to the north-west, and many islands in the river lay between us and their country. Amongst the A-Mezimas I therefore again came in contact with the A-Barmbos living in the district of the Mambanga-Zandehs. It was these very A-Mezimas, under their chief Bazingebanno, who had formerly threatened Dsumbe.

After a short march we reached our temporary destination on the 11th of December, the third day of our journey, and from this spot, the peace negotiations which now took place were carried on. The robbery and plunder committed by our men certainly did not indicate a mission of peace, but it is always the custom of the Arabs to impress the Negroes with a sense of their power and to harass and starve them into subjection. It is certainly not my wish to defend this system of pillage, although I must confess that the Negroes are often by no means inclined to compliance until they have learnt to recognize the full force of their adversaries, and have been tamed by the severe discipline of war. The gradual spread of European influence in the colonial territories finds indeed sometimes other conditions, and the high reputation of Europeans, their omnipotence, and, it is to be hoped, also their humanity, will pave the way for better times, and decrease the necessity of war. But it may be that powder and shot are in certain cases the best means of attaining the end in view.

As soon as we reached the A-Mezimas, every one hurried away in search of food, for the timid and indolent get only the wretched gleanings. I, too—"in for a penny, in for a pound"—had to let my men join in the plundering. Dsumbe prowled about after fowls and tobacco, whilst Dembeh-Dembeh returned with a basket of sesame, and my carriers came laden with maize and such like. It was vain to try to stem the tide of destruction, and whole groves of bananas fell in a few minutes under the blows of the trumbashes. Then the men, taking five or six trunks, placed them so as to form a conical structure, and by covering them over with leaves, had their quarters for the night ready. The felling of these fruit-trees is deplorable under any circumstances, as they are of great importance to the owners. It is of no avail to urge by way of excuse that new branches would compensate in a few months for the trunks which had been hewn down; nor did the end justify the means, for how many hundreds of branches were cut down on the march from mere love of destruction! However, I must do that justice to Hawash Effendi that he gave his men orders to abstain from all deeds of violence against the natives themselves. He also sent offers of peace to the chiefs, some of whom did not long delay coming into the camp, bringing their ivory with them. And these same men who had formerly been moved by the weight of a bad conscience, or by fear, or ill-will to keep away from me, were now

RECKLESS DESTRUCTION OF BANANA TREES. (*Drawn by L. H. Fischer.*)

brought to subjection by real fright and stern necessity, for they well knew that otherwise they would have to face the collective forces of the "Turks."

Accordingly, I again soon saw Senu, who brought in his tribute of ivory with cringing obsequiousness; likewise that very Basansa under whose conduct it was, as had been proved, that out of forty loads several cases had been stolen on a previous occasion. He probably thought I should not spy him out of the throng, and, to further his disguise, had actually changed his name, but I recognized him even at a distance by his slight stoop. Basingebanno presented himself also, but his utterances were now in a much humbler strain than the message which he had sent me by Dsumbe.

I generally kept away from the long discussions between Hawash and the A-Barmbos. There were many complications. Many of the A-Barmbos had escaped at our approach to the north bank of the Welle, where, however, fresh enemies were already in wait for them. There were soon complaints that Mazindeh, the A-Madi Mbittima, the dragomans from Osman Bedawi's station, and other chiefs on the further bank, had taken the women who escaped thither. This naturally provoked Hawash again, and he sent a division across to rescue the victims, and if possible to bring in Mahmud and the Bongo dragomans as prisoners; and the men really brought back twelve slaves from the station, seven of whom, mere children, had already been marked as slaves, with three newly-made cuts in each cheek. Mahmud, Mazindeh, Mbittima, and most of the Bongo dragomans had managed to hide before the arrival of the soldiers.

The immediate result of this expedition of rescue was a counter-cry that our troops had in their turn been robbing and plundering. In a word, there were fresh evils even amongst the A-Madi, without, as we shall see farther on, any plan being carried through. Not all of the A-Barmbos of the district had submitted; on the contrary, many of them were in hiding after concealing their property on the islands. So that very peremptory measures had to be taken, and there were skirmishes between the A-Barmbos and our people, who often went out in small parties, in which sometimes blood was shed. Dsumbe, for instance, on being surprised by the A-Bukundas when he was sent soon after our arrival with a few soldiers to Mambanga-Zandeh, shot one of the natives and brought back the pierced shield as a trophy. Mambanga was naturally overjoyed in this way to get nearer the goal at which he had long been aiming, and once more recover his authority over the A-Barmbos.

In this chaos of constant negotiations, complaints, processes, capture and exchange of women, despatch of skirmishing parties, and infliction of punishment, still further aggravated by the din and tumult of camp-life, the days passed noisily away. One specially abominable and deplorable scene occurs to my mind. One day the soldiers thought they recognized amongst the A-Barmbo rabble a man who had once during a sally from the station (Hawash) killed one of their own men; mad with rage, they rushed in a body on the luckless yet innocent man, belabouring him with the butt-ends of their guns; whenever he attempted to escape, his tormentors raised a yell of triumph, and once more felled him to the ground. Before I heard of the occurrence and could intervene, the victim of this cruel treatment had breathed his last in the midst of the infuriated mob.

I experienced a greater sense of justice in the diligent search which resulted in the return of some of my stolen property. The receivers, indeed, denied having anything still in their possession, but the goods were found hidden away on an island with other articles, including four boxes of English powder, some linen, and many other sorts of things, some of which I now gave away as presents. So Senu and Bamadsi had still further compromised themselves by their denial; the former managed to escape just in time, whilst his accomplice was punished by being put in the pillory. I must allow that I now demanded, as some compensation for the inconvenience and vexation the rascals had once caused me, that Hawash should order the culprits to give me ten trumbashes and thirty lances. My demand was complied with, and I felt a certain malicious pleasure in dividing the implements amongst my Makaraka carriers and the subalterns.

Of course I was still more rejoiced by the arrival at last of the long and anxiously-expected box from Khartum, of which Dsumbe had already received intelligence at Ndoruma's. At first sight I thought it contained provisions, but the contents were far more precious, consisting entirely of printed matter—bundles of newspapers, one volume of Petermann's *Mitteilungen*, the lately published maps of my first travels, and best of all these good things, a charming little budget of letters; but my enjoyment was again clouded by sorrow, for my letters brought sad intelligence from home.

Orders arrived about this time from Bahit Bey, who was at Tangasi, that Hawash should return in order to start for Makaraka in accordance with Emin Bey's commands. The real cause of the order lay in complaints made as to certain arbitrary proceedings of Hawash when at Tangasi, against Niangara. The consequence of this sudden recall of the expedition was, unfortunately, that the work begun in the A-Barmbo territory remained incomplete, and neither now, nor, as events will show, at a later period, did the injured natives receive indemnification by a settlement of their affairs and assurance of peace. I did not allow myself to be thwarted by the retreat of the whole band, which shortly ensued, but seized this opportunity to carry out an old plan, namely, the undertaking of a solitary journey to Bakangai. Basingebanno did not refuse any longer to provide me with messengers and even carriers, and so I immediately despatched some men to Bakangai, sending Dsumbe with them to anticipate any possibility of false intelligence.

Meanwhile I made an excursion on the Welle, gaining thereby a new landmark on the river, which would be useful as a connection between my present journey and that to be undertaken in February. It was about forty minutes' march from our camp to the river, and about the same distance thence in a north-westerly direction to the point where I had previously crossed on the way to Mambanga-Zandeh's. Numerous rocky ledges here rose above the clear water, for the Welle had by this time, the 19th of December, already sunk six feet. A number of hippopotami disported themselves in the river, exposing their huge heads above the surface, but never for more than a minute. It is often useless to hunt them, for, when badly wounded or killed, the animals drift far away down stream and are lost to the sportsman, while it is pure chance if they fall into the hands of the natives. When shot by a good marksman their unwieldy body rises suddenly out of the water, only to disappear with the same rapidity. If slightly wounded they hide in the thick grass on land, where they can breathe more freely than in water.

Even before the order to retreat had reached the expedition, messengers had departed westwards with some of Mambanga-Zandeh's men to Bakangai's brother, Kamsa; they now returned with a few of his people, bringing ivory, to express their chief's delight at the determination of the Government to enhance his power amongst the A-Barmbos, and to state that he was now awaiting Hawash Effendi. My messengers also soon returned with good tidings; they were accompanied by envoys from the chief, who were to present me with a chimpanzee and three elephant tusks, and to escort me to him with all speed. Meanwhile I had already made all necessary arrangements for my departure, even to finishing my letters and reports for Europe, and was thus able to start next day without any delay. Hawash at the same time moved his camp farther back to the east, where he was to await news of my arrival at the Bomokandi and safe passage over the river with Basingebanno's carriers. The first orders sent to Hawash had been quickly supplemented by a second, conveyed by thirty soldiers from Tangasi, so that now the return of the expedition appeared still more urgent.

The Embatas had meantime refused the troops the use of their boats, but the opportunity was taken to seize ten of them; and the ivory and other goods besides were for the first time transported by water from those western districts to the station on the Gadda, thus proving beyond all doubt that the whole distance of about one hundred miles is free from rapids and quite navigable. I also took this opportunity of sending my chimpanzee and newly-made collections up the river. I intended to make my way to the east again by another and more southerly route from Bakangai, and so sent my invalided servants, who had been left behind at the station with Buru, as well as the packages which had remained there, to Tangasi.

Thus on the 26th of December, my long-cherished wish was at length fulfilled, and it was in a most contented frame of mind that I followed my small company of fifteen A-Barmbo carriers to the south. My retinue was strengthened on this journey by the accession of the dragoman Dembeh-Dembeh and a small

A NIGHT IN THE FOREST. (*Drawn by L. H. Fischer.*)

maid, besides a girl whom Dsumbe had procured from Hawash.

During the next few days, and beyond the Bomokandi as far as Bakangai's, our way led constantly southwards with few deviations. Shortly after our departure we passed by Basingebanno's huts, and traversing the country of the A-Mezimas, reached Ngillima's abode. We were delayed some hours by the necessity of procuring supplies, for a wild desert stretches away to the south from this place. Farther on in the same direction succeeds a hilly district which parts the rivers falling into the Wel'e-Makua from the tributaries of the Bomokandi, its southern affluent; the divide reaches its greatest elevation, an hour's walk to the east, in the Bongotu mountain chain running south-south-east and north-north-west. Behind it lay the route to Bakangai, which Osman Bedawi had taken the previous year. The first stream that flows into the Bomokandi is the Gadsi, ten yards broad. I was obliged to recross it the following day at a point where there was a bend to the south-west. All the smaller streams found their way to it during the first half of our journey from the east, and afterwards from the west. The road from the A-Barmbos as far as Bakangai's had been very little used, and was completely concealed by the grass which rose above our heads, so that we found it easier to strike through the tracts of forest, which gradually increased as the woodlands bordering on the small rivers became more dense. The first night we encamped in the depth of the forest; but the men being too lazy to build a hut, and there being little likelihood of rain, I settled myself as best I could under the leafy crests of the huge trees.

The moon was in the second quarter, and now and then its beams burst through the rifts of the majestic forest dome, which resounded with the merry shouts of the men. I, too, was in a happy frame of mind, and eagerly devoured the simple evening repast of kisra with chicken and manioc root, and afterwards, indulging in a cigarette, unconsciously counted the cheerfully glowing camp-fires, while my thoughts were in reality hurrying on to my long-desired goal. But soon the mirth and laughter around grew silent, and weariness quickly succumbed to sleep. I alone was unable to sleep, and in its place came the forerunners of fever.

I had neglected for several days to dose myself against its attack with quinine, and had to bear the consequences. I lay under my woollen blanket with my teeth chattering; then this cold fit was succeeded by one of heat, until the gentle, monotonous sough of the wind in the leaves so far lulled me that I fell into a light sleep, in which, however, my excited fancy found no real rest.

I had not long enjoyed this doze, when I was suddenly awakened by a loud rustling and crackling as the trees swayed to and fro in the wind, for a storm was approaching. Things looked dismal enough. Masses of black cloud rolled up, smothering the light of the moon save for a few gleams which died away in the glare of the southern heavens shining like a sea of fire beyond the narrow limits of the forest. A raging fire had evidently broken out in the far-distant steppes, which was being driven on by the fury of the storm.

There was little time for meditation, every moment was precious, for the thunderstorm might burst upon us any minute. The wind was already rushing madly through the trees, hurling foliage and dry branches down upon us, and in another second we felt the first heavy raindrops. I hurriedly took measures to roll up the rugs with all speed, and to put them in the waterproof cover, placing the feet of the angareb on some boxes, and protecting the whole with a piece of oilcloth. I then crept underneath to seek shelter against the drenching rain. The glare in the sky soon vanished, for the rain quickly quelled the flames; our camp-fires went out too, and, while the moon was hidden by the heavy clouds, the pitchy darkness of night reigned supreme, save when for a moment the dense darkness was illumined by flashes of lightning crossing one another in all directions, and causing trees, men, and all other objects to appear suddenly like ghosts and again vanish. Thunder drowned the rustling of the trees, and there was often a crackling sound above us like that of grape-shot, all the more terrible since I again momentarily experienced the suddenly increased pressure of the atmosphere, as I had done before during many similar thunderstorms. Besides all this, the rain rattled down incessantly on the foliage of the trees, deluging us poor mortals below. However, in half an hour's time all was at an end; the ashes of the fires were speedily kindled again, and whole mountains of wood piled upon them, so that the Negroes were enabled thoroughly to warm their stiffened limbs, whilst I dried my soaked clothes, and, finally wrapped in my cloak, snatched a few hours' more sleep.

VIEW OF THE BOMOKANDI. (*Drawn by L. H. Fischer.*)

In the early twilight of the next morning all were ready again, awake and gathered round the fires, for a heavy day's march lay before us; so making an early start, we reached the Bomokandi on the same day, the 27th of December. Next day we crossed the Gadsi, later on one of its lesser tributaries, and then another small stream which flows directly into the Bomokandi. In places there are broad ridges of high rising ground, and from one of these I saw Mount Mandyema, to the south of the Bomokandi. This day our way still led constantly through deep tracts of forest, where our advance was much hampered and often only possible by stooping. It would have been almost impossible to make any progress had it not been for the foot-paths which are to be found here as in most other parts of our route, and where these are occasionally blocked, there is certainly no lack of obstacles. Often these ways are only the tracks of animals, of which, however, men too are glad to make use. The roads continually led again from the thin woodland of the steppe into dense tracts of forest, where the natives sometimes hunt for things which are not to be found in the former region, such as roots, fruits, honey, &c.; but the search for certain species of termites is carried on even in the most remote districts.

But it is specially the great hunts which attract whole troops of natives into the least inhabited parts, and hence the foot-paths originate. Sometimes huts of refuge are erected in these places, and one of them was very serviceable to us on this very occasion, for in the afternoon another thunderstorm burst over us before we reached the Bomokandi. Most of the carriers hurried on, the rest remaining behind with me to seek shelter from the rain. In spite of this we reached the Bomokandi long before sunset, but there were no boats for the passage, though notice of our approach had already been given by messengers despatched on the previous day. So we had to spend another night on the damp ground which had been flooded by the river, for the northern bank was flat and showed traces of the water, whilst the southern bank still rose six feet above the level of the river. The breadth was about two hundred yards, and both banks were bordered by a broad belt of forest, as along the smaller streams. In this respect also the Bomokandi differs essentially from the Welle, whose steep banks have but a narrow fringe of trees. A splendid picture, set in a beautiful, appropriate frame, was that offered by the calm, clear expanse of water, from which arose two little islands; the nearest one, indeed, consisted merely of a single mass of rock with one solitary tree, but the other was fully a hundred yards long and thickly wooded. The main course of the Bomokandi here is to the north-west, and near Kamsa's it joins the Welle. There was a bend to the south a little below the point where we crossed, and the view across to the east was narrowed. We were again threatened with rain at night, but it did not fall; my sleep was, however, disturbed by cramp in the legs, caused by the weariness of creeping through bush and forest. Although December cannot be included in the rainy season, the last few days had shown me that in these latitudes heavy rains may occur even in this month, for such was my experience in the year 1881, on the 9th, 13th, 26th, and 27th of December.

On the following morning, whilst waiting for the boats, we tried to catch some fish which were at play under the shade of the bank. At last the baggage was carried over the river, and in an hour's time we reached the settlement of an A-Barmbo chief. I could not proceed farther for want of carriers, so the natives soon came to stare at me, and by way of a change I was able once more to entertain a dusky tribe with music and pictures.

The land south of the Bomokandi is inhabited by numerous A-Barmbo tribes. Their territory reaches westwards to the Makongo, a tributary of the Bomokandi, and is there bounded by the A-Babuas. In the east they cross the Pokko, also a southern tributary of the Bomokandi, but there only form solitary colonies amongst the A-Zandehs. In Bakangai's domains, however, conditions were reversed, the A-Zandehs forming colonies amongst the A-Barmbos, all, however, being vassals of Prince Bakangai. The A-Bayas and A-Mbarandis live near the ferry, and to the east follow the A-Mokubios,

ZANDEH WARRIORS. (*Drawn by Fr. Rheinfelder, from a photograph by R. Buchta.*)

A-Miaros, &c.; to the west are situated the A-Mangales, A-Beliforos, A-Balis, and a whole succession of other tribes.

Messengers from Bakangai continually arrived, requesting me to come to the prince as quickly as possible; they were easily recognized at a distance as messengers from the chief by the loud jingle of bells. My first requirement was to have carriers, but they were not easy to obtain, in spite of all the shouts and noise of bells calling down the wrath of the prince on all who proved refractory. However, some of my A-Mezima carriers had returned to Hawash Effendi with the news of our arrival at the Bomokandi; the rest accompanied us to Bakangai under my protection, in return for which they willingly acted as carriers. We managed to obtain the remaining carriers somehow from the A-Barmbos on the spot.

Shortly before our departure on the 29th of December more messengers arrived, bringing with them as a present from the chief an Akka boy, from the dwarf race living in the south. He was called Akangai, and remained with me for a few years.

The land we now passed through on our way southwards is in part undulating and in part a tableland, well watered by streams flowing westwards chiefly into the Zeseh, a tributary of the Bomokandi. The forest now increased in denseness, so that our march lay more through the characteristic fluvial avenues than in the open wooded steppe. The high grass, still green in parts, was another proof that December may be counted among the rainy months south of the Bomokandi. The country was thickly populated, with settlements occurring every ten or fifteen minutes; first came the A-Bayas, then the A-Mappurus, and then the A-Banyas. The A-Zandehs are chiefly concentrated round about their ruler, and during the last few hours of our march, till we reached the prince's abode, we met with their settlements exclusively.

Up to the very end of my journey, Bakangai kept on sending messenger after messenger to meet me, and as they always returned in the greatest haste to inform him of my approach, I was all the more disappointed by my reception at his place of abode. I had expected to be led straight to the place of assembly, whereas I was simply escorted by his people to a couple of wretched huts, which they gave me to understand were assigned by Bakangai for my residence. In my indignation I determined to have my baggage put down under a neighbouring tree, and a camp pitched there, but received information that the prince himself would shortly appear on the scene. He did actually approach immediately, surrounded by his notables. Contrary to my custom, however, I remained sitting mute on my chair, while the chief established himself at some distance on his stool. Some minutes of perfect silence followed, but, when the prince seemed on the point of breaking it by speaking to his attendants, I interrupted him, saying that, " It was unseemly for him, an absolute ruler, to come to me, especially to these half-ruined huts, instead of receiving the stranger in his own mbanga, which was the proper and customary course. As for the huts which he had assigned to me, they were not good enough even for my servants, and for this reason I preferred to encamp in the open air under yonder tree. Moreover," I added, "he was not to take me for a 'Dongolawi,' an Osman Bedawi, an Ali, or a Mayo." (It was with the two last-named Arabs that Miani had made his journey to Bakangai.) " Nevertheless I would bear him no grudge on this account, as he was not yet sufficiently acquainted with us 'white men.' Therefore, having now said as much as was necessary, I saluted him as the all-powerful sovereign of his country." With these words I rose, and going up to him, gave him a hearty shake of the hand. Bakangai was evidently embarrassed by my speech, and, pleading ignorance as to the badness of the accommodation, gave instant orders for the erection of a large new hut. By the co-operation of many hands this was actually accomplished by the evening, while the day after an awning was put up for me, besides other huts for my people.

Thus at last, almost at the end of the year 1881, I attained the goal at which I had been aiming for a year past, viz., the domain of Prince Bakangai. It is true that a long space of time had elapsed between my first unsuccessful attempt and its present issue, and besides that, the material which I had obtained for my maps was but small in comparison with the extent of the regions which had been explored; but, as a set-off to this, a long stay at various places had afforded me a deeper insight into the customs, way of life, and whole activity of the tribes in those parts, so that I might venture to say, "This year has not been lost."

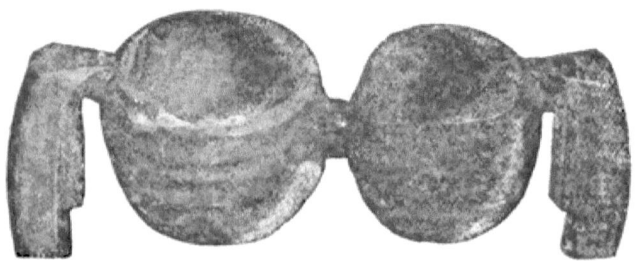

DOUBLE WOODEN COOKING UTENSIL OF THE A-ZANDEHS.

INDEX.

A

ABD ALLAH, settlement under, 109, 111
Abd el-Min, 256, 257
Abd es-Set, settlement under, 111, 127
Adatam, 225, 244, 251, 255
Akka tribe, 260, 469
Albinos, 240
Ali, 253, 264
Animals, 69
    Antelopes, 293, 381, 442
    Apes, 129, 363
    Baboons, 123
    Bats, 119
    Buffaloes, 290, 347, 357
    Chimpanzees, 65, 179, 300, 313, 374;
        nest of the, 377
    Dogs, 151, 305
    Elephants, 431
    Flattermaki, *Galeopithecus*, 423
    Goat, buck, 234
    Golunda Barbara, 382
    Hippopotami, 458
    Leopards, 130, 297
    Mouse-catching, 381
Arab monk, 303
Arabs' treatment of the Negroes, 453, 454
    Nubian, 229, 255, 256
    reception from the, 394
    services of the, 369
    wisdom of, 299
Arithmetic, negro, 329
Artes Africanæ, 94
Atrush Bey, 71

B

BAHR EL-GHAZAL, province of, 81, 361, 425
    populations of, 94, 96, 110
    See River.
Bakangai, Prince, 298; with, 469, 470
Bakit Bey, 428, 433, 452
Barometer, 61
Bastinado, 431, 432
Beer, negro, 278
Berber, road to, 18
    town of, 19
Birds, 69
    Balæniceps Rex, 45, 46, 64, 75
    Cosmetornis Spekei, 175
    Darters, 43, 47
    Numida vulturina, 422
    Parra Africana, 42
    Peacock crane, 78
        in the vicinity of the Werre, 153
    Poultry, 273, 274
    Spur-winged goose, 66
Blood brotherhood, ceremony of, 405
Bohndorff, 9, 294, 298
    excursion near the Werre, 311, 341
    his career, 33
Botanical notes—
    ambatch, 45, 48
    Bania, 391
    bread-fruit tree, 377
    Durra, 107
    Eleusine coracana, 107, 161, 272, 278
    Erythrophlæum guineense, 84
    European plants at Lacrima, 161, 295
    forest, 110, 117
    in A-Madi lands, 370, 373, 375
    indigenous plants, 15, 42, 113, 116, 119, 145, 161, 190, 271, 309, 312
    Meluchia, 342
    mushrooms, 338
    palms, 43, 193, 252, 257, 401
    rokko tree, 447
    south of the Welle, 230
    water plants forming the *sudd*, 57
    wild rice, 304
Buchta, Richard, 22

INDEX

C

CANNIBALISM, 233, 248, 398, 449
Carriers, negro, 267
Casati, Captain, 414, 419
Christmas Day, 306
Collections, fate of, 3
Commerce, 17
Congo, characteristics of the, 117
    affluents of the, the Welle, &c., 114, 199. *See* River.
Copper, 246
Criminal punishments amongst the negroes, 257, 310, 353, 363

D

DAR-FERTIT, 94
Dem Bekir, zeriba of, 95, 107, 115
Dem Guju, 92, 94
Dem Soliman, 79, 85, 86, 92
Divination amongst the negroes, 137, 206, 220, 246, 363, 380, 402, 407, 416
Drar, zeriba, 77
Dress, negro, 163, 226, 241, 245, 249, 288, 447
Drum (*nugara*), beating the war, 140, 217, 314, 366
Dry season, temperature in the, 293, 305, 313

E

EL MAAS, 96
Embata tribe, 324, 328-334, 350, 448, 459
Emigration, negro, 116
Emin Bey, 255, 418, 438
Equatorial provinces, trade in the, 28

F

FARAG ALLAH, 33, 105, 348, 353, 362
Farmán, 4
Fashoda, 35-37
Fire on the steppe, 38, 46, 462
Fish in the Welle, 328
Forests, 117
    in the A-Madi Land, 375

G

GADDA, station on the, 253
Gauda station, 84, 85
Gangura, territory, 186
Genealogy, royal negro, 194
Geological notes, 79, 116, 120, 321
Gessi, Romolo, 20, 22, 60, 71-76, 83-89
    death of, 92, 418
    policy, 63, 151, 160, 304, 428
    triumph of, 79, 81

Ghaba Jer Dekka, 44
Giegler Pasha, 21, 23
Gnani Bey, 83, 85
Gordon, General, 3, 14, 16, 22, 67
Government economy, 78, 448
Grass lands in Zandeh, 185
Grass thatching, 145
Gugas, or granaries, 82

H

HADÉNDOAS tribes, 18
Halima, 296, 386
Hawash Effendi, 378, 386, 393, 396, 417, 426, 432, 434, 452,
    recalled, 458
Hawash station, 393, 416
    mutiny at, 434
Hints for travellers' food, etc., 15, 84, 89, 109, 171, 300, 306, 323, 324, 339, 342, 347, 358, 370, 371, 380, 393, 447
    frequent source of illness, 380
    packing goods, 27
    packing salt, 298
    useful stores, 24, 105, 154, 168, 352
House, author's, in Khartum, 21
    at Lacrima, 143
Hunts, 180, 377, 465
Huts of banana leaves, 405

I

IDI-EL-KEBIR, 432
Industries, negro, 94, 266, 285, 420, 447
Insects, notes upon—
    annoyance from insects, 247, 269
    gadflies, 36
    harvest, 340
    locust gathering, 278
    rare beetle, 450
    robber ants, 159
    termite, 140, 147, 171, 333, 338
Islands in the Welle, 391, 392, 443
Ismailia, on board the, 32-46
    rats on the, 36
Ivory, 138, 151, 200, 209, 214
    ornaments, 288

J

JABAI, Sheik, 77
Jur Ghatta, 61, 70-76
Jussuf es-Shellali, 271

K

KAKA, 35
Khartum, 19
    old friends in, 21, 23
    leaving, 31

INDEX. 475

Khedive, audience with the, 3
Khor Deleb, 43
Khor el-Arab, 43
Khor el-Ghanam, 86
"Kit," 49, 50
Kohn, Herr, 14
Kommunda, 127
Kuru, 85, 86
   geographical importance of the, 95

L

LACRIMA, station of, 149
   life at, 143, 167, 290
   return to, 293, 294
Lado, 81
Lupton Bey, 63, 100

M

MAHDISTS, 64
Mahmud, 321
Maiyeh bita el-Deleb, 45
Maiyeh bita Komundári, 41
Maiyeh bita Signora, 38
Marno, Ernest, 19, 37, 53
Marquet, M., 2, 16, 18, 21, 23
Maximo, Herr, 3, 14
Mbanga, negro meetings, 157, 188, 281
Meshra er-Req, 49, 50, 60
   need of a station at, 62
Miani, Italian traveller, 243, 258
Mill, negro, 169
Missionaries, 22
Mohammed Effendi, 84
Moqren el-Bahār, Lake, 38, 41
Mount Angba, 322, 326, 388
   Baginse, 272
   Balimassango, 326
   Du, ascent of, 112
   Ghasa, ascent of, 120
   Girro, 326
   Keddede, 131
   Lingua, 321, 388
      ascent of, 325
   Madyanu, 391, 441, 442, 443, 465
   Magaragare, 443, 450
   Majanu, 322
   Malingde, ascent of, 321, 360
   Saba, 280
Mountain group, 442
Mudir Mani Bey, 18
Muhammed Kher, 270, 271, 275
Muhammed weled Abdu, 256, 259
Mula Effendi, 254

N

NEGRO, forced labour from the, 7, 64, 97, 147
   tribute paid by the, 98
   industries, 79, 94, 246, 447
   slave trade by, 93, 100, 209, 369, 384, 456
   human sacrifices, 100
   dress, 163, 226, 241, 245, 249, 288, 447
   abuse of authority by the, 113
   capacity, 154, 155
   characteristics, 140, 173, 233, 419
   treachery, 449
   superstitions, 366, 451
   suicide amongst the, 248
   messengers from the, 149
   native government, 157
   dissensions amongst the, 160, 213, 279, 286, 318, 335, 336, 358, 366, 383, 393, 421
   variations of skin amongst, 239, 369
   dances, 237, 384, 408, 430
   festivities, 382
   songs, 384
Negro tribes, unimportant, 244, 266, 327, 336, 338, 352, 391, 392, 393, 441, 453
   A-Bisangas, 249, 251, 421
   A-Barmbo, 127, 204, 217, 222, 226, 324, 433, 443, 456
      land of the, 334
      inhospitality of the, 337-350, 397, 407
      customs of the, 420, 449
      singing of the, 378
      tribes included in the, 466
   Bassansa, chief, 329
   Boboli, chief, 412, 420, 448, 449
   Buru, chief, 220, 237, 250, 394-407
   Manda, chief, 388
   A-Madi, 199, 280
      land of the, 317, 321, 325, 346, 424
      government, 426
   Buru, chief, 364, 387
   Fero, chief, 268, 274-279
   Mazindeh, chief, 359-388
      at Hawash station, 424
   A-Zandeh, 71, 92, 96, 107, 120
      huts, 146, 164, 170
      customs, 189
      princes, 193, 280
      industries, 282
      alliance, 285
      honesty, 287
      criminal code, 310
      loyalty, 425
      summer temperature in land of the, 163
   Abdu'lallahi, Prince, 160, 255
   Binsa, chief, 277, 287, 293
   Hokwa, 160, 271, 275, 276
   Mbittima, 160, 263
   Mbio, 129, 151

Nasima, chief, 203, 209, 218
Ndoruma, chief, 72, 129
    reception by, 132
    mbanga under, 153
    parting from, 174
    return to, 269, 290, 309, 313
Ngerria, chief, 278, 281
Palembata, chief, 193, 197-201, 313
Wando, Prince, 160, 270, 274, 276
Zassa, Prince, 297, 308, 342, 349-355
Zemio, Prince, 92, 151, 396
    reception by, 197, 203
    leaving, 229
Bongo, 77, 83, 85
Dai, 253
Digga, 110-112
Dinka, 62, 67, 68, 90, 100
Embatas, boating tribe, 230, 253
    fishing by the, 328
    extortions by the, 330, 335, 337; 355, 447, 459
Golos, 85, 108
Jur, 77, 79, 82
Krey, 89, 94, 95
Mangballe, 202, 207, 209, 210
    preparing for war, 217, 218
    boats, 221, 397, 430
Mangbattu, 203, 205, 225
    huts, dress, 241, 244
    debates, 242
    weapons, 246
    customs, 366, 411
    history during my absence, 396
Mambanga, chief, territory of, 205, 206; 213, 217, 220, 229
    meeting with, 225
    my residence with, 230-253
    presents from, 314
    his duplicity, 341, 342, 348, 351
    war made upon, 378, 396
    my overtures to, 398, 401, 403
    council of subjects, 412
    his cupidity, 416
    obstinacy, 422
    danger, 428
    defeated, 448
Munsa, King, 254, 258
Niam-Niam, 71, 97
    type, 102, 233
New moon, 293
New Year's day in Khartum, 23
Nile, affluents of the. *See* River.
Nile basin, 275
Nile-Congo basins, 114, 117, 131
Nile, the Blue, 60
    the White, 35
    obstructed by *sudd*, 38
    origin of name, 60
Nuer, 43

O

OPTICAL delusion, marine, 13
Osman Bedawi, 138, 191, 296, 318, 342, 417, 426

P

Palestina, on board the, 10
Palm-oil packing, 325
Papers, useful, 4, 259
Pirona, M., 2
Prime Minister, audience with the, 7
Python, 206

R

RABAY, 124
Rainy seasons, 77, 244, 392, 439, 451, 466
Rauf Pasha, 22
Ringio, dragoman, 437, 451
River Congo system—
    Akka, 222
    Anakaba, 255
    Badua, 117
    Boku, 119, 127
    Bomokandi, affluent of the Welle, 257, 335, 450, 453, 461-466; two tributaries—Gadsi, 461; Zeseh, 469
    Bua, 266
    Duru, affluent of the Welle, 269, 272
    Gadda, affluent of the Welle, 254, 257, 265
    Gurba, 185, 199, 204, 213, 269, 290, 294, 317; Buoli, affluent of the, 293
    Hekke, affluent of the, 317, 360
    Kapili, 267, 269, 272
    Kibali, source of the Welle, 265, 266
    Kibongo, 441
    Kliwa, affluent of the Welle, 251
    Mbruole, 213, 217, 269, 280, 281, 288
    Mombo, affluent of the Welle, Makua, 119, 131
    Rongo, 118
    Tau, 287, 288
    Tong, 387
    Tonj, 69
    Tota, affluent of the Welle, 442
    Welle, affluents of the, 217, 257, 265, 269, 317, 322, 327, 328; 334, 353, 393
        river valley of the, 253
        islands in the, 391
    Welle Makua, 119, 131, 185, 186, 312, 314
        affluents of the, 461

Welle-Makua-Mobangi, 114
Warra, 453
Werre Welle, 313, 317
River Nile system, 114
  Bahr el-Ghazal, 114, 131
    affluents of the, 275
  Bahr el-Jebel, 41, 53
  Bikki, 131, 309, 310
  Buole, 293
  Buseri, head water of the Wau, 109
  Duma, 310
  Duro, 96
  Gitti, 83
  Jih, 108, 114
  Jubbo, 275
  Jur, 49, 50, 79, 80, 275
  Hako, affluent of Werre, 192
  Mbomu, 131, 310
  Swamps draining to the Werre, 182
  Pai, affluent of the Gurba, 201
  Such, 275
  Wau, 79, 109, 114, 275
  Werre, 294
  Yubbo, 280, 294
Route between Egypt and the Sudan, 16
  to Korosko, 17
  Sawakin and Berber, 16-18
  to Kassala, 17
  from Jur Ghattas, 71
  from Wau to Biselli, 82
  to Dem Soliman, 83, 84
  the Shekka from Dem Soliman, 89
  from Dem Soliman, 92
  from Dem Guju, 94
  by the Buseri, 109
  value of shorter, 149
  in the depression of the Welle, 253, 254
  to Tangasi, 255, 257
  through Hokwa's territory, 269
  to Bakangai, 324
  from the Werre to the Deleb, 341
  to the south, 460
Rubattino Company of steamers, 10

S

SAATI EFFENDI, 85
Saida, 33, 296, 345, 353
Salt, 169

Sawakin, 14, 16
Schweinfurth, 102, 254, 258
Slave trade, 29, 93, 100
Snake, 251
Sobat, 54
Soliman Zibèr, 79, 259
Solongo, 123
Sounding stone, 373
Storm, sudden, 61, 347, 465
Sudan officials, 427
Sudd, the grass barriers in the Nile, 19, 37, 38, 44-46, 48, 53, 55

T

TANGASI, 259, 452
Tobacco, 373, 414
Topographical notes, 322, 360
Traps for animals, 297, 326, 424
Travellers who preceded the author, 107
Troops enter Hawash station, 437

U

UNIFORM of the Sudan army, 438

W

WAR between Mambanga and the government, 396
Wau, 79, 81
Wizard Zandeh, 137
Woman—A-Barmbo dancer, 439
  A-Madi, 382
Women, mourning of African, 420
  Bongo, 83
  Mangbattu, 233, 241
  dress of the, 245, 411
  Zandeh, 154, 158, 169, 189, 277, 369

Y

YAPATI, 208

Z

ZANDEH land, grass in, 185
Zassa, 345, 348, 361
Zeriba Awet, 79